JEWS IN THE SOVIET UNION

The USSR, 1929
Soviet Socialist Republics (SSRs)
ARMENIAN SSR
AZERBAIJAN SSR
BELORUSSIAN SSR
GEORGIAN SSR
RUSSIAN SFSR
TAJIK SSR
TURKMEN SSR
UKRAINIAN SSR
UZBEK SSR
IRELAND
UNITED KINGDOM
60°N
ARCTIC CIRCLE
80°N
90°N
40°
North Sea
NORWAY
SWEDEN
FINLAND
Barents Sea
ARCTIC
Murmansk
Nova Zemlya
Kara Sea
KARELIAN ASSR
6
GERMANY
LITHUANIA
ESTONIA
LATVIA
EAST PRUSSIA
CZECHOSLOVAKIA
POLAND
Leningrad
Archangel
Pechora R.
Minsk
BELO-RUSSIA
Severnaya Dvina R.
Volga R.
HUNGARY
Moscow
R
U
Omsk Province
Kyiv
Kama R.
ROMANIA
BESSARABIA
9
Dnipro R.
UKRAINE
UNION OF SOVIE
Don R.
5
Odesa
1
Tobol R.
Kharkiv
BULGARIA
Volga
2
11
7
West Territo
Black Sea
Stalingrad
Rostov-on-Don
Ural R.
Omsk
Novosi
Ishim R.
Irtysh R.
3
TURKEY
10
GEORGIA
Caspian Sea
12
KAZAKH ASSR
ARMENIA
Aral Sea
AZERBAIJAN
Lake Balkhash
SYRIA
Baku
UZBEKISTAN
Syr Dar'ya
TURKMENISTAN
Amu Dar'ya
Alma-Ata
IRAQ
Tashkent
Frunze
KYRGYZSTAN
SINKIA
CHINESE
TAJIKISTAN
PERSIA
SAUDI ARABIA
KUWAIT
AFGHANISTAN
INDIA
LUCIDITY INFORMATION DESIGN, LLC

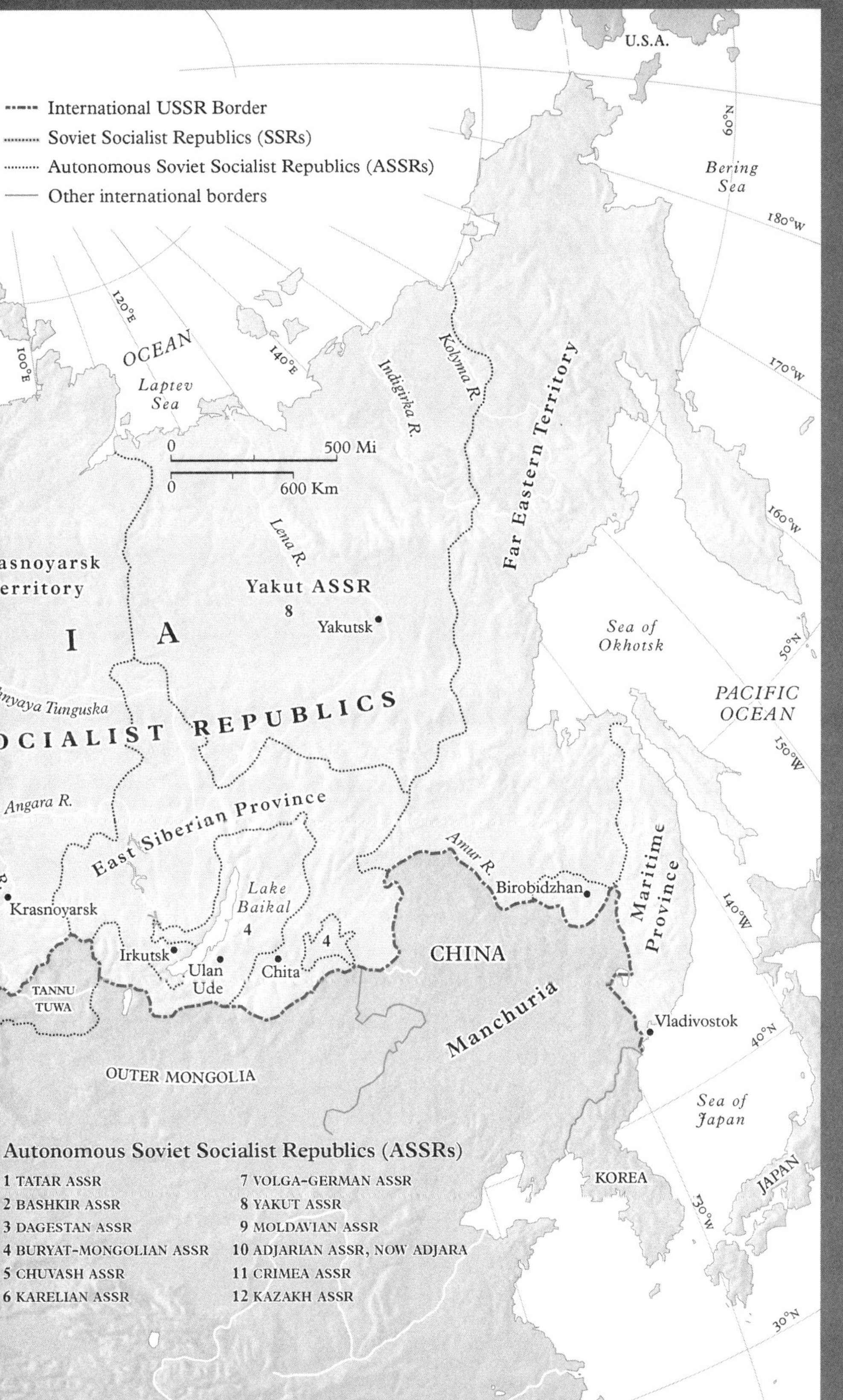

Autonomous Soviet Socialist Republics (ASSRs)

1 TATAR ASSR
2 BASHKIR ASSR
3 DAGESTAN ASSR
4 BURYAT-MONGOLIAN ASSR
5 CHUVASH ASSR
6 KARELIAN ASSR
7 VOLGA-GERMAN ASSR
8 YAKUT ASSR
9 MOLDAVIAN ASSR
10 ADJARIAN ASSR, NOW ADJARA
11 CRIMEA ASSR
12 KAZAKH ASSR

JEWS IN THE SOVIET UNION

A HISTORY

GENERAL EDITORS: GENNADY ESTRAIKH AND DAVID ENGEL

Volume 1:
Revolution, Civil War, and New Ways of Life, 1917–1930
Elissa Bemporad

Volume 2:
Dictatorship and Terror, 1930–1939
Deborah Yalen and Arkady Zeltser

Volume 3:
War, Conquest, and Catastrophe, 1939–1945
Oleg Budnitskii, David Engel, Gennady Estraikh, and Anna Shternshis

Volume 4:
Post-War Hopes and Continued Terror, 1945–1953
Anna Shternshis

Volume 5:
After Stalin, 1953–1967
Gennady Estraikh

Volume 6:
The Final Years, 1967–1991
Zvi Gitelman

JEWS IN THE SOVIET UNION
A HISTORY

REVOLUTION, CIVIL WAR, AND NEW WAYS OF LIFE 1917–1930

Volume 1

ELISSA BEMPORAD

NEW YORK UNIVERSITY PRESS
New York

NEW YORK UNIVERSITY PRESS
New York
www.nyupress.org

Library of Congress Cataloging-in-Publication Data
Names: Ėstraĭkh, G. (Gennadiĭ), editor. | Engel, David (Professor), editor.
Title: Jews in the Soviet Union : a history / editors, Gennady Estraikh and David Engel.
Description: New York : New York University Press, [2025] | Euguene Shvidler Project for the history of the Jews of the Soviet Union. | Includes bibliographical references and index. | Contents: Volume 1. Revolution, civil war, and new ways of life, 1917–1930 / Elissa Bemporad—Volume 2. Dictactorship and terror, 1930–1939 / Deborah Yalen and Arkady Zeltser—Volume 3. War, conquest, and catastrophe, 1939–1945 / Oleg Budnitskii, David Engel, Gennady Estraikh, and Anna Shternshis—Volume 4. Post-war hopes and continued terror, 1945–1953 / Anna Shternshis—Volume 5. After Stalin, 1953-1967 / Gennady Estraikh—Volume 6. The final years, 1967–1991 / Zvi Gitelman.
Identifiers: LCCN 2024039865 (print) | LCCN 2024039866 (ebook) | ISBN 9781479837533 (hardback) | ISBN 9781479837540 (library ebook) | ISBN 9781479837557 (consumer ebook)
Subjects: LCSH: Jews—Soviet Union—History.
Classification: LCC DS134.83 .J494 2025 (print) | LCC DS134.83 (ebook) | DDC 947/.004924—dc23/eng/20241213
LC record available at https://lccn.loc.gov/2024039865

This book is printed on acid-free paper, and its binding materials are chosen for strength and durability. We strive to use environmentally responsible suppliers and materials to the greatest extent possible in publishing our books.

The manufacturer's authorized representative in the EU for product safety is Mare Nostrum Group B.V., Mauritskade 21D, 1091 GC Amsterdam, The Netherlands, email: gpsr@mare-nostrum.co.uk.

Manufactured in the United States of America

10 9 8 7 6 5 4 3 2 1

Also available as an ebook

With deep gratitude to Eugene Shvidler,
whose generosity made possible the research and
preparation of this NYU study.

CONTENTS

FOREWORD TO

JEWS IN THE SOVIET UNION: A HISTORY

DAVID ENGEL AND GENNADY ESTRAIKH

This volume is part of a six-volume comprehensive history of Jews and Jewish life in the Soviet Union, from the establishment of the Russian Soviet Republic in late 1917 through to the Union's formal dissolution on December 8, 1991. The project was launched in 2015 under the auspices of New York University's Global Network for Advanced Research in Jewish Studies, thanks to a major gift from Eugene Shvidler. It has been carried out by an international team of scholars—authors, consultants, archivists, and librarians—based in North America, Israel, and Europe, including several former Soviet states.

The scholars have worked to fill a major need in the study of both Soviet and Jewish history. The prominence of Jews among Soviet elites during certain intervals in the Soviet Union's seven decades, along with pressures to remove them from elite ranks during others, has long been noted as a significant factor in Soviet politics, but the extent of such prominence, pressure, and significance has yet to be explored in detail. Similarly, the Jews of the Soviet Union, though numbering about 20 percent of the world's Jewish population for most of the twentieth century and ranking second or third among Jewish communities defined by geopolitical boundaries, have yet to be incorporated significantly into a broader Jewish historical narrative. Reasons for both phenomena can be found in the very histories from which Soviet Jews have been largely absent. For Soviet ideologues and policy makers, the Jews of their country resisted easy categorization. From a Marxist point of view, their status was confusing. Were they a fully fledged nation? If so, how were Soviet Jews connected to Jews elsewhere in the world, including Palestine, later Israel? Without a clear ideological lens through which to regard them, certain aspects of their situation in the Soviet Union could not be readily explained. How, for example, to account simultaneously for their prominent role in many domains of Soviet life, most notably during the 1920s and 1930s, on the one hand, and for the unofficial but universally evident restrictions imposed, increasingly from the late 1940s, on their educational choices and career paths, on the other? How did it happen that Jews, many of whom had once been enthusiastic supporters of the Soviet way, sought to leave the country in growing numbers during its final three decades? Why were Jews allowed, at various times and with varying degrees of willingness or reluctance, to emigrate, whereas the vast majority of Soviet citizens were not afforded a similar possibility? The state's guardians preferred to leave such questions in repose. As a result, historians living in the Soviet Union (and, after 1945, in the Soviet- dominated countries of eastern Europe as well) were strongly discouraged from taking up such an ideologically treacherous subject.

For historians of the Jews, Soviet Jewry presented a different set of anomalies. The Soviet state purported to act in accordance with a unique set of principles that, its leaders and advocates promised, would offer Jews greater physical safety, material security, and psychological peace of mind than would any alternative set of principles guiding other contemporary states or political movements, including those associated with liberal democracy and with Zionism. The principles' uniqueness made the Soviet Union seem an outlier in the political history of modern Jewry. Moreover, in the highly charged atmosphere of the Cold War, those principles became associated with forces hostile to the countries in which most historians of the Jews resided. Consequently, the handful of Western scholars who displayed sustained interest in Soviet Jewish history tended to investigate the negative, tragic aspects of that history that eventually impelled many Jews to want to depart the country, leaving more quotidian, less dramatic, less controversial, and more successful parts of the story largely in the dark. Lack of sources for studying those parts of the story compounded the problem. As long as the Soviet Union existed, it severely restricted Western scholars' access to relevant documents in Soviet libraries and archives.

Only after its demise did scholars begin to grasp the breadth and depth of the materials they had once been unable to consult. During the three decades that have passed since then, many of those materials have been brought to light. Moreover, the passage of time has been both long enough to offer researchers sufficient distance for evaluating this massive documentary record and short enough to allow them still to benefit from the living memories of the large number of Jews who directly experienced the Soviet regime. Those memories have been and continue to be tapped by several large-scale oral history projects. Thus, a critical mass of new source material appears to have made possible a synthesis of the Soviet Jewish past with a degree of accuracy, inclusion, understanding, and refinement unachievable even a generation ago. That is the outcome the current project has sought.

The project's findings suggest that the results of the Soviet Union's approach to matters of Jewish concern and the attitudes of different parts of the heterogeneous Soviet Jewish population toward the Soviet Union were mixed. At first, many Jews were great supporters of the new regime that replaced the oppressive tsars. Yet it was not long before Soviet Jews faced the dismantling of their religious life. Some aspects of Jewish culture were suppressed, while others were promoted. For some Jews, these features of life under the Soviets were profoundly distressing; for others, they were less so. Some found ways to maintain certain religious and cultural practices despite official disapproval. At the same time, the regime pursued policies that helped some Jews achieve Soviet-style prosperity and reach the highest levels of Soviet society, though often simultaneously heightening tensions between Jews and some of their non-Jewish neighbors. After 1941, the Soviet Union fought the Nazis and sheltered Jews who had escaped to the East, with Soviet Jews playing a significant role in the war effort. Shortly thereafter, however, the regime intensified its own repression of the sharpened Jewish consciousness that World War II had aroused. Even under those conditions, Soviet Jews developed multiple mechanisms for excelling in this difficult environment and for preserving a Jewish identity. Some Jews became dissidents, campaigning for the right to emigrate and contributing to the Soviet regime's eventual downfall. Other Jews strove to prosper within the Soviet system, despite difficult circumstances. Some of them were more successful than others.

Accordingly, the authors of the six volumes have tried to present the multiple, changing situations in which Soviet Jews found themselves over seven decades and more as much as possible through the eyes of all the various actors in those situations, Jewish and non-Jewish alike. In doing so, their aim has been to help readers understand how the various ways in which different groups of Jews adjusted to the policies and practices of the Soviet regime at different times could make sense to their members and how the changing policies that the regime adopted at different times could make sense to the regime itself in changing contexts. They have not sought to take sides in the debates of the times they explore, to evaluate the actions or attitudes of the participants, or to identify heroes and villains. Instead, they have endeavored to fathom and to represent an intricate, multifaceted history as fully and fairly as available documents and available space allow.

EDITORS' NOTE

The opening volume of *Jews in the Soviet Union* explores how the revolutionary experiments in governance and social organization introduced by the Bolsheviks after 1917 affected the lives of the nearly three million Jews who became subject to them during the 1920s. Among those experiments was a conscious effort to change the terms of the relationship between Jews, the state, and the surrounding society, based on recognition of some Jewish collective interests and denial of others. By the end of the decade, the Soviet regime abandoned or modified central aspects of that effort. This volume tells the story of those changes and relates how Jews built their lives around them.

In this book, places are referred to by the official names that were in force at the time under discussion: hence, Petrograd until 1924 and Leningrad thereafter. In keeping with the tendency of the Soviet regime during the period treated in this volume to promote national consciousness among ethnic minorities, the names of cities and towns outside of Russia are rendered in the local languages: hence, Kyiv instead of Kiev, Mahiliau instead of Mogilev. Individuals' names are rendered as the individuals were accustomed to Romanize them. Absent evidence of preference, names are transliterated according to the language in which the person wrote most frequently. Languages using Cyrillic alphabets are generally transliterated according to Library of Congress standards, except for omission of diacritics and of some hard and soft signs. Yiddish is transliterated according to the system adopted by the YIVO Institute for Jewish Research, and Hebrew is transliterated according to an internal scheme that aims for a reasonable balance between the most common orthographically and phonetically based systems currently in use.

INTRODUCTION

It Was the Best of Times, It Was the Worst of Times . . .

The momentous world events of the first decades of the twentieth century transformed entirely the vast territories of what was known as the Russian Empire, alongside the lives of the many peoples that inhabited the cities, towns, and villages within its confines. World War I, the two Russian Revolutions of 1917, and the subsequent civil war initiated a chain reaction that engendered the reconfiguration of the geopolitical order in much of Eurasia. The changes that occurred over the span of seven years, from the summer of 1914, when the Russian Imperial Army entered World War I, through the democratic revolution of February 1917, the revolutionary coup of October 1917, and the long and bloody civil war of 1918–1921, set the stage for the establishment of the Soviet Union, a political and economic system that would survive in the region for seventy-four years.

"Soviet Union" was short for Union of Soviet Socialist Republics, or USSR. The name stemmed both from the term "soviet," or council—which referred to the political organization of workers who participated in the revolutionary activities before 1917 and became the primary unit of government in the new system—and from the term "union," indicating the new system's organization as a federation of territorial nationalities consolidated into republics. The Soviet Union was established at the end of 1922, when the delegations of four constituent socialist republics that emerged out of the turbulent years of the civil war—the Russian and Transcaucasian Soviet Federated Socialist Republics and the Ukrainian and Belorussian Soviet Socialist Republics (SSRs)—approved the creation of the new country.

New Soviet socialist republics were created over the course of the 1920s, including the Turkmen and Uzbek republics in 1924 and the Tadzhik republic in 1929. By the 1950s, the Soviet Union would include a total of fifteen union republics and several autonomous republics, provinces, and districts.

Driven by a passionate and uncompromising commitment to the principles of Marxism, internationalism, and anticapitalism, the Bolsheviks—the radical faction of the Russian Social Democratic Labor Party that seized power in October 1917—formed the new revolutionary government at the head of the new country. Sustained by a powerful utopian vision of a just and modern society that would rise like a phoenix from the ashes of its economically and politically backward predecessor, the Bolshevik Party, which became the Communist Party of the Soviet Union, established the first socialist society in human history.

Wars and revolution generated sweeping political and economic changes, evoking powerful emotions among the inhabitants of the territories of the future Soviet Union. The abdication of a tsar exacerbated the political upheaval and intensified class resentment among workers and peasants; the substantial losses experienced by the Russian Imperial Army at the front in World War I deepened the soldiers' discontent and led to a crisis within what at the time constituted the largest military in the world; the unprecedented violence of the civil war, sparked by the overthrowing of the Russian Provisional Government—established after Nicholas II's abdication—and by the October Revolution, caused massive fatalities and produced a cataclysmic refugee crisis that transformed the social and economic landscape. Grievances over the status quo had fermented throughout the region long before these events and in fact dated back to the second half of the nineteenth century, culminating in the political terror that led to multiple assassination attempts on the tsar's life. In the context of the widespread discontent, socialism eventually became the preferred protest movement of many people. It attracted large sections of the working class and disillusioned middle-class intellectuals in the urban centers of the European regions of the Russian Empire in particular. The Bolsheviks strategically rode this feeling of political and socioeconomic discontent but imposed on it their own version of a utopian world: resorting to violence and playing on the allure for a world revolution, Vladimir Lenin and his comrades established a political system that strove to create new subjectivities, to invent new understandings of time and space, and to relegate capitalism and religion to the dustbin of history.

Arising from the expansive, multiethnic, and multilingual tsarist empire, the Soviet Union became a major political and military actor on the twentieth-century world stage, its revolutionary vision of socialism eliciting simultaneously intense criticism and hostility and boundless enthusiasm and support at the international level.[1] In its commitment to promoting ethnic consciousness among national minorities and granting an official status to their national languages, the new state conveyed to the members of ethnic minorities that it would behave differently from the Russian Empire, as well as from other European nation-states: it would protect their well-being not only more reasonably than the tsar had done but also more thoroughly than neighboring Poland or Romania were doing.[2] At least on paper, then, the Soviet nationality policy stood out as significantly distinct from the violent Russification policy imposed by the tsar on all ethnic minorities. Similarly, it diverged substantially from the general strategy adopted by the European nation-states that emerged in the wake of World War I, based on promoting and imposing exclusively the majority group's national language and culture.

Even despite the territorial losses endured in World War I and the civil war, like its predecessor, the Soviet Union was the world's largest country. Its western lands, which constituted the country's political and cultural center, bordered with the new independent nation-states of Poland and Romania that emerged out of the wars; in the north, the Soviet Union shared a border with Finland and two of the new Baltic states, Latvia and Estonia, established in the wake of 1918; its eastern and southern lands, which included Central Asia and the Caucasus, bordered with Turkey, Iran, Mongolia, China, Afghanistan, and Japan, which occupied Korea. Of the approximately 147 million residents inhabiting the immense territories of the Soviet Union, stretching from the Pacific Ocean in the far east to the cities and towns on the western borders of Soviet Ukraine and Belorussia, who belonged to about two hundred different ethnic groups, spoke hundreds of different languages, and identified with different religious confessions and cultures, lived also one of the largest Jewish communities in the world.[3] This book tells the story of the ways in which members of the Jewish ethno-religious group endured, came to terms with, adjusted to, and participated in the Soviet system both as individuals and as part of a Jewish collectivity during the first decade of its existence. In doing so, the volume traces Jewish experiences both of hope and excitement for the building of a new world and of anguish and despair because of the devastation of the old one.

Before the Bolshevik revolutionaries came to power and established the first socialist society on Earth, the majority of the Jews living in the Russian Empire resided in the so-called Pale of Settlement. Composed of fifteen provinces in the western regions of the empire and ten provinces belonging to the Kingdom of Poland—integrated into the Russian Empire in 1815 in the wake of the Congress of Vienna—the Pale constituted the area where Jews were permitted permanent settlement.[4]

The enlightened despot Tsarina Catherine the Great had set up the Pale in 1791 to contain the Jewish population inherited by the empire following the three partitions of the Polish Lithuanian Commonwealth at the end of the eighteenth century.[5] The decision to limit the movement and residence rights of the Jewish minority stemmed from a combination of lingering religious prejudices and economic pressure from Russian merchants who feared the competition of their Jewish counterpart. From the late eighteenth century through the first decade of the twentieth century, residing in an area covering approximately 386,000 square miles between the Black and the Baltic Seas, the Jews in the Pale generated a relatively uniform religious and ethnic culture, albeit not devoid of regional variations. Whether they lived in the Ukrainian lands, in the territory of present-day Belarus and Lithuania (which Jews referred to as Lita), or in the Polish lands, they overwhelmingly spoke Yiddish, used Hebrew in their religious and/or cultural life, and, depending on where in the Pale they resided, became increasingly literate in Russian or Polish. Of course, we can hardly talk about a perfectly homogeneous whole with harmonious affinities only. Socioeconomic and cultural gaps certainly existed between Jews living in cities like Warsaw and Odesa and those residing in the surrounding shtetls. By the same token, a Jew from the town of Uman, in central Ukraine, could understand only with difficulty the Polish Yiddish spoken by the Jews living in the city of Lodz.[6]

Beyond the Pale of Settlement, a growing Jewish community—mostly made of privileged, middle-class or wealthy, and Russified Jews—took root in the province and city of Saint Petersburg.[7] In 1897, approximately 21,200 Jews, or 1.01 percent of the city's population, lived in Saint Petersburg (on the other hand, only 8,749 Jews, or 0.36 percent of the population, lived in the province and city of the second empire's capital, Moscow).[8] Non-Ashkenazi communities dwelled in regions far removed from the European lands of the Pale of Settlement. While the non-Ashkenazi communities were notably smaller in size compared to their counterpart in the Pale, they boasted an especially long history that dated back centuries. In the Caucasus and Trans-Caucasus, the history of Georgian Jews, who were incorporated into the Russian Empire in 1810, went back at least two thousand years. Mountain Jews, whose descendants probably moved to the Caucasus from ancient Persia, came under Russian control during the nineteenth century, when tsarist forces conquered the region. Bukharan Jews too, who descended from Babylonian and Persian Jews and who moved to Central Asia in ancient times, became subjects of the Russian Empire in mid-nineteenth century. The Krymchaks constituted another ancient Jewish community: with their own language and customs, they had lived in Crimea for at least a thousand years and came under tsarist rule in 1783, when the region was formally annexed in the wake of Russia's imperial ambitions.[9]

By the early twentieth century, these different "Russian Jewries" residing within the vast confines of the empire had generated a variety of political views and movements, shaped by Zionism or socialism or a combination thereof, and of different cultural-linguistic and religious identities, with varying levels of acculturation to their neighboring populations (which were not especially pronounced in the Ukrainian, Belarusian, and Lithuanian lands, let alone among non-Ashkenazi Jews).[10] The years of revolution and war brought about the breakdown of the Russian Empire and, with it, the establishment of new borders. "Russian Jewries" came under a new geopolitical order, which in turn promoted the construction of new national and regional identities. Once united under the umbrella of an overarching empire, these Jewries were now divided among different nation-states, some of which nurtured opposite political worldviews. Smaller segments of the Jewish population of the former Russian Empire came under the new nation-states of Romania, Lithuania, Latvia, Estonia, and Finland. On the other hand, independent Poland and the Soviet Union split among themselves the bulk of the Jewish communities, with three and a half and three million Jews, respectively. The establishment of a Soviet federation of republics reinforced old regional and cultural identities while at the same time forging new ones that intersected with an all-Soviet identity, rooted in ideology as much as in geography. In other words, the existence of a Ukrainian, a Belorussian, an Uzbek, or an Azerbaijan Soviet Socialist Republic strengthened preexisting notions of Jewish regional identities while shaping new ones *ex novo*. In the new Soviet context, then, "Russian Jewries" eventually yielded to "Soviet Jewries."[11]

This book discusses how different Jews, in different geographical contexts, fared in this comprehensive experiment in noncapitalist modernity: socialism. It narrates the lived experiences of those Jewish men and women who became enthralled with the power of the revolutionary dream, of those who agonized because of the havoc that the new system wreaked on their previous lives and communities, and of those in between who adapted to and even succeeded in the new society regardless of their political engagement with communist ideology. The possibilities to resist the system, to circumvent its principles, to continue practicing Judaism, or to support an underground Zionist organization officially deemed as anti-Soviet, but also the possibility of hastening change and rising to a position of political power, hinged on all kinds of variables. The recognition that place, gender, and age matter to understand the ways in which the Jewish experience in Soviet society unfolded underpins the following chapters. The encounter with the new regime not only unfolded differently based on the age group and sex of the individual but was also contingent on whether this encounter unfolded in a Soviet metropolis, in an agricultural settlement, in a Belorussian shtetl, or in a small town near Samarkand.

While the purpose of the volume is to explore how different Jewries became Soviet in the 1920s, our story also pays close attention to the response of world Jewry—including personalities, organizations, or the common folk in North America, Europe, and Palestine—to the establishment of the new system. By tracing some lines of contact that remained open between Jews in the Soviet Union and the outside world, the volume reveals how these reactions fluctuated between open antagonism and impassioned support.[12]

Without succumbing to a common tendency among historians of trying to interpret the Jewish experience overall as exceptional, this volume does acknowledge some unique aspects that marked the encounter between Jews and the Soviet regime. One of these aspects pertains to the way in which Jews, more than any other group, went from being a marginal minority, oppressed by numerous legal restrictions under the tsar, to becoming a remarkably visible, prominent, and even influential one following the Bolsheviks' commitment to their emancipation.[13]

The exploration of rupture and continuity in Jewish life from the prerevolutionary years to the Bolshevik era is one of the broad themes that runs through this volume. The following chapters probe how and to what extent the new Soviet system transformed prerevolutionary Jewish religious, cultural, and political identities and life, as well as how and to what extent the new government succeeded in contending with the tsarist legacy of official anti-Jewish discrimination and amending popular violence and active expressions of hostility toward Jews. Zooming in on questions of continuity in the midst of revolutionary breaks, and investigating how new and old ways of life coexisted, enriches our understanding of the Jewish experience in the Soviet Union of the 1920s.

Furthermore, by drawing comparisons between the process of modernization and assimilation of Jews in Soviet society to that of Jews in Europe and North America, this volume endeavors to integrate the study of the Soviet Jewish experience into the broader context of modern Jewish history. If, for instance, there certainly were similarities in the ways in which the Jewish minorities of Europe, the United States, and the Soviet Union integrated into their surrounding societies in the early decades of the twentieth century, there also were significant differences. The forceful role played by the state as a driving (and often) violent force compelling assimilation and imposing conformity remained unique to the communist context. The tempo of change was sudden and brutal. Only in the Soviet Union, moreover, did the state rely on internal colonizing agents to coerce through communism the modernization and assimilation of the different ethnic groups. In the Jewish case, the state mobilized the population through the Evsektsiia, or the Jewish section of the Communist Party.[14] By carrying out the Sovietization of the Jewish masses, spreading among them the ideas of Marxism, and enforcing on them the official campaigns against Judaism, Hebrew, and Zionism, the Evsektsiia also actively promoted their modernization, secularization, and assimilation into the socialist system.[15]

Overall, this volume relies on published literature and archival sources that allow us to reconsider the Soviet Jewish experience by pushing back against the victimization narrative crafted during the Cold War. This narrative favors the reading of Jewish life in the Soviet Union as one of mere suffering, destruction, and martyrdom. While in many respects and for many Jews, the Soviet experiment did indeed represent the "worst of times," in other respects and for many other Jews, it represented "the best of times." Without ignoring the heavy toll that the brutality of the new system took on many aspects of Jewish life, this volume also recognizes some key aspects that informed the Jewish experience beneficially or at least constructively. More specifically, this book chronicles four original features that epitomize the experience of Jews in the wake of the establishment of the Soviet Union.

First, what stands out is the extraordinary upward mobility and rapid success achieved by Jews in different spheres of Soviet life. If under the tsar, the Jewish minority advanced through an anomalous status of being a relatively and sometimes even highly educated, mostly urban population within a largely rural, illiterate society, whose social mobility was hindered by legal restrictions, under the Soviets the lack of official constraints governing Jews' lives allowed them to achieve a far greater degree of mobility and attain remarkable feats. The accomplishments of Jews in the economic, cultural, and political sectors of Soviet society seem comparable only to the heights reached by German Jewry at the time of the Weimar Republic. This impressive process started out in the 1920s and paved the way for a future successful trend that persisted in the 1930s and even 1940s. Second, the official campaigns against antisemitism endorsed by the Soviet government to combat the tsarist legacy of anti-Jewish violence and discrimination, supported through extensive state funding, existed nowhere else in Europe. Organized efforts to harm members of the Jewish minority and even expressions of animosity against them, which under the tsar had become culturally acceptable, were generally criminalized by the Soviets. Third, as part of the state's process to Sovietize its inhabitants, it championed the establishment of numerous organizations and institutions that operated in a Jewish language—in particular, but not only, in Yiddish—thus promoting the flourishing of Jewish cultures. Finally, in the push to "normalize" Jewish economic life and employment patterns and to adjust them to the socialist system through productivization, the state funded the establishment of hundreds of agricultural colonies. In an unparalleled development in Jewish economic life in modern times, this process eventually attracted 10 percent of the overall Jewish population living within Soviet borders. Thousands set about farming the land, thus giving rise to an actual revolution in Jewish life, comparable only to the agricultural experiment launched by the Jewish pioneers who reached the Land of Israel in the early decades of the twentieth century.

As the following chapters make evident, for three million Jews in the Soviet Union, the 1920s would be simultaneously "the best of times and the worst of times."

1

THE JEWS IN REVOLUTION

At the end of the nineteenth and beginning of the twentieth century, an impressive number of political parties and movements, with a remarkable range of newspapers, organizations, and clubs, came into being in the larger and smaller Jewish settlements of the Russian Empire. A new Jewish political life emerged with full force, making the radical choices of nationalism and socialism, or the combination thereof, appealing for many young men and women. Several developments had led more and more Jews to feel increasingly impotent in Russian society, which in turn made alternatives to liberalism, like socialism and nationalism, more and more appealing: first, the occasional eruption of anti-Jewish violence in the cities of the Pale of Settlement, which had culminated in the pogroms of the 1880s, 1901–1903, and 1905; second, the harsh May 1882 anti-Jewish decrees adopted by Tsar Alexander III, which drastically curtailed Jewish socioeconomic growth and diversification and which remained in effect until 1917; and third, the quota system in institutions of higher learning enacted against Jewish students in 1887, which restricted their upward mobility until it was removed in the spring of 1917.[1] As different shades of Zionism and socialism became real options and won over the support of thousands of Jews, the relationship with the Russian state began to change and deteriorate.

The path to solving the Jewish question through emancipation and integration, in which so many Jewish intellectuals and thinkers had placed all their hopes, collapsed via a ripple effect, first with the assassination of Tsar Alexander II, who as a consequence never granted Jews the full-fledged equality they claimed, and then with the conservative political turn that enveloped Russian society under the reigns of Alexander III and Nicholas II, accompanied by anti-Jewish legislation and the radicalization of an increasingly frustrated opposition, as well as with growing popular animosity against the Jewish minority. Popular anger brought anti-Jewish violence, which tsarist authorities generally ignored. All this corroded the hope that Jewish emancipation was imminent, and the loss of faith in prospects of emancipation forced Jews to rethink their political program.

The 1903 pogrom in Kishinev played a key role in the rethinking process. The anti-Jewish riots unleashed in the capital city of the Bessarabia *guberniia* of the Russian Empire resulted in forty-seven Jews killed, almost one hundred critically wounded, as many women raped, and hundreds of Jewish houses and stores destroyed. Russian officials made no attempt to put an end to the violence until the third day of the pogrom.[2] Writing about the Jewish response to the events, the cultural and political Jewish activist S. Ansky noted at the time, "The Kishinev pogrom . . . met a new Jewish people, very sensitive to its human dignity, holding an enormous store of militant energy within itself. . . . In everybody, and before all else, there emerged the thirst for revenge."[3]

In the wake of the pogrom, Jewish people turned increasingly to movements and ideologies that favored socialism and nationalism; these included, for instance, the Bund—or the General Union of Jewish Workers in Lithuania, Poland, and Russia, established in Vilna in October 1897—and Labor-Zionism, along with the Jewish Social Democratic Labor Party (Poale-Tsiyon), established in Poltava in 1906.[4] Meanwhile, the Russian authorities concluded that they would gain more from ostracizing and marginalizing Jews than from taking after the states in western and central Europe and emancipating the Jewish minority. As radicalism and anti-state activities in tsarist Russia crystallized among Jews, the term "patriot" became a synonym for a rabid antisemite: this was the case especially at the time of the first Russian Revolution of 1905, with mass Jewish politics in action and a new outburst of bloody pogroms.[5] The editors of the Russian-language Jewish journal *Voskhod* (The dawn) captured this moment of profound change as follows: "These pogroms, coming now at the height of the Russian revolutionary struggle, on the day of the triumph of Russian freedom, confused, discouraged and disappointed the Jews who had thrown themselves with such enthusiasm into the struggle for freedom. . . . Jewish impotence and alienation were again underlined, and faith wavered in those steps to political freedom already undertaken."[6] Alienation grew during World War I, as government repression increased and Russian troops committed horrific acts of violence against Jews in the battle zone.[7]

In February 1917, the tsarist state collapsed suddenly, perhaps even unexpectedly.[8] Food queues in the capital city of Petrograd turned into political demonstrations, and peasants, soldiers, liberals, and socialists demanded in unison the end of autocracy.[9] The February Revolution turned out to be a spontaneous, popular insurrection: while socialism had grown into an absolute movement with a large consensus, especially in the cities, the support for autocracy gave way among most social classes, including the peasantry in the countryside. A socially polarized empire, with a weak tsar and new political forces on the horizon, was furthermore caught up in the military disaster of World War I, when an unprepared imperial army faced the German army, at the time the most modern military in Europe. In the midst of the horrendous destruction produced by the "war to end all wars," in which almost two of the twelve million soldiers mobilized into the Russian army lost their lives, the expectation that the February Revolution would usher in a better world imbued the hearts and minds of everyone, everywhere.

On March 15, in the midst of World War I and the February Revolution, Tsar Nicholas II abdicated in a railroad carriage outside the city of Pskov, in the northwestern region of the empire. The news spread quickly throughout the world. On that same day, a crowd of fifteen thousand people gathered in New York City in Madison Square Garden (which at time would have been an overflow crowd) to celebrate. In the Lower East Side, a neighborhood of Jewish immigrants, thousands met in Seward Park "to read the bulletins of the Yiddish dailies which were being posted hourly."[10] On March 16, the *Forward* greeted the news with great jubilation: "That which has long been awaited has finally come! A free Russian people, a free Jewish people in Russia! Is this a dream?"[11] Back in Russia, the workers, peasants, soldiers, professional elites, intellectuals, and socialists of all parties, who had grown profoundly dissatisfied with the status quo, shouted, "Down with the tsar!" and truly meant it. While the emotions fluctuated along with the events, most residents of the former Russian Empire, including Jews, agreed that there was no going back to the Russia of the tsars. But if there was no going back, what then should come next?

Two centers of power emerged from the collapse of the tsarist government: on the one hand, the Provisional Government, which retained formal authority and was led first by the Constitutional Democratic Party, better known as the Kadets, and later by the Mensheviks and Socialist Revolutionaries; and on the other hand, the workers of Petrograd (as Saint Petersburg was renamed after the outbreak of World War I), who together with the soldiers of the city's garrison, established the Soviet of Workers' and Soldiers' Deputies, a representative body of the capital's workers and soldiers.[12] The very existence of a "dual power" split between the Provisional Government and the Petrograd Soviet confirmed the intense polarization existing in society between the upper and lower strata of the population. The soviets, or councils, which had emerged as political bodies to lead workers and organize strikes before the revolution, offered only conditional support to the Provisional Government. If at the beginning of the revolution the Socialist Revolutionary Party and the Mensheviks largely controlled the Soviets, with the war progressing and the ongoing defeats of the Russian army, the Bolsheviks eventually came to dominate both of them. Lenin's party took advantage of the Provisional Government's failure to establish an industrial peace and guarantee good conditions of work and fair wages for workers and, most importantly, of its inability to obtain peace terms with Germany and withdraw from the war. Without the war, the Bolshevik seizure of power remained highly improbable. Shouting the slogan "all power to the soviets," the Bolsheviks began to grow in support and promised to overthrow the Provisional Government.

Jewish Voices in the Russian Revolutions

The Russian poet Osip Mandelshtam, who was born in Warsaw in 1891 to a wealthy Jewish family, captured the complexity and ambivalence of the mood and passions generated by the events of 1917 in his poem "Vek" (The age). Expressing his hopes and apprehensions for the future of post-revolutionary Russia, Mandelshtam referred to rebirth as well as rupture. "And the buds," he wrote, "will swell again, and the green shoots will sprout, but your spine has been smashed my beautiful, pitiful, age."[13] In Mandelshtam's words, the revolution's seeds of redemption were intertwined with its destructive power.

Jewish reactions to the events sparked by 1917 were both inconsistent and dynamic. While the majority of Jews may have agreed that the end of tsarism could not be undone, the revolution elicited different and even contradictory responses ranging from enthusiasm to fear. In the midst of the tumultuous course of events, political choices, tactics, and allegiances changed rapidly from month to month. The many voices of Jewish activists and leaders of the Jewish communities located in different areas of the former Russian Empire can be best captured through the image of a seesaw, oscillating between belief in the prosperous future of a more democratic Russia and the realization that violence was deeply entrenched in the events of 1917 and could be expected to continue through the years to come. Max Goldfarb, a Bundist living in New York on the eve of the revolution, captured the great expectations and dread tied to the events of 1917. He experienced simultaneous ecstasy and deep concern that 1917, like 1905, would unleash pogroms and that the counterrevolution would "use Jewish blood to quench the fires of the Russian Revolution."[14] For Goldfarb, the impulse for freedom seemed to be closely interconnected with the possibility of anti-Jewish violence.

The Provisional Government had introduced freedom of speech, press, and assembly for all citizens. It had also granted Jews an array of political and civil rights, ending their decades-long legal segregation. This legislation also marked the long-awaited abolishment of the Pale of Settlement.[15] An editorial from a Russian newspaper issued in Moscow at the time declared that "the act abolishing religious and national restrictions should be considered as the greatest conquest of the revolution."[16] Jews across the political spectrum, and regardless of their class allegiance, greeted the end of tsarism with enthusiasm.[17] The months following the February Revolution offered a space of opportunity for all, unleashing high hopes and generating frantic political, national, and cultural activities.

In the absence of legal curtailment, the already impressive number of Jewish parties, movements, and organizations stirred with a frenzy that before the revolution had been inconceivable both in scope and in quality. Especially in larger urban centers, Jewish political life emerged with full force as young people strove to partake and have their voices heard in society, in culture, in politics. Issued just three days before the Jewish holiday of Passover, the emancipation decree was hailed by many Jews almost with religious fervor. In the words of a contemporary, "The Jewish masses viewed the February Revolution as the advent of the Messiah."[18] In Petrograd, some Jewish families celebrated the decree as a modern "exodus" and chose to read its text at the seder table instead of reading the traditional Haggadah, the chronicle of the Jewish liberation from slavery in Egypt.[19] All the major publications in Petrograd, whether liberal or conservative, hailed the emancipation of the Jews. Even the editors of *Novoe vremia* (New times), which had relentlessly spread anti-Jewish propaganda in the later imperial years, welcomed the emancipation decree with the following statement, "Nothing aroused such hatred in society towards the authorities as this persecution of ethnic minorities and religious denominations."[20]

Far removed from the revolutionary centers of Petrograd and Moscow, the news about the revolution reached the provinces as well, albeit with some delay. The presence of the retreating German army on the eastern front slowed down the transmission of information from the capital. Writing from Mohyliv-Podilskyi, in the Vinnytsia region of Ukraine, Max Sadikoff, a member of the local Jewish community, recorded the enthusiasm that broke out when the news about the revolution finally reached the city.[21] For the first time, he recalled, Jews took to the streets en masse and together with local Poles and Ukrainians displayed their support for the revolution and flew the blue and white Jewish flag. No longer illegal in their activities, Bundists and Zionists engaged in the intensive cultural and political work of opening libraries, writing creative works of fiction, organizing theater productions, and establishing youth clubs, publishing houses, and evening schools.[22] This remarkable outpouring of cultural work took root in the cities as well as in the shtetls located in the heart of the former Pale of Settlement. By World War I, new ideas, values, texts, and commodities had reached the most remote Jewish small towns, some of which even had makeshift movie theaters.[23]

More than six hundred kilometers north of Vinnytsia, the city of Minsk too became a theater of stormy events. Joy and panic quickly spread through the city and simultaneously seized Jewish and non-Jewish workers as reports about the February Revolution reached the city. Many Jewish workers cheered the revolution; others, out of trepidation, refused to participate in the demonstrations in favor of Lenin scheduled to take place in the city. As support for the revolution grew, fear abated somewhat, and workers' demonstrations moved from the factory kitchen to the city theater and onto the street.

In Minsk, like in other cities and towns of the former Pale of Settlement, Jews took advantage of the new freedom introduced by the Provisional Government. Different Zionist groups in the city issued different publications, including the Yiddish weekly *Dos yidishe vort* (The Jewish word), the Yiddish biweekly *Der yid* (The Jew), and the Russian-language publication *He-khaver* (The friend), published by a local Zionist youth organization. On the other end of the political spectrum, the Bund consolidated its position through the support of prominent local leaders. In June 1917, it issued the party's central organ—the Yiddish daily *Der veker*—and the organ of the local section of the youth organization Yugend Bund: the Yiddish journal *Der yunger arbeter* (The young worker). In the fall of 1917, Minsk held the official celebration for the twentieth anniversary of the founding of the Bund, with concerts, plays, a public session of the Central Committee, and a street demonstration.[24]

But amid the extraordinary vitality of the many Jewish cultural and political projects that materialized in 1917, some bad omens were on the horizon. Back in Vinnytsia, Max Sadikoff, who would eventually become head of the Committee for Relief of Pogrom Victims in Mohyliv-Podilskyi and lead the local efforts to collect eyewitness accounts of the violence that would soon be unleashed in the region, acknowledged the growth of a palpable anti-Jewish sentiment. For one, right-wing groups dismissed the Provisional Government as an abortive institution by falsely branding its leader, the moderate socialist revolutionary Alexander Kerensky, as a Jew.[25] On the other side of the political spectrum, left-wing activists made the same false accusation to scorn the opposition. Some Bolshevik leaders conveyed to the voters queueing up to vote for the All-Russian Constituent Assembly's elections that they should cast their vote for Bolshevism because of Kerensky's Jewishness.[26]

The bloody coup d'état launched by the Bolsheviks in October 1917 was not inevitable. However, the onslaught of World War I and the February Revolution did set the stage for Lenin's seizure of power, for the ensuing violence that erupted during the civil war years, from 1918 to 1921, and ultimately for the failure of a possible liberal path for Russia. While the Provisional Government set the date for the election to the Constituent Assembly on November 12, 1917, the voting never took place: the October Revolution, which broke out on October 25, ended the Provisional Government, and Kerensky, who headed the Provisional Government from July to October 1917, was overthrown by Lenin. If the "Judaization" of the revolutionary events of February never became a mass phenomenon, the perception of the Bolsheviks' rise to power as a Jewish coup became widely accepted among different political forces. The fact that one of the prominent leaders of the October Revolution, and the people's commissar for military and naval affairs, was a Jew by the name of Leon (Bronstein) Trotsky certainly encouraged that association early on.

Many leading figures of the Bolshevik and Menshevik factions were in emigration or in exile on the eve of the revolution. The February events drew them back to Russia with force. Trotsky himself, who had moved to New York in January 1917 and lived in the Bronx for ten weeks, reemigrated to Russia, heeding the call of the revolution.[27] In the fall 1917, a needle-trade journal issued in New York lamented that as a result of this great migration of Jews back to Russia, the industry would be taken over by other ethnicities, including Greeks, Hungarians, and Italians.[28] One of the editors of the Yiddish *Forward* described the formidable allure he felt toward revolutionary Russia as follows: "Life is strange: my body is in America. My heart and head and soul and life are in that great wonderful land, which was so cursed and which is now so blessed, the land of my youth and revived dreams—Russia."[29] While retrospectively such comments might seem naïve, at the time, their author made these remarks genuinely and sincerely.

For some émigrés and exiles who returned to Russia at the time of the dramatic events of 1917, the messianic call unleashed in the revolution yielded to disillusionment once it came face to face with the Bolsheviks' rejection of any compromise with other socialist movements and parties. In the wake of 1917, at the age of seventy-four, the Russian anarchist Peter Kropotkin returned to his native Russia from Great Britain, but his enthusiasm quickly turned into disappointment. He famously noted that the Bolsheviks "buried the Revolution."[30] Alexander (Sasha) Berkman and Emma Goldman—both Russian-born Jews who became involved in the anarchist movement in New York but were arrested and deported back to Russia in 1919 due to their politics—voiced their initial support for the Bolshevik Revolution. However, the violent suppression of any real or imagined criticism of the Bolshevik path to the revolution, in particular the ruthless quashing of the 1921 Kronstadt Rebellion (the revolt launched by sailors and civilians against the Bolshevik authority in the city of Kronstadt), disenchanted the anarchist couple.[31] In September 1921, on the eve of leaving Russia under the nascent Soviet regime, Berkman confided to his diary, "One by one the embers of hope have died out. Terror and despotism have crushed the life born in October. The slogans of the Revolution are forsworn, its ideals stifled in the blood of the people. . . . The Revolution is dead, its spirit cries in the wilderness. . . . The Bolshevik myth must be destroyed. I have decided to leave Russia."[32]

From afar, however, many Jewish activists and institutions remained keen in their support for the revolution, even following the Bolsheviks' coup. When in May 1918, Abraham Cahan, the editor of the *Forward* and a prominent voice in the Socialist Party of America, found out that the Bolsheviks decided to erect in Moscow a monument to Karl Marx to mark his hundredth birthday, he conveyed his "affection and enthusiasm" for them. "Truly, it reads like a story of the coming of the Messiah," he wrote. And he added, "How, then, can one bear the Bolsheviki a grudge? How can one experience anything like a hostile feeling against them? . . . Is it not about time for all of us to cast off our former bitterness and venom?"[33] In the post-October months and years, organizations like US labor unions, the International Ladies' Garment Workers' Union, and the Jewish daily *Forward* declared their support for Lenin's government.

Jewish Choices in the Russian Revolutions

In October 1917, a small but fiercely committed and highly organized group of Social-Democrats gradually took over the core of the tsarist dominion. Under Lenin's leadership, the revolutionary vanguard of the Bolshevik Party began to create a one-party political system, a state-controlled economy, and an official atheistic culture wherever it extended its power. On the one hand, the Bolsheviks did nothing else but assert their ownership over a vocabulary and a vision that, abundant in violence and in antiauthoritarian ethos and shared by most socialists, permeated the general atmosphere at the time. The Bolsheviks relied on keen organizational skills, talked the good line of "peace" in the midst of a bloody, unpopular world war, and encouraged people to express their rage full voice against the previous government and centers of authority.[34] But unlike other social-democratic ideologies, Bolshevism explicitly embraced the principle of centralized rule by the select few: as the vanguard of the proletariat, the Communist Party's rule should remain unchallenged and unquestionable. It was not by chance that in March 1918, the Russian Social-Democratic Party (Bolsheviks) adopted the name the Russian Communist Party (Bolsheviks), excising the word "democratic."[35] The Bolsheviks identified their enemies based on class and political allegiances (real or imagined), while they largely disregarded ethnicity or nationality as defining features of potential adversaries. Hence, members of ethnic minorities, many of which, including Lithuanians, Poles, Georgians, and Jews, had been banished from tsarist politics, could now join the political leadership and serve as the vanguard of the proletariat.

One Jew who did so was Adolph Joffe, who under the tsar was exiled to Siberia for his revolutionary activity. Born in 1883 in Simferopol, Joffe joined the Bolshevik faction and served as the chairman of the Petrograd Revolutionary Committee, which overthrew the Provisional Government. From November 1917 until January 1918, Joffe headed the Soviet delegation that was sent to Brest-Litovsk to end the hostilities with Germany; following talks there that lasted for two months, Soviet Russia officially withdrew from World War I. That a Jew could lead peace treaty negotiations with the Central Powers (Germany, Austria-Hungary, Bulgaria, and the Ottoman Empire) on behalf of Soviet Russia would have been unthinkable before 1917.

In the city of Minsk, for instance, which during World War I became the headquarters of the Western Front, there was no strong Bolshevik faction at the time of the February Revolution. A separate Bolshevik group appeared in the city soviet only in May 1917. Yet, Lenin's supporters, many of whom were dissatisfied soldiers and workers, easily defeated their opponents. On November 8, following the Bolshevik takeover in Petrograd, local Bolsheviks organized a Revolutionary Committee and declared all power to the soviets, while different factions of Mensheviks, Socialist-Revolutionaries, and Bundists issued a declaration condemning the revolution and called for the transfer of authority to the Municipal Duma. Aron Vaynshteyn, known by the nom de guerre Rakhmiel, who had been elected chairman of the Bund's Central Committee in April 1917, headed the Minsk Duma. On November 9, the whole city was an armed camp, and a bloody clash between the Bolsheviks and those who opposed them seemed inevitable. The two sides ultimately reached a compromise and signed a truce—the Bolsheviks fearing a setback in case of a direct clash with their opponents. However, as soon as they got hold of reinforcements from Red Army soldiers on the Western Front, they broke the truce and reinstated the Revolutionary Committee. On November 22, the Minsk Soviet of Workers and Soldiers dissolved the Municipal Duma.

Compared to most ethnic groups scattered across the territories of the former Russian Empire, Jews were more involved in politics. This phenomenon grew mostly out of their higher literacy rates and their overwhelming concentration in urban areas. Nevertheless, it would be an exaggeration to argue that every Jew took part in the stormy events in and after 1917. It would also be misleading to argue that those who did partake in the events did so out of a clear ideological conviction, as Trotsky or Joffe did. Political views did not always determine the resolve to support the Bolsheviks, the Ukrainian forces that opposed the Soviets and strove to gain control over the southwestern region of the former empire, or other socialist parties that rejected Lenin's view of the revolution. Let us consider, for example, the city of Berdychiv: the fourth largest city in Ukraine; after Odesa, the second major commercial center in all of southern Ukraine; and the most Jewish city in Ukraine. An important Hasidic center, where even tsarist policemen spoke Yiddish, it was dubbed "the Jewish capital" or the "Jerusalem of Volin" (the Yiddish name of Volhynia, the historic region in western Ukraine in which it was located) and, by those who left the city for Palestine in the early 1920s, the "Tel Aviv of Goles," a reference to the fact that its population was overwhelmingly Jewish: here Jews constituted the bulk of the city population.[36] Here, from late 1918 to early 1919, the city's mayor was Jewish: the Bundist activist Dovid Lipets (also known as Max Goldfarb, mentioned earlier in this chapter), who also served as head of the local Jewish community.

In Berdychiv, most Jews did not support the Bolshevik faction or those forces that sought to establish an independent Ukraine (from 1917 to 1920, the city came for the most part under Ukrainian rule).[37] While the Bundist and Zionist movements canvassed conspicuous support in the city, overall the political life of Jews took up small, narrow circles. Not everyone was involved in politics, even in this most political of times. For many, the only politics that really mattered related to commerce, the preoccupation with which dominated everyday life even in 1918.[38] In Zvi Kaminski's memoir about Berdychiv, he skipped over the revolution entirely.[39]

A deep-seated myth about massive Jewish support for the Bolsheviks crystallized in these years. Yet, very few Jews actually backed Lenin's party.[40] According to the 1922 Bolshevik Party census, only 958 Jews had joined Lenin's party before 1917.[41] While the October Revolution confirmed the legal emancipation of Jews, allowing them to join the political system, become citizens of the state, and participate in the newly established socialist society without quotas or discrimination, in 1917–1918 only 1,175 Jews joined the Bolshevik Party.[42] Compared to the many socialist and Zionist parties competing for the vote of the Jewish population before the outbreak of World War I, the Bolsheviks enjoyed the lowest amount of support. The fact that many Jews served in the leading ranks of the Bolsheviks made no difference, insofar as for most of them, Jewishness (whether in its religious or national manifestation) had no bearing at all on their identity. For Bolsheviks like Lev Kamenev, Grigory Zinoviev, and of course Trotsky, Jewishness was nothing more than an (unfortunate) accident of birth.[43]

A month after the October coup, Benzion Katz (a journalist and the former editor of the prominent Hebrew newspaper *Ha-Zeman* [The time], issued from 1903 until World War I first in Saint Petersburg and then in Vilna, and editor of the anticommunist Hebrew weekly *Ha-am* [The people], issued in Moscow until June 1918), from the capital of the Soviet state voiced his unwavering rejection of Bolshevism as follows: "The Russian revolution surpasses in its savagery all the negative features of the French revolution. . . . We have only one hope, that the reign of this inquisition will not last long."[44] Obviously, the meaning of the October Revolution differed significantly according to geographic location, age, sex, and social background of the individual who was directly or indirectly affected by the events. Depending on whether they lived in an urban or rural setting, Jewish soldiers, the wives of Jewish merchants, Jewish peddlers, or young Jewish revolutionaries viewed the Bolshevik coup differently. However, most Jews shared some common political views. By early 1918, the majority of Jews living in the territories of the former tsarist empire supported the Zionist movement. The results of the January 1918 elections to the national Jewish congress confirmed this both at the local and at the all-Russian level. The majority of the votes cast by Jews were in favor of the Zionist parties, with 60 percent of the electorate voting for Zionist parties and organizations. While different non-Zionist socialist parties received a quarter of the vote, Orthodox religious groups won 12 percent of the vote. Jewish party politics expressed the same commonality in the All-Russian Constituent Assembly elections: Jewish public opinion overwhelmingly backed coalitions of Jewish parties in the political center, while overlooking Lenin's party.[45] Zionist and religious parties received 417,215 of the 498,198 votes cast, while the socialist parties (including Socialist-Zionists) received a total of 80,983 votes (31,123 votes for the Bund and 20,538 for Poale-Tsiyon).[46]

Zionism had been the dominant political force among the Jews of Russia and the main adversary in vying for control over the Jewish community before October 1917. The Bund, for instance, which had an impressive number of charismatic militants with great oratorial skills, never quite managed to represent the Jewish masses as its leaders argued it did. In competing for mass support, the Bund had to contend not so much with Orthodox groups and other socialist parties but with Zionism. In the summer of 1917, the Zionists could count on 140,000 members (and many more unofficial supporters), while the Bund only had 30,000 members.[47] If the Zionist influence on the Jewish street grew significantly in the frenzied months that followed February 1917 and the ensuing outburst of political and cultural work that accompanied the decree on freedom of speech, press, and assembly, it was the Balfour Declaration that swayed the political views of thousands. The British government's commitment to establishing a Jewish national home in Palestine, publicly endorsed on November 2, 1917, came to dominate Jewish political expectations. The message of national salvation took on a new redemptive meaning. By the end of 1917, the organization of Russian Zionists included 300,000 members and 1,200 local branches.[48]

Besides the support for Zionism, other factors explain why many Jews did not back the Bolsheviks in the early phase of the revolution. First, Lenin's avowed atheism and uncompromising rejection of "the opium of the people"—as Marx defined religion's power in blinding the masses—probably dissuaded many Jews. Second, the Bolsheviks had long denied to the Jewish minority the status of nation. Stalin voiced this position very clearly in 1913, when in an essay titled "Marxism and the National Question," he argued that Jews lacked the primary attributes of nationhood, namely, one common language, one common territory, and one common economic life. He argued, "The question of national autonomy for Russian Jews assumes a somewhat curious character: autonomy is being proposed for a nation whose future is denied and whose existence has still to be proved!"[49] His comments, which targeted in particular the Bund and its claim for Jewish national-cultural autonomy, must have alienated the supporters of those Jewish parties across the political spectrum that asserted that Jews constituted a nation. Third, the majority of the Jewish population rejected the Bolshevik rise to power out of economic reasons: insofar as most Jews belonged to the lower or middle class, they feared that the Bolshevik victory would result in their loss of status and their property.[50] This negative attitude toward the Bolshevik Revolution, which was shared by many non-Jews too, was overturned during the civil war.[51] The brutality of the pogroms and the genocidal impulses they unleashed forced the Jews to reconsider their view of Bolshevik power.

The Turning Point: The Pogroms of the Civil War

The dean of Russian Jewish historiography, Simon Dubnov, was cautious in his enthusiasm from the very beginning and feared the eruption of anti-Jewish violence and pogroms as early as March 8, 1917. While the Jewish families in Petrograd were reading the emancipation decree in lieu of the Haggadah, Dubnov wrote in his diary, "This revolution has in it something that appears to be very strange: it is like a spring sun in a tough winter cold, just like today's weather. There is light but no warmth . . . and the soul bounces between hope and worry."[52] He sensed that the revolution's theoretical attempt to create a better world was inherently flawed and grounded in violence.

It was the extreme violence unleashed during the years 1918–1921 that ultimately swayed the overwhelming majority of Jews—including many

Zionists and Bundists—to support the Bolshevik cause. The pervasiveness, extraordinary brutality, and unprecedented nature of the anti-Jewish pogroms that followed the revolution influenced and reshaped the relationship between Jews and Bolshevik power, sparking a new alliance, the Soviet Jewish alliance.[53] The unintended consequence of the violence, and the Bolsheviks' official condemnation of the pogroms, was for Jews to move closer to the new state and to central authorities. Pledging loyalty to the nascent Soviet state and joining its infrastructure not only meant empowerment and, for many, revenge for the suffering endured during the violence; for the Jewish minority siding with the Bolsheviks, it primarily meant protection from further indiscriminate attacks. The absence of pogroms perpetrated by the Red Army became a compelling factor in enticing Jews into supporting the Bolsheviks.[54]

The civil war that engulfed the territories of the former Russian Empire was a chaotic and ruthless conflict among a variety of more or less organized troops and armies that hoped to gain political and territorial control following the downfall of the tsar and the October Revolution. Led by Leon Trotsky, the Red Army fought on behalf of the Workers' and Soldiers' Soviet for the victory of Bolshevism. The Reds faced the White Volunteer Army, a union of anti-Bolshevik forces committed to the return of the monarchy to the territories of the former Russian Empire and to the ultimate defeat of Lenin's party.[55] Symon Petliura, the head of the Directory of the Ukrainian People's Republic, which existed as an independent entity from 1917 to 1920, spearheaded the Ukrainian troops in a ruthless battle for sovereignty against the Red Army. Fighting on behalf of the Second Polish Republic, Polish troops also faced the Red Army from late 1918 until March 1921 in what came to be known as the Polish-Soviet War, with the war's main territories of contention being present-day Ukraine and Belarus. In addition to the military forces involved, a host of paramilitary and anarchist bands with fluctuating loyalties also took part in the war, launching insurrections that destabilized the control exerted by different armies and troops at any given time. The Ukrainian lands, in particular, where the overwhelming majority of the Jews of the former Russian Empire lived at the time, became one combat zone and the epicenter of the violence and ethnic conflict.[56]

All troops and military units perpetrated atrocities against the Jewish population. These pogroms were new and stood out in the long history of anti-Jewish violence in eastern Europe: they combined messy mob attacks with highly organized military operations that grew out of wartime violence. The White forces, often relying on their Cossack units known for their militaristic brutality, systematically terrorized Jewish communities and are blamed for 17 percent of the pogroms.[57] Forces proclaiming loyalty to the Ukrainian Directory perpetrated approximately 40 percent of the pogroms against Jews on Ukrainian territory. While officially committed to combating attacks on Jewish civilians, in fact even the Red Army became complicit in instances of anti-Jewish violence, perpetrating approximately 9 percent of the pogroms in the early months of the war.[58]

The violence became unprecedented both in nature and in scale. Approximately fifteen hundred pogroms—which developed as military pogroms but which also saw the overwhelming dynamics of intimate violence of neighbors killing neighbors—were carried out in more than eight hundred towns and shtetls, most of them located in Ukraine: as many as 150,000 Jews died as a result of the violence, with thousands of Jewish children orphaned, hundreds of thousands of Jewish men and women wounded or permanently disfigured, thousands of women raped, and Jewish homes looted or destroyed in their entirety.[59] The violence was perpetrated by military and paramilitary forces, but in the context of the power vacuum left by the collapsing state and the ensuing growing lawlessness, local peasants too often took part in the violence attacking their Jewish neighbors. In many places, the fragile and often strained relationships between Jews and their non-Jewish fellow residents resulted in massacres that were almost as deadly as the ones carried out by the military forces that occupied the town or shtetl.[60]

The pogroms occurred at a time of political uncertainty and sudden change of power, in the absence of a state that could deter or prevent the violence: when the advancing troops forced the retreat of the troops previously in control of the town, violence erupted. In the words of a survivor, "Our shtetl was at the center of a cat and mouse game, when the Ukrainian forces came in, the Poles fled, when the Poles came in, the Ukrainian fled."[61] In this never-ending game of power change, in a constant pursuit of near captures and repeated escapes, violence was most likely: this was the time when all contenders sought to reaffirm and reestablish power, often by looting, raping, and murdering.

The motivations for the violence differed vastly. The impetus was often rooted in anti-Jewish stereotypes and false rumors, which even included the traditional notion of Jews as Christ-killers or perpetrators of ritual murder. The neighbors' motivation for participating in the violence could range from ideological convictions to social pressure or the simple appeal of plunder. The following anecdote, which emerged at the time of the civil war, captures the role that looting played in triggering the pogroms, especially in the countryside in the context of desperate economic conditions: "During the civil war, a villager shouts hurrah for the incoming troops; and to the question 'Whose side are you on?' he answers: 'The ones coming in.'"[62] But in general, soldiers and civilians attacked Jews and plundered their property for two main reasons. On the one hand, the desperate economic conditions engendered by war since 1914 egged on soldiers and local peasants to loot the "Jewish capitalists," exploiters and archenemies of the proletariat, targeting Jewish-owned shops and plundering Jewish property. Emotions ran high due to the deadly combination of food shortages and rationing, which convinced the rioters—farmers, workers, and soldiers—of the existence of a Jewish plan to exploit their neighbors.[63] Anti-Jewish sentiment, which was widespread in late imperial Russia and intensified during World War I, became so embedded in everyday life during the civil war that it influenced the views of individuals regardless of the ideological camp to which they belonged. The same soldier who served in the imperial army may have joined the Red Army two months later and may eventually have sided with the White forces. In other words, soldiers—many of whom were poor peasants—often joined different armies based on the possibility of personal enrichment and access to food and clothing, rather than belief in any ideology.[64]

At the same time, anti-Jewish rhetoric repeatedly shifted from a focus on Jewish economic exploitation to a growing fear of Judeo-Bolshevism, the myth that conflated Jews with Bolshevism. Exclusivist nationalism, which scapegoated other ethnic groups, usually minorities, as dangerous threats to the nation's survival, had been on the rise since the late nineteenth century and peaked during World War I.[65] As such, it encouraged political leaders and military personnel on all sides to label the Jewish minority as disloyal and treacherous toward the Ukrainian dream of nationhood, the Polish reestablished nation-state, and the Russian Whites' vision of revitalized empire.[66] In the midst of a fierce war over land and political sovereignty, the troops and civilian population often imagined Jews as interlopers tearing at the heart of the nation's fabric, as compromised political actors who committed acts of espionage or spread communism, often notwithstanding their actual political choice. Jews could not fit in the different campaigns of ethnic homogenization.[67] The idea that Jews supported the Bolshevik Revolution served as a prime justification to attack Jewish communities.[68]

The myth of Judeo-Bolshevism possibly became the deadliest motivation for the pogroms of the civil war. The belief in a Judeo-Bolshevik conspiracy reached many people through a growingly sophisticated propaganda effort, which relied on newspapers, brochures, leaflets, and posters; it was put in place rather effectively by the White Volunteer Army but was employed also by other armies. Even local peasants in remote villages came under the spell of the Judeo-Bolshevik conspiracy. More than anyone else, Leon Trotsky, who led the Red Army, personified the specter of an alleged Jewish political symbiosis with communism. Slogans such as "This is for you because of Trotsky!" accompanied many pogroms.[69] In some places, when the Jewish community's delegates protested to the occupying forces against the ongoing violence, they were told to "go and complain to Trotsky" or that the violence would continue "as long as the Jewish youth and the Jewish working class back the Bolsheviks."[70] But Trotsky only represented the tip of the iceberg of a larger phenomenon. For instance, when the Ukrainian or White militias returned to a town that had been under the Red Army's occupation, Jews were often "remembered" as the only supporters of Bolshevik power. In the summer of 1919, the Red Army retreated, and the Ukrainian forces took control of a shtetl near Uman. A young Jew, who was also a committed Zionist and who had worked in the city administration under Bolshevik occupation, was remembered as the "Communist Jew," who planned to take over Ukraine. On the other hand, the new authorities in charge "forgot" about the young Ukrainian who had been appointed chief of police under the Bolshevik occupation of the shtetl. While nobody doubted his political allegiance to the Ukrainian cause, everyone doubted the political allegiance of the young Ukrainian Jew.[71]

Distinct waves of anti-Jewish pogroms ensued one after another in a continuum of violence, with each successive wave turning more violent than the previous one. The first wave of pogroms was carried out by the Russian army in the early years of World War I. The war provoked the brutal displacement of at least one million Jews and fueled an unprecedented humanitarian crisis of epic proportions that mobilized international relief organizations to provide medical and financial resources to aid the refugees.[72] World War I also destabilized the ethnic and religiously diverse borderland region, in particular the provinces of Volhynia, Podilia, Kyiv, Warsaw, and Galicia, where it caused the destruction of trade networks and local economies. Here, plunder and ethnic violence against different minorities became pervasive. Thousands of Poles, Armenians, Germans, and Jews living in the war zone faced the consequences of brutal deportation, which was frequently accompanied by indiscriminate violence at the hands of the Russian army. Jews were often singled out and charged with profiteering, which further mobilized civilians to commit acts of violence against the Jewish community. It was in the context of World War I that the pogroms became military actions. The experience of extreme brutality during World War I also removed the inhibition to kill civilians and desensitized everyone to the horrors of witnessing murder. In this climate, pogroms were not only the consequence of organized military violence; they also became the upshot of neighbors killing neighbors.

The Jews became victims of a second wave of violence in the wake of the Bolshevik Revolution: while contesting the existence of the newly independent Ukraine, the Red Army soldiers carried out brutal pogroms against the Jewish population from the end of 1917 into mid-1918. Although the nascent Soviet power would eventually rally around the slogan of opposition to antisemitism, it did not do so at first. In the context of a widespread upsurge in popular hostility against Jews, the Bolshevik leadership chose to ignore anti-Jewish violence. A prevailing antibourgeois sentiment dominated the residents of many towns and cities in the former Russian Empire and accelerated anti-Jewish violence: Red Army soldiers could be heard hollering, "smash the Yids," branding Jews as speculators and agents of the bourgeoisie, as they attacked Jewish merchants and traders, mostly to loot food and merchandise. In March 1918, the Red Guards—a volunteer regiment made of workers and poor peasants—perpetrated violent pogroms against the Jews of Hlukhiv, a city in Chernihiv *guberniia*, and Ekaterinoslav

(Dnipro). Hundreds of Jews, including children, were murdered under the slogan "We are going to slaughter all the bourgeoisie and the Yids," while the peasants from neighboring villages looted Jewish homes.[73] Red Army soldiers did not refrain from engaging in anti-Jewish violence, but unlike the members of the other troops involved in the conflict, they were publicly punished for their deeds.[74] Often the punishment was harsh: in one instance, in mid-1918, 138 Red Army soldiers who were found guilty of taking part in anti-Jewish pogroms in the region of Podilia were shot, and 28 were sentenced to life in prison or forced labor.[75] Yet, despite the later attempts to silence this aspect of the civil war in the Soviet memory of the events and to blame exclusively Petliura's forces and the military units of the Volunteer Army, the Red Army was indeed complicit in anti-Jewish violence.

The third and most intense wave of anti-Jewish violence began in late 1918, reached its peak in the summer of 1919, and continued through the end of 1920. The pogroms were perpetrated mostly by the White Army and Ukrainian militias and in certain areas by the Polish troops.[76] Almost everywhere, peasant insurgent groups and neighbors took part in the anti-Jewish violence. The pogrom carried out by the Ukrainian forces in February 1919 in the city of Proskuriv (now Khmelnytsky) became emblematic of the scope and breadth of the violence. Sixteen hundred Jews—including children, women, and the elderly—were killed in less than four hours for their alleged Bolshevik sympathies.[77] The killing became systematic, as neighbors and military troops together strove to eliminate as many Jews as possible, in the shortest amount of time possible. The perpetrators believed that the fight against Bolshevism demanded the elimination of the Jews.[78] The lawyer-investigator Arnold Hillerson, a member of the investigatory body of the Central Committee for Relief of Pogrom Victims, described the violence as follows in his report on the Proskuriv pogrom: "Proskuriv has the dubious honor of heralding a new era in pogrom execution. Prior pogroms had looting as their primary goal, meaning the pilfering of Jewish property; killings would follow the looting, but nonetheless remained secondary. . . . From Proskuriv on, the primary goal of pogroms in Ukraine was the wholesale slaughter of the Jewish population."[79]

The pogrom disrupted preexisting notions of time, upsetting the slow pace of life that marked the quotidian in times of peace in the hundreds of small towns where the region's Jews lived. One witness in the shtetl of Smila, Kyiv province, explained, "To be honest, it is challenging to determine when exactly the first pogrom ends and the second begins. The four months that the savage volunteers had their way in the town constituted one continuous pogrom. The Jewish population did not even have a moment of peace."[80] The shorter the time of occupation, the more intense the violence: "They stopped in the town for no more than 1.5–2 hours. But during that short time, they managed to get so much done and worked so zealously that the next day 107 casualties were brought to the Jewish cemetery. There were around 600 wounded. The number of rape victims was terribly high (according to some local doctors, the figure is over a thousand). . . . The destruction in the town was staggering. Suffice to say that [many] Jewish homes lost even their hearths and chimneys. Floors everywhere were torn up and ruined, the dirt in cellars dug up, often up to fifteen feet down."[81] Ukraine became the main stage of the battlefront, and here the small towns became the epicenter of the pogrom. Here, acts of violence and ethnic cleansing against Ukrainian Jews were so extraordinary that they foreshadowed the genocidal violence that would engulf the region some twenty years later, at the time of the Holocaust.[82]

Chronicling the destruction of the shtetl of Dubova, located a few miles southeast of the city of Uman, Rokhl Faygnberg, a Yiddish writer and a refugee who fled the pogroms near Odesa, explained how in May 1919 the violence resulted largely from neighbors joining the Ukrainian forces. As she wrote in her account of the destruction, "They were all locals. . . . Many smeared their faces so that they would not be recognized by Dubova Jews, but the Dubova Jews recognized them, [they were] the doctor's assistant, the mailman, the young Christian lads, who killed them with cold steel," at night, with pitchforks and axes.[83] At the same time, Faygnberg managed to escape the violence by going into hiding with her newborn son among the peasants of nearby villages, who provided assistance: they helped her disguise herself with a folk dress and a little cross to put around her child's neck. After all, there were still signs hanging from the telephone poles on the roads between Odesa and Balta, "calling on people to kill all little Jewish boys, because when they grow up they will all be communists."[84]

Like other places, Dubova experienced more than one pogrom, with each episode intensifying in brutality as local inhabitants became accustomed to carrying out mass murder. Three main pogroms succeeded each other from May to August 1919, with the quiet pogrom first, a display of intimate violence carried out mostly by local peasants who, following the Bolsheviks' retreat from the shtetl, attacked their Jewish neighbors. The second pogrom was accompanied by extensive looting, triggered by the critical loss of economic stability among all social classes in and around town: the second time around, the violence escalated, became more public, became ritualized, even carnivalesque, and turned into a sort of circus luring the bystanders' curious eyes, including the public spectacle of mass rape, which grew precisely at the time when looting was no longer an option and nothing else of value was left to take. On June 17, the Cossack detachment that supported the White forces killed a number of Jews in assembly-line fashion: forced toward the basement of the home of a local Jew, they were decapitated as they approached the staircase. The third time around, the violence intensified even more. The pogrom, referred to by survivors as the "great one," was carried out in early August 1919 by insurgent forces, who fought against the Red Army, with hundreds of Jews murdered at the site of the clay pit and "tortured like communists."[85] In due course, the perpetrators not only killed nearly the entire community of Jews, numbering approximately twelve hundred people, but proceeded to destroy important symbols of Jewish life, such as the Jewish cemetery, along with the gravestones, plowing through it and planting it with grain, fields, and gardens—thereby removing the "place and consciousness of Jewish Dubova." They excised the memory of Jewish Dubova, eradicating, in a way, the time when Jews had lived there.[86]

The ways in which pogrom victims experienced the violence during the civil war varied. Survivors took stock of the brutality either by inscribing these pogroms into the long history of anti-Jewish violence, drawing on similarities with previous waves of pogroms, or rather by emphasizing their difference from anything that had ever happened in Jewish history. Some survivors compared the brutality of the civil war to the massacres carried out centuries before, in the context of the 1648 Cossack uprising against Polish rule in Ukraine led by Bohdan Khmelnitsky's forces or during the 1768 rebellion of Ukrainian peasants and Cossacks against the Polish-Lithuanian Commonwealth, led by Ivan Gonta, who massacred thousands of Jews in Uman in retaliation for their alliance with the Polish forces.

Others made sense of the violence by removing it from the Jewish past: one survivor's account compared a pogrom carried out by the White troops to the St. Bartholomew's Day massacre, during the French wars of religion, when the Catholic mob massacred the Huguenots. For some, it was clear that these pogroms did not belong in the temporality of anti-Jewish violence and were unconnected to the past: "It is impossible to imagine what happened here on Saturday, February 15, [1919]. This was not a pogrom. It was like the Armenian slaughter," wrote a witness to the violence unleashed in Proskuriv.[87] The witness could only compare it to the systematic extermination of one and a half million Armenians, at the hands of the Young Turks, which took place from 1915 to 1917 in the context of the collapsing Ottoman Empire. Perpetrators also built their actions on memories of previous waves of anti-Jewish violence. In launching the attack against the Jewish population of Proskuriv, the perpetrators' shouts of "Yids, we will remind you of the times of Gonta and Khmelnytsky!" echoed through the city streets; the massacres perpetrated by Bohdan Khmelnytsky and Ivan Gonta in the seventeenth and eighteenth centuries were connected to the pogroms of the civil war via an established culture of anti-Jewish violence.

As a rule, however, witnesses and victims seemed to concur over the unparalleled nature of the violence. When in June 1919 a Jewish medical team traveled to the shtetl of Kytaihorod, in Kyiv province, to provide relief to the pogrom victims, it began to assess the loss of life, the trauma, and the damage that resulted from the attack. A member of the medical team noted in his official report that there was blood everywhere in the shtetl: "Kytaihorod is literally covered in blood. There is clotted blood on the pavements, on the walls, on the street."[88] He also remarked on the unprecedented violence he witnessed, in which entire families had been massacred, including children before their parents' eyes. The medical worker's report tragically summarized what he saw as follows: "We have reached the tragic conclusion that the carnage in Kytaihorod is unparalleled, even in the history of anti-Jewish pogroms."[89]

The Lesser of Two Evils

> The Jewish masses see in the Soviet power their protector, who saved them . . . from physical annihilation.
>
> —Petition to the People's Commissar of Justice by the Jewish religious community of Moscow, 1922

As the different armies and troops involved in the conflict waged against each other an exceptionally brutal war to control the territories of the former Russian Empire, the violence engulfed at least nine hundred Jewish settlements, intensifying at each stage of the conflict. In many places, the violence targeted all members of the Jewish community, indiscriminately and without exception. In a desperate attempt to plead for their lives, Jewish community leaders petitioned officers and generals of the invading armies, bemoaning "the systematic and more or less complete annihilation of the Jewish population." Compared to previous pogroms, sexual violence against Jewish girls and women, often carried out in public, in the presence of parents and neighbors, became a common feature of the violence. In many instances, rape of Jewish women was employed as a systematic weapon of war to instigate ethnic cleansing. Sexual violence may have been as common as murder: perhaps as many as one hundred thousand—or one in twelve—Jewish women and girls became victims of sexual violence in Ukraine alone, where the intraethnic clashes and paramilitary conflict reached its peak.[90] The progressive intensification of violence was accompanied by an ensuing rise in the number of rapes, which may have occurred in two-thirds of the pogroms.[91] And while rape occurred during the earlier waves of anti-Jewish violence of the late nineteenth and early twentieth centuries, it lay mostly at the periphery of the pogrom script; mass rape increased in frequency during World War I, in the context of the brutal expulsions of Jews branded by the Russian Imperial Army as enemy aliens; and during the civil war, sexual violence reached massive proportions, often serving as a form of plunder, especially in those impoverished communities in which, following multiple raids, no other form of ransom was available.[92]

In this context of growing violence, traumatized by loss and terror, most Jews chose to support the Bolsheviks. Not all did at first, however. Some continued to side with the White forces, fighting on behalf of General Anton Denikin, deputy supreme ruler of Russia during the civil war; well-off Jews in particular, who owned shops or factories, tended to prefer the White forces over the Bolshevik dictatorship, which posed a threat to their private property.[93] There were even extreme cases in which Jews took part in the looting of other Jews, probably enticed by class allegiance to the members of peasant groups and by the absence of links to the Jewish community under attack.[94] Some Jewish bandits, who knew well the social composition of the town's Jewish population, helped identify the wealthiest families so that the peasant bands and paramilitary groups could plunder their homes. In the shtetl of Rzhyshchiv, in Cherkasy province, a Jewish bandit even killed the daughter of a Jewish neighbor and helped murder a young Jew who organized the local self-defense unit to oppose the pogroms.[95] But these choices were unusual and represented the exception to the rule.

Seeking protection or revenge, and hoping to see an end to the looting, rape, and murder, most Jews made the practical choice of supporting Soviet power. The choice had very little to do with ideology and very much to do with survival or reprisal. The historian Leonard Shapiro recalled his surprise seeing in mid-1919 a Red Army company composed entirely of Jews: "they were yeshiva students from Proskuriv who joined the Red Army after Petliura's riots in order to take revenge."[96] Many youngsters joined the Red Army even when they resented the Bolsheviks. The words of a contemporary from Kamyanets-Podylskyi—capture the necessary choice made by most Jews at the time: "Every day, and every hour, the news of more and more pogroms perpetrated by Petliura's forces reached my native city. . . . 300 Jews had been killed or wounded in Balta . . . , in the shtetl of Felshtin, so close to us, 600 Jews had been murdered. . . . From day to day we awaited . . . in terror . . . [until] the Bolsheviks succeeded in their strategic maneuver and forced the Ukrainians to leave Kamyanets [without a pogrom]." Even when the neighbors' behavior hindered the scale of the pogrom, deterring the violence by assisting Jews as opposed to escalating it, the short- and long-term emotional effect of terror swayed many into supporting the Bolsheviks. And while accepting the Bolsheviks seemed almost impossible, in 1919 it became inevitable: "The knowledge that [the Bolsheviks] had saved them from the day-to-day expectation of death at the hands of the Haidamaks, forced them to forget about everything that the Bolsheviks stood for. The majority of the Jewish population welcomed the new ravishers and chose the lesser of two evils."[97]

The pogroms changed the Jewish political landscape, altering the views of the Jewish political elites, who had been consistently anti-Bolshevik. If in the beginning very few Jewish activists supported the Evsektsiia, the Jewish section of the Communist Party established by the Bolsheviks in the fall of 1918 to spread communism among the Jewish masses, by 1919 a growing number came to support the communist organization. Loyal Bundists—and resolute anti-Bolshevik activists—like Moyshe Rafes and Ester Frumkin eventually adjusted their political orientation and became more compliant with Soviet power. They eventually reversed their position not only as a result of the growing allure of a world revolution, which grew especially in the wake of the November 1918 events in Germany, when the military defeat of the German Empire in World War I triggered a naval mutiny in the country; the extreme anti-Jewish violence perpetrated by the Ukrainian militias, the Polish legions, and the White troops also swayed them into supporting the Red Army and Bolshevik power. When in 1919, on the eve of Jozef Pilsudski's troops' invasion of Belorussia, the Red Army organized armed militias to defend the city of Minsk from the Poles, Ester Frumkin not only helped create the combat units but also participated in the military training sessions, during which she occupied the front row because of her height.[98]

Young members of the Bund and Poale-Tsiyon switched allegiances and came to support the Bolshevik Party solely because the Red Army stopped carrying out pogroms. And even though the decision to condemn anti-Jewish violence came late in the game and grew out of the Jewish initiative to put pressure on Lenin rather than from within the Party itself, the July 27, 1918, decree outlawing antisemitic incitement was uncompromising.[99] Issued by the Council of People's Commissars, the decree clearly stated, "Pogromists and pogrom-agitators are to be placed outside the law."[100]

Some Jewish activists openly acknowledged that what drove them to join the Red Army was the prospect of avenging family members and friends who had been murdered in the pogroms. Dovid Lipets, the Bundist leader and mayor of Berdychiv, who during the early stages of the revolution had warned that "freedom and Jewish pogroms have a strange connection, a wild insanity," eventually put aside his criticism of Lenin and joined the

Communist Party.[101] Whereas in 1918 he endorsed with resolve the Ukrainian directorate and its struggle for independence, by early 1919 the bloody pogroms carried out under Petliura forced him to reconsider his position. With the attack on the Berdychiv Jewish community, perpetrated by the Ukrainian Battalion of Death headed by Colonel Mykalo Palienko, it seemed that the directorate's militias viewed the plundering and killing of Jews as inherently linked to the fight for an independent Ukraine.[102]

Even though the massacres in the Belarusian territories can hardly compare to the ones perpetrated in the Ukrainian lands, they still strengthened pro-Bolshevik tendencies among the Jews. In Minsk, anti-Jewish violence reached its peak at the time of the Polish army's retreat from the region, in early July 1920.[103] In describing the violent pogrom carried out in the city, Rabbi Yechezkel Abramski voiced his despair, admitting, "I doubt that the world will ever believe that such horrendous crimes were committed by human beings."[104] The violence endured by the Jewish population under the Polish legions invigorated popular support for the Red Army, and many Jews welcomed the establishment of the Belorussian Soviet Socialist Republic (BSSR) in the summer of 1920. A few months after the Bolsheviks came to power in Minsk, a proclamation issued in a local communist Jewish publication reminded Jewish workers of what would happen if they fell "again in the murderous hands of the Polish 'aristocrats'": "Pogroms . . . slavery and abuse. . . . Take the rifle and sword into your hands and set out in a heroic struggle for the final victory against your bloody enemies."[105] Sore Rejzen—the younger sister of the better-known cultural activists Avrom and Zalmen Rejzen—hailed the revolution with great fervor in a poem published in September 1920: "Well, a' la guerre comme a' la guerre, Our victory is long-since guaranteed, Because we know what we want, Because our goal shines bright like the suns, Because this is our last struggle, before humanity is freed, The International calls to us, like a heavenly voice from on high."[106]

In Minsk, like elsewhere, the choice to side with "the lesser of two evils" was fueled by the sense of powerlessness experienced by Jews more than by others during the frenzy of 1918–1920, with the Bolsheviks in power, then the Germans, then the Bolsheviks again, then the Poles, and finally the Bolsheviks once more. The sense of relief and security experienced by most Minsk residents in 1920 following the establishment of the Belorussian SSR was probably more intense among Jews than it was among other national groups in the city precisely because of the official condemnation of the pogroms. At the outset at least, Soviet authorities showed their commitment to punish the perpetrators of anti-Jewish violence—some of whom were arrested and prosecuted—to document the massacres, to establish memorials, and to publish witness accounts to honor the victims.[107]

If Lenin's public refutation of the pogroms encouraged many Jews to side with the Bolsheviks, the political choice to combat anti-Jewish violence also backfired by further bolstering the widespread perception of a special affinity between Communism and Jews. The fact that the Bolsheviks condemned the pogroms confirmed the alleged role of the Jewish group as a compromised political agent that could be perceived as a threat to the social norms governing the relations between the majority and minority groups.[108] What made the situation even worse was the fact that many Jews joined the Reds in warding off the attacks or created their own self-defense units to protect the Jewish communities. This was often seen as a provocation, as proof of their role as dangerous and disloyal interlopers in the national fabric of Ukraine, Poland, or Russia. Men and women who survived the pogroms joined the Red Army to retaliate against their families' murderers.[109] This was the case even in areas far removed from the epicenter of the conflict. Once Denikin's troops reached the Caucasus, the White forces attacked the communities of Mountain Jews (the Jewish communities living in the eastern and northern Caucasus, mainly Azerbaijan), systematically looting and destroying their property. Dispossessed and displaced, some fled the region as refugees, while others joined the Red Army and fought on behalf of Soviet power. Once the war ended and they returned to their homes, they found that most of their property and land had been taken over by neighbors.[110]

Many young Bundists and Zionists, but also Jewish soldiers who had fought in the Russian Imperial Army during World War I (some of whom may have been Bundist or Zionists themselves), rushed to establish self-defense units, engaging in battle with the rioters and troops, at times successfully.[111] As early as October 20, 1917, a Jewish military detachment was established in Petrograd to protect Jews from the anticipated violence: the detachment's tasks included organizing self-defense units in the event of a pogrom and recruiting Jewish fighters.[112] Zionist and other Jewish soldiers formed paramilitary organizations and played a role in establishing self-defense in many cities and towns across Ukraine. One of the most effective self-defense units protected the Jews of Odesa and succeeded in averting pogroms while the city changed hands eight times from 1917 to 1921. By early 1921, a Jewish armed force of fifteen thousand uniting fifty localities operated in central Ukraine, drafting local Jews and guarding the shtetl settlements against the insurgent bands.[113]

The pogroms destabilized relations between Jews and their neighbors in many places, harming the largely peaceful socioeconomic balance that predated the years 1918–1919. The extraordinary degree of suffering experienced by the peasantry, impoverished and ruthlessly starved through the Bolshevik grain requisitioning policy, served as the backdrop for their involvement in the violence: looting became a key incentive for taking part in the pogroms. Most accounts reveal the surprise and the resentment on the part of Jews for the sudden change in the relations and attitudes of their non-Jewish neighbors in the midst of violence. A survivor of the deadly Proskuriv pogrom of February 1919 confirmed, "The relationship between Jews and peasants . . . [was] excellent and most friendly throughout the thirty-two years I lived in the city. . . . I never heard of any tensions between Jews and non-Jews."[114] Describing the events of the July 1919 pogrom in Uman, one survivor stated, "This is what happened in Ladyzhenko, Mankovko, Dubova, Ivanko, Buki, Talnom and wherever else Jews lived. . . . Together with the peasants who arrived from the surrounding villages, those who participated in the pogrom and in the murder were also the peasants who were fellow villagers of the Jews, often their neighbors, who had known them for decades."[115]

The pogroms of the civil war could not be easily forgotten from one day to the next. Rather, their encumbered memory remained intensely alive and haunted survivors, perpetrators, and witnesses for years to come. The violence experienced and executed retained an afterlife that influenced neighborly relations following the establishment of the Soviet Union in 1922 and that profoundly shaped the Jewish experience throughout the interwar period.

The Memory and Legacy of the Pogroms

The weeks and months that followed the pogroms were the time when hundreds of thousands of refugees, displaced by the violence, began to come to terms with the trauma of loss and destruction. Witnesses and survivors mourned and buried their dead through private or collective ceremonies, marking the burials with memorials erected in the Jewish cemeteries or at the site of the mass grave where the perpetrators had murdered the victims, thus forging a private and collective memory of the events. While hundreds of thousands of Jews managed to reach the Romanian border and eventually made their way to Palestine, to independent Poland, to western Europe, or to North America, most of those who experienced the violence of the civil war remained in what would become the Soviet Union. Their experience of the violence is key to understanding Jewish responses to the October Revolution in the ensuing decades of the Soviet experiment.

Those displaced Jews who, for a variety of reasons, could not or did not want to leave the country were forced to begin a new life amid seemingly insurmountable challenges often without the support of the local Jewish communities, which were in ruins. Whether they moved back to their city or town of residence, settled there from nearby shtetls, or fled the town, wrapped in the memory of violence, for the larger Soviet metropolises, they faced catastrophic living conditions.[116] An international uproar had accompanied the massacres and the humanitarian catastrophe. Protests, strikes, and demonstrations were held in various cities in Europe and North America, while a diverse group of intellectuals, mainly historians and poets, produced an impressive paper trail as they tried to make sense of the violence while seeking justice, revenge, and commemoration. If the push to flee and forget was overwhelming for many, for others there was a conscious attempt to make sense of the violence, document it, and memorialize it through the written word. Many Yiddish writers—some of whom would become prominent in the Soviet Jewish cultural landscape over the course of the 1920s—experienced the violence firsthand. The Yiddish poets David Hofshteyn, Itsik Kipnis, and Leyb Kvitko wrote verses and novellas about the deadly encounter between neighbors at the time of the civil war, chronicling through the written word the brutality of 1919 in the Ukrainian lands.[117]

Hundreds of relief workers, doctors, nurses, and activists connected to the Jewish Public Committee to Aid Victims of Pogroms (Evobshchestkom), the Organization to Promote Health among Jews (OZE), or the American Jewish Joint Distribution Committee saw as their goal the revitalization of Jewish life and, in particular, the enhancement of the sanitary conditions and mental health of the thousands of Jewish children who had been orphaned during the war. Yet, even after an extraordinary international relief effort launched by the Red Cross and other humanitarian organizations to reconstruct the devastated communities, traumatized Jewish refugees confronted extreme shortages in food and medical supplies and ravaging diseases that caused worsening of health conditions and contributed to a lingering high mortality rate. Thousands of men and women fled the countryside in despair, seeking refuge in larger urban centers, where they faced starvation and disease and where they were often forced to turn to smuggling, the black market, and prostitution.[118] The Russian Red Cross Committee to Aid Victims of Pogroms estimated that one million Jews in Ukraine had suffered from pogroms and their consequences.[119] The great famine of 1921–1922, which affected primarily the Volga region but had broad repercussions throughout other areas as well, causing the death of millions, did not make things easier. The idealism and enthusiasm that set on fire the hearts of young Jewish communists, many of whom settled in Kyiv in the winter of 1921 from the nearby smaller towns in Ukraine and Poland and who would play an important role in the newly established Soviet Yiddish institutions, clashed with the daily chronic lack of food. "We longed terribly for a piece of plain bread. We were always very hungry. It seemed to us, that we couldn't even dream of the possibility that at some point we would ever be able to eat our fill," wrote the teenager and future member of the Evsektsiia Hersh Smoliar.[120]

There were other challenges for those thousands of Jewish refugees who returned to their cities and towns of residence. They often had to struggle to reclaim their looted property, which meant turning to and relying on the new Soviet authorities. The property restitution crisis was so pervasive that Soviet law had to acknowledge it, and in early 1921, an official decree deemed that legitimate property owners from the years prior to the civil war had the legal right to reclaim their homes. However, this was not always easy. Many local authorities—who might have themselves taken over Jewish homes vacated in haste by the refugees or might have been related to the perpetrators or the looters in the pogroms—tended to disregard the law. Issues of restitution exacerbated ethnic tension. The Jews had then only one option left: to turn to the central authorities of the new Soviet state, who would usually enforce the law and redress their grievance.[121]

Those victims, perpetrators, and bystanders who continued to live in the same town or region affected by the violence preserved the memory of the pogroms and at times recalled it to confront the adversities of Soviet life. The memory of the violence was preserved in the private sphere of the family or in the town lore through the numerous memorials that were set up in different places in Ukraine at the end of the civil war. In the town of Trostianets, in Vinnytsia oblast, for instance, the presence of a massive monument, which had been erected after the Soviets reoccupied the area, nurtured the encumbered memory of the violence of 1919 among neighbors. The memorial stood on the site of the mass grave where hundreds of Jews were buried. The inscription on the Trostianets memorial, which appeared both in Russian and in Yiddish, captured the essence of the relationship between Jews and the new state forged through the violence of the civil war. It read, "Here rest 337 Jews of Trostianets brutally murdered on May 9–10, 1919, by the enemies of the Soviet state."[122] The message conveyed to anyone who passed by the memorial was unambiguous: the Soviet state commemorated, remembered, and guarded Jews against anti-Jewish violence.

For those Jews who opted to remain in Trostianets following the pogroms, the memory of the violence remained vivid and embedded in everyday life, so much so that it came to measure time: throughout the interwar period, Jews referred to the great pogrom as "the catastrophe" (*khurbn*) and understood and remembered all events in their personal life as well as in the life of the country through the lens of the pogroms. It was not the revolution that measured time; it was the violence of the pogroms. For the town residents, the year that changed everything was not 1917, the year of the Bolshevik Revolution, but 1919.[123]

If some memorials, like the one commemorating the pogrom in the town of Trostianets, were remarkably large and imposing, others, like the one in the Jewish agricultural colony of Novopoltavka, were small and modest.[124] Hundreds of tombstones in the many cemeteries in the towns and cities of the former Pale of Settlement commemorated the victims of the violence.[125]

Many years later, Jewish collective farms were named after those who were murdered in the pogroms. Some Jews carried with them the memory of the pogroms for the rest of their lives: "I was born in March 1919. I was named Asia for the first letter in my name was the same as in the name of my father's brother Arkadiy who was killed during a pogrom."[126] Many years later, traces of physical destruction were still pervasive. In late 1927, during the Yiddish writer and journalist Hersh Dovid Nomberg's travels through Ukraine, he noticed the omnipresent ruins from the civil war. He acknowledged the sense of eeriness and loss that still lingered in the region: "How can one be in Ukraine and not be reminded of the massacres [*di shkhites*], perhaps the greatest, perhaps the most horrible ones in our ancient history."[127]

It was also in order to escape the spaces of violence and the enduring memory that so many Jews fled the smaller towns of the former Pale of Settlement, triggering one of the greatest demographic revolutions in modern Jewish history. In a remarkable process of internal migration, hundreds of thousands of Jews flocked to Moscow and Leningrad, as Petrograd was renamed in 1924, and to other larger urban centers in the Soviet interior, fleeing the confines of the shtetl, the town, or the city where they had experienced the pogroms. In search for a future, a time ahead, deprived of violence, they fled the destruction and murder, which had often been carried out with the complicity of some of their neighbors. Many towns in the territories of the former Pale of Settlement experienced a momentous drop in their Jewish population from prewar numbers. The demographic decline resulted from the physical and psychological trauma associated with the violence: the general mortality rate, the lower birth rate among Jewish women, distressed by the legacy of rape, and the mass relocation movement toward the Soviet interior.[128] If in the 1920s Moscow became the new Berdychiv, "the new Jewish capital" attracting thousands of Jewish refugees from Ukraine and Belorussia, it was also because of the pogroms.[129]

A native of the shtetl Korsun, in Cherkasy oblast, the young Anna Spektor witnessed three pogroms there. Once the shtetl came under Bolshevik control, at the end the civil war, together with her mother and sisters, she fled Korsun, which, "with the exception of nature, could show her little of beauty": after all, she had been chased and nearly killed by a neighbor who suspected her of supporting the Bolsheviks and who was eventually killed by the Jewish self-defense unit. Anna resettled in Moscow, where she lived with other pogrom refugees and eventually managed to emigrate to the United States.[130] Different patterns of memory and oblivion, of remembering and forgetting the experience of the pogroms, seemed to crystallize among those immigrants who reached North America and those who left for Palestine. Most Jewish refugees who relocated to the United States became caught up in the trials of integration and acculturation into the American dream. The yearning to fit in often resulted in the erasure of the memory of violence. On the other hand, those Jews who settled in British Mandatory Palestine from 1919 to 1923 may have drawn from their experience of the civil war to make sense of the new geopolitical context, made of new neighbors and new authorities.

Those Jews who stayed in the cities and towns of the former Pale of Settlement were more likely to hold onto the memory of violence, carry it with them, and pass it on to the next generation. But the genocide of European Jewry perpetrated by the Germans and their collaborators some twenty years later in the same lands expedited the removal of the pogroms of the civil war from official and popular memory. Those Jews who preserved the memory of violence, who remained in the territories of the former Pale of Settlement, in the towns and cities of Ukraine and Belorussia, including Trostianets, were annihilated, together with their memories, at the beginning of the summer of 1941, during the German occupation of the Soviet Union.

Those Jews who left for the Soviet metropolises were more prone to forgetting the violence of the pogroms, some of them consciously hoping to erase the trauma through a successful socialization, in alignment with Soviet power. They relied on the new state to protect them from future violence. As the civil war did for Soviet society and culture, it represented a seminal experience in modern Jewish history, in particular for those Jews who remained in the territories that would come under Soviet control. Violence became a driving force in the urbanization and therefore in the modernization and Sovietization of the Jewish population. The unintended consequence of the anti-Jewish violence of the civil war was the making of Soviet Jews.

2

A SOVIET STORY OF ACCULTURATION

Jews, Social Mobility, and Empowerment

The urbanization, modernization, and Sovietization that followed the Bolshevik Revolution and the civil war became a source of extraordinary and unprecedented opportunities to hundreds of thousands of Jews. The new Soviet state offered them access to positions of prominence and influence in the political, cultural, and economic spheres of the recently established system. Many came to hold top leadership positions in the government and in the Communist Party. The state allowed Jews to join the professional, legal, academic, and medical elites of the country in the thousands. As they made the most of the new educational opportunities, many rapidly moved up the Soviet social ladder and gained access to managerial and administrative positions. Like never before, the Jewish white-collar state employee appeared in the cities and towns of what had once been imperial Russia. The open doors unleashed great hopes. The open doors also gave many Jews access to unparalleled power in the political, cultural, and economic life of the new country.

Some Jews took advantage of these open doors because they genuinely believed in communist ideology. Like many true believers in the Marxist doctrine, they were eager to partake in the project of building a great future for humanity, the closing phase of which seemed to be just around the corner in the new socialist society. On the other hand, many were driven primarily by ambition unconnected to ideology or by economic necessity and in some cases by the sheer lack of real alternatives. The destitution and despair caused by the violence and chaos of war and revolution enticed many into taking advantage of the open doors to Soviet society. Regardless of the motivation, countless Jews benefited from the political transformation, quickly seizing new opportunities to succeed and empower themselves.

But who exactly were the many Jews who benefited from the creation of the first socialist society, and where within the vast territories controlled by the Soviet state did they live? How did they take advantage of the new opportunities offered to them by the new state? Did they do so by favoring their Jewish identity? Or did they opt for a more universal Soviet identity? Or did they do so by forging a new identity, which was Jewish and Soviet at the same time?

First, during the 1920s, the process of upward mobility and socioeconomic empowerment concerned primarily those Jews who lived in the territories of the newly established Russian, Ukrainian, and Belorussian republics. According to the 1926 census, 97.9 percent of Jews were living in the European regions of the new state, with less than 3 percent living in Central Asia and the Caucasus.[1] Moreover, Jews in Central Asia and the Caucasus were at first less integrated into the new Soviet system than their European counterparts were: there, full-blown Sovietization was not carried out until the second half of the 1920s. Second, many of those who initially crossed the threshold into Soviet society, by joining the Communist Party or finding a job as government employees or civil servants, were Jews by birth, and maybe by upbringing, but were Russian by cultural affiliation—their language was Russian, and their culture was Russian; and they were also Soviet by ideological commitment. Their choice to embrace the ideals of the revolution thus comes as no surprise.[2] The Bolshevik Party not only represented an outlet for their revolutionary drive but also allowed them to become part of the society surrounding them and its Russian culture.[3]

However, and this is the third point worth mentioning, many more Jews acculturated and eventually integrated successfully into the Soviet system almost inadvertently, because of circumstances and not out of conviction or as a result of a conscious decision. They joined the revolution by chance or lack of other options, usually through the back door: they were not driven by ideology and were not inspired by Vladimir Lenin's words or Leon Trotsky's deeds. These were thousands of Jews who picked up the threads of the overarching urbanization process of the late imperial years, as they moved from villages to towns, from towns to cities, and then to larger cities. Most of those who moved to Soviet cities were nonbelievers in the supreme universal good of socialism. They resettled to larger urban centers as a result of the destruction of the civil war and the ensuing economic misery that took hold of the region. And by doing so, they strove to adapt to the new system and its ideals and thus take full advantage of the privileges that came with Party membership or through the social status that resulted from employment.

Fourth, many Jews, particularly those who had been affiliated with Jewish socialist parties before the revolution—in particular the Bund and the Poale-Tsiyon, the Marxist Zionist workers organizations founded in different cities of the Russian Empire at the beginning of the twentieth century—actively joined the Bolshevik project in order to reform Jewish life. Within the new communist framework, their mission became the destruction of bourgeois Jewish life and its reconstruction according to the principles and values of Marxism-Leninism, in particular atheism and socioeconomic reform. To do so, they took up positions of political and cultural responsibility through the Evsektsiia, the Jewish section of the Communist Party, or other Soviet Jewish institutions and organizations established after October 1917. At the same time, there were Jews who chose to cast off entirely their prerevolutionary connection to Jewish political activities and cultural life, who chose to benefit from the new system and partake in its creation by keeping a low Jewish profile, some of them even choosing to hide everything Jewish, including their name, their deeds, and their family ties.

Whether driven by belief, faith, choice, hope, advantages, careerism, ambition, appreciation, lack of alternatives, want, or despair, hundreds of thousands of Jews became productive and successful members of the new Soviet system, many by joining the Communist Party and serving at the vanguard of society, others by filling positions of political and cultural leadership, and others yet by entering educational, military, and economic institutions and contributing to reshaping the academic and artistic Soviet landscape. The new government and Party institutions certainly favored the employment of politically trustworthy individuals (namely, those who had not supported autocracy before 1917 or joined the ranks of the counterrevolution during the civil war), who were possibly literate and who, given the state's commitment to Soviet internationalism and rejection of the tsar's policy of Russification of non-Russian peoples of the empire, were not members of the prerevolutionary dominant Russian ethnic group. Jews fit this profile to perfection.

The number of Jews who joined the Communist Party, which represented a unique source of power, influence, and privilege and the best path to a well-paid job, grew more than twofold over the course of the 1920s. According to the 1922 membership census, there were 19,564 Jews in the Party, or 5.21 percent of all Communist Party members were Jewish (compared to 3.1 percent of ethnic Germans and 2.53 percent of Latvians).[4] According to the 1927 census, there were 49,627 Jewish members, or 4.34 percent (compared to 0.49 percent of ethnic Germans and 1.66 percent of Poles).[5]

Jews held important positions in the higher echelons of the Communist Party, with four out of nineteen members of the Central Committee being Jewish in 1918 and in 1919 and five of the twenty-five members in 1921. By the mid-1920s, several members of the Politburo, the highest policy-making authority within the Communist Party, were Jewish (ranging between 23 and 37 percent), including Leon Trotsky, Lev Kamenev, and Grigoriy Zinoviev. After 1926, when Stalin quashed the power struggle within the Party and defeated Trotsky's opposition, no Jews remained in the Politburo through the end of the 1920s. Yet, Jews continued to hold important positions in the Organizational Bureau (Orgburo) and in the Secretariat of the Central Committee of the Communist Party, including Lazar Kaganovich, one of the most powerful figures in Ukraine in the late 1920s, and his older brother Mikhail Kaganovich. In 1927, 60 Jews were members of the highest legislative and administrative body in the country, namely, the Central Executive Committee of the Soviet Union (a number that is relatively low, similar to the 42 Latvians who served on the Central Committee but high in comparison with nine ethnic Germans and seven Poles). By 1929, the number of Jews on this body had declined to 55 (as did the number of Latvians), while the number of Germans and Poles grew to 12 and 13 respectively, with a total of 402 Russians and 95 Ukrainians.[6]

One of the most striking consequences of the revolution was the role that

Jews came to play—together with members of other national minorities, Latvians in particular—in the Cheka, the All-Russian Extraordinary Commission for Combating Counterrevolution and Sabotage. Established in December 1917, the first Soviet secret police organization, under the leadership of Felix Dzierżyński, a Polish aristocrat who embraced Bolshevism, had the goal of protecting communist forces from its many (real and imagined) enemies. The Cheka was first and foremost a punitive body that carried out thousands of arrests and ordered the torture and execution without trial of perhaps as many as one hundred thousand class and political enemies of the revolution during the years of the Red Terror. After the end of the civil war, the Cheka was replaced by the State Political Administration, or GPU, renamed OGPU in 1923 and in existence until 1934. This body, which became a permanent dreadful factor in the lives of Soviet citizens, maintained the same punitive functions of the Cheka and remained under Dzierżyński's chairmanship until 1926.

Many Jews joined the Cheka out of idealism and many more, perhaps, to avenge the pogroms, most of which had been carried out by the counterrevolutionary White forces. In September 1918, for example, the proportion of Jews among Cheka investigators was significant: of the twelve investigators of the Department for Combating Counterrevolution, the most important structure in the Cheka, half were Jewish.[7] At the end of 1920, Jews made up 9 percent of the fifty thousand employees in the Cheka provincial branches.[8] In 1923, a significant percentage of Jews were employed at the higher levels of management and secretariat of the OGPU, the heir of the Cheka. Many of them satisfied the employment prerequisite of a degree in higher education. In 1924, 8.49 percent of employees in the OGPU central apparatus were Jewish (against 8.66 percent Latvians and 3.75 percent Poles); and in 1927, Jews made up 14.7 percent of the directors of the regional branches of the OGPU (against 10.8 percent Latvians and 3.9 percent Poles).[9]

Overall, in the mid-1920s, of the 417 members in the Soviet ruling elite bodies (including the Central Executive Committee, the Party Central Committee, and the ministers and chairman of the Executive Committee), there were 27 Jews, or 6 percent. In many ways, in the early Soviet period, Jews took over the position in the central administration previously held by ethnic Germans in tsarist Russia, as their share in the government was more than double the proportion in the population.[10] In the economic elite (senior administrators of factories and state enterprise), where their share was even more remarkable, Jews reached 10 percent. In 1926, 24.7 percent of clerical workers employed in commerce, industry, and public institutions were Jewish (20.6 percent in Ukraine and 17 percent in Belorussia).[11] Many Jews—especially those of destitute background—joined the Red Army, a vital stepping-stone for socioeconomic mobility (the percentage grew from 1.4 percent, or fifty thousand people, in 1920, to 2.2 percent in 1923). In 1926, the proportion of Jews in the High Command of the Red Army reached 4.57 percent (compared to the 4.37 percent of Belarusians, who had a significantly larger population).[12] Their overall proportion in military academies reached 8.8 percent.[13]

One of the most spectacular indicators of the Sovietization of the Jewish population was enrollment in universities and research institutions. In 1927, Jews made up 14.37 percent of the total Soviet student body (namely, 23,405 Jewish students versus 994 ethnic Germans and 1,034 Poles) and constituted 13.6 percent of all scientists in the 1920s. In Ukraine alone, Jewish students made up for 47.4 percent of all students in institutions of higher learning (versus 24.7 percent of young Ukrainians) in 1923. By 1929, the proportion was still high, amounting to 23.3 percent. The high percentage of young Soviet Jews who attended institutions of higher education in the 1920s would bare long-term consequences for the social structure of the Jewish population in the next decades.[14] Similar disproportions were noticeable in Poland and Romania in the 1920s. The difference was that those countries soon imposed a *numerus clausus* legislation, whereas the Soviets did not regard the situation as a problem.

The intense social mobility of Jews in the Soviet Union during the 1920s produced remarkable success and visibility. Most members of the Soviet elites were not Jewish, and most Jews were not members of the Soviet elites; but comparatively speaking, with the exception of Russians, Jews had a much higher proportion of members in the elites than did any other ethnic group in the Soviet lands.[15] The seeming overrepresentation in the share of government, educational institutions, and the arts and sciences of this exceptionally urban and educated minority group, which constituted by far one of the most literate, if not the most literate, minority groups in the Soviet Union, grew out of different and profoundly complicated considerations on the part of the regime and of Jews themselves, considerations that changed over time during the course of the 1920s.[16] Whether it was the upshot of a conscious ideological decision or it resulted from the attempt to escape poverty and despair, joining the Soviet social order inevitably accelerated acculturation and assimilation.

Who's Who and Why?

If we consider who's who in the early years of Soviet Jewish history and ponder why and how Jews from different walks of life partook in the new system and shared in the advantages it offered, whether from its center as elite figures or from its sidelines as ordinary Soviet men and women, we notice that the boundaries between opportunism, careerism, and belief were blurred and often conflated. Belief in the communist dream could easily justify opportunism and careerism in Soviet society.

Born in Zhytomyr in 1898, into a family of Jewish artisans, Aleksander Bezymensky was among the small minority of Jews who had joined the Bolshevik ranks before the revolution; he joined the Party in 1916. After the Bolsheviks rose to power, he became a legendary personality in the Komsomol, the Young Communist League first established in 1918 as the political youth organization of the Party. In 1922, following the establishment of the Soviet Union and the transformation of the Komsomol into an All-Union agency, Bezymensky authored the organization's official song, titled "The Young Guard" (Molodaia gvardiia).[17] As a true believer in the revolution and an enthusiastic supporter of the Soviet state (his brother had been killed in Kyiv in 1918 when the city was under the German forces and Hetman Pavlo Skoropadsky, the military commander of the Ukrainian People's Republic), he eagerly and passionately contributed to the forging of a new culture. He helped nurture the ideal communist youth who would consume and eventually produce this new culture for decades to come. Bezymensky acquired the influential name of "Komsomol poet." His poetry was read and learned word for word by millions of young Soviets throughout the country. In his capacity as poet, editor, and journalist, he became "one of the Party's most uncompromising crusaders against old age and degenerate art." In one poem, he even rejected his own mother:

My very old mother,
who is but a speck in our struggle,
Cannot understand that my Party card
Is part of me.[18]

Born in Białystok in 1876 into a Jewish middle-class family, Meir Henoch Wallach joined the Russian Social-Democratic Workers Party in 1898 and changed his name to Maksim Litvinov. After his arrest in 1901 and his exile to London, where he remained—with short breaks—for more than a decade, he tirelessly worked in émigré Bolshevik cells, becoming secretary of the London Bolshevik group as well as Bolshevik representative at the Second International. In London, Litvinov met Ivy Low, an English Jewish novelist and a charismatic personality, whom he married in 1916. Following the revolution, Litvinov returned to Russia with Ms. Litvinoff, as Ivy Low would become known to foreign diplomats in Moscow, and began a remarkable diplomatic career that would turn him into the key figure in interwar Soviet foreign policy.[19] He started out in 1921 as first deputy people's commissar of foreign affairs and throughout the 1920s worked hard to establish Soviet diplomatic relations with the West, advocating for diplomatic agreements leading toward disarmament. Few, if anyone, in the Ministry of Foreign Affairs in late imperial Russia could have imagined that a Jew would eventually emerge as the top diplomat in the first socialist state. While it was not inconceivable for a Jew in other European countries at the time to rise to the position of foreign diplomat, it was indeed impressive that a Jewish man could do so in the same territory that just a few years earlier denied Jews all political and civil rights.[20]

On the other side of the spectrum, someone like Solomon Grinberg applied to join the Party in 1927 not so much out of belief in communism but in order to fit in, gain some of the socioeconomic advantages associated with Party membership, and also perhaps out of appreciation for the new system, which had lifted him out of destitution and illiteracy. Grinberg was born in Babruysk, Belorussia, in 1900. His grandfather was a carpenter, and his father was a *melamed*, a teacher in a Jewish traditional primary school. His father died when he was young, and to make ends meet, Grinberg began to work as an apprentice hairdresser, from eight in the morning until eleven at night. As he wrote in his application for Party candidacy, in poor

Russian (his mother tongue was Yiddish), the long workday forced him to remain illiterate and prevented him from understanding anything about the February Revolution. But as he noted in his autobiography, when the October Revolution broke out, "I instinctively felt that this was my revolution. . . . I immediately sided with the Bolsheviks, supported their conspiratorial work . . . [and] enrolled as a volunteer in the Red Army . . . , where I served until 1923. . . . I [now] work as a hairdresser in Minsk." He concluded his application by beseeching the local cell of the Communist Party to accept him, resorting to the following cliché statement: "I recognize the Party as the vanguard of the working class and believe it the duty of every conscious worker to join it . . . and fight against world capitalism . . . for a world revolution." Whether Solomon applied for Party membership out of conformity or opportunism, the revolution gave him the option to become part of its elite and open the path to potential success in Soviet society.[21]

While some Jews accepted the regime as legitimate, others participated in the system out of self-interest and not because of ideological convictions. The beneficiary of the revolution did not always remain loyal to it. When the February Revolution broke out, Herman Shub, a well-known economist who had served as adviser to the tsarist regime in Petrograd before siding with the Mensheviks, was overjoyed. He did not feel the same about the Bolsheviks seizing power. And yet, he became part of the system: thanks to his reputation and skills as a technocrat, he was employed by Gosplan, the central planning agency that coordinated the communist economy. But he continued to celebrate the anniversary of the February Revolution, privately, throughout the 1920s.[22]

Born in 1886 in Berdychiv, into a family of well-to-do merchants, Dovid Lipets was drawn to the revolutionary movement early on in his life and joined the Jewish labor party the Bund in 1902. Following his arrest by tsarist authorities in 1906, he left Russia and began his wanderings through London, Brussels, and France. When he returned to Russia, he was arrested again and eventually expelled from the country. Lipets then settled in New York City, where he conducted work among the Jewish working class. There, he also became a member of the Central Committee of the Jewish Socialist Federation of America, a member of the Socialist Party of America, and one of the editors of the Yiddish *Forward*, for which he wrote under the pseudonym Max Goldfarb. But the outbreak of the October Revolution drew him back to Russia: after his election to mayor of Berdychiv, where he witnessed the horrors of the pogroms of the civil war, he became an agitator for the Red Army and joined the Bolshevik ranks. His turn of faith allowed him to embark on an extraordinary career as a Soviet civil servant and rise as a key figure in the country's military educational institutions, where he oversaw military training and education. Lipets was also elected Comintern representative in the Communist Parties of Great Britain, France, and the United States.[23] These positions granted him security and prestige and a glamorous life in Moscow and other European capitals. His career path involved changing his name, first to David Petrovsky and then, during his Comintern mission abroad, to David Bennett. As he helped build and strengthen the Soviet economy and military in the interwar years, Lipets/Petrovsky/Bennett never looked back on his Jewish work and left fully behind his prerevolutionary commitment to the Jewish masses and to Yiddish culture.[24] He all but created a new Soviet persona, largely turning away from his Jewish past.[25]

Following a similarly illustrious career in the Bund, Ester Frumkin, who was born in Minsk in 1880 and had joined the Jewish socialist party in 1901, serving as one of its most committed and efficient propagandists, editors, and policy makers, embraced the Bolsheviks by joining the ranks of the Communist Party in 1921. Under the Soviets, she became an esteemed Party activist committed to bringing the revolution to the Jewish masses through words and deeds. She served as the only female member of the Central Committee of the Evsektsiia, the Jewish section of the Communist Party, and was the author and editor of numerous books and publications in Yiddish. She helped forge the revolutionary minds of Jewish children who read her work in Yiddish. In a short book titled *Follow in Lenin's Footsteps*, published one year after Lenin's death in Yiddish for Young Pioneers, the All-Union youth organization for children aged nine to fourteen established in 1922, Frumkin promoted reverence for the Bolshevik leader in a quasi-religious fashion. She comforted the youth and reassured them that they would eventually meet Lenin again: "Those of you who do not die a heroic death prior to the victory of the working class will eventually come to Lenin's place [*getselt*] where he rests quietly and awaits you, and you will tell him that capital has been stifled throughout the world, that over all the major cities of the world his banner, Lenin's banner of communism, is waving. The international Soviet republic which he prophesied has come to pass. You will say to him, 'Our dear, devoted one! With your weapon we have won the victory, we have won. You have won, Comrade Lenin.' "[26] Frumkin also served as rector of the Communist University of the National Minorities in the West, which made her deeply knowledgeable in issues pertaining to the communist parties in different countries, as she forged close connections to the Central Committee of the Communist Party. It is impossible to imagine a Jewish woman playing such a leading role in public life in prerevolutionary Moscow. As a beneficiary of the Soviet system, Frumkin climbed the Soviet ladder. But she also remained actively involved in Jewish work.

If many Jews Sovietized by inaugurating an entirely new chapter in their lives, which did not include any connection with the immediate Jewish concerns they had had before the revolution, others, like Frumkin, remained committed to working on the Jewish street. Among them were, for instance, those writers who chose to write in Yiddish and who came to constitute the backbone of the Soviet Jewish cultural elite. For the Soviet Yiddish poet Peretz Markish—who was born in 1895 in Polonnoe, Volhynia, and who from 1921 had wandered through the literary capitals of Europe, including Berlin, Paris, London, and Warsaw, where he was mostly based until 1926, when he returned to the land of his birth—it was gratitude that drove his support for the new system. At least according to his wife, Ester Markish, he "exalted the Soviet regime, not for personal gain or out of opportunism but because it was his unshakable conviction that the regime had emancipated his people, had torn down the walls of the ghetto, so that they, his people, could blossom anew and flourish in an atmosphere of freedom."[27]

The Great Demographic Turn: From the Pale to Moscow

Joining the Communist Party, seeking employment as a civil servant in the new state apparatus, or reshaping Soviet culture and the arts as a ballet dancer and choreographer in the Moscow Bolshoi Theater, as a leader of the Russian Association of Proletarian Writers (RAPP), as a painter whose work would eventually serve as the blueprint for Socialist Realism, or as a violinist and conductor was the outcome of one of the greatest Jewish migrations of the twentieth century and, indeed, of all time.[28] This migration was not headed toward the United States or Palestine, but it developed as an internal exodus from the territories of the former Pale of Settlement to Moscow, Leningrad, and the many other major cities of the newly established Soviet Union. This population movement not only involved the shift from smaller towns to regional centers but also generated the distinct settlement patterns of Jews in the larger cities and the continued clustering of Jews in certain districts. Manifold reasons set the Jewish demographic revolution in motion, and non-Jews too streamed in the hundreds of thousands into Soviet cities for similar reasons but also for very different ones.

Perhaps one of the most glaring results of the Jewish demographic revolution that followed the end of the civil war was the astonishing growth of the Jewish population in Moscow, which, in some contemporary accounts (negatively inclined toward Jews), was referred to as a "Jewish city." If in 1912 Jews made up less than 1 percent of the city's population, numbering 15,353, in 1923, they reached 86,000, and by 1926, 131,000, making up 6.5 percent of the city's total population.[29] Traveling to Moscow, a Jewish correspondent from Poland noted, "There is not one shtetl in Russia, one village with a Jewish community that is not represented in Moscow." He added, "At times on the street you might be under the impression that you are actually in Berdychiv and 100 meters later that you are in Zhytomyr, Minsk, or Kaunas."[30]

The overwhelming majority of Jewish migrants were young: more than 90 percent were fifty and under, and one-third were in their twenties. They usually left for the larger cities without their families but, like their fellow non-Jewish migrants, depended on social networks to adjust to urban life, relying on relatives and acquaintances from the same shtetl or town to help them with housing and with finding a job. If before the revolution, peasants in particular had journeyed to Moscow and other large urban centers to work as seasonal laborers, during the 1920s, they moved to Soviet cities in search of permanent settlement. But the urban unemployment crisis forced many more to return to their villages empty-handed; the impact of the revolution and the subsequent civil war caused rising unemployment in the cities.[31] For the Jews, the legacy of the pogroms of 1918–1921 paved the way for the resolve to relocate to larger urban centers: thousands of young Jewish men and women made this decision based on the trauma of recent massacres and the fear of new ones, swayed by the Soviets' commitment (at least on paper) not to tolerate pogrom violence and hopeful of better opportunities in the wake of the economic ruin generated in the civil conflict. Those Jews who moved felt a greater degree of security in larger urban centers away from the former Pale. Relocation, then, would almost certainly lead to acculturation into and even support for the Soviet system.

The Jewish demographic resettlement was also a spin-off of the steady trend of Jews moving into urban centers, which had picked up in pace in the first decade of the twentieth century. Its chief motivation was fleeing the economically stagnant countryside regions of the former Pale of Settlement: the combination of demographic growth and need for jobs forced large numbers of Jews to look for new occupations in the cities.[32] In the aftermath of the revolution and the civil war, younger Jews especially continued this trend as they poured out of the territories of the former Pale of Settlement and relocated to larger and more modern cities, this time not only in pursuit of upward mobility and a more profitable and satisfying employment but also because many of them enthusiastically embraced communism, enticed by the promise of social justice and national equality, as they readily rebelled against their Jewish mothers and fathers. Without doubt, the new system also represented an outlet for the ambitions that had been frustrated during years of discrimination under the tsar. The new regime, which urgently needed loyal cadres, was unquestionably impatient to employ and engage young Jews. Based on the events of the civil war, the Soviets had reservations about the political allegiance of Poles, Ukrainians, and even Russians. On the other hand, they probably saw in the Jews a potentially loyal ally because of the specific treatment they had endured under the tsar.

The utter collapse of the countryside and the shtetl, which in many cases was wiped out by war and revolution, provided a strong impulse for both Jews and non-Jews to leave their place of residence.[33] Following the 1917 revolution and the civil war, perhaps as many as five hundred thousand Jews left the nascent Soviet Union and settled in Europe, the United States, or Palestine. Many wished to leave the new Soviet territories terrorized and traumatized by the pogroms; others were driven by pressing economic considerations. What drove others to flee Soviet power was the fundamental aversion to communism.

Rokhl Faygnberg managed to reach the border with Romania, fled to newly independent Poland, and eventually made her way to Palestine with her newborn son. But before leaving Russia, Faygnberg spent some time in Odesa, where thousands of refugees from nearby cities and shtetls roamed the streets. There, she met with survivors and collected their witness accounts of anti-Jewish violence, which she then sent to the historian Elias Tcherikower, who devoted his life to gathering evidence about the civil war pogroms. Faygnberg also met with other Jewish intellectuals who pledged to flee Bolshevik power, including the Yiddish writer and editor Mordechai Spektor, the Hebrew national poet Chaim Nachman Bialik, and Bialik's first editor and publisher, Yehoshua Ravnitski. With the Bolsheviks in power, soldiers who had supported the White Army or fought with the Ukrainian forces against the Reds were also among those desperate "to leave the Russian hell [*gehena*]." In fall 1919, the Odesa Palestine Office rented ships from the remnants of the Russian imperial Black Sea fleet to take refugees to Yaffo. However, the Palestine Office required that only those who could give proof of some connection to the Land of Israel, whether via previous visits there or by virtue of relatives, could register to leave. Overrun with applicants and aware that some registered to leave for Palestine with the intention of traveling elsewhere, including the United States, the office wanted to assure that those whom it paid for would actually stay in the Land of Israel.[34]

Among the stories of those who were desperate to leave, Faygnberg overheard the account of a middle-aged Jewish woman, whom she described as "a real Odesite, not typically religious, with a full head of white hair." While she was no Zionist, she was desperate to see her three adult sons, "who were as tall as giants" and who "have always been in danger of being killed at the hands of this or that ataman," to leave for Palestine.[35] To get permission for her sons to leave, she pleaded with local bureaucrats, trying to convince them that she indeed had a close relative in Palestine: "a mother, our Mother Rachel [*Rachel imenu*]," as she referred to one of the matriarchs in Judaism. When everyone in the Odesa Palestine Office broke out in laughter, "she insisted that she meant it seriously, and was willing to take the matter to the city's military commander." Faygnberg does not tell us whether the Odesite Jewish mother managed to see her three sons leave for Palestine. Indeed, many did not make it onto the ship, especially once the city came under Bolshevik occupation: thousands of Denikin and Petliura supporters took over the ship, scuffling to get on board with their stolen goods, frantic to flee the vengeful hand of the Red Terror.[36]

Many Jews then attempted to illegally cross the Dniester River, reach the city of Rybnitsa (today in Moldova), get to Poland, and from there travel to the United States or Palestine, but only after they sold all their goods, usually to acquaintances only, so as to keep their border crossing a secret.[37] And while thousands managed to cross the border, most of those who experienced the violence remained in what would become the Soviet Union. It was here, then, that parents encouraged their sons and daughters to undertake a new path and leave the ravished shtetl, where the market place, the private businesses, and the artisanal activities had ceased to play their prerevolutionary socioeconomic function. In a report from the mid-1920s, the Commission for National Minorities of the All-Ukrainian Central Executive Committee noted with concern the grim conditions of the Jewish population of the shtetls around Kyiv, which, as a result of war and pogroms and the ensuing refugee crisis, lacked almost entirely an economic base. The report noted, for instance, the significant loss in population (by 24 percent) in thirty-six Jewish agricultural colonies in the regions of Volhynia and Podilia: here, the population declined from thirty-nine thousand in 1916 to twenty-nine thousand in 1922, with 19 percent of all buildings destroyed and 70 percent of horses and 57 percent of cows and stock perished.[38] The situation was desperate. The outbreak of cholera and the 1921 famine crisis just added to its gravity. In the fall of 1921, the American Relief Administration (ARA), an organization formed by the United States Congress in February 1919 to provide war relief in ravaged Europe, came to the rescue and delivered 450 tons of food to Moscow, 30 trucks with 15 tons of food each to Petrograd, Samara, and Kazan.[39]

Young Jews who wished to enroll in institutions of higher learning, acquire professional training, or simply learn Russian left smaller settlements for larger urban centers in order to access education. The numerous autobiographies by young Jews submitted as part of the application materials for Party candidacy noted the appeal of the new system because it supported education. Born in 1906 in the Mazyr region of Belorussia, Chaim Zaretskii remarked that when in late 1922 a small Komsomol Party-cell was established in his shtetl, what enticed him the most to join the organization was the prospect of education: "I almost did not know any Russian since I had never received any kind of education."[40] We can be sure that among the 98,823 Jews who were Komsomol members by the late 1920s, many had joined the organization for similar reasons.[41]

In a 1926 statement, the chairman of the Central Executive Committee of the Soviets, Mikhail Kalinin, acknowledged the educational aspirations of Jews in the new system. The many educational opportunities and their accessibility represented a powerful driving force for Jewish women too. Under the tsar, in order to get a residence permit and circumvent the quotas on the admission to institutions of higher learning, some Jewish women pretended to be maidservants or in some cases even chose to take out the "yellow ticket" (*zheltiy bilet*), the personal identification document they received once they registered as prostitutes with the police and medical authorities. In the 1890s, Ester Frumkin, the future leader of the Evsektsiia, in order to attend the Advanced Pedagogical Courses for Women in Saint Petersburg, obtained official permission to reside in the Russian capital by feigning that she was a prostitute. To make sure her yellow ticket did not run out, Frumkin had to register at the local police station once a week.[42] Under the Soviets, Jewish women (and men) no longer faced such obstacles: no state legislation prevented them from living in certain areas and having access to higher education.[43]

More than ideology, then, it was the pursuit of education and the attempt to escape chronic poverty that lay at the heart of the great Jewish migration to Soviet cities. The sons and daughters of small peddlers, mill owners, or poor craftsmen, especially those who were branded class enemies because they employed one or more apprentices, moved to larger cities—hoping that the anonymity would allow them to blend in—in search not simply of education but literally of food. The letters sent to relatives by Jewish adolescents who had left their towns in different parts of Ukraine to move to Odesa and enroll in one of the professional schools for Jewish workers and artisans established in the early 1920s are a powerful testament to the utter socioeconomic distress experienced by so many Jewish families.

In the letters of the young students, they reassured their families that their living conditions were decent and better than the ones they had fled from and that they had access to enough food, since they received three meals a day. Some were proud to show off their newly acquired literacy, as they wrote for the very first time in Yiddish or in Russian, like young Yudl, who on May 12, 1924, informed his parents that he had just learned how to write: "I can write to you that I am OK but I miss you, I can write to you that I am learning how to write and read in Yiddish and in Russian. . . . I can write to you that I'm not going to die of hunger."[44] Like others, he also voiced the emotional challenge that leaving home, family, and siblings—perhaps for the first time—entailed. This emerged as a leitmotiv in most of the letters: "I am angry at you, dear father and mother, because you do not answer my letters"; or "Please answer me"; or "Please write to me." In broken Russian, a young girl thanked her parents for sending two rubles—a trifling amount indeed—and also informed them that the school would take the students to visit Moscow in June of that year, a place that her parents had probably never been to.[45] When young Lev Fridliand wrote to his mother on March 16, 1925, he thanked her for the letter, noting that the one ruble she said she sent him "was not included in the envelope," and dutifully informed her, "they've already given me two outfits, one for the winter and soon one for the summer: I now work in a locksmith workshop."[46] In a letter that Rakhmiel Zinger wrote to his younger sister, dated March 14, 1925, he described upward mobility in his own words, encouraging her to follow in his footsteps: "Dear Bashale, write to me and tell me how you are doing, write to me and tell me if you are reading books and if you are learning how to write on your own. I am healthy. I am learning a profession. I am a pioneer. . . . Mother writes to me that you cry. . . . You were born in 1917, the year of the October Revolution, so you must be strong. You can ask mother to buy you some little cookies to encourage you to learn how to read and write by yourself."[47] These words conveyed the hope in a brighter future, one complete with access to education, to a profession, and to better economic conditions but also a future made of Soviet rituals, values, and institutions.

The NEP: Good for the Jews or Bad for the Jews?

In March 1921, Lenin announced to the hundreds of delegates attending the Tenth Party Congress in Moscow the New Economic Policy (NEP). Pragmatism drove the decision to adopt the new economic plan. Under

Lenin's leadership, the Party acknowledged that War Communism—the centralized economic policies introduced during the years of the civil war and based on the abolishment of private trade, the nationalization of large-scale industry, the requisition of foodstuff, and the control of labor—was no longer sustainable. War Communism had to give way to more liberal economic policies. Therefore, in order to overcome the chronic food shortages, the drop in the country's industrial and agricultural output, and the unrest of peasants and soldiers, the new state had to introduce a mixed economy, allowing for the reappearance of private property and free commerce. Although Party leaders were ambivalent (and some even reluctant) about giving into market forces and were concerned about the retreat from central economic planning, they were also well aware that only these measures could save the revolution. Small-scale industries were thus denationalized, food surpluses could be sold on the open market, and some concessions were granted to foreign investors. Lenin and Trotsky clearly understood the New Economic Policy as a temporary measure to rescue the country's economy. Its transitional nature served as a palliative for the ideological compromise and the about-face made by the Party in indulging in capitalism.[48] In 1921, a communist activist remarked about the NEP, "We created you and we will destroy you!"[49]

Given the historical socioeconomic structure of the Jewish population, which was largely concentrated in small peddling and trade, with a minor percentage being part of the industrial working class, many Jews took advantage of the economic liberalization of the NEP years. Many continued to work as independent artisans and small businessmen and did so by joining the new cooperatives, known as *arteli*. These were artisanal or agricultural voluntary associations of individuals who joined upon contributing capital and labor, paid membership fees, and in turn received the profit from selling the finished product. Many of the cooperatives established in the cities and towns of the former Pale of Settlement operated as Jewish ethnic spaces: not only were they overwhelmingly Jewish, but Yiddish was often the main work language and Sabbath was the day of rest.[50] Because the cooperatives retained a degree of autonomy from the state, several attracted members who were committed to religious life and who knew that working in the artel instead of in other state-owned enterprises would allow them to abide by Jewish religious practice. In some rare cases, Jews were employed in cooperatives that yielded Jewish religious objects. In early 1929, for instance, in the small town of Sudilkov, in the Shepetivka district of Kamianets-Podilskyi, Ukraine, the members of a textile artel "that was officially producing bedsheets actually turned out prayer shawls."[51]

A new Soviet bourgeoisie emerged under the NEP, and it was largely Jewish. In 1926, Jews made up 40 percent of all Soviet artisans and 20 percent of private traders.[52] While most just managed to get by, some accrued wealth and property and joined the economic elites in the spheres of trade, industry, and services. This phenomenon made the association between Jews, speculators, and affluence widespread among those who were not sympathetic to Jews. The expensive high-quality furniture, clothing, and jewelry accumulated by the most successful entrepreneurs—some of whom were Jewish—could trigger resentment against Jews among neighbors and competitors.[53] In 1923, an entrepreneur from Kharkiv by the name of A. L. Meyerovich bought a house worth thirty-eight thousand rubles and furnishings for eighteen thousand rubles.[54] At the time, these were extraordinary sums, especially for factory workers who faced unemployment and housing shortages in the cities and struggled to make ends meet.[55]

While the state tolerated the new bouts of partly controlled capitalist entrepreneurship, it also loathed them. The official press echoed this position and regularly confronted the "NEPman spirit" as hostile to communist society.[56] Thus, if to some extent the NEP helped recover the economic disaster wrought by War Communism on Jewish traders and peddlers and even helped revive Jewish religious and cultural life by relaxing the rules on religious practice, publishing, and cultural activities, it also egged on some antagonistic tropes tied to the Jewish NEPman.

In general, the tension between economic liberalization and ideological condemnation of the mixed economy favored chaos and uncertainty. What the state allowed and what it forbade were not always apparent, and regional and local authorities could easily take advantage of the ambiguity. This happened, for instance, with regard to the status and treatment of *lishchentsy*, namely, those who were disenfranchised by the state. On the grounds of their real or alleged bourgeois origin, their occupation, their political orientation, or their membership in the clergy, many Soviet citizens were branded as *lishchentsy* and thus deprived of civil rights. Not only did Soviet authorities deny them electoral rights, but they also forbade them to register at the Labor Exchange, which left them without the right to work and earn a living.

In addition to limited access to food and housing (only trade-union members had access to co-op stores and housing allotment), the disenfranchised had no right to free medical services. If a family member fell ill, they would not be treated in the city hospitals, unless they paid high fees. Finally, whenever a family member became disenfranchised, then children and siblings too faced restrictions over access to education; this penalty in particular represented a major setback for young Jews who saw in education one of the great perks of the revolution, which had cast off the late imperial anti-Jewish quotas. Being labeled a *lishchenets* jeopardized one's position in Soviet society, hindering the path to integration and upward mobility.

Because of the prerevolutionary employment structure of the Jewish population, as well as the new positions that many came to occupy during the early years of the NEP, more Jews than non-Jews were likely to face legal restrictions as *lishchentsy*. Whether one was susceptible to disenfranchisement depended to a large degree also on local authorities, who could determine if someone's rights should be revoked. At times, this verdict was driven by anti-Jewish sentiments, which could be easily disguised as commitment to the Party line.

In the early years of the NEP, many bankrupt and economically ruined Jewish merchants and peddlers moved to Moscow in the hope of starting a new life and a new business. A reporter for a Polish-Yiddish newspaper who passed through the city in 1926 noted, "Jews from all corners of Soviet Russia, including Homel, Babruysk, Berdychiv, Minsk, and Odesa, flow relentlessly to Moscow, . . . but they don't come for pleasure, or to visit the city, they come out of despair as the shtetl has pushed them to Moscow to seek a livelihood." The reporter also noted, "Moscow has become a city of Jewish livelihoods and Jewish troubles"; here, "the majority [of Jews who moved to Moscow] are peddlers, perhaps fifty thousand; as many as thirty thousand cannot take care of themselves; and barely ten to fifteen thousand are employed in offices, factories, and other Soviet institutions." Only a small percentage of the new migrants who moved to the city to engage in commerce and crafts did not struggle daily and managed to take advantage of the opportunities offered by the NEP policies, making some profit. But, as the reporter acknowledged, "they remained fully aware that everything could change in the blink of an eye."[57]

Things began to change in 1926, when the state partially backed away from the initial economic liberalization, and—while not outlawing them—introduced new restrictions on private trading and credit to the private sector.[58] This change further enhanced the public resentment toward the NEP bourgeoise and traders, many of whom were Jews and many of whom could be reproved for their business and their real (or imagined) success through disenfranchisement. In 1926, 68.8 percent of Jews in Ukraine were categorized as "traders" and deprived of civil rights, and 20.8 percent did not earn a living by working; the remaining were either those who profited from hired labor ("exploiters") or religious personnel.[59] By the late 1920s, in the Minsk province, 40 percent of Jews and 5 percent of non-Jews were disenfranchised.[60]

Whether in search for education or an occupation or simply a way out of the desperate conditions at home, migrating to a metropolis entailed real-life struggles and emotional challenges, which varied according to the age and gender of the migrants. Some of these challenges echo through the works of literature produced at the time. The Soviet Yiddish writer Shmuel Godiner, for instance, who had himself moved to Moscow in 1921 from a shtetl in Belorussia after serving in the Red Army during the civil war, captured in his work some of the emotional trials connected with moving to the big city. The short story titled "A Shklov Moon over Arbat," which Godiner wrote in the late 1920s, describes the journey from the shtetl to the metropolis of a déclassé Jew, who went from being a successful accountant in Shklov to losing everything after the revolution: he left for Moscow in search for a better livelihood but ended up as a street vendor during the NEP years. He remained an incorrigible bourgeois, who could not adapt to the new ways of communism and continued to stumble. While he came under the influence of religion, through none other than the Lubavitcher rebbe, his wife left him to become what she regarded as a productive member of Soviet society.[61]

Assimilation and Jewish Women

Bolshevism was arguably a "men's movement," which despite its rhetorical commitment, ultimately failed to liberate women from the domestic sphere.[62] Yet, women did take advantage of the new system, and many actively partook in this project, whether they conceived of it as male in nature or not. Compared to non-Jewish women, some Jewish women might even have been better equipped or at least more at ease in gearing up for a career or even simply in participating in the political life of the new society. This difference not only grew only out of the comparatively higher literacy rates of the predominantly urban minority but was also the direct result of the role Jewish women played in different political parties before the revolution. Therefore, if the revolution entailed empowerment for disenfranchised groups, including Jews and women, then Jewish women could certainly take part in this process too.

Born in Moscow in 1880 and a graduate of the prestigious Bestuzhev Women's Institute of Higher Learning in Saint Petersburg, Tatiana Varsher became a professor of ancient history at the Petrograd Pedagogical Institute, and during War Communism, she served as a "cultural enlightenment" lecturer in different Soviet institutions, before fleeing the country for Latvia in 1921. In her memoirs, which she published in 1923, Varsher captured the profound difference between the Bolshevik stance on the women's question in the early years of the revolution and the position of European feminism regarding women's liberation. To illuminate the difference, Varsher first reminded the reader of a slogan popular among enthusiasts of feminism in Europe: "If a woman is worthy of a place on the scaffold, then give her a place in Parliament." But to pinpoint the new regime's commitment to emancipate women and entrust them as builders of the new system, she added, "the Bolsheviks went much further along the road to women's equality: not only did they give women their 'place in parliament,' as well as some of the highest positions in the republic—they also gave them the job of executioner."[63] While we do not know how many Jewish women were members of the secret police organs, whether the All-Russian Extraordinary Commission, or Cheka, or its successors, the GPU and the OGPU, like their male counterparts, they acted with or at least accepted violence as a necessary means to implement the revolution.

Varsher might have even been referring here to Rozalia Zemlyachka (born Zalkind), a member of the Russian Social Democratic Party and a committed revolutionary long before 1917, who during the civil war was appointed commissar and head of the political department of one of the Red Army's divisions and participated in the military campaign in Donbas and who, in November 1920, as a member of the Crimean Revolutionary Committee, was responsible for ordering mass executions of captured soldiers and officers of the White Army.

Many Jewish women who became active in public life under the Soviets had partaken in the pre-1917 revolutionary movement.[64] Russified educated Jewish women had joined revolutionary organizations, often surpassing the proportion of non-Jewish women, swelling the ranks of the Menshevik and Bolshevik Social Democratic Parties, as well as the Socialist Revolutionary Party, eager to rebel against gender inequality and the Jewish traditional society they felt alienated from. Many Jewish women, especially in the cities of the western borderlands of the empire, joined the Bund, with one-third of its members being women, as well as different socialist Zionist organizations.[65] By attracting young women to their rank and file, Jewish parties served as an important stepping-stone for young Jewish women, especially those who were less Russified and who would have hardly considered so quickly and eagerly to participate in the political and social life of the Soviet Union without their previous Bundist or Socialist-Zionist political experience. In other words, having served in the Bund or in the Poale-Tsiyon allowed Jewish women, perhaps even more than it did Jewish men, to gain footing in the new system. After all, women who were active in socialist politics were atypical and stood out from the masses of womankind by virtue of their commitment to socialism, as well as their political activities. The Poale-Tsiyon, for instance, acknowledged its role in facilitating women's active involvement in public life. In the summer of 1921, while carrying out party work among Jewish women, party leaders sent questionnaires about women's participation in politics and inquired about ways to consolidate it, by gauging from its members, for example, "How many of you can speak publicly at interviews, lectures, rallies and in which language, Yiddish or Russian?"[66]

The new Soviet system pledged to transform the lives of women, liberating them from the "dark forces" of religion, drawing them to the Party, and enticing them into playing an active role in the newly established Soviet institutions. The political agency that dealt with women's affairs, envisioning for them political agency in Soviet society, was the Zhenotdel, the Women's Department of the Secretariat of the Central Committee of the Communist Party. Established in 1920, with branches throughout the cities of the Soviet Union, the Zhenotdel intended to eradicate women's illiteracy, to attract them to the social and political life of the new Soviet system, and to provide them with a firm knowledge of communism. Equating their "ignorance" with danger to the cause, the Zhenotdel contended that only by virtue of communist education could women fulfill their vital role of caretakers of the younger generation. The Soviet political system created a new category for women interested in participating in the political arena: the *delegatka*, or woman delegate, was elected by other women and coordinated propaganda on behalf of the Zhenotdel in the agency or factory in which she worked. Delegates met regularly to discuss topics related to women's everyday life, such as hygiene, children, wedding laws, unemployment, religion, nationality policy, and schools. They were also responsible for monitoring the social conditions of other women. Finally, delegates were expected to discuss women's questions in political brochures and wall newspapers and to participate in the literary and political circles organized for women.[67]

With the exception of the prerevolutionary Bund's meetings, most of which took place illegally and underground, for many Jewish women, work in the Zhenotdel constituted the first time that they participated in a public political forum and debated questions related to the status of women in a male dominated and oriented world. More than Ukrainian or Belarusian women, Jewish women served prominently as delegates in Party-cells and agencies.[68] Because of the higher level of literacy, urbanization, and tradition of political activism compared to their non-Jewish counterparts, from the beginning Jewish women occupied most of the newly created positions for women and were more engaged in Party work. In some cities with a large Jewish demographic concentration, only Jewish women participated in the Zhenotdel initiatives. In some places, the Women's Department operated as a Jewish ethnic space and could bear a stronger resemblance to other Jewish agencies than to general Party organizations. In a heavily Jewish city like Minsk, for instance, not only did the Zhenotdel address specifically Jewish concerns and interests more than it did Russian or Belarusian ones, but it also convened general women conferences in Jewish institutions because of the identity of a large segment of the audience.[69] In many cities, the high percentage of Jewish women active in the Zhenotdel persisted throughout the 1920s and into the year 1930, when the Party deemed the women's question solved and eventually liquidated the department.[70]

In general, whether young Jewish women hoped to improve women's conditions or were keen on being part of a project that went beyond the walls of their homes and enabled their voices to be heard in public, many became enthusiastic supporters of the regime. From different towns and cities in Belorussia, Ukraine, and Russia, young Jewish women attended the All-Union Congress of Women Workers and Peasants, which was held in Moscow in October 1927. Many had reached their position in public life thanks to the Zhenotdel and had become members of the city soviet or of the presidium of the shtetl's soviet. E. Goldberg, one of the young Jewish women workers who participated in the Moscow congress and who was the chairperson of the soviet of a small village in Belorussia, spoke in Yiddish at the congress, making this the first time ever that the Jewish language sounded through the cavernous Andreevsky Hall in the Kremlin (a reporter admitted that, with the exception of the German delegation of women workers, most of the congress attendees did not understand the speech, until it was translated into Russian).[71] A photograph taken at the end of the congress portrays the Jewish delegates surrounding Avel Enukidze, the prominent Georgian Old Bolshevik and secretary of the All-Russian Central Executive Committee.[72] For some of these young women, this public moment in their political activism represented a memorable one in their lives.

The success and failures of the Zhenotdel varied from place to place. In the European regions of the Soviet Union, the Zhenotdel's most remarkable achievement on the Jewish street resulted in the creation of a new elite of Jewish women eager to partake in the building of the socialist system and educate other women in the spirit of communism and equality with men. Mostly untouched by politics in the past, they now learned the basics of political and cultural organization, monitoring factory conditions, fighting against female unemployment and prostitution, and teaching literacy classes. Moreover, Jewish women who became active in the Zhenotdel could act simultaneously as communists, Jews, and women, interweaving these three identities in a new distinctive unity, harmonious and contentious at the same time. Finally, for the first time, Jewish women were able to attain social mobility through the Party and not through their fathers or husbands. For many Jewish women, becoming a delegate and joining the Women's Department was the first stage in their rise to high positions of responsibility and power in society. And even though female empowerment eventually met and collided with male empowerment, as Jewish men who found Bolshevism exhilarating also viewed Jewish women as dangerous competitors for power, it was still real and had some long-term consequences for the Sovietization of Jews.

On the other end of the Soviet geographic landscape, in the largely Muslim regions of Central Asia and the Caucasus, despite the fact that gender was central to the revolutionary vision, carrying out the Soviet emancipation of women lagged significantly behind. The attempt to educate and emancipate the "female dark masses" through the promotion of literacy with the help of the Zhenotdel fell short due to the lack of funding, with a trifling budget allocated to the region and to local cadres. A 1922 report from the Mountain Republic in Northern Caucasus complained that the Zhenotdel was active exclusively in the city of Vladikavkaz with no work in the surrounding rural area. Anastas Mikoyan, a member of the Central Committee of the Communist Party and future commissar of trade, lamented the insignificant progress made in the sphere of the women's question.[73] An additional concern complicated matters in Central Asia in particular. There, Zhenotdel activists were more often than not Russian or Jewish women, who were more likely to be literate and politically active.[74] Moreover, the Soviet campaign to encourage women in the regions of Central Asia and the Caucasus to forgo wearing the traditional veil favored the involvement in politics of Jewish women over Muslim women. In the Bukharan community, for instance, the unveiling of Jewish women was not met with too much hostility. A special investigation report from the late 1920s about women in Uzbekistan emphasized the difference between Jewish and Muslim women, pointing out, "Jewish women veil themselves when someone traditionally dressed is approaching, even if he is Russian, but do not veil when a man dressed in western style comes by, even if he is Uzbek." In other words, unveiling did not represent a problem for Jewish women because it did not constitute a violation of any specific religious commandment but was, rather, embedded in local customs.[75] The absence of a religious proscription gave Jewish women more leeway to partake in the political sphere. But the theme of women's emancipation emerged strongly in some of the cultural productions at the time. Both Bukharan Jewish drama and Mountain Jewish poetry approached the theme by contrasting the Soviet commitment to liberate women from bondage with the actual fate of "the subjugated women" in the domestic realm of the prerevolutionary years.[76]

By the end of the NEP era, communist work among women lost most of its momentum and became somewhat relegated to the margins of the Party's political initiatives. Questions about women all but disappeared from Party protocols and the press. The frequency of women's columns declined; they typically appeared only on specific occasions, in particular March 8, International Women's Day. This change might have been an indication of the imminent liquidation of the Zhenotdel, a process initiated by the Secretariat of the Central Committee in Moscow in late 1929, primarily, but not exclusively, for lack of funds.

The Evsektsiia: Upward Mobility, Power, and Violence on the Jewish Street

When the Bolsheviks rose to power, many Jews who had served as activists in reforming Jewish life before the revolution faced persecution, as the revolution destroyed not only political parties but lives as well. Many Bundists fled to neighboring Poland. Others faced repeated arrest and torture. Some committed suicide, like the Bundist Sore Foks, who in a desperate act of protest took her own life by throwing herself into the Dnipro River. Like the leaders of other socialist parties, many Bundists were forced into exile abroad or sent to Siberia.[77] Many former Bundists opted out of Jewish work: they embraced communism and, overcoming (or silencing) their criticism of Lenin's vision of the revolution, joined the Communist Party and settled for power and influence. But in settling for power and influence, many decided to remain committed and connected to Jewish work, primarily by joining the ranks of the Evsektsiia, the Jewish section of the Communist Party.

Established in the fall of 1918, the Evsektsiia grew out of Lenin and Stalin's revision of their previously held position on the identity of the Jewish minority group: if before 1917, in their passionate opposition to the Jewish labor Bund, the Bolshevik leaders argued that Jews did not constitute a nationality or an ethnic group and that the Jewish proletariat should assimilate entirely, following the October Revolution, they realized that compromise might be the most practical approach. In order to bring Marxism to the Jewish masses, they needed to rely on Jews who were knowledgeable about Jewish life and of the language of the Jewish masses, namely, Yiddish, eventually reaching the agreement that Jews constituted a nationality after all. Consequently, alongside the different commissariats for Polish, Lithuanian, Estonian, Armenian, and Muslim affairs, under Stalin's leadership, the Commissariat for Nationality Affairs, established a Commissariat for Jewish National Affairs (EVKOM). Unlike the other commissariats, the Jewish commissariat was designated as temporary.[78] The Evsektsiia grew out of the Commissariat for Jewish National Affairs. In the midst of the early debates about its existence, including, for example, the opposition of someone like Yakov Sverdlov, chairman of the All-Russian Central Executive Committee, who, despite being Jewish, argued against "separate forms of Jewish work," it was Lenin himself who intervened. He argued that the creation of a Jewish section within the Bolshevik Party constituted an indispensable instrument to promote the Sovietization of the Jewish minority group.[79]

One of the main challenges on the Jewish street was finding reliable cadres who could bring the revolution to the Jewish masses. Trustworthy Jewish communists from the European regions of the Soviet Union were dispatched to Central Asia and the Caucasus to bring communism to the non-Ashkenazi local Jewish communities. In the Soviet Republic of Turkestan, for instance, a Turkestan branch of the Evsektsiia was established soon after the Jewish section was founded in October 1918. In lieu of local Jews, young Jewish activists from Ukraine and Belorussia, who had little or no knowledge of the life and culture of Bukharan Jews, were given control over the Bukharan Jewish community of Turkestan.[80] The members of these potential cadres were the men (and some of the women) who before the revolution had thrown themselves into Jewish political life as members of the Bund, of different socialist Zionist parties, and even of territorialist and autonomist parties. These parties had a relatively strong foothold in the borderland regions of the new Soviet empire in formation, in particular in Belorussia and Ukraine; for this reason, especially in the early stages of its establishment, the Evsektsiia reached out to the Bund for support and relied heavily on the Jewish party to organize propaganda activities, appointing from its ranks the new communist cadre.[81] The year 1921 became a turning point in this process: as the Communist Party abolished almost all Jewish parties, members of the left wings of the Bund, the United Jewish Socialist Workers Party (Fareynikte), and the Poale-Tsiyon joined the Communist Party and then the Evsektsiia. Going from being a Bundist to a Bolshevik was not only about swapping party cards; it entailed a change in worldview, commitments, and priorities. As for other Socialist Revolutionaries and Mensheviks, Bundists too had to renounce, at least publicly, the emotional loyalty of a tight-knit family that had characterized its members' relationship during the first two decades of the twentieth century.[82]

In particular, many Bundists who ultimately embraced communism envisioned the Evsektsiia as something more than a mere section of the Bolshevik Party, as something truly akin to an autonomous Jewish organization. This perception, however, turned out to be in glaring conflict with the Party's view of the organization. The Evsektsiia seemed to be committed to modernize and Sovietize the Jewish population while preserving its specific ethnic identity; on the contrary, the Communist Party remained unconcerned with the survival of a particular Jewish identity.[83] This tension between the stated official goal of carrying out propaganda and agitation in Yiddish among the Jewish masses and actually hoping to foster and spread a secular Jewish culture and thereby retain a Jewish ethnic identity would characterize the Evsektsiia's existence until its liquidation, in 1930.

Regardless of how the approximately fifteen hundred Jewish activist who joined the Evsektsiia viewed the future of Soviet Jews and the nature of the culture they intended to shape for them, they knew that in order to bring the revolution to the Jewish street, they had to restructure Jewish life according to the tenets of socialism. This entailed destroying the foundations of prerevolutionary Jewish life, including Zionism and its different organizations, Judaism and religious institutions, and Hebrew language and culture. Because of their potentially suspicious background, many members of the Evsektsiia implemented the mission to Sovietize the Jewish population through Yiddish, the language accessible to most Jews, and "vanquish" all bourgeois Jewish parties and communal organizations with ruthlessness. The violence stemmed from their insecurity about their prerevolutionary political careers, which had made them latecomers to communism. Ex-Bundists in particular strove to wash off their political sin by carrying out the revolution on the Jewish street with further brutality.[84]

Of course, Jewish communists were also operating in a general zeitgeist of violence. After coming to power, the Bolsheviks stimulated a revolution in civil society by allowing citizens to express anger and antiauthoritarian feelings. The Bolsheviks relabeled the violence as counterrevolutionary, delegitimizing it; at the same time, they institutionalized authority and antiauthoritarian violence in the context of the Red Terror in the socialist state. This general atmosphere also influenced the ways in which the former Bundists and Socialist-Zionists who joined the Evsektsiia dealt with those who opposed its mission, embracing violence as a mode of discourse and a mode of action.

The rush for power and the need to express it, combined with the frustration over the inability to fully tame the Jewish masses, led to an intensification of brutality. The Evsektsiia embraced with pathos the Bolshevik path to violence and redemption and played a crucial role in hastening the demise of independent Jewish life, including religious institutions, Hebrew-language education, and Jewish political movements and organizations. If the Evsektsiia's first large-scale effort encompassed putting an end to the old order on the Jewish street, helping disintegrate traditional structures and values, its second round of priorities was to promote the social mobilization of the Yiddish-speaking masses by way of creating a new secular Jewish culture. This effort built on a network of Soviet Yiddish cultural institutions, including newspapers, magazines, journals, schools, clubs, and theaters, as well as the dissemination of the Yiddish language in Soviet political and legal institutions, including the Party, the Soviet courts, and trade unions. By supporting the process of cultural construction, the Evsektsiia fostered the enlistment of Jews in the new system, promoting their modernization, upward mobility, and political integration.

The great majority of Evsektsiia members were men: a collective photo of the first conference of the Jewish section, held in Moscow in October 1918, depicts almost exclusively men.[85] But there were also women who came to play a key role in the Jewish section, as they rushed to realize their ideological priorities and fulfill their personal ambitions. Besides Zlata Litvakova (sister of Moshe Litvakov, the de facto commissar of Soviet Yiddish culture), who was active in the Ukrainian Main Bureau of the Evsektsiia, or Ester Frumkin, who was the only woman to assume a high leadership role in the Evsektsiia's Central Bureau in Moscow, there were other women who assumed middle-level leadership roles.[86] Sara Mariasina, whose name often appears in the Evsektsiia protocols in Minsk, was one of them. She became successful in the 1920s and attracted others to Sovietize. Born in 1890, Mariasina had been a member of the Bund prior to the revolution. In 1920, she joined the Communist Party, and in 1921, she became a member of the Minsk Evsektsiia and of the Jewish section of the People's Commissariat for Education. A well-educated woman, who besides Yiddish and Russian knew French and German, Mariasina had worked as a pedagogue before the revolution and had been the director of the local Professional School since 1916. A member of the Minsk city soviet, she was active in the Zhenotdel and participated in the debates regarding the status of Jewish women and the use of Yiddish in the city factories with a high percentage of Jewish women workers. In 1925, she became director of the Cultural Department of the Union of Education Workers. At the end of 1925, at the age of thirty-five, she applied to law school at Belorussian State University. In 1929, while acting as a supervisor for Jewish culture in the District Education Department, Mariasina published a book on the new Soviet pedagogical system, titled *The Old and New School*.[87] While Mariasina's success story as a Soviet and Jewish woman during the 1920s is exceptional, it is also indicative of the breadth of new opportunities available to Jewish women in the fields of politics, education, and social life in a Soviet city, precisely to those women who chose to work on the Jewish street and, by doing so, to mobilize other Jews.

So What's the Plan? Sovietization through Settling the Land

Besides destroying the ostensibly bourgeois foundations of prerevolutionary life and giving shape to a Soviet Yiddish culture, which, following Stalin's conception would be "national in form and socialist in content," the Evsektsiia worked to rectify the unhealthy socioeconomic structure of Jewish communities. The question of how to modernize and redeem Jews through productive work, an all-too-common question that had occupied the hearts and minds of many *maskilim* (enlightened Jews committed to educational and cultural reforms) and Jewish political thinkers from a range of positions since the second half of the nineteenth century, was now a preoccupation of Jewish communists too.[88]

How should the Evsektsiia address the question of rebuilding the economic structure of a population that was for the most part not engaged in Marxist activities? What to do with the thousands of Jews who had been deprived of civil rights, and thus livelihood, after the revolution? How to Sovietize the young unemployed Jews who roamed the streets of Soviet towns and cities? And how to integrate and politicize those Jews living in the regions of Central Asia and the Caucasus? The Evsektsiia could certainly not encourage residents of Soviet cities to rely on help from relatives in the United States—even though many did. As noted by a visitor from the United States to the Soviet Union in the second half of the 1920s, "Wherever I met a Jew and asked him what his source of livelihood was, I got the same answer: American relatives send me money."[89] Similarly, the Evsektsiia could not allow families that had lost their income to turn to profiteering and black marketing and could not encourage them to become successful NEPmen.[90]

Brutalized by war and revolution and economically broken by the endless waves of refugees, the shtetls and their inhabitants continued to pose an ideological threat to the success of the Soviet experiment on the Jewish street. Unemployment rates soared in the shtetls, as their "bourgeois" residents, mostly small merchants, peddlers, and artisans who were unable to take advantage of the New Economic Policy, were left without an income. Those who were excluded from the local job registers could not become employed and support their families. Some turned to trading as a way out of abject poverty; some even managed to earn a comfortable livelihood despite the burden of exorbitant taxation. But eventually many gave in: they either went bankrupt because of rising taxes or escaped their pariah condition of *lishchentsy* by fleeing their place of residence. In general, Jews more than non-Jews suffered from unemployment in the 1920s because, as a largely lower-middle-class urban group, they were underrepresented in the proletariat and the peasantry, the two classes favored by Marxism. In 1926 in Ukraine, 38.9 percent of Jews were gainfully employed (compared to 61.8 percent of the total population), and 37.1 percent of Jews in Belorussia were gainfully employed (compared to 63 percent of the total population).[91] Overall, more than 72 percent of Jewish youth in the small towns of Ukraine and Belorussia were without work in the second half of the 1920s.[92] Many would have wanted to leave and move to larger cities. As noted by a visitor from the United States to the Soviet Union in the early 1920s, "In general it may be said that the smaller the town, the greater the proportion of Jews who wish to leave."[93] But work options were limited.

Jews in Central Asia and the Caucasus were also heavily affected by unemployment and disenfranchisement. Mountain Jews from the Caucasus, primarily from Dagestan and Azerbaijan, who constituted the second-largest non-Ashkenazi Jewish community after the one in Georgia, numbered twenty-six thousand in 1926.[94] As of 1927, 26.7 percent of all the Jews in Dagestan were categorized as nonworking elements, a status that made their children last on the list for school matriculation and gave them little chance of entering government service. An alarmed account at the time noted that the situation for Mountain Jews "was so dismal that there was no escape. . . . The only deliverance was resettlement on land."[95]

Resettlement on land indeed became a plausible prospect for the Evsektsiia. Promoting the establishment of Jewish agricultural colonies seemed like the best way to Sovietize and rescue the young Jews of the shtetl, the disenfranchised Jews in the cities and towns throughout the Soviet lands, and those Jews who, in the confusing context of the NEP policies, strove to make a living by returning to commerce. Evsektsiia leaders also showed a preference for rescuing Jews from extreme poverty and resettling them on land over absorbing them into new industrial plants: the establishment of Jewish colonies had the potential of modernizing and Sovietizing Jews while at the same time retaining the Jewish identity of their residents by virtue of the nature of their largely homogeneous ethnic spaces. On the other hand, industrialization in the large factories of the Soviet urban hubs would inevitably speed up the assimilation process of the Jewish group, making the retention of ethnic identity and culture more problematic.[96] Some non-Jewish political figures also voiced their condemnation of Jewish assimilation. Mikhail Kalinin, president of the Soviet Union, publicly supported preserving the existence of a Jewish nationality through an agricultural and territorial base in one region only.[97]

In summer of 1924, a mass colonization project to productivize Jews was endorsed by the All-Union Central Committee with the establishment of the Committee for the Settlement of Jewish Laborers on Land (KOMZET in Russian; KOMERD in Yiddish). As the Soviet state sanctioned Jewish productivization by supporting the creation of agricultural colonies, the American Jewish philanthropic organization the American Jewish Joint Distribution Committee (JDC) established the American Jewish Joint Agricultural Corporation, or Agro-Joint, to help resettle Jews on land.[98] According to the plan, the Soviet government would assign to Jews, mostly free of charge, stretches of land in Crimea, southern Ukraine, and Belorussia, while the JDC would pay the bills of agrarianization and the purchase of modern machinery. By 1926, Komzet committed to settle on land one hundred thousand Jewish families.

Many Jewish activists, both within and without Soviet borders, hailed with enthusiasm the resettlement of Jews on land. In a 1926 memorandum for the Soviet Foreign Office, the New York Yiddish-language communist newspaper *Frayhayt*'s leading journalist, Moshe Katz (former editor of the Kyiv *Naye tsayt*), reported, "no other campaign of the Soviet government has made there [in the United States] such an exceptionally good impression as it does the land settlement of Jews."[99] In celebrating the endeavor, Moshe Litvakov, one of the foremost Yiddish cultural activists at the time and editor of the central communist Yiddish daily *Der emes* since 1921, compared the establishment of Jewish colonies in Crimea to the creation of a new Palestine.[100] He wrote about Crimea as "our Palestine" and reminded his readers that "the Jordan could not be compared with the Dnieper, nor were the friendly Crimean Moslems like the hostile Palestine Arabs."[101]

The JDC had already offered massive nonsectarian relief to the country; as early as 1921–1922, it assigned $4 million toward the American Relief Administration, more than $1 million to purchase food and clothing for pogrom victims, and $2,000 a month to cover the expenses of the children's homes under the auspices of the Commissariat for Jewish National Affairs.[102] In March 1926, the JDC approved the allocation of an additional $1.1 million in support of Jewish colonies: headed by Joseph Rosen, the Agro-Joint (the JDC agency to promote Jewish resettlement on land) sponsored 7,091 farming families, 3,631 of whom settled on the land in 1925 and 3,460 additional families who would embark on agricultural life in early 1926. The funds would cover house building and the purchase of seeds, livestock, and agricultural implements, as well as the cost of medical relief, administrative training, and tractor courses.[103]

The triangular relationship between the Soviet government, the JDC, and the Evsektsiia was fraught with strain. If in order to see colonization succeed the Evsektsiia desperately needed the financial support from the JDC, from an ideological point of view, Jewish communist were wary about accepting and rejoicing over US "capitalist" funding. Furthermore, they probably felt threatened by a foreign non-Soviet organization that in certain ways displaced them in their role of chief agents of change in charge of Jewish life. At least publicly, some Evsektsiia leaders tried to contend that relief should be dispensed according to the class principle only. From their own vantage point, JDC leaders mistrusted Jewish communists, fearing that they harmfully interfered with and even tried to sabotage the project; at times, they preferred reaching out to non-Jewish Soviet leaders.[104] Some foreign Jewish leaders who supported the colonization project highlighted the Evsektsiia's harassment of the JDC and admitted that in order to ease the tension, the US relief organization should resolve to promote communist cultural activities in Yiddish and fund libraries, presses, and newspapers.[105]

There was an ongoing conversation, which often triggered tensions and disputes, among American Jewish leaders regarding the amount of funds that should be funneled to the Soviet Union. Many American Jews resisted the idea of interfering in the Jewish question in the Soviet Union, particularly out of suspicion of the Bolshevik position.[106] In 1926, for example, the allotment of funds to support the establishment of colonies for Soviet Jews was discussed at a luncheon at the luxury New York Biltmore Hotel. Presided over by the banker Felix M. Warburg, who was honorary chairman of the JDC's New York drive campaign, the luncheon's guests included prominent leaders such as Louis Marshall, William Fox, David M. Bressler, and James Rosenberg. The journalist Louis Fischer, who had recently visited Ukraine and Belorussia, spoke in favor of the resettlement endeavor by reminding the guests that the JDC's support for the project would solve the huge social problem afflicting Jewish life in the Soviet lands. He acknowledged that "reproaches of their children because they are leading non-productive lives, the governmental policy of exterminating the merchant class, and the precariousness of urban existence, are the three leading factors which are causing large numbers of Jews in Russia to become farmers." Fischer also made some exaggerated statements that involved propagandistic selling points. Even though there was no anti-Jewish violence in the mid-1920s, he argued that those who settled in the colonies "felt undoubtedly safer from pogroms and counterrevolutionary uprisings than the Jews in the cities."[107] Louis Marshall, founder of the American Jewish Committee, also solicited support for the cause by drawing on the pogrom rhetoric. "Jews are as safe in Russia as they are in any other part of the world," he pointed out, reminding his audience, "The policy of the present government is distinctly opposed to pogroms."[108] In Fischer's comments, he exaggerated the positive influence that productivizing Jews on land would have on ethnic relations, noting, "As farmers they had been able to demonstrate to the neighboring peasantry that the tales that Jews are parasites are myths. By their own arduous labour they have demonstrated to the peasantry that Jews are also producers. . . . They have added to the prosperity of the neighboring country, and the extension by the Joint Distribution Committee of the use of its tractors and breeding stations to the peasantry without discrimination has established a new cordiality between non-Jewish peasants and the new Jewish farmers."[109]

Both the JDC and the Soviet state invested significant resources and effort (in the case of the American partner, substantial capital too) in publicity strategies to support colonization. These included silent movies. Two promotional silent movies were produced in 1927 to appeal to potential donors and supporters. The JDC sponsored a film titled *Back to the Soil: A Story of Jewish Hope, Struggle, and Achievement*. It chronicled the visit to the Jewish colonies of the German-born American banker Felix Warburg, showcasing the success of the project. The Soviets, on their end, produced a movie titled *Evrei na zemle* (Jews on land), intended to promote the resettlement of Soviet Jews on land but also to combat unfavorable stereotypes. It became popular thanks to the involvement of a stellar cast of caption writers; these included Vladimir Mayakovsky and Viktor Shklovskii, two major literary personalities, whose work is, respectively, associated with the rise of the Russian futurist movement and Russian formalism. Mayakovsky's beloved muse in his work of poetry, Lili Brik, worked on the film as assistant director.[110] Shortly after the movie's release, it was shown in trade-union clubs across Moscow and introduced by lectures about Society for Settling Toiling Jews on the Land (OZET) and its mission.[111]

The Jewish colonization project faced severe challenges well into the late 1920s. For one, it largely failed to attract, and thus reform through Sovietization, small traders and the unemployed: the majority of those who were drawn to the project included artisans and factory and agricultural workers and were thus, at least in theory, already deemed productive elements in society.[112] In the late 1920s, for instance, many of the Mountain and Georgian Jews, most of them living in rural or semirural areas and already land farmers, were incorporated into the collective farm system.[113]

Second, for Ashkenazi Jews, Soviet Yiddish culture never became the backbone of Jewish ethnic identity in the colonies as the Evsektsiia had hoped it would. Rather, to the dismay of Jewish communists, the colonies may have helped retain, at least to a certain degree, Jewish religious practice and Zionism. Third, despite the ongoing financial support from the JDC, infrastructure in many colonies was deficient, with a number of settlements lacking basic equipment and livestock. Several families had left the colonies by the end of the 1920s: in 1928, in a colony near Kryvyi Rih, for example, 33 percent of the farmers returned home.[114] Reporting about a recent visit to the Soviet Union, the American Zionist leader Rabbi Abba Hillel Silver, who was positively inclined toward the colonization plan, acknowledged the precariousness and transience of the project as a whole when he wrote in 1927, "I am still of the opinion, however, that it will not prove permanent. Should there be an extension of the NEP policy, the Russian Jew will simply not stay on the soil."[115]

The ideological clashes and tensions that cyclically erupted between the leaders of the Jewish agricultural settlements, who strove to apply strict Marxist tenets to life in the colonies, and the colonies' residents also muddled the possible success of Sovietization through resettlement on land. Denied bread cards and expelled from cooperatives and industrial enterprises, déclassé Jews had fled the shtetl for the colony, just to be shortly thereafter accused of engaging in blackmail and kicked out as unproductive elements. All they could do was return to the shtetl. Agro-Joint representatives expressed their concern over the fact that alleged Jewish *kulaks* (from the Russian for "fist," a term used to identify wealthy or prosperous peasants) were being expelled from the colonies.[116] Finally, the colonization project had to contend with Stalin, who had taken over as the new leader of the Soviet Union and the Communist Party after Lenin's death in 1924, and with his Great Turn, namely, with the political decision made at the end of 1928 to reject the NEP and implement a violent push for industrialization and collectivization. In particular, the collectivization of the countryside involved a campaign to internationalize Jewish colonies—with Ukrainians and Belarusians moving to Jewish colonies and Jews settling in Ukrainian and Belarusian ones—a campaign that both Jewish communists and Agro-Joint activists opposed since it made countering assimilation all but impossible.[117]

And yet, despite all the great and many challenges that the campaign to resettle Jews on land faced, it remained an extraordinary experiment in modern Jewish history by virtue of both its scope and its appeal. At the peak of the movement to settle Jews on land, 10 percent of all Jews living in the territories of the Soviet Union were engaged in agriculture.[118] To grasp the revolutionary nature of this proportion, it is useful to compare it to the percentage of Jews who settled on the kibbutzim (agricultural collective communities) in Palestine, which also amounted to 10 percent of the total Jewish population of that country. Even though most Jews in the Soviet Union and in Palestine never moved to the colonies and the kibbutzim to toil the land, in both contexts, the Jewish farmer and their ways of life came to constitute the ideal of future Jewish generations, the symbol of the New Jew, and the promise of success and productivity in the communist as well as in the Zionist system. In the Soviet Union, then, Jewish resettlement on land embodied the aspirations and the future accomplishments of the new Soviet state and its Jews, even of those who had no intention of leaving the city. Not unlike the kibbutz in the Zionist project, the Jewish colony in the Soviet Union guaranteed that, in a not-too-distant future, Soviet Jewry would emerge triumphantly.

In the 1920s, the last stage in the plan to Sovietize and productivize Jews through resettlement on land became closely connected to the problem of mounting popular antagonism toward Jews. More and more peasants, in Crimea especially, came to perceive the establishment of Jewish colonies as an unjust process, which was sponsored by wealthy US organizations that bought up or, in the peasants' eyes, illegitimately stole their land. At an OZET-sponsored lecture on Jewish resettlement on land, held in the district of Odesa in late 1928 for workers in the transportation sector, unrest suddenly broke out as one of the seaport truck drivers voiced his discontent over colonization: "While Ukrainians are sent to Siberia, Jews are sent to Crimea, where it is warm. . . . Let the Jews go to Siberia to work [the land] a little; the land in Crimea has already been toiled [by us]." The event was disrupted, and resuming it became impossible.[119] In the wake of growing friction between Jews and their neighbors, Soviet authorities and Jewish communists began to look away from the historical demographic centers of Jewish residence in Ukraine and Belorussia and search elsewhere for an alternative and less problematic location for Jewish colonization. They found it in the Soviet Far East, along the border with Manchuria. Called Birobidzhan, a territory of approximately thirty-six thousand square kilometers that the Central Executive Committee of the Soviet Union designated in March 1928 as the largest Jewish agricultural colony on Soviet territory. According to the resolution, which the Soviets made to promote the political and military expansion of a largely underdeveloped region, the resettlement of Jews to the region of Birobidzhan would allow for the establishment there of a Jewish autonomous national unit.[120]

Propaganda efforts to promote the Birobidzhan project began in full swing immediately. But the number of Jews it managed to attract remained trivial compared to the country's total Jewish population. Most families that moved there did so exclusively for economic reasons and not out of ideological conviction. Of course, there were exceptions, and those are the voices recorded in the sources. The early settlers included, for example, a woman who moved to Birobidzhan with her husband because she no longer tolerated being called by the derogatory term *torgovka* (market woman); another settler, who had moved to Crimea first, opted for Birobidzhan because he envied non-Jewish peasants who "had land."[121] Only 950 people moved to Birobidzhan to become Jewish farmers in 1928, and of them, 35 percent of them left shortly thereafter. In 1929, 1,875 Jews settled in the "New Soviet Promised Land," a slogan used in Soviet propaganda to neutralize the Jewish connection to Palestine or at least to redirect the emotional and historical bond that Jews nurtured for the Land of Israel to Birobidzhan and attract Zionists.[122] Non-Jews outnumbered Jews in the so-called Soviet Jewish homeland throughout the Birobidzhan project, and many of the Jews who settled in the region eventually moved to its cities and towns.[123]

Besides the general difficulty of convincing an exceedingly urban population to resettle to underdeveloped rural areas, the failure of the project depended largely on the fact that the land in Birobidzhan was not suited for agriculture, had a horrible climate, and was too far from the Jewish demographic centers. Yet, the establishment of Jewish colonies in Birobidzhan, which in 1934 was designated as the Jewish Autonomous Region, would remain at the heart of official Soviet Jewish policy throughout the 1930s. Leftists across Europe and the US came to support the project too. In 1929, Franklin Harris, an agronomist and president of Brigham Young University, organized an American expedition to Birobidzhan and voiced his support for establishing agricultural settlements in the region, as expressed through the film reel shot by the expedition during his travels.[124]

The choice of Birobidzhan as the preferred territory to settle Jews, productivize them, Sovietize them, and perhaps even normalize them through the establishment there of a Jewish republic was based also in the hope that agrarianization there would help improve relations between Jews and non-Jews. The hostility against Jewish farmers in Crimea and other areas of Ukraine and Belorussia from the Tatar and Ukrainian longtime settlers, who felt duped by the fact that the new settlers received modern machinery, land, and financial support, might have diminished. In the Soviet Far East, Jewish farmers did not generally face the opposition of an angry and frustrated surrounding population that experienced their settlement on land as an attempt to take over and step out of line. But the idea that Jews somehow stole land in Crimea resisted the test of time and reemerged following World War II. Anti-Jewish feelings grew proportionally with Jews' upward mobility and integration into Soviet society. As in any other context, even in the new Bolshevik one, social mobility involved a shift from a subaltern group to one that occupied an equally dominant position to that of the majority group. The sense of Jews transgressing their position of minority group became intolerable for many non-Jews, in the new rural settlements just as in the cities. And because most Jews moved to new cities or remained in their native one, the problem did not go away.

3

THE SOVIET STATE, THE JEWISH QUESTION, AND RETHINKING ANTISEMITISM IN SOVIET SOCIETY

> Here [in Odesa] one can now observe a degree of violence unheard of in history. This is because the Jews are in power, and they want to choke all other nations, especially the Russian one. They want to be the superior nation, persecute workers and peasants; therefore, they torment the peasants, steal from them, drive them from Soviet housing, and leave them without clothes and blood.
>
> —"Special summary of workers' conversations in the factories in Dnipropetrovsk and Odesa, 1926"

> Can one hate the Jews here? No . . . After all, this is a Jewish government.
>
> —H. D. Nomberg, *Mayn rayze iber rusland*

Among the new Soviet regime's many boasts was the claim that it could eliminate all tensions between Jews and non-Jews. As part of the effort to carry out this goal, in 1926, the secret police (OGPU) in the Ukrainian Soviet Socialist Republic collected detailed information about expressions of anti-Jewish animosity, which had been recorded prevalently in urban centers over the course of that year. These expressions captured the angst experienced by many non-Jews over what they perceived as the sudden empowerment of Jews in Soviet society, over an alleged commonality of interests that Jews shared with the new Bolshevik government, and over the ostensibly secretive and dangerous ethnic allegiance that brought them together against non-Jews. The secret police recorded countless conversations, statements, and comments in which neighbors and coworkers identified Jews as a political and economic threat.

A group of water workers in the Odesa region voiced their frustration over what they defined as the most astonishing and disturbing event of the 1917 revolution. They referred to the position that Jews came to occupy in society, which they understood as an unlawful usurpation of power. One said, "Yids emancipated themselves in the October Revolution, while they enslaved Russians. In the central government there are exclusively Yids with Russian names."[1] Workers in different plants in other large cities of Ukraine expressed similar views. In mid-August, employees in a Kharkiv factory reprimanded Jews for ethnic tensions at the work place; they were responsible because "after taking up positions [of power] everywhere, they lead the government." Anti-Soviet and anti-Jewish sentiments frequently coincided in the comments and complaints recorded by the OGPU. For example, an engine driver in a Kyiv heavy industrial plant explained to a group of fellow workers, "Jews took over power in their hands, and [non-Jewish] workers are fearful and dance to their tune. . . . Jews command." In the same city, construction workers expressed analogous sentiments: "We must beat up all those ruling Jews who don't give us the possibility to work, while they fill up their pockets. There's no need for Jewish workers here."[2] A group of unemployed workers in Kyiv vowed to rise up against the purported rule of Jewish communists to show them "how powerful and resilient" the Russian people are: "Have fun for now, drink up our blood, because you will no longer reign over us."[3]

The distress over a secretive powerful entity that disenfranchised the majority was conveyed again in Kyiv, during a meeting with two hundred unemployed workers: "Jewish communists have penetrated our unions and organizations, they eavesdrop on our conversations and then pass them on to the GPU and the police. . . . We must organize a union of Russian workers only, and not allow Jews to join since they will sell us out, and betray us." Jews were perceived not only as spies and agents of the new state but also as the only ones who benefited from the economic crisis that enveloped society in the mid-1920s. Typographers in Mykolaiv agitated, blaming Jews for unemployment: "Jews are such a people that it never happens that they are without work, they are the only ones who carry a wallet."[4] In the fire brigade's courtyard in Uman, firefighters complained that few workers were accepted into the Party and that there were too many Jews: "more than eighty percent of the membership, and they . . . all have briefcases and make 200 rubles every month."[5]

The idea of organizing a pogrom as a legitimate act of revenge became rather widespread among frustrated workers in the mid-1920s. Lamenting that there were no Jews among the unemployed, Odesa construction workers suggested that the only way to put an end to this situation was through a pogrom: "A pogrom against the Yids in the near future will allow us to be free and live well."[6] A transportation worker in Kherson voiced his criticism of the "powerful Jew" by calling for payback through violence, commenting, "Right now Jews spin the carousel; but we are waiting for the time when there will be an anti-Jewish pogrom."[7] Food workers in Mykolaiv also spoke about the need for an uprising against the Jews. There were leaflets at a local plant that called for a rebellion, and a local policeman confirmed that if an insurrection were indeed to take place, then he would eagerly participate "and would beat them up."[8]

The comments collected by the OGPU in Ukraine in the 1920s are a reminder of the mounting resentment that a social class and ethnic group (in this case, Russian and Ukrainian workers and peasants) experienced toward another ethnic group (Jews), whose social status, visibility, and access to privilege had suddenly and deeply changed over a short period of time. As in late-imperial Russia, in Soviet society too, class and ethnic categories could not be easily separated when dealing with Jews, even more so since the Bolshevik leadership itself deployed profoundly racialized categories in class analysis. "Bourgeois" and "exploiter" were often code-words for "Jew" in the Bolshevik lexicon, and Jewishness remained overdetermined by both class and ethnic elements.[9]

But the context remains crucial in pondering attitudes toward Jews in Soviet society. Anxieties triggered by change unleashed unprecedented emotions. Not only was the change was swift, but it also took place in the midst of other epochal changes—social, economic, political, and cultural ones—which disrupted the lives of all Soviet citizens. These changes inspired the search for a common enemy, as a backlash against Jews turned into the dark side of the Bolshevik project. After all, in the eyes of many people, in particular of disenfranchised ethnic Russians who lost their privileges in the revolution, the Soviets were guilty of sanctioning the unjust emancipation of Jews.

As was the case elsewhere in Europe, following the Bolshevik takeover, the Jewish question ceased to be the question concerning the emancipation of the Jews and became instead the plea for emancipation from the Jews.[10] One difference between the Soviet Union and other European countries like France and Germany lies in the abruptness of the change. In French and German societies, the social and legal emancipation of Jews progressed over the course of several decades and was not as hasty as it turned out to be in the Soviet lands. This hastiness became furthermore noticeable when compared to the pervasiveness of anti-Jewish sentiments in tsarist society and governing circles on the eve of 1917. The March 22, 1917, decree issued by the Provisional Government in the wake of the February Revolution, which was later confirmed by the October Revolution, annulled all legal discrimination and restrictions against Jews. But it certainly did not eliminate anti-Jewish prejudice. World War I and the civil war had led to intensified fears and myths of Jewish domination and had exacerbated and exponentially fueled animosity against a "Judeo-Bolshevik enemy." Building on the assumption of a Jewish leading role in the Russian revolutionary movement and on the fame of the claims made in the *Protocols of the Elders of Zion* (the popular text that described an alleged Jewish plot for global domination published in Russia in 1903), the 1918 Soviet official condemnation of antisemitism and anti-Jewish violence only reinforced ideas of Jewish power and secrecy. These ideas in turn intersected with the vexing reality of a uniquely violent system like the one created by the Soviets.

Stereotypes of Jewish power enforced through communism not only were widespread among anti-Bolshevik forces at the time of the civil war but became a broadly accepted cultural mind-set throughout Europe. The British journalist Robert Wilton, who served as the Russian correspondent for *The Times* of London and who insisted that Bolshevism had no roots in Russian culture, argued that the October Revolution was the making of a Jewish conspiracy. In 1920, Wilton explained the destructive force of Bolshevism by linking it to the Jews and even argued that the killing of Tsar Nicholas II and his family was nothing else than a Jewish ritual murder.[11] That same year, E. Pellegrinetti, responsible for the Vatican affairs in Warsaw, commented on a dossier put together by the apostolic nuncio

Monsignor Achille Ratti, who became Pope Pius XI in 1922, referring to the danger of Jewish power and domination in Poland. "Poland is the most Judaized state in the world," he wrote. "The Jews certainly represent a great cause of weakness for the Polish state. Insofar as they control the banks, the press, . . . and are sustained by their international organization, their goal is to create a Judeo-Poland (Giudeo-Polonia)."[12] The myth of a deep-seated affinity between Jewishness and communism was one of the features of the alleged Jewish scheme to overpower the newly independent Polish nation.

Finally, unlike in France and Germany, the emancipation of Jews by the Bolshevik Revolution took place in the midst of actions that literally wiped out the country's historical elites, who were by and large ethnic Russians. These political, economic, and cultural elites were often replaced with the overwhelmingly literate and urban Jew, who had generally opposed the counterrevolution and monarchism and was thus potentially trustworthy in the eyes of the new regime.

The fear that Jews could violate their position of subaltern minority and assume power in society had taken hold of the hearts and minds of many Russians on the eve of 1917. Between February and October 1917, newspapers reported hundreds of attacks on Jews; a third of all recorded acts of violence against national minorities at the time targeted Jews. Pogrom agitation became widespread. The fear of impending anti-Jewish violence was felt in Petrograd: in April and June 1917, people openly called for anti-Jewish violence in the capital.[13] But the nightmarish fear of Jewish empowerment materialized with the October Revolution. It first took the shape of violent pogroms carried out by all forces involved in the civil war, often in cooperation with neighbors, and once the Soviets forbade pogroms, it crystallized in the mounting social and political discontent against the Jewish minority group.

After the revolution, growing numbers of Jews appeared in places and spaces from which they had previously been largely absent. Their presence in new places of residence, economic and political posts, and social spaces alarmed many people and elicited insecurity, especially in the midst of the Bolshevik attack on familiar structures and traditional norms. A Soviet author, who condemned antisemitism, captured the frenzy over Jewish visibility in the Soviet capital: "Now you might see the physiognomy of [a Jew] on Tverskaia [Street], . . . on Petrovka [Street], and then that same evening you might run into him at the theater, at the movies, or at the pub; he is nimble, mobile, brave, and free. . . . It's almost as if he alone fills out all of Moscow with his persona."[14] Another writer captured the anger and frustration over the growing presence of Jews in Moscow as follows: "The real Moscow-born patriot and resident cannot bear that his city is full of Jews, that the Jewish language resounds through its streets, it pains his ears to hear Russian spoken with a Jewish accent there. . . . It offends him even more to see Jews buried by the Kremlin Wall, . . . where every stone is shrouded in Russian history and blood, and now becomes a Jewish cemetery, . . . as his Moscow with . . . its churches, old monasteries, old Kremlin, old traditions, becomes a second Berdychiv."[15]

It was not only Jews who lay at the heart of the problem, of course. The new Soviet state was equally, if not more, responsible in the eyes of those who complained: while the tsar had maintained the Jews in their proper place, the Soviet state allowed them to achieve growing visibility in different sectors of society, turning them into purportedly active agents of disruption of tradition, socioeconomic order, and politics. By confirming their emancipation, the state promoted the breaking down of the social and cultural boundaries between Jews and non-Jews that had marked many aspects of the life of the country for decades. The wrath against the Soviet state and the Jews could thus harmoniously coincide. Confirmation of a suspected commonality of interests that brought together the new Soviet state and the Jewish collective came in the words of the revolution's leader. Lenin applauded the break from the tsarist period by outlawing antisemitism and pogroms. The struggle against antisemitism and the commitment to its successful eradication became proof of the new regime's disassociation from tsarist Russia and alleged support of the Jews. This fueled the perception that Jews constituted an untouchable political force, a mysterious elite that rose to power thanks to communism, something that never should have happened according to the accepted and historical relationship between the majority and minority group in tsarist Russia. What was most troubling, thus, in the wake of the revolution was that the Soviet state upset the mechanism of justice, disqualifying the traditional modes of punishment against those who deserved it. How could punitive acts of retaliation against the disloyal Jew, who had immorally empowered himself against the interests of the majority, be carried out if the new state no longer tolerated pogroms?

The Soviet Context

The scale of suffering experienced by the general population made the 1920s particularly ripe for the perception of Jews as a harmful force in society. The Ukrainian countryside, in particular, depleted and ravished by terror and war, in 1924–1925 faced a poor harvest and famine, with ensuing growing cases of suicide and the strengthening of criminal banditry, with looting, murder, and raids.[16] The Soviet decision to export grain despite the famine and an outbreak of hunger-induced typhus, which hit heavily the Ukrainian countryside, led to mounting popular frustration with the "predatory government." "No . . . the entire harvest must stay in Russia," stated a clandestine anti-Bolshevik flier. "Not even one lb. should be taken out. . . . Go on strike and don't pay the taxes. . . . We do not fear the GPU. . . . Let them open fire on us."[17]

The economic crisis and the social changes imposed by the new regime during War Communism and then during the NEP years fueled popular disappointment throughout the Soviet territories. Thousands of peasants were forced to move to the cities in search of a livelihood. Here, often for the first time, they encountered Jews, who had themselves resettled from the small market towns to the more industrialized regions and found employment in heavy industry. This new employment pattern, coupled with the prominent role Jews came to occupy in many governmental bodies, turned the encounter between in-migrant Jews and non-Jews into an economic and political clash. Peasants and workers (the latter were often peasants who moved to the cities temporarily to be employed as seasonal workers) accused Jews of holding too many positions of prominence and responsibility; on the other hand, the Soviets explained the rise in popular expressions of hostility toward Jews by pointing a finger at the influx of peasants into the cities, who brought with them prejudices, religious stereotypes, and political backwardness. Negative conjectures about the peasantry and the unpolitical *Lumpenproletariat*, which were inherent in Marxism and Leninism, also played out in the shaping of this view. By blaming the newly urbanized peasantry, which lacked knowledge about the official Party position on the Jewish question, the regime dismissed that hostility toward Jews could in any way emerge as a result of the conditions of life under communism, thus uprooting it from the Bolshevik project.[18]

However, while anti-Jewish feelings became a serious social problem among industrial workers, many of whom were of peasant background, such feelings were just as widespread among the new Soviet elite. This included Party members and Komsomol activists, all of whom should have been, at least in theory, well-read in Marxism and aware of Lenin's rejection of expressions of antisemitism, including discrimination against Jews in employment and education, verbal insults, and physical violence. In 1926, the Politburo member Mikhail Kalinin noted that the new elites were more likely to discriminate against Jews than were their precursors under the tsar.[19] Indeed, 1926 marked a turning point in the approaches of Party and state to the Jewish question. While a ruthless power struggle within the Party seemed to tolerate discrimination and expressions of hostility against Jews from above, the state launched—as we will see—the largest campaign against antisemitism in modern European history.

In the fall of 1926, Stalin, who was tightening his grip on the Party machine as Lenin's successor, was up in arms against the so-called United Opposition. This Party faction rejected the political economy of the NEP and identified wealthy peasants, traders, and retailers (contemptuously referred to as *kulaki*, a derogatory term used to describe "wealthy" peasants and NEPmen) as a major threat to the future of the country. Founded in the summer of 1926, the group resulted from the merging of Trotsky's Left Opposition and the new opposition led by Grigory Zinoviev and Lev Kamenev. Several members of the United Opposition's leadership were Jewish. Besides Trotsky, Zinoviev, and Kamenev, they included Karl Radek and Adolph Yoffe. As part of Stalin's ultimately successful campaign against them, he attacked his opponents' Jewish background, which may, in turn, have fueled a spike in anti-Jewish animus among the Party constituency.[20] Ideas of a Jewish political conspiracy trickled into society via Party meetings and discussions, collective readings of press releases among workers, and quickly traveling rumors. Workers in the First State Tobacco Factory in Kremenchuk, for instance, seemed convinced that all Jewish communists would be expelled from the Party since the Opposition was supposedly made up of Jews only.[21] Contrary to the former understanding of the events, rumors in the Uman district established that the Opposition took shape within the Party itself to protest the alleged domination of Jews.[22]

After Trotsky's and Zinoviev's banishment from the political leadership, caricatures of them became widely available in the press. The satirical magazine *Krokodil* published caricatures of the two Opposition leaders: the exaggerated large noses and ears allowed readers to unmask the hidden Jewish roots of the political enemies, thus making invidious public representations of Jews seemingly acceptable.[23] Identifying Jews as a foreign and threatening political force generated among Uman students the suspicion that Zinoviev actually headed the Zionist movement: "After all we know that all Jews are strong nationalists. . . . They stand for each other and it is quite possible that Zinoviev's case is closely linked to Zionism. . . . There are many enemies in the Party and in the event of war, the internal enemy will grow stronger."[24] Assumptions of an imagined Jewish political opposition took the form of campaigns against Trotskyism, which intermittently exploited antisemitic slurs during the late 1920s and into the 1930s. Trotsky himself noted, "Antisemitism and anti-Trotskyism reared their head simultaneously."[25]

Stalin and his allies were willing to use anti-Jewish images for certain political purposes but did not want those images to prompt widespread public hostility toward Jews. Party leaders understood the dangers in stimulating mass anger against Jews and in challenging Lenin's condemnation of anti-Jewish violence.[26] To counter the impulses promoting attacks on Jews from above, the government launched a robust and unprecedented campaign to fight against antisemitism. After collecting extensive evidence that confirmed the growth of antisemitism, the authorities tried to put the cat back into the bag. But keeping antisemitism at bay proved much more difficult than expected, especially in the context of the Party's ideological war against the NEP.

In theory, the mixed economic policies of the NEP era would provide the economic foundation necessary for socialism to thrive in the Soviet Union. And yet, the ideological resentment against these policies was widespread, so much so that a state-approved continuation of capitalism and foreign investments developed in tandem with a harsh refutation of the same trade and private business it tolerated. In other words, the NEP enterprises and entrepreneurs coexisted within the ideological commitment to the socialist project, which rejected their very essence. Private ownership subsisted while coming under attack as a retreat from socialism. The taxes levied by the state on small-scale and more substantial private traders were astronomical. Consumption, for example, was not meant to be a private experience as it was under capitalism; rather, Soviet publications and advertising agencies exhorted the consumer to behave as a Soviet citizen. Advertising from the 1920s encouraged consumers to buy and use state-produced commodities only, while staying away from the dangerous privately produced NEP goods, which were irreconcilably at odds with the new great socialist enterprise.[27]

The ideological condemnation of the NEP added a new layer to pre-existing canards about Jewish economic exploitation. The image of a corrupting middleman minority that took advantage of the Russian peasants was deeply embedded in age-old cultural notions about the money-grubbing Jew as well as in nineteenth-century tsarist legislation.[28] During the years of the civil war, Jews became the principal signifier of antibourgeois sentiment and were attacked and killed as "speculators" in defense of the revolution.[29] At the time of the Red pogroms of 1918, fighting for Soviet power and the revolution while attacking Jewish exploitation could be in harmony, not in contradiction. Calls to smash the Jews and the bourgeoisie could overlap, and revolutionary Bolshevism could merge with counter-revolutionary antisemitism.[30]

Arguably, the top Bolshevik/Soviet leaders were of two minds about the support they received from the Jews. On the one hand, they were not about to scoff at the considerable assets Jews were prepared to bring to their cause, but on the other, they understood that the prominence of Jews among their supporters impeded the efforts to expand their base among other, more numerous, sectors of the populace. This situation created tensions in the ways in which Soviet leaders regarded the impacts that different actions by the regime had on Jews and their relations with other social sectors.

During the 1920s, the term "NEPman" became synonymous with "Jew," and the new Soviet bourgeoisie was perceived as a Jewish phenomenon. Assumptions of ethnic and class solidarity among Jewish entrepreneurs operating in closed economic networks and niches fomented anti-Jewish hostility. While these networks might have existed, their influence and impact were trivial and disproportionately blown up by the socioeconomic tensions at the time. During the NEP years, the tendency in the Soviet project to conflate Jewish economic practices with the workings of merchant capital came to the fore.[31] Comments about the Soviet-Jewish bourgeoisie included statements such as, "The wives and daughters of the Jewish NEP-man-ness [*evreiskaia nepmanstva*] buy beautiful jewelry, dolls, and makeup, embodying the bourgeois spirit." Allegations were made by Soviet citizens that the powerful Jew par excellence, Trotsky, had orchestrated the NEP so that Jews could take advantage of it.[32]

To restrain the class-driven anti-Jewish sentiment, some writers tried to demonstrate that despite the fact that many Jews did engage in commerce, the majority of them belonged to the working and not the exploiting class in the 1920s. Writing in 1927, a Soviet author emphasized the harsh living conditions and poverty of the Moscow Jewish small peddlers. He described the wretched small traders as "an eyesore to all of us; they inhibit our movement on the Kuznetsky bridge, on Petrovka and Tverskaia streets; they deafen us with their outcries about better quality merchandise, such as stockings, socks, laces, bras, lampshades, toys for kids, sensational novels (for 50 kopeks instead of one and a half rubles). They get wet when it rains and when it is minus twenty, they suffer in the heat, and then they usually have to pay one ruble to the police, which is usually 75 percent of their income. Tell me how many of them would turn down a different job as a courier, janitor, or a watchman . . . ?"[33]

The mixed economy of the NEP years also gave rise to a thriving black market and to crime. In many places, racketeering became more and more widespread and targeted small businessmen. Every so often, members of the Jewish group had been portrayed as criminals driven by greed since the Middle Ages, and there were indeed times and places that saw Jews deeply involved in crime. The legendary Jewish gangster Benja Krik, also known as "the King of Odesa," hailed as a local hero in Isaac Babel's *Odessa Stories*, was one such example in the NEP years. Based on the real-life gangster Mishka Iaponchik, a well-known extortionist who was also called the Robin Hood of the Moldovanka (the Jewish neighborhood in Odesa) and who was killed during the civil war, Benja Krik became the subject of a Soviet-produced silent movie, released in 1927 and based on Babel's 1926 screenplay.[34] Underworld songs (*blatnaya pesnya*)—a prerevolutionary apolitical urban genre, which alongside gypsy romances, jazz, and foxtrots, was forbidden under the Soviets as part of the deplorable NEP musical culture—were still sung at parties and informal gatherings. Jews appeared as the heroes in many a criminal folk song, which may have affected their social image in a negative way.[35]

The 1928 Party decision to reject the NEP as a retreat from socialist policies and embrace forced collectivization and industrialization as a path to success was accompanied by the arrest of "bourgeois elements" and a crackdown on private enterprises and cooperatives. In the summer of 1928, the Soviet secret police arrested all members of the Jewish artisan association in Vitsyebsk, charging them with connections with speculators and with actively harming state institutions by helping private commerce. Whether there was a connection between the state's suppression of the private sphere and preexisting antisemitism (namely, Jews being targeted for discrimination because of their Jewishness or/and because of their economic role) is impossible to establish. But being Jewish and being involved in trade was not promising at this time and in some instances could lead to dire consequences. Moisei Galperin, who managed the customs department of the Soviet Transportation Organization, "was sentenced to death for allegedly supporting foreign concession firms to obtain credit from the government bank, and thus operate on Soviet funds without investing their own money."[36]

According to a reporter in the Yiddish daily *Der emes*, in some places the rejection of the NEP triggered anti-Jewish discrimination among local authorities: in Kyiv, the Housing Committee targeted for eviction from municipal dwellings Jewish families whose members were not former NEPmen but who had been working for less than five years and were hence classified as nonworking elements.[37] Officials and clerks, who in prerevolutionary years had been used to tsarist anti-Jewish legislation and who after 1917 were forced to work next to Jews or may have had their positions in Soviet society taken over by Jews, exploited anti-NEP sentiment to express their resentment.

Ethnic tensions and anti-Jewish animosity grew in the period of transition from the NEP to the Five-Year Plan (1928–1932), Stalin's economic policies to modernize the country through the collectivization of agriculture and rapid industrialization. The general crisis unleashed by forced collectivization and industrialization became fertile ground for expressions of antagonism toward Jews by Soviet citizens, especially in the form of class resentment. The reality of one Jewish NEPman who conducted an above-average lifestyle or a relatively higher proportion of Jewish Party members in one city or factory could channel rumors and assumptions about Jews occupying the most lucrative positions in society. Complaints about the fact that unemployment never affected the Jews, who as skilled workers received higher salaries, were commonplace: "The whole politics of the USSR is one of privileges for Jews."[38] Disguised under the attack on the NEP and on the bourgeoisie, expressions of covert anti-Jewish animosity became all too ordinary (and may have been akin to negative sentiments regarding the *kulaks*). Respectable antibourgeois accusations and rhetoric could conceal expressions of precisely the long-standing common antipathy toward Jews that the state openly rebuked. Some Soviet citizens could also take advantage of the anti-NEP feelings to vent on the Jews their frustration, as their lives became disrupted by the Party's program of breakneck industrialization and collectivization. But ultimately, the position of Jews in Soviet public opinion (or the degree to which people chose to draw on hostile images of Jews for public or private purposes) depended also on the ways in which the state, at different times and in relation to different internal or external pressures, chose to challenge or to ignore the social problem of antisemitism.

"Shame on Those Who Sow the Seeds of Hatred against the Jews!"

Many Soviet citizens regarded the war against antisemitism as one of the markers of change of the new system, something that set it apart from tsarist Russia. Many Jews supported the Soviet system precisely because of its stated commitment to obviate the Jewish question altogether. By the same token, many conservative and anti-Bolshevik voices criticized the system for this very same reason. The fact that pogroms, accusations of ritual murder, and anti-Jewish legal and social discrimination, all of which had been tolerated to a greater or lesser degree under the tsars, were now banned represented a startling novelty and a source of exasperation for many people. Of course, intellectuals and writers had spoken out against anti-Jewish prejudice and expressions of anti-Jewish violence under the reigns of Alexander III and Nicholas II.[39]

The Russian writer Maxim Gorky was one of them. He poignantly described his childhood encounter with a Jewish boy in his autobiographical writings and condemned anti-Jewish violence in his widely read short story "Pogrom."[40] In 1915, in the midst of World War I, Gorky also coedited, together with the prominent members of the intelligentsia Leonid Andreev and Fyodor Sologub, a literary anthology with statements in defense of the Jews, which decried how they had been treated in tsarist Russia. Other intellectuals who publicly condemned the treatment of Jews in late imperial Russia and championed Jewish emancipation included the internationally renowned writers Vladimir Korolenko and Leo Tolstoy.

Under the Soviets, the novelty lay instead in the state's commitment to and involvement in restraining, at least on paper, public manifestations of anti-Jewish feeling. For many people, its success in this endeavor served as a test to measure whether the Soviet state had truly distanced itself from the tsarist system. And yet, while seemingly crystal clear, the Bolsheviks' position on Jews was fraught with ambivalence from the very beginning. There is a noteworthy difference between condemning violence against Jews while being on the sideline of political power, as Lenin was, for instance, in 1906 when he denounced unconditionally the bloody pogrom in Bialystok, and rebuking any and all expressions of hostility toward Jews while being in power, as Lenin was after October 1917—or, even more so, as he struggled to retain power in 1918–1921, against the backdrop of long-standing antagonisms between Jews and non-Jews in the territories that would become the Soviet Union.

Whether anti-Bolshevik forces identified the Soviets as the saviors or as the hireling of the Jews, the Bolshevik commitment to eliminating hostile actions against Jews was uncertain from the outset. The regime could make certain actions illegal and prosecute offenders for them; but it could not keep people from feeling what they felt: even though it postulated that a true socialist regime would indeed change its subjects' consciousness, it never set out to prosecute private unexpressed thought. Lenin's response to the pogroms of the spring of 1918, most of which were carried out by the Red Army, came late, only in July of that year.[41] Moreover, the official response to the violence followed numerous pleas on the part of Jewish activists in the Moscow EVKOM and the Jewish commissariat to condemn the pogroms. Jewish socialists, most of them members of the Bund and the

Poale-Tsiyon, pressured Lenin and the Party to confront the issue of antisemitism and publicly condemn it. The Committee to Fight Against Antisemitism (a Soviet state institution established in the fall of 1919 to conduct a systematic educational campaign by publishing pamphlets and press articles, condemning anti-Jewish hostility, discrimination, and violence) was the result of a whole year of petitioning by Jewish activists in a desperate attempt to get the Bolshevik leadership to prove that it could indeed remove anti-Jewish behavior from the public sphere.[42] In other words, it was Jews themselves who reminded the Soviets that fighting against antisemitism was their responsibility. At the same time, in opposition to the expressed commitment of the Bolshevik leadership, it contemplated restricting the number of Jews in the Soviet government in the second half of 1919. Because of the overrepresentation of Jews in the state apparatus in Ukraine, for instance, Lenin himself considered reducing their numbers. This evaluation was made in the hope of refuting complaints of Judeo-Bolshevism.[43]

The ambivalence about how to confront tensions between Jews and their neighbors emerged in the language used during the trials against the perpetrators of the pogroms of the civil war. In the immediate aftermath of the civil war, pogromists could indeed be convicted for their behavior and even shot for participating in the violence. Occasional statements and reprimands in the press condemned their actions as an expression of hostility against Jews.[44] At the same, there was a growing tendency to refrain from labeling the participation in anti-Jewish violence with the word "antisemitism." Other terms, like "hooliganism" or "counterrevolutionary actions," were increasingly employed. In many instances, official indictments issued by Soviet tribunals used the term "banditry," sentencing to death the "enemies of the working people" without mention of pogrom activity. The perpetrators' involvement in anti-Jewish violence remained unmentioned.[45] Furthermore, whenever the perpetrators were not well-known leaders of one of the armies or insurgent groups involved in the conflict—in which case Soviet authorities made the effort to take legal action against them—seeking justice largely depended on the initiative of the pogrom victims and their family members. This dynamic remained at play throughout the 1920s: victims of pogrom violence, or of anti-Jewish resentment, had to track down those who were responsible and try their best to turn them over to the authorities (central ones, when local ones seemed unresponsive). More often than not then, investigating crimes of anti-Jewish violence or other sorts of hostile behavior toward Jews depended on the victims themselves. Some of them, however, resisted pursuing the offenders out of fear of retaliation.

The Soviet state's actions occasionally took on a more aggressive tone, as authorities rebuked or arrested those who were deemed responsible for igniting anti-Jewish resentment. This was especially the case whenever the situation of Soviet Jews intersected with issues of foreign policy. In the aftermath of World War I and in the wake of the Genoa conference (1922) and its spin-off, the Treaty of Rapallo (1922), both of which laid the groundwork for Soviet relations with other European countries, the condemnation of antisemitism became essential. The Soviet state was adamant to show the West its commitment to publicly condemn anti-Jewish violence and prosecute perpetrators. Similar dynamics were set in motion at the time of the 1927 Schwartzbard trial, the sensational Paris trial that followed the assassination of Symon Petliura by a Ukrainian Jew: it was apparently in reprisal for the pogroms of the civil war that Scholem Schwartzbard killed the head of the Ukrainian government-in-exile in the French capital.

After Schwartzbard's arrest, the Soviets began to collect eyewitness accounts and personal reports from victims and bystanders. They sent the materials to Paris to be used as evidence in the trial. These included documents from the vast pogrom archive assembled since 1920 by the Soviet Jewish Committee, the Evobshchestkom.[46] And to bolster credibility among the Paris judges, the Soviets even collected evidence of the victims' identity from local rabbis and burial societies, religious institutions whose authority had come under threat in Bolshevik society.[47] They probably did so to corroborate the role that Petliura played in the outbreak of anti-Jewish violence, as well as to confirm their commitment to preventing further pogrom outbreaks. In the wake of wide international coverage of the assassination and growing tensions between the Soviets and Great Britain (which would result in a break of the Anglo-Soviet trade deal of 1921), the Bolshevik government may have been eager to confirm its commitment to combating antisemitism.[48]

But even at this foreign policy juncture, ambivalence remained an intrinsic feature of the Soviets' engagement with Jewish affairs, as the state oscillated between condemnation of anti-Jewish behavior and silence. During the summer of 1926, the secretary of the Central Committee of the Komsomol sent out to the organization's branches detailed reports of instances of antisemitism (the source specifically uses the term "antisemitism") among Soviet youth. While the Central Committee's resolution about the most efficient ways to combat anti-Jewish feelings among the youth was to be made public and released in the press, specific cases were to remain classified. As the Komsomol secret memorandum stressed, "Keep top secret, reprinting or disclosing is prohibited."[49]

Throughout the 1920s, the stated commitment to uproot expressions of antipathy and violence toward Jews presented numerous geographic variables. It depended on the ways in which local authorities understood and implemented the signals coming from above, as well as on the ability and efficiency with which Jewish citizens managed to direct their complaints and petitions to the right organizations and offices. But the effectiveness of the stated campaign against antisemitism ultimately hinged on whether the Party perceived this fight as complying with or defying the raison d'état, namely, the state's commitment to establishing a society grounded in Marxism, atheism, and a utopian brotherhood of peoples.

When combating antisemitism was in the interest of the state, it could certainly take center stage. In the early 1920s, the state launched a campaign to publicly distance the new regime from tsarist Russia's treatment of Jews. The campaign targeted primarily the Red Army. It included publishing popular and more scientific books condemning anti-Jewish animosity. Out of one hundred books and pamphlets published in the early years of the regime, forty-six focused on the topic of antisemitism, its origin, and its counterrevolutionary essence.[50] Perhaps for the very first time in modern history, a state pledged on paper to fight against antisemitism (namely, to uproot prejudice, discrimination, and violence against Jews), investing funds to promote a campaign to counter it, with public lectures and speeches, pamphlets, and theater programs and plays for clubs, schools, and factories. The campaign conveyed to Soviet citizens that Jews were not despicable creatures, that they were entitled to equal treatment, and that they constituted an important element in the new Soviet society. The fact that the commitment to prosecute offenses toward Jews (as ambivalent as it might have been) took shape in the very territories where just a few decades earlier legal discrimination, pogroms, and blood libels were culturally acceptable means to punish Jews for alleged crimes remains remarkable.[51]

New Ideas and Behaviors, Old Ideas and Behaviors

The Soviet campaign against antisemitism of the mid- and late 1920s resulted in layoffs, arrests, official reprimands, trials, discontinuation of Party membership, and prison and labor camp sentences. If antisemitism was construed as the exact opposite of socialism, then making contemptuous comments about Jews could result in dire consequences. When in 1923, a client in the Kyiv restaurant Empire hollered against the musicians, whom he disparagingly called "Yids," asking them to stop playing Yiddish songs and to perform Russian songs only, he was arrested at once. He was sentenced to forced labor.[52] When in mid-1926, in Makhachkala, the capital city of Dagestan, in the North Caucasus, a ritual murder accusation triggered a series of pogroms in the city and nearby towns and resulted in the death of several Jews, Soviet authorities in Moscow dispatched an investigative commission to the city.[53] The investigative commission gathered information also about other instances of antisemitism that had gone unpunished. Arrests ensued. Moscow denounced the local authorities, blaming them for the absence of a campaign to uproot antisemitism.[54]

A similar case that took place that same year in the town of Belyov, in the Russian province of Tula, involved the death of a child, for which his Communist Party–member father accused his Jewish neighbors of murdering him for ritual purposes.[55] The ensuing political investigation confirmed the absence of any inflicted wounds or cuts on the boy's body; but the rumors spread quickly anyway, and some city residents—including Party members—contemplated attacking the Jews to avenge the murdered boy. The escalating tensions almost triggered a pogrom. The allegation that Jews used Christian blood for ritual purposes became a source of embarrassment for the Soviets, particularly when it was uttered by a Communist Party member or a state official.[56]

But while Soviet authorities confirmed the need to fight against such behaviors, in many cases arrests took place only after Jews themselves intervened and denounced the authorities' ineptness at bringing to justice the people responsible. In another instance of an accusation of ritual murder, a Jewish reporter complained in the press against the mild sentence of two months of forced labor and objected to the fact that the offender had not been dismissed from his position. "How was it possible that he was still a member of the city soviet?" protested the Jewish reporter.[57] Soviet authorities were susceptible to Jewish pressure because of the official state condemnation of hostility and discrimination against Jews.

On the basis of secret police reports and press releases, antisemitism grew dramatically in 1926 and 1927. The Party responded with an unprecedented campaign, which exceeded in scope and scale anything ever seen in Europe. "The wave of antisemitism will become a serious political problem in the near future if it does not encounter resistance," the Central Committee Secretariat reported in August 1926.[58] In December 1927, Stalin himself declared to the delegates at the Fifteenth Party Congress, "This evil has to be combated with utmost ruthlessness, comrades."[59] The campaign was conducted from 1927 to 1930 with an impressive financial commitment on the part of the Soviet state, which covered surveillance, agitation, and propaganda, with articles in the daily press, pamphlets, radio programs, publication of books and pamphlets, mass rallies, lectures, Party-cell meetings, and public trials in order to take out expressions of discrimination and hostility against Jews.

In the summer of 1928 in Kharkiv, authorities organized excursions to nearby shtetls for local workers as a way to acquaint them with Jews and dispel antisemitic beliefs.[60] The youth publication *Pionerskaia pravda* organized a radio rally in Moscow for pioneers (members of the communist youth organization for children aged nine to fourteen), encouraging them to fight against antisemitism, by acknowledging their own wrong assumptions about Jews and reporting those of their peers; the publication also sent young communists from Ukraine and Belorussia to visit the Jewish colonies and meet the Jewish farmers in the hope of countering anti-Jewish prejudice.[61] The following year, the Moscow Central House of the Red Army hosted meetings and lectures on the struggle against antisemitism for hundreds of soldiers. The soldiers representing the Moscow garrison were also sent to visit "the shtetl and the Jewish colonies."[62] In some ways, the regime was actually trying to change how people thought about Jews.

From 1927 to 1932, at least fifty-six books against antisemitism appeared in the Soviet Union, some of them with a large circulation.[63] A 1929 short pamphlet on teaching lecturers and agitators how to fight against antisemitism was published in fifty thousand copies.[64] In December 1928, authorities in Luhansk argued that antisemitism constituted such a massive social problem that the only way to address it was by organizing Party-cells devoted to the struggle against antisemitism in every local organization and institution.[65] In 1929, a publication aimed at fighting against antisemitism in Soviet schools was issued.[66] That same year, the Soviet economist Yuri Larin published *Evrei i antisemitizm v SSSR* (Jews and antisemitism in the Soviet Union), which was based on a series of talks he delivered at the Moscow City Committee of the Communist Party.

The Soviets had to confront the rise of antisemitism in new social spaces, such as factories where Jews and non-Jews worked side by side and ethnic tensions could arise. In mid-1929, a public trial was organized in the theater in the small town of Uladovka, in Vinnytsia province. The case involved the workers and managers of a local factory who purposefully restricted the employment of Jewish workers. They did so by verifying the identity of the "little Yids": they checked whether they were circumcised. In the three-day trial that ensued, authorities aimed at uprooting the pre-1917 "legacy of the Potockis [one of the wealthiest and most powerful aristocratic families in Poland]" and at clarifying once and for all that antisemitism was not allowed in Soviet society. One of the defendants explained that the intention to regulate the number of Jews employed in the factory was adopted as a defensive measure to prevent them from taking over the factory itself, especially at the managerial level. They feared that if they employed one Jew, then all the Jews of the surrounding towns would want to be employed in that factory.[67] The workers' action was not motivated by objections to Jewish religious beliefs: checking for circumcision was simply a way of finding out who among the workers were Jews, to whose presence the checkers objected.

According to a 1927 report, handwritten fliers that agitated against Jews or promoted discord between Jews and non-Jews occasionally appeared in Moscow and other Soviet cities. They were glued to the tramway schedule poles or just strewn around city streets. Some called for expelling Jews from Moscow, such as, for example, "In order to reduce cramped housing in Moscow, 150,000 residents must be expelled. . . . Let's kick out the Jews." Some fliers, supposedly written by religious Jews, called for disrupting the social norms at the workplace, as in the following cases: "A group of prominent Jews demands that the day of rest be changed from Sunday to Saturday"; or "We, Moscow Jews, request that stores be open on Sunday and closed on Saturday."[68]

As embarrassing as it might have been for the Party, the ancient accusation against Jews that they murdered Christian (or Muslim) children for ritual purposes was alive and well in what strove to be the most modern atheistic and modern society in the world. The four-year-old daughter of a worker went missing in mid-1929 in a communal courtyard in Moscow. Only ten minutes after her disappearance, the neighbors in the building were already accusing Jews of having taken her "to cut her for ritual purposes." Even after the little girl was found, not far from the courtyard, sucking on some candy, and was returned to her home, rumors of a blood ritual for matzah lingered in the building and reached the factory where her father was employed.[69] In a similar vein, at the end of 1930, three workers in the Khalturin sawmill factory of Rohachiv in Ukraine were put on trial for antisemitism. They were accused of abusing a Jewish worker, first taunting him with nicknames, then forcing him to kiss a wooden-made cross, which they purposely carved at the sawmill factory, and then taking a piece of lard from the cafeteria, smearing it on his lips, and forcing him to eat it. The court sentenced them to prison for two years.[70]

Violence or Not?

In the Soviet Union of the 1920s and 1930s, outbreaks of mass violence against Jews virtually disappeared. In tsarist Russia, pogroms had occurred in waves, beginning in cities and towns and then spreading to the countryside and the surrounding villages during the early 1880s, following the assassination of Tsar Alexander II, and then during the early twentieth century, in particular at the time of the first Russian Revolution of 1905. After the carnage of the civil war, instances of public violence against Jews receded significantly under Soviet rule. But in exceptional cases, hostile feelings toward Jews did lead to hostile action, engulfing the factory shop floor, the classroom, or the street and even crystallizing into mob violence. Rare instances of pogroms occurred in Central Asia and the Caucasus. Accusations of blood libel in Makhachkala in 1926 and in Bukhara in 1928 dovetailed with violent attacks against the Jewish communities. One of the reasons why uncontrolled violence broke out in the region was the arguably weaker Bolshevik state infrastructure, which was not as developed as it was in the European areas of the Soviet Union.[71] The stronger the state, the more unlikely a frenzied violent outbreak.

But rare instances of pogroms did occur in the European territories of the Soviet Union. On September 12, 1928, for instance, a group of seasonal workers in Rudnya, in Smolensk province, attacked two young Jewish men, shattered the windows of the home of a local Jewish resident, and attempted to coerce the policeman into partaking in the violence.[72] Although the authorities arrested twelve people, they resisted defining the incident as a pogrom: for the Soviets, "pogroms" could only be carried out by "members of the Black Hundreds" as in tsarist Russia or by "bandits" and "counterrevolutionaries" as during the civil war. When a similar instance of anti-Jewish violence erupted in the streets of the Belarusian city of Mahiliau and a group of sixty Red Army recruits on their way to report for service attacked the local Jewish population, the Soviet press similarly refrained from branding the incident a "pogrom."[73] While the Soviets acknowledged the "pogrom-like" character of the attacks, they could not quite bring themselves to label them as "pogroms," something that they would have been eager to do had a similar event taken place in neighboring Poland or Romania. The political essence of the Soviet system, based on the celebration of the "brotherhood of peoples" and the condemnation of "incitement of national hatred," was at stake in the label.

If mob violence against Jews abated during the 1920s, instances of violence targeting individual Jews may have escalated, especially in the context of Stalin's forced collectivization and rapid industrialization. Violence and abuse broke out in a university classroom in Voronezh, in a factory in Leningrad, at the construction site of the university campus in Minsk, and in the District Court of Krasnoyarsk.[74] Such actions could constitute an expression of resistance against the radical state policies concerning the reorganization of Soviet economy. The new economic plan of the so-called Great Turn brought millions of migrants to the factories, which became new sites of strained encounters between Jews and peasants. In particular, the new phenomenon of young Jews hired in large factories, especially in heavy industry, sparked harsh economic competition and rivalry that crystallized along ethnic lines, as people scrambled for jobs.[75]

Abuse and murder cases captured the attention of the press. A young worker in the Pskov metalworking factory murdered a young Jewish coworker by the name of Bolshemnikov. The murder was carried out in the presence of five coworkers. Nobody intervened to prevent the crime, which was exceedingly brutal (the young Jew was killed with an axe).[76] Ensuing press reports noted disapprovingly the inaction of local authorities: before Bolshemnikov's murder, he had filed official complaints about antisemitism and ongoing harassment to the Factory Committee and then to local courts. The local courts ignored the case as unimportant.[77] According to one source, during the investigation, the seventeen-year-old perpetrator did not express any guilt and admitted killing Bolshemnikov simply because he was Jewish. He then retracted his confession during the trial when, in front of the one thousand people who filled the courthouse, he conceded murdering the young Jewish worker following a quarrel in the factory dormitory but not because of his Jewish identity. Most factory workers defended the perpetrator, concurring that the murder was not counterrevolutionary in nature.[78] While the official prosecutor demanded the death sentence or, short of that, a ten-year prison sentence, the Pskov court ultimately decided to sentence the defendant to five years in prison, because of his age and lack of premeditation.[79] Some journalists lamented the mild sentence, which seemed to contradict the reality of growing antisemitism.

Another case involving the torture of a young Jewish female worker employed in a glass factory near Babruisk, Belorussia, captured the media's attention.[80] The abuse was perpetrated by the foreman, the factory security guard, and other workers. In describing the incident, a reporter compared it to the false accusation of ritual murder and the ensuing trial against the Jewish clerk Menachem Mendel Beilis in 1911–1913 in Kyiv; he noted, "Not since the Beilis affair has a case involving Jews attracted so much attention . . . as the trial in the Barshay affair." The trial opened in January 1929, in Minsk, as the Supreme Court of Belorussia convened in the city's central workers' club, in the presence of Soviet and foreign newspaper correspondents, including a representative from the Polish consular service. In line with the Soviet conception of antisemitism, the prosecution tried to connect the workers' behavior to counterrevolutionary activities and beliefs. The defense attorneys, on the other hand, tried hard to disentangle the defendants' actions from the accusation of counterrevolution.

For one, they argued that the defendants used the term "Zhid" in lieu of "Jew" not as a derogatory term and racial slur but out of ignorance.[81] Barshay's non-Jewish roommate testified that the term "Zhid" was commonly used by factory workers, "who certainly could not call a Jew 'comrade' or 'citizen' and hence must say 'Zhid.'"[82] In the midst of the campaign against antisemitism, Soviet authorities selected the Barshay affair as an exemplary case to conduct propaganda: it involved sexual violence against a woman, and it confirmed once again the interlacing between anti-Jewish hatred and counterrevolutionary forces. In sentencing the defendants to prison, the prosecution highlighted the wealthy background of the people involved in the case and stressed the participation of one of the culprits in the 1905 pogrom that took place in the Belarusian town of Orsha.[83] The fact that the hearing was held in the capital city of Minsk and not in the local court outside of Babruisk further confirmed the demonstrative purpose of the trial.[84] But extensive reporting in the Soviet press about the Barshay case did not serve its intended purpose: just a few months later, the Homyel Regional Court found eight workers in the paper factory in the town of Dobrush guilty of torturing two female Jewish coworkers; following a long trial that lasted several days, the defendants were sentenced to prison.[85] As one publication noted, these events and the emotions that accompanied them "were reminiscent of the Russian pogrom tradition."[86]

Making Sense of Rumors about Jews: Soviet Publications on Antisemitism

The word "power" stands out in the 1928 data on hostile opinions about Jews collected by the secret police in Ukraine as part of a wider investigation of what the populace thought about the regime. In the Stalinskii district, in the Mandrykino railway station, the train inspector and railroad workers complained about the Soviet system by associating it with Jews: "Only bandits are in power, who are members of the Party, none of them are real communists as far as ideology goes, and no one can apply to institutions of higher learning, only communists and Jews." Workers in the district of Kharkiv also complained about Jewish power, protesting the fact that Jews occupied all the administrative and skilled workers positions: "The whole factory will soon become Jewish." Workers in the meat factory in Prilukii district complained, "Jews and communists have been placed everywhere. They don't allow us to live, they don't leave us alone." The accountant of the Krasnaia Zvezda mill in Kupianskii district conveyed his anti-Jewish feelings in similar fashion: "Jews are everywhere and everywhere they occupy worthy positions, in the highest ranks of power there are exclusively Jews and everywhere they are given good employment."[87] In light of these comments, how should Soviet publications teach the citizens of the new state that hating Jews was wrong? How should it convince them that Jews were not responsible for the crisis in living conditions and employment? That they did not orchestrate the so-called Great Turn or the 1928 new political and cultural direction launched by the break from the NEP in favor of collectivization of the countryside and industrialization in the cities? And, most importantly, that Jews were not agents of extraordinary power?

Didactic in nature, Soviet publications strove to establish the origin of Jewish hatred and show why it was in opposition to Bolshevik ideology. Most brochures and pamphlets opened with a historical overview of the roots of antisemitism: they usually included religious and economic explanations for its emergence and contextualized it within the general persecution of minority cultures under the tsar. The oppression of the Jewish minority through legal decrees, pogroms, and religious bigotry against the "Christ-killers" promoted by the church served as the basis for antisemitism. Most publications explained the persistence of the hatred of Jews by blaming the NEP, which allowed the tsarist legacy to thrive while thwarting the imagined harmony of socialism. The roots of anti-Jewish prejudice lay in the contradictions and inconsistencies of the NEP: "if we had a socialist society, we would not have antisemitism."[88] Moreover, if "antisemitism is a disgusting political phenomenon . . . [and] is the weapon of class enemies," as *Komsomolskaia pravda* wrote in 1927, then the goal was to divorce it from Soviet reality.[89] According to one publication, for example, antisemitism traveled to Soviet territories from abroad. It was an imported phenomenon: it penetrated the Soviet Union through the words of religious leaders, which were broadcast over the radio, as Soviet workers listened to the Mass aired from Warsaw.[90]

One of the key goals of the literature on antisemitism was to reveal the falsehood of the claim that Soviet policy amounted to "the politics of privileges for Jews and politics of Jewish violence."[91] The widespread assumption about a special relationship between Jews and communists hovered in Soviet society throughout the 1920s. Mikhail Kalinin, chairman of the Central Executive Committee of the Soviets, openly addressed the idea of an imagined powerful Jewish elite that subdued Russia through communism in the summer of 1926. He issued a statement on the Jewish question, which appeared in *Izvestiia*, *Krestianskaia gazeta* (The peasants' paper), and the Yiddish-language *Der emes*.[92] The statement was in response to one of the many questions he received from concerned citizens about the relationship between Jews and the Soviet government. It was posed to him by Vasily Ovchinnikov, an eighteen-year-old Post Office employee and Komsomol member in Crimea. While distributing the mail in different villages, the young clerk had come in daily contact with peasants and was himself faced with the question about a state that seemed to favor Jews. He had trouble answering the question and wrote to Kalinin as follows: "It is a question about the Jewish settlers who arrive daily in . . . Crimea and especially in our district. The peasants conveyed to me much indignation and protest. . . . Our sons and brothers, they say, fought at Perekop.[93] Tens of thousands of our brothers lost their lives there. We conquered . . . Crimea and our victory cost us dearly, and now what do we see? Our demands to be settled in Crimea have been rejected and we are told to settle in Siberia. What have the Jews done to deserve to be settled in the Crimea?" In his statement, Kalinin contended that the assumption that the Soviet government was in fact a Jewish government that favored Jews was utter nonsense. He did so by reminding Soviet citizens that the government had not given rights to all Jews but had, for example, systematically confiscated Jewish capital. As he pointed out, "We, whom antisemites consider defenders of the Jews, actually destroyed Jewish capital like all other capital. Let anyone show us a Jewish factory or a bank or other Jewish property that was not confiscated."[94]

To dissipate notions of a preferential treatment of Jews on the part of the Bolshevik state, some of the literature on antisemitism appealed to the readers' emotions. The authors encouraged empathy, instead of hatred, reminding them, for example, that Jewish settlement on land was a delicate process, not devoid of great challenges: the new Jewish farmers, who were city people who lacked experience in toiling the land and who had lost everything during the early 1920s, were real pioneers who had to learn everything.[95] Most publications focused on dismissing the slander of Jews dodging the military. This notion had deep roots in the nineteenth-century rise of the nation-state, which cast doubt on the loyalty of minority groups, as well as in the harsh treatment of Jews in the tsarist army.[96] To show that Soviet Jews were eager to fight, the literature included statistical evidence. Several publications confirmed that in 1927, when Jews constituted 2 percent of the population of the Soviet Union, they also made up 2.2 percent of Red Army soldiers. This meant that the percentage of Jews in the Red Army was statistically higher than in the general population.[97]

Finally, each publication included a celebratory story of the success in the fight against antisemitism, which had proceeded from "the dark middle ages" to the policies adopted in the Soviet Union. Each text celebrated the "light at the end of the tunnel" by quoting, sometimes in its entirety, Lenin's 1918 speech condemning anti-Jewish violence.[98] Lenin's words were recorded and played via gramophones on propaganda trains in the midst of the civil war, at the front, in cities and villages, in clubs, and at meetings and conventions.[99]

In this staged narrative, the words of the Bolshevik leader opened the minds of "Red army soldiers, workers, and peasants who heard . . . [them] and began to understand" that their hearts had been poisoned by the tsar, the landowners, the capitalists, and the priests. "Shame to him who spreads the seed of hatred against the Jews, who spreads hatred against other nationalities!" concluded the speech.[100] Lenin's classical pronouncement served as the ultimate and unquestionable confirmation that the Soviet system remained committed to fighting against antisemitism.[101] Of course, none of these publications mentioned that the speech's text had been drafted not by Lenin but by Semion Dimanshtein, who would become one of the most prominent political and literary figures on the Jewish street.[102]

The literature on antisemitism published in the Soviet Union represented a unique phenomenon in the context of twentieth-century Europe. It grew out of an ambivalent commitment to the fight against antisemitism. As imperfect as this fight turned out to be, it had some long-term consequences. The existing scholarship on World War II seems to confirm that active collaboration with the Germans in exterminating Jews during the Operation Barbarossa campaign was less widespread in the historical regions of the Soviet Union and much more common in the newly occupied Soviet territories, in particular eastern Poland (including present-day western Ukraine and Belarus, which were annexed into the Ukrainian Soviet Socialist Republic and the Belorussian Soviet Socialist Republic in 1945). These territories had not been exposed to the same degree of propaganda against antisemitism.[103] And yet, this literature succeeded only partially in stamping out anti-Jewish prejudice. If by the early 1930s there seemed to have been a decline in instances of discrimination and violence against Jews in Soviet society, the fact that the media discontinued recording them does not necessarily mean that they had disappeared from everyday life.[104]

Jews and the State Struggle against Antisemitism

Our knowledge of cases of hostility toward Jews is largely contingent on the extent to which Jews themselves felt comfortable petitioning and complaining to local and central authorities about their experience. In some instances, the Soviets themselves complained that Jews were too passive and silent and called on them to partake more actively in denouncing antisemitism by speaking up. Others, perhaps out of confusion, as one Meerovich from Odesa, asked whether it was "appropriate for Jews to participate in the struggle against antisemitism," noting to the editors of *Tribuna* that the question deserved further discussion.[105]

In October 1923, Aron Kravets, a Jewish resident of the town of Sidorovichi, in Kyiv district, petitioned the authorities complaining about antisemitism. He protested the fact that during the elections to the village soviet, the representative of the district executive committee openly offended Jews using the tsarist derogatory epithet of "Moshka" and accusing them of engaging in profiteering and speculation. "When I reproached him for this," complained Kravets, "he forced me to leave the meeting. I proclaimed myself an equal citizen of the Soviet Republic, . . . but a second time I was ignored and was ordered to leave the meeting . . . while the speaker carried out anti-Jewish propaganda." Since the local authorities seemed to ignore his grievance, the Jewish resident turned to the regional authorities, asking them to intervene and challenge a view that contradicted the principles of the Communist Party.[106]

Jews would often address their complaints about antisemitism to the Evsektsiia or other Jewish organs, which then served as intermediaries between the individual and the authorities. Moyshe Rozenblar submitted a complaint about antisemitism to the Jewish section of the Provincial Executive Committee in Kyiv when, following the liquidation of one of the synagogues in his town, he turned to local authorities to inquire about whether information pertaining to the Jewish holidays could be sent out to local Jews. The Soviet official immediately replied by saying, "absolutely not." And when Rozenblar retorted by saying that other groups like Baptists and evangelicals were allowed to convey to their communities' members information about religious holidays, the woman cut him short. By crossing from a religious domain to an ethnic one, she remarked, "This is none of your business, what a Jewish manner!" (Ne vashe delo, eto evreiskaia manera!). Rozenblar replied to the woman, asserting his Jewish pride: "I am proud of being a Jew." And he filled out his petition, "protesting antisemitism as a proletarian and as a poor person."[107] His confidence stemmed, at least in part, from knowing that the Soviet state was on his side and opposed antisemitic discrimination.

Indeed, there was room for Jews to take a stand and protest when they felt that their rights as Soviet Jewish citizens had been violated. When one Frolov assaulted a Jewish family on the streets of the city of Penza, shouting, "Beat the Yids and save Russia," he was at once taken into custody by the police and arrested. But the court dismissed his behavior as hooliganism and failed to mention antisemitism. The local Jews were not happy and proceeded to complain about the court's decision. The local newspaper demanded the prosecutor's intervention and called for further investigation in the matter.[108] As a rule of thumb, whenever Jews managed to get the attention of the authorities—central ones in particular—they stood a good chance of seeing their complaints redressed. In November 1929, the local soviet in the village of Kosobrovsk in Ukraine called for "all gypsies, Jews, and thieves to be expelled from the village" as an official measure "to cleanse" the Soviet apparatus from unwanted bourgeois and counter-revolutionary elements. The Evsektsiia heeded the complaints of local Jews and intervened by publishing the resolution in the press and expressing criticism and indignation.[109]

Jews themselves could also take advantage of the state's commitment to apprehend anyone for engaging in antisemitism. Claims of antisemitism could be fabricated to take revenge on a neighbor, an acquaintance, or a coworker, in the hope that by having them removed from their posts, the "Jewish victim" could advance to that position. In some cases, Soviet clerks resisted accusing someone Jewish of a wrongdoing in fear of retaliation. They worried about the consequences of being accused of antisemitism. If non-Jews could exploit the campaigns against speculators and contraband to target Jews, then Jews could profit from the campaigns against antisemitism to target non-Jews.[110]

An additional aspect of the Soviet state's struggle against antisemitism related to its connection to the fight against Jewish nationalism and chauvinism. Most press reports on antisemitism from the late 1920s included the denunciation of Jewish chauvinism as well. Even in the most brutal cases of antisemitism, articles reproaching anti-Jewish hatred were typically accompanied by a statement rebuking Jewish chauvinism; this appeared on the same page of the publication and at times was compiled by the same author. In the case of the axe murder of Bolshemnikov, a Jewish workers' meeting convened after the trial not only condemned antisemitism but also felt compelled to denounce "Jewish chauvinism" in the same breath.[111] Some bemoaned the link between antisemitism and chauvinism and argued that the extravagant focus of the press on condemning Jewish nationalism in fact weakened the campaign against antisemitism.[112] It might even be that the fight against antisemitism elicited attacks on Jewish life, in particular on Judaism. At an evening event held at the Minsk Club for Woodworkers, for example, comrade Slonim spoke about antisemitism and Jewish chauvinism. He blamed the persistence of Jewish chauvinism on the presence of three houses of prayer in the Komorovka neighborhood of the Belarusian capital. "They spread chauvinism among the ignorant masses!" he stated and, by doing so, inferred that closing them down would be in everyone's best interest.[113]

The Jewish response to expressions of hostility varied according to different factors including geographic location and socioeconomic position of both the victims and the perpetrators. When in 1927 in the city of Seredy, in Ivano-Voznesensky district, a fifteen-year-old year Jewish worker at the power station of a local factory became the target of brutal harassment and torture on the part of several foremen, who were Party members, he complained to his older brother. But the brother urged him to keep silent and endure the abuse, fearing that they would otherwise both be kicked out of the factory. The case became publicly known, and the culprits were arrested only after the young Jew fainted because of the beatings and was hospitalized. The OGPU then intervened with an investigation and an ensuing trial.[114]

In the absence of networks of support and out of fear of retaliation, in certain contexts and circumstances, Jews might have chosen to remain silent, especially when local authorities and the police showed some arbitrariness and keenness on "violating the revolutionary legality." But especially at the height of the campaigns against antisemitism, whenever Jews could draw the attention of central authorities and appeal to higher courts or centers of power through individual petitions or by turning to a Jewish organization, then the complaints would be redressed. In light of the formal commitment to "uproot antisemitism," central authorities were more willing to heed complaints and intervene, by stepping in and reprimanding local authorities.[115] But in general, the Jewish response to popular hostility had to be self-monitored and restrained. Because Soviet officials commonly situated the campaign against antisemitism within the broader struggle against chauvinism and bourgeois nationalism, protesting too loudly could easily backfire. Soviet Jews had to carefully walk the fine line between standing up for their rights as Soviet citizens of Jewish nationality and avoiding charges of chauvinism.[116]

Conclusion

There are many factors that shape our knowledge about antipathy toward Jews in Soviet society during the 1920s. The intensity and diligence with which the state conducted the campaigns and dispensed the appropriate punishment play a crucial role. The more serious and thorough about combating antisemitism central authorities appeared, the more responsive local authorities would be in pursuing the offenders and the more at ease Jews would feel in reporting their complaints. The way in which the public discussed anti-Jewish animosity hinged on the Party's approach to the issue. At the same time, however, local authorities, neighbors, and acquaintances retained a degree of agency and could choose, in different contexts, to ignore the Party message of rebuking antisemitism. Local authorities did not always choose to follow meticulously the message coming from Moscow but retained some autonomy in deciding whether to prosecute cases of antisemitism.[117] The lessons imparted at the center and the way in which these lessons were understood at the periphery did not always coincide. Local authorities misread the Party line on antisemitism, pretended to do so, or even decided to enforce a decision that countered Soviet ideology. In the interwar period, therefore, a real clash between popular antisemitism and the Bolsheviks' attempt to tame it took place.

If the growing number of reports about antisemitism during specific years was also a consequence of the state's active role in promoting the campaign against antisemitism, the absence of such a discussion in the Soviet public sphere does not necessarily indicate that the problem did not exist. One writer captured this dynamic. He admitted that the seemingly documented intensification of antisemitism in 1929 depended on the fact that "the press now records much better such instances, that we are more familiar with the idea of fighting against it, that the whole Party apparatus and society is paying more attention . . . so that antisemitic incidents that would go unnoticed before, now draw major attention. . . . They draw the attention and the anger of all proletarian organizations."[118]

The Bolshevik confrontation with antisemitism was inconsistent and contradictory from early on. This ambivalence remained a constant feature throughout the interwar period, but it likewise persisted during World War II and its aftermath, in particular in the newly occupied Soviet territories. Under the Soviets, it happened that Bolshevik leaders themselves deployed racialized categories in their class analysis, which in turn influenced the persistence of a racialized conception of Jewishness, the essence of which was instantly tied to the "speculator," the "bourgeois," or the "exploiter." At the same time, Jews had to walk the fine line negotiating between their visibility and growing antisemitism. Leon Trotsky himself, "the king of assimilation and internationalism," refused to take on senior roles in the Soviet government to escape greater Jewish visibility, which would further fuel antisemitism under the guise of Judeo-Bolshevism.

More traditional strands of antisemitism, often inspired by religious-based myths, resurfaced cyclically in Soviet cities. If the blood libel allegation had largely dissipated in western and central Europe, it retained an impressive vitality in the Soviet Union of the 1920s. The marketplace, the factory, and the club could become spaces of rhetorical and (at times) physical violence against Jews; these could become spaces in which discussing ritual murder, Jewish NEPmanness, or blaming Jewish Bolsheviks for unwanted changes in politics and in social order became socially and culturally acceptable, even normative, especially in micropolities of anti-Soviet resentment. If an open critique of the system was not feasible, then criticizing the Jews, under the veil of disguised antisemitism, was more doable—not in the streets, though, where the state usually prevented spontaneous outbreaks of anti-Jewish violence.

The Yiddish writer and journalist Zalman Vendrovskii, who had been active in the 1919 short-lived Department for the Struggle against Antisemitism in Moscow, compared Soviet antisemitism to anti-Jewish hatred elsewhere in Europe. Writing in 1925 for the Warsaw Yiddish press, he noted that the real question was not to ascertain whether antisemitism existed in Soviet Russia but rather to identify its nature, among which social classes it tended to occur, and, most importantly, how dangerous it was for the Jews. In his analysis, Vendrovskii concluded that while in the new Russia antisemitism remained "a way to fight against the system," carrying out anti-Jewish propaganda or perpetrating a pogrom was considered unethical and illegal; and he added that while antisemitism took hold of wider circles in society than before, "it did not constitute a threat for Jews."[119]

Whether Soviet Jews strove to assimilate or not and whether they did so more or less successfully, their experience was shaped by preexisting cultural notions of Jewishness. Some of these notions touched on the question of allegiance, both vertical, vis-à-vis the state, and horizontal, vis-à-vis other citizens of the new state. Strained by the new conditions of life under the Soviets, the encounter between Jews and peasants took on a heightened economic and political charge. But even when the official condemnation of the NEP made Jews more susceptible to antisemitism, calls to exclude them from the national economy or political life never materialized in Soviet society—something that would happen in other countries of central and eastern Europe in the first half of the twentieth century.

LONGING FOR ZION UNDER THE SOVIETS

Sixteen-year-old Berta Levin took her own life in mid-March 1925. She threw herself into the river running through the city of Minsk and drowned. A member of the local Zionist Socialist Youth League (TS Yugend Farband), which she had joined in the early 1920s, Levin was taken by the Soviet secret police in a wave of arrests to destabilize the Zionist youth groups. The head of the Belorussian OGPU, A. F. Andreev, managed to wring from Levin the information he was after. Although early Soviet prisons generally banned physical torture against minors and tended to release younger arrestees within two weeks of their imprisonment, the interrogation of Levin might have involved torture after all. Into the third day of her hunger strike, and after a lengthy nocturnal interrogation, Soviet authorities released her—but only after she revealed the names of her comrades. Levin's body washed up on the shore of the Nyamiha River the day after her release.[1] She probably could not live with the remorse of having betrayed her comrades.

Those members of the Belorussian Regional Committee of the Zionist Socialist Youth League who managed to dodge the wave of arrests compiled a secret memo to be passed down from hand to hand throughout the cities of the Belorussian republic. They spread the news about Berta Levin's suicide, presenting it as the death of a real martyr. They encouraged other young Zionists not to give in to the "murderous secret police that forced her to take her life." The memo also noted that the ongoing arrests and forced exile of Zionists turned the Soviets into the direct heirs of tsarist Russia. They noted that if torture and starvation were "expected in the prisons of neighboring Poland, they should not be tolerated in the so-called state of workers and peasants."[2] Its authors vowed to carry on the fight for freedom on behalf of the Jewish working masses and issued one of the numerous calls for resistance that echoed through the Zionist underground circles of the 1920s.[3]

The Zionist Socialist Youth League was just one of many Zionist groups that operated in the Soviet Union in a gray zone of semi-legality during the 1920s. They were in desperate need of financial resources, central leadership, and publications, and their work conditions were dire and worsened after 1925. With the help of Jewish activists who supported the establishment of the new communist system, the Soviets clamped down on the activity of all political movements outside of the Communist Party. Yet, some Zionist groups managed to become increasingly popular among certain sectors of the Jewish population, and amid an ongoing struggle for existence, they even flourished in the early years of Soviet rule. Alongside Berta Levin and the authors of the secret circular, thousands of young Jews actively participated in different Zionist organizations, joining them out of hope, despair, or belief.

The deep-seated tradition of prerevolutionary Russian Zionism served as the foundation for the existence of Zionist youth groups and as the fertile ground for their development. After all, in late tsarist Russia, an increasingly significant number of Jews had chosen to identify with one of the many shades of Zionism that had taken root in the towns and cities throughout the Pale.[4] Of course, the messianic hopes unleashed by the February Revolution encouraged this continuity through a remarkable degree of creativity. During the approximately seven months of freedom that separated the Provisional Government from the Bolshevik coup, Zionist organizations and parties produced an impressive array of associations and publications, holding demonstrations and cultural activities in almost every city and town of the old empire. With three hundred thousand supporters, Zionism was the strongest political movement among Jews in the year of the Bolshevik Revolution.[5] Furthermore, when in November 1917 a world power like Great Britain expressed its support for a Jewish national home in Palestine, the idea of settling in the Land of Israel no longer appeared like a mere illusion. The Balfour Declaration sparked great hopes and sustained the longing for Zion even among young Jews in the Soviet Union.

The unprecedented nature of anti-Jewish violence unleashed during the pogroms of the civil war gave new impetus to Zionism. In the wake of the terror, many Jews became desperate to leave the territories of the former Russian Empire and sought out some connection with Zionist groups wishing to see their hope materialize. Of the 2,118 Jewish families still living in Cherkasy, in central Ukraine—a city hit by two pogroms, first in May and then in August 1919—as many as 1,823 favored immediate emigration. All surviving Jewish residents of Novoarkhangelsk, a shtetl in the Kherson *guberniia*—where the White Army carried out a pogrom in September 1919—expressed their wish to leave for Palestine at once. Local Zionist groups moved quickly to establish special offices wherever they could, encouraging Jews to register for resettlement and collecting money to support the endeavor.[6]

Born in Berdychiv in 1906, Israel Kargman joined the Zionist movement at the age of thirteen, shortly after the pogroms. During the early 1920s, he actively participated in Zionist youth groups in the towns of Podilia and Volhynia. The Soviets eventually arrested Kargman in 1926. The longing for Palestine remained at the heart of his commitment to Zionism: after two years in exile, he still kindled an unrelenting faith that he would reach the Land of Israel. From the Arctic region of Komi, in the midst of terrible conditions, he wrote, "We are here strong in our spirit, reinvigorated and full of faith in the victory of our ideal."[7]

For many young Jews, the political or cultural choice of joining Zionist groups during the early 1920s grew out of their upbringing. It is not that surprising that Fanya Zubrin, who was born in 1906 outside of Kyiv, became actively involved in different Zionist youth groups beginning in 1923 until her arrest and exile to Alma-Ata, in 1931. Her father was an instructor of Hebrew before the revolution, and he continued to teach the language and lead a cultural circle for young Zionists until 1920. Together with her sister, Fanya Zubrin studied in her father's school and took part in the Hebrew-language club bearing the slogan "From now on only Hebrew!"[8] Not unlike Zubrin, Zerubavel Yevazrikhin, who was born in the Jewish colony of Nahar Tov—one of the Jewish agricultural settlements established in the Kherson province in early nineteenth century—followed in his parents' footsteps.[9] His father had founded a Zionist-leaning modern elementary school (*heder metukan*) in the colony and had turned their home into one of the Zionist cultural centers of the region. Yevazrikhin joined a Zionist youth group in 1918 and worked toward his goal of resettling in Palestine until his arrest in 1926 and then throughout his years in political exile, where he perished in 1937.[10]

The relative success of Zionist youth movements depended also on the fact that they could offset the sense of despair and marginality experienced by thousands of disenfranchised Jewish teenagers during the NEP years. If the new Soviet policies of a mixed economy brought some prosperity to the country, they did not bring fortune to Jewish artisans, shopkeepers, and small-town residents—or to their children. Unemployed youth from the depleted shtetl, who because of their background could not take part in the socialist project or join communist organizations, found a sense of purpose and social outlet in the underground Zionist groups.[11] Many young Jews who had come of age after the revolution and joined Zionist groups in the early years after 1917 could now self-consciously perceive themselves as the new vanguard of an ostracized Jewish youth. Shimon Vovsianniker was one of them. Born in Starokostiantyniv in 1903, he was deemed by the revolution a member of the "merchant class" and, as such, branded a *lishchenets* and disenfranchised. From the beginning, he feverishly engaged in underground Zionist activities and propaganda among the shtetl youth in the towns of Podilia. Like him, most of the young shtetl Jews were unemployed and possibly in desperate need of a sense of purpose. Vovsianniker was eventually arrested in late 1925 while attempting to illegally cross the border into Romania.[12]

Finally, and perhaps most importantly, these groups expanded also because of the state's surprising ambiguity toward Zionism during the early 1920s. At least in the beginning, the Soviet state seemed to resist the outright categorization of the movement as a political adversary. This, of course, does not mean that Zionist cultural activities and institutions did not come under the surveillance of Soviet authorities and waves of extraordinary harassment. In late 1920, for instance, a Zionist activist in Minsk remarked, "Our [Zionist] . . . activities are being hounded. . . . Our elementary school . . . was taken from us. The teachers and many of the students left the school because a decree was issued forbidding the teaching of Hebrew. . . . Some of our teachers are living in great poverty and don't even have bread."[13]

Yet, unlike for other political groups, Jewish and non-Jewish alike, there was no centrally driven attempt to enact the complete destruction of all Zionist organizations and parties. Until the mid-1920s, the scrutiny, the searches, and the arrests usually grew out of the initiative of local authorities and activists, very often Jewish ones, in particular members of the Evsektsiia.[14] Hence, the persecution of Zionist groups turned out to be more unforgiving in certain areas of the Soviet Union—especially Belorussia and Ukraine—than it did in others.[15] But, in general, even when arrests were made, the sentencing reflected an official uncertainty on the part of the state about policies on Zionism: arrestees were usually not accused of counterrevolutionary activities and were more often than not released from prison after short periods of time.[16]

The state's relative tolerance, then, sanctioned the ongoing development of Zionism, primarily in its socialist expressions. The movement was eventually suppressed, but over time and not suddenly. If religious and political Zionism declined in the general context of the Bolshevik persecution of political parties and religion, as thousands of Zionists were arrested and sent to labor camps during the Red Terror, socialist Zionism in particular produced new ideological strains in a lasting commitment to Marxism, social welfare, and class struggle on the Jewish street.[17] After all, many supporters of Labor Zionism, in their fascination with the events of October 1917, not only had overlooked Lenin's dictatorial tendencies but had also referred to him as "the prophet of the Russian Revolution, its leader and teacher, ruler and spokesman, lawgiver and guide."[18] Many were eager to work with the Bolsheviks.

"There Is Not a Single Jewishly Inhabited Location in Ukraine without Zionists!"

In a liminal space between legality and persecution, socialist-leaning Zionist organizations yielded a new kind of Zionism. With impressive creativity and persistence in adjusting their activities and ideology to the demands of the Bolshevik system, established groups and new movements reshaped themselves into "Soviet Zionism." In 1920, the Labor Zionist party Tseire-Tsiyon split into the Zionist Socialist Party (Sionisticheskaia sotsyalisticheskaia partiia) and the Zionist Toilers' Party (Sionisticheskaia trudovaia partiia). In coming to terms with the new political regime, the members strongly disagreed over their relation to the Bolshevik Revolution and the role that socialism should play in Jewish life. Far from being comprehensive, the groups' doctrines revealed some internal contradictions. Zionist Socialists accepted the right of the workers and the soviets to establish a dictatorship to fight against the enemies of the revolution; they viewed socialism as an essential component of Zionism, and they promoted productivization among young impoverished and unemployed Jews by drawing them into the trade unions and cooperatives. But they fully rejected the Bolshevik dictatorship.[19] As late as 1924, members of the Zionist Socialist Party were still paying their dues to the organization in the form of the shekel.[20] On the other hand, the Jewish national revival in Palestine became the key priority for members of the Zionist Toilers' Party. While aiming to turn Jews into laborers, they snubbed every aspect of the new political regime and fiercely resisted the involvement in all social organizations that existed under the Bolsheviks.[21]

Both parties organized independent youth groups for youngsters between the ages of seventeen and twenty-three. The Zionist Socialist Party created the Zionist Socialist Youth League, the same one that had attracted Berta Levin. The Zionist Toilers' Party united the existing student movements under an umbrella organization called EVOSM (United All-Russian Organization of Zionist Youth), which in turn brought together young Jews ages ten through sixteen in Ha-shomer ha-tsair ha-amlani (The toilers wing of the young guard). Modeled on the scout movement, Ha-shomer ha-tsair ha-maamadi (The class wing of the young guard) also recruited young Jews ages ten through sixteen.[22] A secret memorandum from the early 1920s addressed the significance of providing a "national education to the future generations of [Jewish] people, independently from [the families'] party affiliation with Ha-shomer ha-tsair"; it stated that the movement had managed to engage thousands of Jewish children. The goal was to awaken in them a "national romance" (*natsionalnaia romantika*), teaching them Hebrew and Jewish history and most importantly serving as a barrier against the assimilationist force of Soviet schools.[23]

The Jewish Socialist Youth League (ESSM) and the Zionist socialist federation Dror, originally established in Kyiv in 1914, also organized youth groups with branches in different cities including Moscow, Leningrad, Minsk, and Kyiv. By 1924, at least seven new Zionist youth groups operated underground on Soviet territory, and by 1925, Zionist parties and organizations in the Soviet Union claimed a membership of as many as tens of thousands.[24] Handwritten bulletins and news sheets were secretly circulated through different areas of the Soviet Union, spreading propaganda and providing information pertaining directly or indirectly to the Zionist youth groups. One such handwritten news sheet from Ukraine included information from different cities and towns in the Ukrainian republic, as well as from the Soviet Union as a whole. It captured the challenges and the victories of the movement. It noted, for instance, that in Kam'yanka, a young teacher was fired for spreading the "Zionist plague," by wearing a small blue and white bow to school; that in Kryzhopil the Soviet school expelled seven children on charges of membership in Ha-shomer ha-tsair; and that the number of Ha-shomer members grew to seven thousand in the ninety-three existing branches in Ukraine, "with 300 new members who recently joined . . . from the Komsomol."[25] According to another report, in 1925, on the very same day, Zionist proclamations were issued in twenty-seven different cities located primarily in Ukraine. In some places, like Odesa, they were tossed from the theater gallery or distributed through the city streets. Some read, "Don't believe in the Soviets but hold high the flag of Zionism!" The author of the report condemned this propaganda and compared it to the agitation carried out among the twenty million Muslims who lived in the Soviet lands and who were manipulated by "bourgeois pan-Islamism."[26]

Many young Jews joined the Zionist youth groups while belonging to official communist organizations. As students in the Yiddish schools, they might have been forced to read in class anti-Zionist propaganda, such as, for example, the pamphlet *Zionism as It Is* (*Tsionizm vi er iz*), and after school join Zionist groups.[27] In Minsk, for instance, where by 1925 the members of the different Zionist organizations amounted to more than five hundred, the youth group of Ha-shomer ha-tsair actively recruited members among students in Soviet schools.[28] Operating underground—the Soviets banned Ha-shomer ha-tsair in 1922—the movement emboldened secondary school students into secretly distributing pro-Zionist fliers through the streets of the Jewish quarter, in the synagogue courtyard, and even inside the synagogue buildings during the Sabbath service.[29] Some young Jews chose to join Zionist groups in spite of their families' lack of connection and sympathy for the movement and perhaps even their condemnation of Zionism. After joining Ha-shomer ha-tsair's youth group in the early 1920s, Eliezer Isakin became the group's leader first in Kharkiv and then in Odesa, until his arrest in 1927 and his exile to the northern region of Kazakhstan. On the other hand, his family had integrated fairly well into the new system. His father was employed in a state institution, and his brother was a prominent member of the Komsomol.[30]

Zionist organizations spread their activities and influence well beyond the borders of the former Pale of Settlement, as cells and branches reached deep into central Russia. In 1920, eighteen-year-old Yakov Liberman became a leading member in the Zionist youth groups in Samara, a city in the Russian interior framed by the Volga and Samara Rivers, with a Jewish population of approximately seven thousand only—most of them refugees who had fled the violence of the civil war. A member of the Zionist organization Kadimah (Forward) since 1917, Liberman became active in other Zionist youth organizations in Samara as well.[31] Appointed head of the local branch of He-haver—a semilegal Zionist student organization—he actively contributed to the movement's periodical *Akhdut* (Unity) and then joined the editorial board of the publication *Evreiskii student* (Jewish student), which was widely distributed through the region.[32] Liberman carried out his Zionist activities while enrolled as a student in the local Industrial Economic Institute. But after enduring several OGPU home searches, and the ensuing arrests and releases, being banned from completing his studies, and witnessing the closing down of the local Zionist club, Liberman opted for illegally crossing the border. From Kaunas, he reached Riga and eventually made it to Palestine in 1924.[33]

Moscow too grew into a hub of underground Zionist activity. One apartment in particular become the symbol of the secretive struggle. Located in the city center at Nikitskaia 9, a long rectilinear street leading from Nikitski Gate to the Kremlin, the apartment was the home of two sisters, the university students and Zionist activists Leah (Liza) and Miriam Leyn.[34] The apartment became the meeting point for young activists from the city as well as from the provinces. They came together there to coordinate illegal activities, gather instructions from the movements' leaders, mark the anniversary of Jewish historical events, and sing songs of protest. Leah Leyn, who was a talented actress in the Moscow Sholem Aleichem Drama Studio and who remained in the apartment until her arrest in June 1925, wrote several songs of the Zionist underground.[35] These songs shed light on the nature of Zionist counterculture during the early Soviet period.

Leah Leyn wrote most of these songs in Yiddish, as remakes of classic songs and poems from the Jewish religious and secular tradition. "Af Nikitske 9," for example, was a satiric song about the life and activity in the apartment on Nikitskaia, which followed the playful song sung at the end of Passover, "Chad Gadia" (One young goat).[36] Leyn composed a number of songs to mark the arrest of fellow activists, including "Af Lubianke 2," or "At Lubianka Number 2," the address of the Soviet secret police's headquarters in Moscow.[37] The witty song "Az Merezhin, der Evsek-meylekh," or "When Merezhin, King of the Evsek," mocked the Jewish communist Avrom Merezhin and his role in persecuting Zionism. Based on the well-known "Az der Rebe Eli-meylekh" (As the Rebbe Elimelech), the new anti-Evsektsiia satire by Leyn included the following stanza:

Az Merezhin, der Evsek-meylekh
Iz gevorn lustik, freylekh,
Iz gevorn lustik, freylekh
Undzer liber Evsek-meylekh,
Hot er ongeton di hitl
Un gefunen zikh a mitl
Un geshikt nokh der khevre GPU[38]

When Merezhin the royal Evsek,
Became content and jubilant,
Became content and jubilant,
Our beloved royal Evsek,
He threw on his hat
And he came up with a plan,
And he sent for the GPU gang

Whether these songs were performed in the "Zionist apartment" on Nikitskaia or in exile, they lifted the youths' spirits and served as an inspiration to those committed to the struggle. Leyn wrote "Dos letste vort," or "The Last Word," a remake of Bialik's prophetic poem, in 1926, while she was in exile in the Urals. Dedicated to all Zionist arrestees, the song's last stanza echoed the grand hope of a new day of freedom, which would bring certain doom to the OGPU and the Evsektsiia:

Itst zog ikh "Gepeu" azoy:
"Ir vert tsuzetst khotsh fun geshrey,
Nor doyern s'nisht lang dos shlekhts,
Aroys di zun vet bald fun rekht.
Aroys di zun vet bald fun rekht
Un vet di velt mit likht bagisn,
Un s'veln dan nisht zayn keyn knekht,
Fun frayhayt yederer vet visn.
Tsu redifet kumen vet an ek
Un tsu der gevaldhayt fun 'Evsek,'
Un tsum Cheka un tsum Tshertok,
Er geyt, er kumt, er kumt, der tog!"[39]

Here's what I say to the "GPU":
"Our cries and shouts will smother you
Evil won't reign for many more days
The sun of justice will soon rise
The sun of justice will soon rise,
The world will be covered in light and beauty
And there won't be any more slaves
Everyone will live in liberty
Persecution will no longer be
An end to the Evsektsiia's brutality
Cheka and Chertok will meet their doom.
That day is coming, coming soon!"

The relative success of Zionism in recruiting young Jews from Soviet organizations and in penetrating areas outside of the former Pale alarmed the communist leadership and eventually swayed it into rethinking its lenient policies toward Zionism. In the fall of 1925, the head of the Ukrainian OGPU addressed a secret memorandum to the secretary of the Central Committee of the Communist Party of Ukraine, Lazar Kaganovich. Here, he voiced his concern over the Party's inadequate struggle against the Zionist movement. The distress stemmed in particular from the fact that Zionism seemed to be winning over a younger generation of Jews. As the OGPU chairman acknowledged, "Zionist forces are arising with frightening alacrity from the depth of the Jewish masses and the predominant majority of these forces are the youth." If indeed every city and town in Ukraine regardless of its Jewish population boasted an active Zionist group, as the Party leadership feared in 1925, then the Zionist cells had somehow managed to exert more influence on many young Jews than the Soviet state had through its own Party and governmental organizations.[40] This development indicated a degree of failure on the part of the system.

The wording in the indictments of many Zionist arrestees reflects this change, as Zionist work by left-leaning groups was now branded "anti-Soviet" and "counterrevolutionary."[41] Signed by the same OGPU chairman in the summer of 1926, the indictment against a recently arrested young Zionist read as follows: "Taking into consideration that [he is] an active member of the anti-Soviet organization STP [Zionist Toilers' Party], we declare him a socially dangerous element and . . . sentence him to a period of three years in exile outside of the Ukrainian republic."[42] But the change of language and attitude reflected in the new wave of arrests did not necessarily mean that Zionist activity was beyond redemption. The same young Zionist who had been sentenced to a three-year exile was released one year after his arrest, in the fall of 1927. The new chairman of the OGPU in Ukraine "allowed him to reside freely anywhere in the Soviet Union."[43]

He-Halutz and Its Zions

During the early 1920s He-Halutz (The pioneer) emerged as one of the most influential Zionist youth groups in the Soviet Union. At its first conference, which was held in Moscow in January 1919, He-Halutz leaders defined the movement as a nonpartisan Zionist association of workers who shared the common goal of settling in Palestine. The movement would provide its members with appropriate training in agricultural work and facilitate their transportation to and their absorption in what would eventually become a Jewish state.[44] He-Halutz branches promoting physical labor and agricultural training for young Jews in preparation for their resettlement to Palestine emerged in different areas of the tsarist empire during World War I. Their number increased in the aftermath of the civil war, as the violence of the pogroms triggered a wave of unorganized emigration.

The number of communal farms that attracted *halutzim* also grew out of the coincidental absence of an unsolvable tension between those young Zionists—in particular those who believed in socialism and might even have been sympathetic to the Bolshevik experiment in its early phase—and the Soviet government.[45] From the very beginning, the Soviet state agreed with the goal of productivizing the Jewish population by promoting the establishment of agricultural settlements. New Jewish colonies were established in Crimea, Ukraine, and Belorussia, often next to or on the foundation of the earlier Jewish agricultural colonies, founded under Tsars Alexander I and Nicholas I in the southern regions of the empire. Although the degree of support for Jewish colonies in different areas of the Soviet Union varied, their existence inevitably sustained He-Halutz, so much so that with its emphasis on agricultural settlements and immigration to Palestine, the Soviet He-Halutz movement might have even influenced the nature of the same movement in neighboring Poland—at least until 1928, when Soviet authorities liquidated it.[46]

Like the Zionist Labor Party Tseirei-Tsiyon before it, He-Halutz also split into two factions. The rift harked back to a 1918 petition that the party's headquarters in Moscow had sent to the Bolsheviks seeking official authorization to operate—the Party's response was that no official approval was necessary as long as He-Halutz did not stand in the way of Soviet principles. The tension between He-Halutz members escalated a few years later: on the one hand, those who wished to work with the Soviets were willing to make their ideology conform to the official line of the Communist Party in exchange for an endorsement of their activities; on the other hand, those members who resisted all compromise strove to disassociate themselves entirely from the Bolsheviks and their commitment to class warfare. While traveling through the Soviet Union to attend the Moscow Trade Fair, the future first prime minister of Israel David Ben-Gurion attempted to resolve the rift between the two factions. But he was not successful.[47]

In August 1923, the party split into a legal faction committed to class warfare and an illegal faction committed to the national Jewish workers' movement. The legal faction managed to revamp its branches in different cities, launch an official publication (*He-Halutz*)—which was issued in Moscow and had a circulation of three thousand—and see its members participate in Soviet celebrations and holidays displaying Zionist slogans.[48] The legal faction also joined the two official Soviet organizations established to promote agricultural settlements for Jews, OZET and KOMZET.[49] This was despite the fact that OZET—established in Moscow in January 1925 as a nonpolitical and non-Party body—rejected active Zionists as members.[50]

It is not possible to fully understand the relative success of He-Halutz without contextualizing its development within the early Jewish agricultural settlements. Jewish colonies had existed in Russia since the early nineteenth century, in particular in the region of "New Russia," which included parts of southern Ukraine and Crimea. In the hope that agricultural colonization among the Jewish population would solve the Jewish question, the Russian state had promoted the establishment of agricultural colonies, granting Jewish farmers special privileges. Both legal and illegal He-Halutz factions established training farms, often on the premises of the historical Jewish colonies, located around the Black Sea.[51] These were more successful in attracting local Jewish support than the ones established in Belorussia. Here, the Jewish agricultural experiment had been less effective not only because of the absence of preexisting colonies to build on—it was harder to start from scratch—but also because fewer urban Jews from the Belorussian cities and towns were willing to move to agricultural settlements. This resistance might have grown out of a relatively stronger connection to the Bundist political and cultural memory of rootedness as opposed to the Zionist idea of moving elsewhere to solve the Jewish question, which was historically more ingrained in Ukraine.[52] While this cultural legacy of rootedness might have influenced the older generation, it probably did not have a significant impact on Jewish youths. Many young Jews from the economically ruined Belorussian shtetls chose to move to a nearby larger city like Minsk or to the faraway metropolis of Leningrad for reasons unrelated to ideology and politics. To be sure, economic hardship and material struggles paved the way to resettlement. But it was the quest to pursue an education and achieve self-realization in the new society that swayed young Jews to eschew becoming farmers in the colonies and instead move to large Soviet urban centers.[53]

The Jewish colonies around the Black Sea turned out to be more successful also by virtue of the support and funding channeled through the American philanthropic organization the American Jewish Joint Distribution Committee (JDC). JDC funding came in the shape of modern equipment that was brought to Ukraine to replace, modernize, and fix what had been damaged and destroyed during World War I and the civil war. Given the remarkable shortage of modern technology and the state's interest in the project, the director of the Russian branch of the JDC—the agronomist Joseph Rosen—signed an agreement with the Soviet government to promote the settlement on land of impoverished and disenfranchised Jews. Not only was transforming Jews into productive and loyal citizens in the state's best interest, but the prospect of improved harvesting that would result from the modern machinery, as well as the influx of hard currency, prompted the Soviets to back the project.[54] And so, in 1924, the JDC established the American Jewish Joint Agricultural Corporation, or Agro-Joint, which supported financially the agrarianization of Jews on large tracts of land that the state set aside for the settlers, free of charge. The JDC agreed to invest $400,000 in 1924–1925 on the Agro-Joint project in Ukraine and Crimea.[55] The American Jewish Committee leader Louis Marshall supported the JDC's venture and even donated toward it $100,000 of his own money.[56] While Marshall loathed communism and described the Soviet Union as "a tyranny of absolutism, . . . as abhorrent to [him] as Tsarism," in the mid-1920s, he expressed his firm belief in the colonization project and its relief potential for Soviet Jews.[57] On the other hand, some American Zionist leaders voiced their opposition to the Soviet colonization project not only because it distracted from their primary goal of settling Jews in Palestine but also because of the fear that it would trigger anti-Jewish animosity. After all, non-Jews too needed land.[58] Some foreign Jewish organizations, like the Yiddish *Forverts*, championed the project and even called on their readers to help raise the funds to support the effort, deeming colonization promising especially in the areas that included Jewish colonies established in the nineteenth century or located near large Jewish demographic centers.[59]

Beginning in 1924, thousands of Jewish families settled in Ukraine and Crimea. By 1928, more than two hundred colonies in Ukraine and Crimea were sponsored by Agro-Joint. Before mass production of tractors was launched in the Soviet Union, Agro-Joint purchased John Deere tractors—the most modern American tractors at the time—for the Jewish colonies: the JDC coordinated the first large-scale importation of tractors to the Soviet Union, coordinating the distribution of the tractors, training local peasants to be tractor drivers with American instructors, and organizing mobile repair shops, with a central repair shop set up in the colony of Novo-Poltavka, in Kherson *guberniia*.[60] In 1927, while traveling through the Soviet Union, Abraham Cahan, editor of the *Forverts*, visited the Jewish colonies and noted that many Jews who had flocked to the new agricultural settlements and who "in the prerevolutionary days [. . .] would have mocked at the idea of becoming Jewish 'peasants" did so as a result of the revolution that took place in the Jewish socioeconomic structure during the 1920s. For Cahan, colonization represented the only chance that many Jews had "to carve for themselves a niche in the new economy."[61]

Some of the JDC colonies attracted mostly Zionists and were settled by *halutzim* who considered their agricultural work there a stepping-stone on their road to Palestine. They preexisted the establishment of Agro-Joint, which later sponsored them. Some of the colonies even had Hebrew names.[62] Even after the September 1923 split in the He-Halutz movement—with the legal left wing, which supported the class struggle and was approved by the Soviet state, and the illegal right wing, which identified as a national Jewish workers movement and was thus outlawed by the government—the JDC continued to fund both legal and illegal farms.[63] Writing from Moscow in 1923, Ben-Gurion noted that almost the entire budget to fund He-Halutz farms came from the JDC.[64]

In carrying out this support, the JDC had to conform to the Soviet principle of nonsectarian help. But as for other cultural institutions and activities the JDC subsidized during the 1920s, it did not always abide by this rule. The more the JDC engaged in official forms of relief and welfare and funded Soviet institutions and endeavors, the more it could sponsor—at times even unbeknownst to Soviet authorities—unofficial endeavors. Amid diverse and fairly successful official activities, sanctioned by the Soviet state, JDC representatives could carve out some leeway and generate new opportunities to sustain underground initiatives.[65] These included colonies of the illegal faction of He-Halutz.

Some of these colonies embodied the essence of Soviet Jewishness and combined, without strain, particular and universal identities, Zionist and communist. When Cahan visited Tel-Hai, the largest He-Halutz agricultural settlement in Crimea, he noticed several things: besides the strong communal bond and devotion that reigned among its residents and the fact that many spoke primarily Hebrew, he was struck by the successful pig breeding in the colony. Other visitors to Tel-Hai, including the Yiddish writer I. J. Singer, were similarly impressed by the colony's efficiency and achievements and were surprised by the pig breeding.[66] To a Polish Jew, it seemed noteworthy, even in an atheistic society like the Soviet Union, that Jewish farmers would breed pigs, especially in a Zionist colony.

The *Halutzim* "Didn't Even Know How to Ride Horses!"

Born in 1907 in the Jewish colony of Sede Menuha K'tana (Small field of respite)—exactly one hundred years after its establishment in the region of Kherson, in southern Ukraine—Shterna Ninburg was a fifth-generation Jewish farmer and a proud one indeed. At the age of seventeen, she left Sede Menuha and moved to Crimea to serve as an instructor in the He-Halutz colony of Tel-Hai. Established in 1922, Tel-Hai was named after the place in Palestine where, in 1920, the Zionist leader Yosef Trumpeldor perished while defending the Jewish agricultural settlement from the raid launched by an Arab militia group. Spanning over two thousand hectares of land, the colony included a well, six buildings, a cowshed, horses, pigs, field crops, and a church, which the Jewish colonists used as a dining room. "Tel-Hai was even awarded a prize at an agricultural exhibition in Crimea," remembered Ninburg. As a model colony to train young *halutzim* who settled there from the towns of Ukraine, Tel-Hai was in dire need of instructors like Shterna Ninburg who could train urban Jews and prepare them for resettlement in Palestine. She taught the *halutzim* how to sow, "how to milk cows, how to harvest, even how to plaster houses." "They didn't even know how to ride horses!" she commented in dismay.[67]

At Tel-Hai, Ninburg also worked as a hard-cheese specialist. It was not only the quality of the milk from the nearby Armenian farms that gave Tel-Hai the reputation of a manufacturer of cheese of the highest quality in the region. In Tel-Hai, the JDC (and Agro-Joint) had funded the most sophisticated and technologically advanced dairy equipment in the region.[68] As a cheese maker, Ninburg would wake up at midnight, milk up to ten cows, and then immediately proceed to make the cheese until nine in the morning; following a short rest break, she would milk the cows again at noon, for a total of three times a day every eight hours. "It was hard work," she recalled, "and only the girls milked the cows."[69] While Hebrew classes and study groups related to Zionism and the Land of Israel did exist in Tel-Hai, learning to toil the land remained the priority.[70] Ninburg, who only knew Russian and Yiddish, commented on the centrality of work over culture: "When I came to Palestine, I didn't know any Hebrew. There were very few people who learned Hebrew [in the colony]. . . . We worked very hard. Life was very hard."[71]

Despite Ninburg's young age, as an instructor, she was a central figure in the life of the colony. She not only served as an agronomist who taught the *halutzim* the tricks of the trade but also acted as a counselor, a mediator of tensions and difficulties that arose as the settlers shared their hopes, fears, and sorrows about the new life.[72] As passionate or as desperate as they may have been, transitioning to agricultural labor was not easy for many young *halutzim*. But the influence between the young *halutzim* and the instructors-agronomists must have been mutual. We can surmise that a number of urban Jews who had settled in the colony with the intention of leaving for Palestine, after having learned the trade, decided to stay and toil the land. On the other hand, the farmers and instructors—most of whom had not originally been strong supporters of Zionism—eventually came to share the same dreams and passions of the *halutzim*. Shterna Ninburg eventually moved to Palestine in 1928—as did her parents, in 1933.

The decision to leave coincided with a change of policy and attitude on the part of Soviet authorities. In the spring of 1926, the secret police arrested some of the leaders at Tel-Hai, including agronomists and instructors. Some were given the option to choose between Palestine and exile. Tel-Hai members who, like Ninburg, decided to leave received a visa from the He-Halutz center in Moscow, via JDC secret funding, and departed for Palestine from the port of Odesa in 1928. The Supreme Court of

Crimea sentenced the members of the Tel-Hai administration to prison for two to four years on charges of engaging in counterrevolutionary activities. These included organizing Zionist conferences and spreading pro-Palestine propaganda, as well as expelling Communist Party members from the colony.[73]

One of the leading administrators and agronomists at Tel-Hai, Benjamin Gornstein, was arrested with his wife and assistant, exiled to Novosibirsk for a year, and eventually given a visa to settle in Palestine in February 1927. According to Gornstein, the Evsektsiia destroyed Tel-Hai.[74] Because it considered the colonies—and in particular the ones that thrived through the Agro-Joint funding and had close connections to Zionism—as a dangerous threat to the general agrarianization project of Soviet Jews, the Jewish section exerted pressure on Soviet authorities to intervene and liquidate them. And indeed they did. By 1926, most He-Halutz farms, legal and illegal alike, ceased operating as such; and by March 1928, the state revoked the status of legality it had bestowed on one faction of He-Halutz. The Sovietization of Tel-Hai was followed by the Sovietization of other major He-Halutz training farms in Podolia and throughout Crimea; one exception was the colony of Mishmar, in the Dzhankoy district in Crimea, which in March 1929 still had 140 young people working there.[75]

Eventually renamed Red October, Tel-Hai lost its Zionist spirit. Over time, the number of Jewish residents in the colony declined; in the midst of the internationalization campaign to counter bourgeois nationalism in the colonies, Red October / Tel Hai attracted new settlers, including ethnic Germans, Ukrainians, and Crimean Tatars.[76] The internationalization of Jewish colonies grew out of the political and socioeconomic changes of the late 1920s, when Stalin launched the First Five-Year Plan with the goal of reshaping the Soviet Union into a modern nation through rapid industrialization and the expansion of heavy industry and through the collectivization of the countryside. Collectivization in particular, which the state pursued intensely between 1929 and 1933, was supposed to transform the country's traditional agriculture once and for all by forcing the peasants to join large collective farms. Like many others, Shterna Ninburg's parents—who worked as farmers in Sede Menuha K'tana, where their daughter had been born, and who would have otherwise stayed—decided to leave for Palestine as a result of the policies introduced during the First Five-Year Plan.

During the Great Leap Forward, as the First Five-Year Plan was known, the Soviet countryside, like the Soviet city, was supposed to break with the semicapitalist and semiliberal policies of the NEP years. The violent collectivization of the countryside but also the implementation of a broad cultural revolution, with the goal of crushing, once and for all, religious, cultural, and political identities and behaviors deemed bourgeois and anti-Soviet by the state, determined the choice of Ninburg's parents—and that of many other Jewish farmers—to leave the colonies.[77]

Despite the push to suppress the national distinctiveness of Soviet colonies and promote their internationalization, several Jewish agricultural settlements retained a Jewish majority percentage of the population. Some had Yiddish schools and issued Yiddish newspapers. These included Sede Menuha, which was renamed Kalinindorf in 1927 and became the center of the first autonomous Jewish region in Soviet territories.[78] On the eve of World War II, more than eighteen hundred Jews lived in Kalinindorf. And while the Jewish population decreased steadily over the course of the 1930s and Yiddish institutions were closed down by the end of the decade, life in Kalinindorf, as well as in other Jewish colonies in Ukraine and Crimea, was liquidated by the Germans in the wake of their attack on the Soviet Union in the summer of 1941.[79]

The Evsektsiia against Everyone Else

The head of the OGPU, Felix Dzierżyński, had himself given instructions providing legal protection to He-Halutz.[80] Several times over the course of the early 1920s, he expressed his positive inclination toward Zionism and argued that persecuting Zionists was politically counterproductive.[81] In March 1924, for instance, after reviewing Zionist illegal materials requisitioned by the OGPU, Dzierżyński wrote to his deputies, "I must admit, I do not understand at all why they are being persecuted on the basis of their Zionist affiliation. The majority of their attacks on us are based on our persecution of them. Persecuted, they are a thousand times more dangerous for us than they would be not persecuted. . . . Their party work, therefore, is not at all dangerous for us. . . . We should not bother them, on the condition that they do not interfere with our policy. . . . But then we must mercilessly beat and punish the speculators (scum) and all those who violate our law."[82] At a time when the Soviet Union was struggling for recognition and diplomatic relations with the West, avoiding uproars of protests over the persecution of Zionism was in the best interest of the state. Similarly, Dzierżyński seemed to agree that just like official discrimination or popular animosity against Jews, the persecution of Zionism would inexorably boost Jewish support for Zionism.[83]

But in 1925, the Evsektsiia-driven campaign against Zionist youth groups bore fruit among Soviet authorities. First of all, the push for a stronger anti-Zionist position grew out of the intensifying ideological battle between the Evsektsiia and the Zionist youth movements. In facing the Evsektsiia and other communist agencies, Zionist youth groups became more radical and confrontational. In some cases, in order to cover a strong Zionist presence, Jewish colonies changed their names as a way to deflect the attention of Evsektsiia members. One colony, for example, was renamed Rafes, after Moshe Rafes, a Evsektsiia member in the earlier stages after its establishment; another one was called Kiper, after Moshe Kiper, secretary of the Central Committee of the Evsektsiia in Ukraine; and yet another colony was renamed Kaganovich, after Lazar Kaganovich, who in 1925 became the first secretary of the Communist Party of Ukraine.[84] In many instances, Zionist leaders spoke out at communist meetings and used anti-Soviet slogans at assemblies to mobilize Jews for resettlement on land. In one case, the Zionist Socialist Party managed to distribute one hundred thousand copies of anti-Evsektsiia fliers in Ukraine.[85] The OGPU responded by arresting thousand of Zionists (or alleged Zionists) in different cities and towns of Ukraine. In another instance, in January 1926, EVOSM members took over the Shevchenko Theater in the city of Kamianets-Podilskyi and managed to spread anti-Soviet fliers, chanting the slogans "Down with the Evsektsiia, Down with the Komsomol, and Down with Soviet power!" before they were arrested.[86] Young Jews—some of them Komsomol members—were actively mobilized into participating in the dispute and clashes, as they served as informants, spying and chasing after fellow Jews connected to Zionist youth groups.[87] The editors of the secret handwritten EVOSM bulletin from 1926 called on its readers to engage openly and aggressively in a struggle against the Evsektsiia's "dreadful dictatorship" and to reject the politics of silence that the Jewish section had imposed on the Zionist movement. The bulletin referred to examples of public speeches held by Zionist leaders in Odesa, Zinovievsk (Kropyvnytskyi), Moscow, Kharkiv, Kremenchuk, Poltava, and Balta.[88] Interrogated by the OGPU in September 1925, David Farbshtein, a member of Ha-shomer ha-tsair in Kamianets-Podilskyi, admitted to being loyal to the Communist Party and to the Soviet Union but to loathing the Evsektsiia.[89]

This heightened tension between young Zionists and Jewish communists echoed what had been the Evsektsiia's intention from the very beginning. The wrath against the Zionists grew out of a desperate attempt to exhibit their loyalty to communism and whitewash their prerevolutionary sins.[90] Moreover, the many former Bundists who joined the Evsektsiia were eager to finally put an end to the fierce conflict between them and the Zionists, which had dominated Jewish politics before 1917: by destroying Zionism, they asserted themselves as the only credible voice on the Jewish street.

Actual clashes between the Evsektsiia and the Zionists had started early on. In the summer of 1918, former members of the left Zionist parties—including the United Socialist Party and Poale-Tsiyon—who eventually joined the Evsektsiia came together in Moscow, in the Poliakov hall adjacent to the Great Synagogue. There they apparently declared that "the blood of the Zionists will soon be spilled like water and the Zionist movement will be heavily punished."[91] In 1919, the Maccabi sport organization in Moscow hired a number of young Russian sportsmen to help offset the attacks carried out by the Evsektsiia, essentially creating a self-defense unit, not against pogromists but against other Jews.[92] In the veritable civil war that waged on the Jewish street, Evsektsiia leaders took full advantage of the ignorance that existed in general communist organizations about the nature of Jewish political and cultural life. This way they could get a hold of soldiers, storm Jewish institutions with revolvers, and arrest "dangerous" members of the Jewish bourgeoisie.

In 1920, in Saratov, following Evsektsiia orders, Red Army soldiers arrested a group of Zionist activists accused of having supported General Denikin during the civil war. When shortly thereafter GPU officials released the arrestees with an apology, they asked one of them to provide a clear definition of the meaning of "Zionist" and "Zionism."[93] The same form of anti-Zionist lobbying was carried out at the 1920 Zionist convention in Moscow: at the Evsektsiia's behest, armed soldiers stormed the assembly hall on April 23, arrested all the delegates, and took them to the Butyrka prison.[94] People's Commissar of Education Anatoly Lunacharskii clearly stated in his meeting with Rabbi Yaakov Mazeh in Moscow, during which he discussed the closing down of Hebrew-language institutions, "the vandalism comes from your people, not from us."[95] A few years later, a communist leader captured these same dynamics by remarking, "Where Jewish affairs are concerned, our comrades of the Evsektsiia are our highest authority and they virtually go crazy where Zionism is concerned."[96] The Evsektsiia played a crucial role in hastening the tempo of destruction of Zionism. It is also true, however, that the total suppression of the movement was inevitable under the Soviets. This became apparent with the regime's consolidation under Stalin's leadership, which encompassed the decline of those who, like Dzierżyński, had been positively disposed toward Zionism.

Substitution Emigration

Before being arrested on February 5, 1925, the nineteen-year old Nahum Goldin—a member of Kadimah since 1922 and of EVOSM since 1923—had regularly contributed to the underground weekly publication *Be-olamenu* (In our world), issued in Yiddish and Russian.[97] When state political agents broke into his home, he barely managed to destroy his secret notes. He was first taken to the Minsk prison and then to the special OGPU cellar. Two weeks later, charged with belonging to a Zionist organization, Goldin was given three years in exile. Together with other Zionists—most of them members of He-Halutz and the Zionist Socialist Party who had been arrested in different cities of Belorussia and Ukraine—he was taken to Kyzylorda, in Kazakhstan.[98] But after four months in exile, he "received the *zamena*, the substitution," the official document that substituted exile abroad for deportation and exile within the Soviet Union; thus, instead of spending more time in exile, he could leave for Palestine. And on December 17, 1925, alongside twenty-three young Zionists, Goldin left the port of Odesa with a Sovtorgflot steamship bound for the Land of Israel.[99] Zionists used to refer to substitution using a play on words from the liturgy: "because of our sins we were exiled to our land."

Between 1924 and 1934, hundreds of arrested Zionists took advantage of the substitution immigration agreement and opted for "deportation" to Palestine in lieu of prison terms or exile to minus towns in the Soviet empire.[100] Perhaps as many as three thousand Zionist political prisoners left during this decade. This was a rather small, highly complicated, and arbitrary endeavor that materialized thanks to the indefatigable support of Ekaterina Peshkova (the wife of the Soviet writer Maxim Gorky), who headed the Committee to Aid Political Prisoners, or Pompolit, and coordinated all aspects of the process.[101] Many of those who managed to reach Palestine through substitution recalled Peshkova's efforts as she "familiarized herself with the different shades of Zionism . . . and took care of the arrestees' family members, bringing them food, clothes, drugs."[102] The mediation of the renowned pianist David Shor, who often performed at the Kremlin and was a teacher at the Moscow Music Conservatory, was also key to the legal resettlement of arrested Zionists from the Soviet Union to Palestine. This agreement between international bodies, including the British government and the World Zionist Organization, allowed a small but committed contingent of Zionists to reach Palestine and thus play a role in creating a new life for Jews in the Land of Israel.[103] From the Soviet vantage point, substitution produced an influx of hard currency. At the same time, it allowed the regime to remove from society the most radical Zionists, while appeasing international Jewish organizations.

Nahum Goldin was more fortunate than most. The overwhelming majority of Zionist political prisoners were denied substitution and remained in the Soviet Union. Chaim Koserovskii, for instance, applied for substitution twelve times and twelve times was turned down.[104] A much more common experience for Zionist arrestees included the OGPU authorities pressuring them into forsaking their political allegiance to Zionism. The secret police often coerced them into signing a public statement that acknowledged the anti-Soviet nature of their illegal activities and in which they renounced any future participation in the movement. These statements were then released in the Russian and Yiddish press. When the eighteen-year-old S. Dranovska found out that the statement in which she rejected her Zionist views was published in the press, she took her own life.[105]

Those who refused to renounce their party membership and who never received substitution ended up spending years in exile or lived with residency restrictions but with the right to study and work.[106] They established Zionist microcommunities, maintaining strong ties among each other, at times even marrying among themselves.[107] A tiny minority of those who managed to escape exile continued to work in small underground Zionist cells and were eventually arrested in the late 1930s. But whether in exile or not, most young Zionists who did not reach Palestine eventually adjusted to Soviet life. Arrested in 1924 as a leader of the left wing of Ha-shomer ha-Tsair, Solomon Liubarskii signed a public statement renouncing his Zionist activity and was released. He then tried—without success—to cross the border into Latvia and was finally arrested and sentenced to three years in exile. But after graduating from medical school, he eventually became the director of a Soviet hospital in Siberia, where he worked until his death in the 1970s.[108]

On the other hand, some Jews who had moved to Palestine eventually returned to the Soviet Union, drawn back by a combination of frustration over life in the Land of Israel and the ongoing appeal of the new communist system. Born in a small Lithuanian town near Kaunas, Shira Gorshman, who would later become a well-known Yiddish writer, was evacuated with her family to Odesa during World War I. After becoming active in Zionist circles, she decided to emigrate to Palestine in 1924 with her first husband and young child and there joined Gdud Ha-avodah (Workers' battalion), a socialist Zionist work group established in 1920; its members settled kibbutzim, built infrastructure, and lived together with no personal property. When Gdud Ha-avodah split in the late 1920s and a small left faction departed Palestine for Crimea to found a new agricultural colony, Gorshman joined the group and settled there in 1928. As she later captured in her memoirs, in which she chronicled life in Voya Nova, or New Way, as the pioneers called the new collective farm in Esperanto (the international language created by the Jewish physician and Yiddish grammarian Ludwik Lejzer Zamenhof), the connection and commitment to Zionism dwindled. Gorshman ran the farm's diary operations and voiced her pride in being able to "oversee five hundred head of cattle." She eventually left the collective farm in the early 1930s, after marrying Mendel Gorshman, a Soviet artist and book illustrator, and moved to Moscow, where she began her career as a Yiddish writer.[109] In a way, the establishment of settlements like Voya Nova marked the end of the "Zionist period" in Crimea, and the choices made by people like Shira Gorshman confirmed the enduring allure of the Soviet experiment.

Conclusion

The Evsektsiia's obsession with the "dangers" of Zionism included fears that Zionists would restore Jewish petty bourgeois organizations, influence the resurgence of Ukrainian and Belorussian nationalist organizations linked to the anti-Bolshevik Petliura and to the Polish general Stanislaw Bulak-Balakhovich, and even perhaps rekindle the Kadets and the Socialist Revolutionaries.[110] Throughout the 1920s, Jewish communists blamed Soviet authorities for their lack of assertiveness in dealing with Zionism. They noted that the state's ambivalence led to the legal existence of the left wing of Poale-Tsiyon and He-Halutz, which in turn encouraged the activities of other illegal Zionist groups, conveying the general message that feeling a connection to Zionist ideas was still acceptable. This criticism on the part of the Evsektsiia may have had a basis in fact.

A club named after the ideologue of Marxist Zionism, Ber Borochov, was established in 1922 in Baku, the capital city of Azerbaijan.[111] It operated under the patronage of the Caucasus Regional Committee of the Poale-Tsiyon and hosted the performances of an amateur theatrical company founded by Mountain Jews. The head of the theatrical company, Herzl Ravvinovich-Gorskii, was the son of the chief rabbi of the Mountain Jewish community in Baku and the editor of *The Toiler*, the organ of the Caucasus Regional Committee of the Poale-Tsiyon and its youth organization.[112] Presumably, when local Jews came together to watch theatrical performances in an official Zionist space like the Borochov Club in Baku, they might also have come under the impression that Zionism could endure in Soviet society. Its official existence, albeit in modified form, might even inspire some illegal Zionist activities as well.

When in 1927 a group of Jewish students celebrated the twenty-fifth anniversary of the establishment of Poale-Tsiyon by marching in front of the building of the main university in Minsk with flags and banners, someone asked, perplexed, "Why are members of the Poale-Tsiyon allowed . . . if they are considered Zionists?"[113] While Poale-Tsiyon remained a legal organization in the Soviet Union, open support for a political party other than the Communist Party in a public space was considered especially problematic for students at a Soviet university. A year later, local authorities barred students who belonged to Poale-Tsiyon from enrolling at the university and joining other communist organizations. In the summer of 1928, the last legal vestige of Zionism in the Soviet Union and the last legal independent party in the country disappeared, as Poale-Tsiyon was banned.[114] The American Zionist Leo M. Glassman, who traveled to Moscow three days before the organization was liquidated, arranged a secret meeting with one of the leaders of the Left Poale-Tsiyon, who showed him a copy of the protest that he drew up together with other activists. They protested the "arbitrary and unjustifiable actions of the GPU." "Soon after that," noted Glassman, "my informant was exiled to Siberia and, so far as I know, he is still there."[115]

In cities across the country, Poale-Tsiyon members were forced to sign a statement, often reproduced in the local and national press, in which they acknowledged the counterrevolutionary nature of Labor Zionism. Like former Bundists a few years earlier, former Poale-Tsiyonists who signed the document could join the Communist Party without recommendations. Soviet citizens would now be able to express their support for Zionism only in a clandestine fashion, limiting their connection to the Zionist idea to the privacy of their homes, to the few, if any, Zionist publications still in their possession, and to secretive conversations with restricted groups of friends.

But the great majority, who did not manage to leave and could no longer face the burden of social marginalization, decided to conform. As the youth groups progressively disappeared during the second half of the 1920s, disrupted by the ongoing waves of arrests, many young Zionists joined communist organizations in an attempt to fit in.[116] Even when their previous association with Zionism made their political loyalty to the Party questionable, with occasional complaints about Zionists who joined the Komsomol, most youngsters enrolled in the Communist Youth League, attracted by the universal message of the ideology and tired of feeling rejected. Many publicly acknowledged their mistakes in the local press. Only a small minority maintained a secret allegiance to Zionism while successfully partaking in Soviet society well into the 1930s.[117] And even when the Soviets raised the idea of an autonomous Jewish region in the Russian Far East in 1927 and vowed to eventually establish a Jewish national homeland in the Soviet Union, very few Zionists acquiesced to resettle to Birobidzhan and morph their longing for the Land of Israel into the yearning for Stalin's new Zion.[118]

In December 1929, the American Jewish Congress organized a conference condemning the persecution of Judaism and Zionism in the Soviet Union. In front of one hundred delegates representing twenty-three different organizations, the Zionist leader and reform rabbi Stephen S. Wise pled to end the silence by the American Jewish community regarding the suffering of Jews in the Soviet Union. Wise encouraged American Jews to speak out against the treatment of their brethren and passionately (but also inaccurately) stated that "against no religious group in Russia is there the merciless ferocity of attitude that there is against the Jews." Different talks addressed the problem of exile and imprisonment of Zionists, as well as the closing down of synagogues and the persecution of rabbis. Congressman Hamilton Fish vowed to make the American public (Jews and Christians alike) aware of the desperate situation and pressure the US government into resisting the establishment of full diplomatic relations with the Soviet Union. In the end, the conference adopted a resolution, which included a commitment to likewise pressure Soviet authorities into putting an end to the persecution. The resolution included the following statement:

> We must promptly and unremittingly proceed to bring to an end methods and practices calculated to make spiritual orphans of the Jewish children in Russia. There must be no further converting of synagogues and religious schools into warehouses and clubs. We can no longer tolerate the profane uprooting of Jewish cemeteries, the hounding of rabbis and scholars, and the exile and imprisonment of Zionists. The horror of all this is not mitigated by its perpetuation in the name of freedom and of high humanity. And the one way that lies open to us is the way to the court of public opinion. The facts must be made available to the larger masses of our people and must be circulated beyond the mere confines of the Jewish community, so that all right-thinking men and women of every race and faith may join hands with us.[119]

As valiant as these efforts on the part of American Jewry might have been, they could not reverse the Sovietization process, which seemed truly unstoppable under Stalin's regime. This process, which was imposed from above but also more and more accepted from below, not only led to the progressive dwindling of Zionism in what used to be one of its greatest centers since the late nineteenth century but also caused the irreversible transformation of Judaism, Jewish religious life, and identity.

5

"DOWN WITH THE SABBATH!"

Reconfiguring Judaism One Campaign at a Time

In Ilia Ehrenburg's 1927 satiric novel *The Stormy Life of Lazik Roitshvanets*, the writer mocked aspects of the Bolshevik campaign to uproot religion on the Jewish street. Ehrenburg taunted the display of ideological passion, devoid of real substance, with which some "godless" activists understood the campaign to end religion. In the city of Homyel, in southeastern Belorussia, where the novel takes place, the activist Levka, who was a hairdresser by profession, yelled so much during the campaigns to spread atheism that he would lose his voice. He would run to the synagogue and shout at the top of his lungs, "Down with the Sabbath! Long live . . . Monday!"[1] Ehrenburg underlined the absurdity of Levka's commitment to uprooting Judaism by emphasizing his shrieking and his suggestion to do away with the Jewish traditional day of rest in favor of Monday. While each militant atheist "stormed the heavens" with a different degree of belief and solemnity, which could range from Levka's hollow theatrical passion to a real pledge to wage a lifetime war against religion, the campaigns to seize synagogues (and, with them, churches and mosques) and persecute their believers became a priority for the state and the Party immediately following the revolution.[2]

The curtailment of religious life and the systematic harassment of religious leaders in Soviet society grew out of Marx's often-quoted maxim of religion being the opiate of the masses. Communist ideology was inherently atheistic and hostile to any form of religion. From the vantage point of the Soviet state, religion represented first and foremost "an obstacle to its monopoly on political, ideological, and spiritual authority."[3] Therefore, the existence of a Soviet communist state hinged on the establishment of a world without religion. The disruption of religious life also gained traction through the preexisting tensions typical of any secularizing society. Challenges to the role that religion played in everyday life were not a complete novelty for the Jews of the Russian Empire and did not suddenly materialize with Lenin's rise to power. The socioeconomic and political crises that cyclically shook the Jewish communities of tsarist Russia often set off waves of criticism of religious authorities. For instance, the 1827 conscription decree, which made Jews liable for military service, unleashed unprecedented strains between Jews of different socioeconomic backgrounds, insofar as sons of destitute families were more likely to be drafted. These strains elicited the ensuing criticism of the religious elites, supposedly on the side of the community's leaders. Similarly, the emergence of nationally and socially inspired secular Jewish movements and parties during the late nineteenth and early twentieth centuries sanctioned the opposition to the status quo, which went hand in hand with rebuking religious authorities and religious practice.[4] The tsarist state intermittently intervened to settle these internal conflicts, at times promoting secularizing tendencies within the communities, usually supporting or snubbing religious authorities. Overall, the process of secularization had made significant inroads in the life of the Jewish communities of eastern Europe during the nineteenth and early twentieth centuries.

But never before and nowhere else did the state become so invested in hastening the waning of religious life and the demise of religious authorities as it did in the Soviet lands. Compared to the Jews of neighboring interwar Poland or of the United States, the Jews in the Soviet Union experienced a uniquely violent and sweeping push to secularize and conform to general communist practices. Of course, Polish and American Jews experienced secularization as well, but it was not promoted or enforced by the state. Many Polish Jews might have, for example, adopted the practice of selling and buying tickets for cultural events near the entrance of synagogues, on the holy Sabbath, in front of scandalized rabbis.[5] But state authorities did not encourage, discourage, or mandate this practice. They regarded it as none of their business. In the Soviet Union, on the other hand, the unrelenting propaganda and terror devices employed by the state boosted the drive toward secularization and the decline in religious observance.

Under Soviet pressure, the tensions between Jewish religious authorities and the Jewish population grew dramatically. The pressure elicited an unusually rapid shift toward a mostly secular and ethnic-based identity, thus altering the dominant prerevolutionary relationship existing between religion and ethnicity among Jews. If most Jews living in the Russian Empire had typically experienced religion and ethnic identity as harmoniously intersecting and overlapping phenomena, in the Soviet context, more than elsewhere in eastern Europe, Jewish ethnicity came to divorce itself from Judaism. The process unfolded not without difficulties and challenges: not only were religious practices and customs deeply embedded in Jewish life, but religion in general represented a fundamental legal and cultural category in the Russian confessional state.[6] Doing away with it entailed some effort on the part of Jews. Eventually, however, Soviet political and cultural pressures spurred the rejection of many aspects of religious life, intensifying generational conflicts between those Jews who wished to embrace the Soviet integrationist option and their parents. While these pressures and their ensuing consequences began to slowly crystallize also in Soviet Central Asia and in the Caucasus, during the 1920s they remained mostly circumscribed to and particularly intense within the urban centers of European Soviet territories.

The success with which Soviet authorities managed to enforce onto society the campaigns against religion depended on the regime's immediate priorities. First, the state never singled out for persecution Jewish religious institutions and clergy during the 1920s but rather equally oppressed Christianity, Islam, and Judaism. Orthodox Christianity may have been identified as the primary source of counterrevolutionary thinking and behavior, as well as a potential political threat to the Bolshevik system given the strong relationship between the tsar and the church that existed in imperial Russia; after all, the tsar was the head of the Orthodox Church.[7]

Second, the ways in which Soviet citizens (Jews and non-Jews alike) experienced the war on religion varied significantly according to an array of factors. Geographic location and whether they lived in a metropolis, in a small town or village, or in an agricultural settlement marked their experience of and response to the antireligion campaigns. The ways in which Soviet citizens experienced the war on religion also differed based on gender, age, and class. On the Jewish street, for instance, many exhibited a notable degree of resilience, as they endured the attack on Judaism and its institutions with ingenuity and persistence. While their resilience did not counter the Bolsheviks' ultimate intent to uproot religious rituals and customs, it remains a powerful indication of the degree of agency that many Soviet citizens retained in the midst of persecution. Their ability to accommodate to the new system, while exploiting its language and mind-set in order to safeguard religious life, remains impressive.

Conversely, many on the Jewish street responded to the war on religion with enthusiasm, while others chose to actively repudiate Judaism out of conformity. Some, like the young activist in Ehrenburg's novel, participated zealously in the campaigns against religion out of belief. Others were more cognizant of the reasons for their activism than Levka appeared to be and were eager to humiliate their parents for their religious observance. While many partook in the propaganda efforts out of political and ideological convictions, for others the participation in the attack on Judaism stemmed from their socioeconomic background and was pragmatic in nature. Working for the state to destroy Judaism could serve as an outlet for careerism. To be sure, the state relied on Jewish "godless activists" to persecute Judaism. It actively sought out their participation in order to anticipate and circumvent any complaints about antisemitism both from within the Soviet Union and from abroad, as Jewish communities around the world observed the Bolshevik war against religion with great unease.

"Let Us Deal a Crushing Blow to Religion!"

The Bolsheviks held religious beliefs, institutions, and leaders responsible for preventing the masses from becoming aware of class structures and oppression. Consequently, religion represented an insurmountable impediment to the success of the revolution. As early as 1908, Lenin identified the elimination of religion in favor of atheism and materialism as a fundamental ideological goal of the new communist state that would eventually emerge.[8] But if according to Marxist theory, social change would eventually force religion to disappear, Lenin saw the active pursuit of its eradication as a crucial step toward molding the new Soviet person. Predictably, thus, in the very midst of the turbulent years of the civil war, as the Red Army fought to gain control over the territories occupied by the Polish army and General Denikin's White forces, the Soviets launched their campaigns to tear down the hated prerevolutionary legacies. Religion, in its institutional essence as well as in its cultural and spiritual core, represented one of the most dangerous legacies of prerevolutionary Russia and as such was perceived as a real mortal enemy for the Soviets.

In January 1918, the Bolsheviks issued a decree on the separation of church and state, which declared Russia a fully secular state. The decree denied religious institutions the same legal standing they enjoyed before the revolution, declaring that all civil acts could be performed exclusively by the civic authorities in charge of the department for the registration of marriages and births, certifying that church and religious societies had no right to own property, and forbidding the instruction of religion outside the home.[9] Soviet law declared religion to be a matter of the citizen's personal conscience only, something that had no bearing whatsoever on public life. A second decree, issued in July 1918, denied the full rights of citizenship to the clergy of all faiths, who were identified as exploiters alongside capitalists, merchants, and former members of the tsarist police.[10] These decrees set the stage for years of violent confrontations between the state and its citizens, which began with the arrest of religious leaders, who were ipso facto accused of supporting the counterrevolution.

The Russian Orthodox Church and its leadership instantly turned into public enemy number one. Many members of the Orthodox clergy had openly sided with the counterrevolution and shown public support of the White forces against the Bolsheviks. Furthermore, because of the Orthodox Church's symbiotic relationship with the tsar, it constituted an obvious adversary and target in the war against the ancien régime. Thousands of bishops, priests, and believers were put to death or sent to concentration camps during the Red Terror, the campaign of political repression and executions launched by the Bolsheviks in September 1918.[11] And even though politically it was easier to direct the antireligious struggle against the leadership of the Orthodox Church, communist authorities applied the principle of equality in persecuting all clergy. According to one account, after executing a group of Orthodox priests in Kyiv, the Bolsheviks put to death a number of rabbis the following day, in the name of equality.[12]

The violence did not come to an end in 1921. Fearing that the moderation of the NEP would boost religious life and institutions, which it did, the Soviet state intensified the antireligious campaign throughout its territories. In March 1921, during the same Party congress that approved the NEP policies, the Soviets countered the liberalization of the mixed economy with a legislative measure about propaganda and agitation work involving the struggle against religion. Extensive financial and material resources were allocated to carry out widescale antireligious propaganda and agitation among the citizens of the new state, through lectures, pamphlets, booklets, museums, processions, movies, and plays. Antireligious propaganda became a key component of the "cultural front," the regime's project of cultural transformation of the 1920s.[13] While the intensity and perseverance with which the Party tackled the struggle against religion throughout the 1920s varied from place to place and from year to year, the elimination of existing religious institutions and the triumph of state atheism remained constant priorities on the regime's agenda.

"Down with the Rabbis!"

In 1922, Lenin, from his dacha, would ask to be informed "on a daily basis" how many priests had been shot.[14] On the Jewish street, it was the rabbis who were singled out for persecution and discrimination. The "godless activists" who worked among the Jewish masses justified their actions by emphasizing the rabbis' "faithful service" and abhorrent allegiance to the tsar. Available to the Soviets after 1917, the tsarist secret police archives revealed, for example, that in the town of Orlov, in the Kirov oblast, Rabbi Katzenelson "actually worked as an informant for the Okhrana, the tsarist secret police"; that at the time of the 1905 Russian Revolution, the rabbi of Skvir, in the Kyiv *guberniia*, disclosed to the tsarist police the names of Jewish revolutionaries, who were eventually arrested; that the chief rabbi of Lodz, Rabbi Maisel, received the prestigious "golden sword" from tsarist authorities because he helped the police pursue Jewish workers who were linked to the revolutionary movement.[15] For the Soviets, the strongest evidence of the fact that rabbis, not unlike all other clergy members, served the world bourgeoisie was the blessing for the tsar, a prayer held on behalf of the monarch and his family in most synagogues until the revolution.[16] In fact, prayers in support of the ruling authorities constituted a very old tradition of praying for the welfare of the government, which was practiced by Jewish communities not only in imperial Russia but throughout Europe and beyond.

Furthermore, to demonstrate the existence of the clergy's united front, "godless activists" in charge of the antireligious agitation underscored instances of collaboration between Christian and Jewish religious leaders. In the second half of the 1920s, in the Russian city of Smolensk, the local Orthodox priest cosigned the petition by religious Jews opposing the local authorities' requisition of one of the city's synagogues. One of the priorities in the campaigns against religion was the expropriation of buildings (and other property) of religious institutions in order to turn them into communist spaces. In Moscow, the second Baptist community occasionally shared its building with religious Jews who no longer had access to their synagogue.[17] Rabbis were not only accused of being closely involved with the ideologically repulsive, yet tolerated, entrepreneurial activities of the NEP years. They were also depicted as degenerate miracle workers who competed with modern Soviet hospitals and doctors in curing the sick.[18] One of the most outspoken warriors for the preservation of Judaism in the Soviet Union of the 1920s, the Lubavitcher rebbe, Rabbi Yosef Yitzchak Schneersohn, who helped establish underground Jewish educational institutions in numerous Soviet cities, was disdained by the Bolsheviks as a shaman.[19]

But not all rabbis opposed Soviet power. While the so-called Bolshevik rabbi, Avrom Yankev Zhitnik, might have been an exception, it is worth mentioning him. Born in 1890 in a small shtetl in the Zhytomyr province, Zhitnik grew up in a Hasidic family. During the civil war, he moved to Kyiv, where he hailed the Bolshevik Revolution as the triumph of the poor and the oppressed over the wealthy and exploitative and saw October as the upheaval that would put an end to corruption in the Jewish community. When in 1918 the Red Army occupied Kyiv, Rabbi Zhitnik organized a "Council of Jewish Workers," which took over the offices of the local Jewish community, smashing and wrecking them.[20] In 1919, when the Whites, who had returned to Kyiv, fled and the Bolsheviks took back the city, the "Red Rabbi" established an organization called SETMAS, or the Union of the Jewish Working Masses (Soiuz evreiskikh trudiashchikhsia mass), which provided assistance to Jewish religious workers and artisans. Through the de facto support of the Soviet government, SETMAS distributed kosher meat, matzah, and other religious items to impoverished religious Jews, while spreading among them the idea of class struggle and social justice.[21] As a champion of Marxism and Soviet power, Zhitnik shaved his sidelocks and moved to Moscow, where he began to publish two newspapers to disseminate the anticapitalist message to indigent religious Jews and made plans to establish artels and agricultural communes.[22] In 1921, SETMAS was eventually closed down on the initiative of Evsektsiia, which saw the organization led by a rabbi as a threat to its rule on the Jewish street. Zhitnik managed to reach the United States, where he continued to serve as a radical rabbi in Chicago, under the name Z. Abrams.

While Ehrenburg's Levka the hairdresser carried out antireligious propaganda only nonchalantly and might have been enticed to do so merely because of monetary compensation, many Jewish "godless activists" tyrannized the rabbis with passion and initiative. This was true in particular for those activists with a suspicious prerevolutionary past. Many of them were former members of Jewish socialist parties, in particular the Bund, who had advocated for atheism and opposed religious leaders even before they joined the Evsektsiia or other Soviet Jewish organizations. In the early 1920s, they participated in the campaign against Judaism to prove their loyalty to the Bolshevik cause and avoid being branded bourgeois or even being purged from the Party. The pressure to pursue the war against religion with greater decisiveness also came from without. In some instances, non-Jewish communists reprimanded Evsektsiia activists for failing to do enough to uproot Judaism.[23] In turn, Jewish activists, often insecure in their new position of leadership and authority, would put their foot down on the accelerator.

During the earlier stages of the 1920s campaign against religion, several rabbis openly challenged communist activists. After all, according to paragraph 4 of the 1924 Soviet Constitution, antireligious and religious propaganda were equally permitted.[24] But this consent pertained only to the theoretical realm and had very little to do with Soviet reality. In many instances, the conflict between religious leaders and Jewish communist true believers turned into something akin to a civil war on the Jewish street, which was not devoid of public attacks and even clashes. When Jewish communists launched the campaign to close down and requisition synagogue and heder buildings and turn them into factories, clubs, dorms, and dining halls, some rabbis openly protested. Rabbi Mordekhai Barishanskii, who had served as rabbi in a large congregation in the Belorussian city of Homyel for thirty years, was one of them.[25]

In mid-1922, Rabbi Barishanskii actively protested the Evsektsiia's verdict—endorsed by the Commissariat of Education of Belorussia—to close down heders and yeshivas, branding them anti-Soviet institutions. Unlike synagogues, heders and yeshivas were effectively outlawed by the 1918 law separating church from school. Acting on the Soviet People's Commissars decree on the separation of church and state, the Homyel Provincial Executive Committee proclaimed that all heders and yeshivas "must be closed" and that "those who organize or study in educational institutions in which religious instruction is given, as well as those who allow . . . religious schools in their homes . . . , will be punished with the full severity of the revolutionary laws."[26] The rabbi called on local Jews to publicly reject the verdict and to participate en masse in the meeting that the Evsektsiia organized in the city theater, on the Jewish holiday of Shavuot, to "discuss" whether the heder should be closed down.[27] Led by Barishanskii, the angry crowd attacked the members of the Evsektsiia. The Jewish communists responded by summoning a group of armed young Jewish students from the local Party school. A violent clash ensued. Several people were arrested. Rabbi Barishanskii was also arrested and, alongside ten defendants, prosecuted in a grandiose, five-day public trial. This was the first criminal prosecution against Jewish religious officials, who were charged as counterrevolutionaries who had resisted the closure of the heders and yeshivas.[28] Barishanskii was eventually found guilty of plotting against the Soviet state. He was sentenced to two years in prison. Following an international uproar unleashed by the arrest, Barishanskii was pardoned, after having spent several months in prison, and in 1923, he left the country for the United States.[29] The Barishanskii case received wide coverage in the Russian- and Yiddish-language Soviet and US press. While the anticommunist press heeded this case as representative of the resilience of religious Jews in resisting the Soviets, the communist press exploited it as a propaganda instrument and underscored the threat posed by the religious leadership to the Bolshevik state. Instances of clashes and massive protests of the antireligious decrees and of the activists who implemented them were recorded throughout the cities of the Soviet Union.[30]

Rabbis were not alone in facing the war against Judaism. Ordinary residents in the Jewish neighborhoods of Soviet cities joined in the clashes with communist activists. Jewish workers, artisans, and small peddlers, most of whom were committed to some Jewish religious practices, showed their rage against the "godless activists" who confiscated their synagogues and transformed them into clubs and warehouses. In the city of Vitsyebsk, in Belorussia, angry crowds of congregants faced the Evsektsiia, in a desperate attempt to stop the confiscation of Jewish houses of prayer. Local Evsektsiia leaders responded by calling in a cavalry brigade to seize religious property.[31] When in mid-1922 a group of Jewish communists took over the building of the Minsk Talmud-Torah, the traditional Jewish school established by the Jewish community in the early nineteenth century for the education of the poorest children in the city, local residents became enraged. The Jewish activists turned the building into a communist training college. Local Jews, who viewed the building as their own collective property, expressed their bitterness over the seizure of the Talmud-Torah by storming the building and disrupting classes. The "red students" tried to chase out of the "new Communist institution" the local Jews who had stepped into the building uninvited. The guardians of the "new communist space" and the guardians of the "old religious space" came to blows. Stones were thrown at the students and at the building's windows, while a large group of local residents gathered in protest, shouting, "Communists are thrashing children!" With the intervention of the authorities, the restless crowd eventually dispersed.[32]

In other instances, Jews opted for a less confrontational response and chose to petition Soviet authorities to protest the requisition of religious buildings. On April 7, 1922, in the shtetl of Uzda, in the Minsk district, the members of the local synagogue sent a petition to the Central Executive Committee of the Belorussian Communist Party requesting that the confiscated building be returned to them. They identified themselves as citizens of Uzda—workers, craftsmen, artisans, farmers, and merchants. The local union's decision to seize their synagogue and convert it into a club offended them. "We are crushed by despair . . . and shaken in the depth of our souls. . . . Our religious feeling has been offended and our grief has no limit. We've been left with one spacious synagogue only, . . . since the largest ones were destroyed [during the civil war]. Please keep in mind that among those who attend the synagogue there are many members of the working class, and that the synagogue itself does not have a bourgeois character." The petitioners also reassured Soviet authorities that they would continue to support the Bolsheviks and cooperate with the local and central government. As they noted, when the campaign for the confiscation of synagogue treasures began, they willingly opened the synagogue's doors and complied with the confiscation committee's activists. The congregants concluded, "[We call on] the sense of justice proclaimed in the Soviet Constitution, the justice inscribed in the glorious pages of our revolution, and the . . . pledge of the Soviet government not to interfere in the religious matters of citizens professing a religion. Appealing to that sense of justice, . . . we hope that . . . our request will be granted . . . so that, once again, an act of social justice will be performed." There were 379 shtetl residents who signed the petition. They did so as "religious proletarians."[33] In a system that valued most of all a proletarian social background, they were defining themselves as Soviet workers, who happened to be religious Jews. While we do not know the outcome of the petition, it is noteworthy that the shtetl residents took on the identity of Soviet workers: to appease the system, they emphasized their political allegiance to the new state and their proletarian background as parishioners.

Keeping the Sabbath and Other Jewish Holidays

When it came to certain aspects of Judaism, Jewish workers backed the rabbis in their attempt to preserve religious life. As members of the proletariat, they were expected to publicly display their loyalty to the state and Communist Party, while openly renouncing religious practices and authorities. Many Jewish workers did not attend synagogue services regularly, if at all. Others observed some religious practices, especially those rituals that were more deeply entrenched in their families' cultural habits or that were considered essential in the social environment in which they lived. The reluctance to work on the Sabbath, the Jewish traditional day of rest, and the tendency to produce and consume matzah during Passover confirm that the public display of devotion to communism by many Jewish workers was far from ideal. For most of the 1920s, keeping to religious traditions won out over the demands of the state.

In the early twentieth century, in the cities and towns of the Pale of Settlement, most Jews did not work on the Sabbath. But not everyone went to synagogue on that day, nor were they strict Sabbath observers. In 1909, a Jewish journalist described Sabbath observance in the Pale of Settlement as follows: "in nearly all cities, Jewish shops were closed on the Sabbath, but most Jews did not go to synagogue; in Odessa, Jewish shops were actually open on Saturdays, and Yiddish theaters performed on Saturday afternoon in Warsaw and Vilna."[34] Yet, whether the Sabbath was linked to religious observance or not, it represented an essential element of self-identification for a large segment of the Jewish proletariat. For the families of many Jewish workers and artisans, the Sabbath exemplified a crucial marker of ethnic and cultural identity and continued to do so during the 1920s.

Therefore, under the Soviets, many members of the Jewish proletariat opposed transferring the day of rest from Saturday to Sunday. The workers argued that to abolish the Sabbath meant to discriminate against Jews. After all, Sunday was the Christian day of rest, which too had a religious origin. When in September 1921 the workers of the heavily Jewish tobacco factory in Minsk met to discuss the ways in which they could make their contribution to the welfare campaign "A Week to Help the Hungry," the Party-cell leaders proposed to organize a *subbotnik*, or a working day, on Saturday. One worker spoke in favor of the proposal, emphasizing, "indeed it is not a sin to work for the hungry on the Sabbath." She added, however, that she supported the decision "only as long as [the *subbotnik*] is not [organized on] the Sabbath before [the Jewish] New Year [i.e., Rosh Hashanah]." Another worker drew on Jewish law to oppose the *subbotnik* and stated, "It is permitted to work on the Sabbath in order to help the hungry. But only if it is unavoidable. In the present case there is nothing unavoidable. Therefore, it is perfectly possible to [help the hungry] . . . another day [i.e., not on the Sabbath]." Only ten workers out of seventy-five voted in favor of organizing a *subbotnik* on the Sabbath.[35]

In a city like Minsk, which had a large Jewish population, most factories and workshops with a sizable proportion of Jewish workers remained closed on Saturday until 1923. In March of that year, the authorities launched a campaign against the Sabbath: nearly all state enterprises, even those that employed almost exclusively Jewish workers, introduced Sunday as the official day of rest.[36] Despite the shift to the Sunday rest, however, in many workers' collectives, which operated independently from the state and where Jews constituted 50 percent of the workforce, on Friday Jewish employees usually left the workplace two hours before the onset of the Sabbath. They generally rested on Saturday and worked on Sunday. Those who chose to work on the Sabbath were apparently the exception rather than the rule.[37] In private enterprises, some Jewish employees rested on Saturday morning to attend synagogue for Sabbath services, and most of them refrained from working because of the sociocultural norms ingrained in the milieu in which they lived rather than out of commitment to religious observance. They considered not working on the Sabbath a custom, a cultural convention, not a religious obligation.[38] In a Jewish city like Berdychiv, for example, Jewish workers employed in state-owned factories accepted the Soviet norm to shift from Sunday to Saturday as the day of work, and thus to adjust to the "general proletarian calendar," only in 1924.[39] It took some time on the part of state authorities to systematically and successfully implement these changes throughout the towns and cities with a large Jewish population.

There was a notable difference with regard to Sabbath observance between larger urban centers and smaller towns. As a visitor from the United States to the Soviet Union reported in the early 1920s, Saturday was the day of rest throughout the colonies in Crimea and Ukraine. He noted, "I met several young men in Simferopol who were representing a Homyel collective [farm]. They seemed to be modern men of the world, yet they would not ride on the Sabbath. They had decided, they said, to begin their new life by abstaining from work on the Jewish day of rest." The visitor also mentioned, "In some of the settlements they have a Sefer Torah, and almost everywhere a minyan is convened on the Sabbath," and he admitted that while the state forbade the teaching of religion to minors, it might have been easier to circumvent this law in the colonies than in the cities.[40] While traveling through the Jewish colonies of Crimea and Kherson in 1926, the artist Issachar Rybak—a major figure in the Jewish art renaissance, who was born in Ukraine and became a prominent member of the Russian and Jewish avant-garde movement first in Kyiv, then in Moscow, and eventually in Paris—noticed how on the Sabbath, Jewish farmers would stop working in the field if it rained and would pray and then return to work "as soon as the sun came out."[41]

The US-based Yiddish writer Peretz Hirschbein visited Jewish colonies and shtetls during his travels through the Soviet Union and confirmed the influence that geography and Jewish population density exerted on religious practice. Hirschbein remarked that as late as 1928, Saturday rather than Sunday continued to be kept as the day off in most Jewish towns and colonies. In particular, the agricultural settlements that enjoyed the support of Western sponsors such as the Agro-Joint were reluctant to implement some of the harsher antireligious restrictions, fearing to turn away American donors.[42] In some shtetls, some employers allowed Jewish employees to take off the Sabbath but only if they managed to keep quiet about it.[43] As late as September 1929, the Moscow Yiddish publication *Der emes* reported that the town of Kapulye had become the first shtetl to shift the day off from Saturday to Sunday.[44]

The Lubavitcher rebbe, Yosef Yitshak Schneersohn, who left the Soviet Union for Riga in 1927, expressed his deep concern over keeping the Sabbath under the Soviets. But he also offered a creative—even if somewhat naïve—solution to preserve the keeping of the Sabbath. In April 1928, he sent a memorandum to the American Jewish scholar Cyrus Adler, urging the JDC to fund artisans' workshops as a way of guaranteeing the continuation of religious practice among Soviet Jews. According to Schneersohn, it was preferable to support handicraft in lieu of resettlement on land, due primarily to the location of the agricultural colonies. The latter were too far removed from the larger Jewish demographic centers and from any Jewish institution that might have still existed there. Conversely, the support of artisans and craftsmen (*kustary*) would rescue the Jewish small towns, where synagogues already existed, thereby strengthening the religious life of the Jewish family. As Schneersohn conveyed to Adler, perhaps with excessive optimism, "The handicraft requires the participation of the whole family, working together. . . . The son and daughter remain in the family and do not want to go to the Komsomol where they get lost to Judaism."

However, Schneersohn was indeed correct in arguing that the sanctification of the Sabbath (*shmires shabbos*) was more likely within the context of small artisan workshops, which, as we have seen, thrived under the liberal policies of the NEP. Here, work could be performed any time of the day, from home, and was therefore not subject to the official changes in shifting the day of rest from Saturday to Sunday. Schneersohn's plan entailed collecting funds through the JDC to establish, in a number of small towns in Ukraine and Belorussia, workshops for hosiery, tinware, and shoemaking. Each workshop would register a maximum of one hundred artisans. Such enterprises, argued Schneersohn, "would be suited to keep the Sabbath and preserve religious life."[45] His strategy would eventually reach an impasse and clash with the push to industrialize the country and drive artisans into large factories, launched in 1928 by Stalin's First Five-Year Plan to expand the country's heavy industry and steel production and catch up with the more advanced capitalist countries.

During the 1920s, keeping major Jewish holidays remained rather widespread among Jewish workers. With some regional differences, not working and resting on Jewish religious holidays was guaranteed by Soviet law. For instance, in the summer of 1923, the Belorussian People's Commissariat of Labor issued a resolution granting Jewish workers the right to stay home on specific religious holidays. The officially recognized "days of rest for workers and employees of the Jewish faith, employed in state and private businesses," included two days for Rosh Hashanah, one day for Yom Kippur and Sukkot, three days for Passover, and two for Shavuot. Of course, the resolution guaranteed the aforementioned days of rest as long as "the [workers'] absence did not interfere with the regular work productivity."[46] The Belorussian Commissariat of Labor was simply formalizing a preexistent situation. In most factories, small workshops, and state enterprises located in the cities and towns of the former Pale of Settlement, Jewish and non-Jewish workers rested on major religious holidays. In 1923, for example, it could happen that a Jewish communist newspaper—namely, an official organ funded by the state—would not be issued on a Jewish holiday (by contrast, American Jewish socialist publications at the time, like the *Forverts*, did appear on such days). Needless to say, the editors and journalists who contributed to the Soviet publications did not observe the Jewish holiday; but many of the workers in the print shop that issued the newspaper almost certainly did.

The social pressure to desist from keeping Jewish holidays and to go to work instead weighed heavily on Jewish workers, especially in larger cities within the setting of the state factory. When a worker employed in the factory of a larger city decided to rest on a Jewish holiday, his fellow workers and factory managers, Jews and non-Jews alike, could regard his behavior as a deviation from Soviet norms. The worker himself might then realize that "religious behavior" clashed with the expectations of state authorities and Party leaders and could therefore thwart his prospects for a successful career in Soviet society. Over time, the social pressure and the intensity of the Sovietization process produced a plunge in absences from the factory due to Jewish holidays. And yet, we can certainly assume that many of those who, for instance, attended synagogue on the holiday of Yom Kippur in 1928 belonged to the working class. According to one account, the twelve existing synagogues in Moscow that year were at full capacity during the holiday. At the time of the Kol Nidre prayer, which opens the Yom Kippur prayers before sundown, hundreds of people could not enter the large Moscow Choral Synagogue but had to stand on the building's stairway or listen from the street.[47]

Resilience and Strategies of Rabbinic Leaders

Soviet publications applauded the ongoing arrest of rabbis. In the fall of 1923, a special issue titled *Der apikoyres* (The freethinker), dedicated to the struggle against the celebration of Jewish holidays, appeared in Kyiv. The publication included a short story to be performed by Jewish activists in clubs and schools across Ukraine. Titled "The Black Rabbi or the Hellish Fire" ("Der shvartser rov oder di helishe sreyfe"), the story took place in a shtetl where the good Soviet policeman arrested the bad rabbi for breaking the law and engaging in economic exploitation. The rabbi's wife ran through the shtetl's streets protesting the arrest and comparing it to the Beilis affair, the notorious 1913 trial in Kyiv of Menachem Beilis, who was falsely accused of the ritual murder of a Ukrainian boy. The short vignette concluded with the generational conflict between the rabbi and his son: once he was released from prison, the rabbi directed his son Hershl to spy on the enemies by pretending to be a member of the Komsomol. In the end, and in tune with the imparted message of the Soviet victory over religion, the young Hershl joined the other side and became a true member of the Communist Youth League.[48] An excerpt from a poem by the Yiddish writer Leyb Kvitko—who at the time lived in Germany and was a member of the German Communist Party—concluded the vignette. It underscored the generational nature of the antireligious war on the Jewish street: "We've already come to blows with our fathers. . . . Now we can burn down the old rags." The drawing accompanying the excerpt depicts a rabbi in distress over the destruction of the synagogue's dome, the Torah scrolls, and the candelabrum; holding a book, a young Komsomol member smiles in defiance to the rabbi and shows him the new Soviet path, pointing at the synagogue's building turned into a workers' club.[49]

By the end of the 1920s, hundreds of rabbis were either arrested or forced to leave the country. In 1914, there were 1,059 rabbis in Ukraine; in 1927, there were 830.[50] Many rabbis resigned from their position; some did so publicly, denouncing their title of religious leaders in the press, while others acted quietly. Most feared the dangers and repercussions connected to serving in such positions, not only for themselves but also for their families. During the 1920s, one rabbinic figure in particular stood out for his notable resilience and astute strategies to counter the antireligious decrees.

Rabbi Schneersohn was the leader of the Chabad-Lubavitch movement in the Soviet territories. While it had been the largest Hasidic group in imperial Russia, it is unlikely that the majority of Jews who were committed to some form of religious practice in the Soviet Union identified with the movement and its strict adherence to Judaism. However, because of the specific dynamics in place under the Soviets, which prompted major rabbinic leaders to emigrate to Poland or the Land of Israel, Schneersohn was able to rise to a position of prominence. The sudden creation of a leadership vacuum, in combination with his decision to stay and fight, turned Schneersohn into the key figure for the preservation of Judaism during the 1920s.[51]

In 1922, Schneersohn established the Committee of Rabbis of the USSR, a highly centralized (and illegal) organization to support Judaism throughout the Soviet territories: it funded heders and yeshivas, which were closed down by the Soviets in 1922; it distributed prayerbooks and Hebrew Bibles to communities in need; and it trained rabbis and other religious personnel such as *shokhtim*, ritual slaughterers, who faced constant harassment on the part of authorities.[52] To do this, Schneersohn relied on a network of hundreds of faithful followers who eagerly heeded his word and promoted the struggle to preserve Jewish religious life. Furthermore, he counted on funding from different Jewish aid organizations, including the American JDC, the French Alliance Israélite Universelle, and the German Hilfsverein der Deutschen Juden.[53]

As chairman of the Committee of Rabbis, one of Schneersohn's foremost goals was to defy the Soviet attempt to cut off the younger generations from Judaism by forcibly closing down religious schools. At least one thousand heders were liquidated in 1922–1923 alone.[54] The committee made funding underground religious schools and providing support to its teachers, the *melamdim* (religious teachers), an absolute priority. And while it is hard to measure the success and long-term effect of Rabbi Schneersohn's effort and strategy, the available data show significant accomplishment. In 1928, the Committee of Rabbis funded underground heders in sixty-six towns and cities (which enrolled 8,700 children) and underground yeshivas in eighteen towns and cities (with 468 students enrolled).[55]

To circumvent some of the restrictions imposed by the Evsektsiia on Jewish life in the European territories of the Soviet Union, Rabbi Schneersohn promoted the establishment of underground religious institutions in Central Asia as well. Here, at least during the early 1920s, the Soviets were more careful and less forceful in uprooting religion and destroying religious institutions as a way of easing in Sovietization with caution.[56] Hence, the possibility to preserve Judaism and fund heders and yeshivas may have been greater. In Tashkent, for instance, the students in the Bukharan Jewish Teachers' seminary, founded in 1920 to train the teachers of the Bukharan Jewish educational network during the 1920s, were served kosher food.[57] Schneersohn dispatched his emissaries primarily to Samarkand, in Uzbekistan, and Kutaisi, in Georgia.[58] Over the course of 1926, 1927, and 1928, he sent to Samarkand one of his leading followers, Rabbi Simha Gorodetskii, who worked with great enthusiasm to preserve Judaism among Bukharan Jews.[59]

Rabbi Schneersohn and his network of activists faced ongoing harassment and intimidation. In 1921, the authorities raided his home in Rostov, in southern Russia, the city to which his family had fled at the beginning of World War I; they confiscated his belongings, closed the Lubavitch Tomchei Temimim yeshiva in Rostov, and arrested its staff.[60] In 1924, he was forced to move from Rostov to Leningrad, where he continued his counteroffensive on the war on Judaism. In 1927, he was arrested in Moscow for counterrevolutionary activities, namely, for collecting funds to maintain Jewish religious institutions, but released shortly thereafter following an international protest. He eventually resettled in Riga, Latvia, and from there continued to promote his strategies and encourage resilience among his followers in the towns and cities of the Soviet Union.[61]

A Woman's Rage, *Der kas fun a yidene*: Women in the Antireligious Campaigns

Jewish women too could show an unusual degree of dedication in the campaign to destroy Judaism. A former prominent Bundist and the only woman leader in the Evsektsiia, Ester Frumkin became a prime mover in the systematic antireligious propaganda as she trailblazed the struggle to uproot Judaism. She was among the first activists to set foot in the Great Choral Synagogue in Minsk to seize the building and turn it into a workers' club. On the face of it, she was not concerned about the fact that the onslaught on Judaism could elicit the fear of antisemitism and violence among the Jewish masses. In light of the extraordinary degree of destruction suffered during the civil war, when synagogues had been extensively looted and destroyed, the attack on Jewish religious institutions and leaders could be interpreted by Jews as a new wave of pogroms. But Frumkin had other priorities, or rather her concern was expressed differently. By attacking religious Judaism, she was actually trying to defend Jews against the slander of Judeo-Bolshevism.

In 1922, she wrote one of the most ferocious pamphlets against Judaism to appear in the context of the Bolshevik assault on religion. Published in Russian in 1923, *Doloi ravvinov!*, or *Down with the Rabbis!*, appeared in two editions. What stands out in this text is the resentment and the fierce rhetoric. While largely understudied, women's active participation in the antiauthoritarian anger that was channeled against all vestiges of the ancien régime should not be surprising.[62] In the new socialist state, women were not immune to the rage. Zlata Litvakova, for example, sister of Moshe Litvakov, one of major players in the communist Jewish camp, was an eager participant in the confiscation of Hebrew books preserved in the Jewish libraries across the cities and towns of Ukraine. Apparently, on one occasion, Litvakova, who had joined the Ukrainian Executive Committee of the Evsektsiia, discovered that a Jewish library in Kharkiv was secretly hiding books in Hebrew; she flew into a rage and ordered the books to be burned at once.[63]

In *Down with the Rabbis!*, Frumkin described and celebrated what she referred to as the "war of terror" that took place on the Jewish street in the cities of Ukraine and Belorussia between religious leaders and young Jewish communists and workers. She recorded the clashes between the activists who stormed the synagogues on the day of Yom Kippur in 1922 and the believers who attacked them as the Soviet armed forces intervened to protect the Jewish commissars.[64] She wrote, "we must liquidate the heder with a death sentence" and destroy "the clerical vermin"; and she reveled in describing how in different cities, the chanting of the International welcomed the "death" of the heder and, at the same time, silenced the protesting voice of those who attempted to chant Hatikva, the as-yet-unofficial anthem of the Zionist movement. Finally, as she chronicled the arrest of Rabbi Barishanskii and of other rabbis who had shown a remarkable degree of courage in resisting the Soviets, Ester Frumkin mocked the petitions that Jews from abroad made in protest.[65] Letters were sent to the Soviet ministry of foreign affairs and to Lenin himself. In Frumkin's opinion, the rabbis should "be punished and sentenced to the concentration camp."

Frumkin's inquisitorial zeal in carrying out the war against Judaism and its leaders was driven by a combination of factors. First, as a committed Marxist, she believed that human civilization would thrive without religion. Second, the choices that Frumkin and so many others made under Bolshevism were also shaped by their pre-1917 experiences. Promoting the destruction of "bourgeois" Jewish life was a way to redeem herself from her Bundist past. Moreover, the unforgiving war was a way to wash off other sins from her pre-Soviet life, including a rumored liaison with a former rabbi that predated the revolution and occurred while she lived in exile in Astrakhan, in the city of Chernyi Iar.[66]

Compared to the rich antireligious literature produced in the Soviet Union during the 1920s, which was more often than not published in Yiddish in order to reach and educate the Jewish masses, *Down with the Rabbis!* addressed a Russian (namely, non-Jewish) audience. While Frumkin enlightened the non-Jewish readers about the peculiar practices of the Jewish religion (she explained, for example, in great detail the *kapores* ritual practiced by some Jews on the eve of Yom Kippur), she also reassured them that a ruthless civil war was taking place on the Jewish street. Frumkin actually argued that the war on the Jewish street was much more uncompromising and incisive than the one that was taking place among the Christian population against the Orthodox faith. In other words, Frumkin meant to quell the widespread notion that the Soviet state supported and protected the Jews and that the Jewish commissars shielded Judaism. Frumkin wanted to confirm the absurdity of the claim of Jewish Bolshevism, which gained credibility in the aftermath of the civil war.[67] In other words, she strove to prove that the campaigns against religion were not, as many non-Jews believed, a Jewish-Bolshevik attack on Christianity and that Jewish religious institutions and leaders were not being given preferential treatment in the Soviet war against religion.

At the same time, Frumkin nurtured some bitterness toward the religious leadership and infrastructure that survived the early 1920s: religious Jews, and Judaism in general, ultimately offered greater resistance and showed a greater ability to adapt to the regime than the Bund had. As she poignantly noted in the mid-1920s, "no Jewish socialist party . . . fought for its principles with as much vigor and devotion as these Jews wrapped in their prayer shawls."[68] This remark by the former Bundist and Jewish communist leader not only conveyed the depth of her antireligious feelings but also acknowledged the nearly accomplished defeat of Jewish political parties compared to the fairly dynamic life that Judaism retained against all odds throughout the 1920s.[69] Frumkin's attack on Judaism reminds us that while the antireligious campaigns were sanctioned by the state from above, they also retained some specific features that depended on the biographies and initiatives of those who decided to "storm the heavens."

Holy Places, Holy Spaces, Holy Warriors

The systematic confiscation of church valuables marked a crucial stage in the legislative implementation of the antireligious campaigns. The looting of churches and the confiscation of religious valuables was initially justified as a means to bring help to the victims of the terrible famine of 1921–1922, which killed an estimated five million people primarily in the Volga and Ural River regions. In fact, there is no evidence that the regime used the confiscated church valuables for famine relief. The real issue was both ideological and political.[70] Thousands of religious institutions, in particular churches and synagogues, were closed down in a sweeping attempt to cleanse the Soviet public spaces from bourgeois remnants because of their unacceptable spatial closeness to "holy" Soviet institutions, such as factories, schools, or workers' clubs. A synagogue located within walking distance of a Party institution could be shut down because it contaminated a holy Bolshevik space. The exceedingly high taxes also forced religious communities, ostensibly tolerated by the Soviets, to renounce their agreements with local authorities and to close down.[71]

Jews and non-Jews alike strove to quickly learn how to "speak Bolshevik."[72] The hope was that speaking the jargon of the new power structures would guarantee some agency in implementing the reorganization of society. Whether Soviet citizens believed it or not, they appealed to Soviet authorities using categories of speech that they hoped would be successful in facing the struggle on the antireligious front. We have hundreds of petitions that Soviet citizens addressed at this time (and later) to Soviet authorities in response to this campaign. While the petitions to reopen heders and yeshivas were ignored, some petitions asking to return to the Jews of that city or town the synagogue building or the *mikveh*, the bath used for ritual immersion, were indeed successful, as the Evsektsiia activists were bypassed, at least temporarily.

Replacing the traditional holiness of religious places and acts with a new form of Bolshevik holiness entailed not only taking over religious institutions but also occupying the streets and other public spaces in an open display of antireligion in action. Carnival-like processions of students and working-class youth singing the International and burning images of religious "cult" figures took place in major Soviet cities. In Kyiv, the so-called anti–High Holiday committee, established ad hoc in 1923, organized "massive entertainment" on the first night of Rosh Hashanah. These shows, which resembled the anti–Yom Kippur ceremonies that Jewish anarchists organized decades earlier in North America and England, took place in the workers' club in the historic Jewish neighborhood of Podil; they featured some of "the best concerts and drama artists in the city."[73] In lieu of *tashlekh* (a ritual performed during Rosh Hashanah during which the worshipers symbolically throw their sins into a source of water), the committee organized "exciting excursions by boat along the river Dnipro."[74] To undermine religious customs, at the time of the High Holidays, the Jewish theater collective of Berdychiv performed the play *Reyzele dem rebns* (Reyzele, the rabbi's daughter) in the city theater.[75] The play was about the children liberated from the yoke of the heder and the brutal *melamed*; and it was about Reyzele, who fled her father's home, scoffed at the traditional Jewish wedding ceremony, and got married without a chuppah or a rabbi. According to a review of the play, the chorus performed beautifully the duets and the couplets.[76] Antireligious culture, argued the reviewer, could indeed aspire to attain beauty and thereby win the hearts of many people.[77]

The twelfth Congress of the Communist Party, April 17–25, 1923, temporarily broke off the first intense phase of the antireligious campaigns. The state-sponsored program to convert everyone to atheism continued, of course, but in a less violent fashion. From 1924 to 1928, the requisition process of synagogue buildings and the persecution of Jewish religious leaders slowed in pace. In Berdychiv, for instance, a dozen synagogues had been closed down after the revolution, but by 1928, over fifty other synagogues still functioned in the city.[78] The relatively moderate oppression of Judaism made possible the thriving of underground religious education and institutions, with a growing number of students who secretly enrolled in heders and yeshivas.[79] When the Polish-born Yiddish writer Joseph Opatoshu, who had moved to the United States in 1907, visited the Soviet Union in 1928, he met with children who attended a regular school during the morning—some of them were members of the communist organization Young Pioneers—and attended one of the local heders during the afternoon. The heder operated illegally, although "everyone, including the authorities, knew about its existence."[80] During the 1920s, the largest underground yeshiva in the Soviet Union operated in Minsk, with the impressive number of seventy students.[81]

At the same time, the establishment in 1925 of the League of Militant Atheists, a new public body created by the Party to lead the struggle and to actively promote atheism throughout the Soviet Union, helped retain the vigor of the war against religion through fierce rhetoric and by enticing young activists. On the initiative of the prominent Bolshevik Emilyan Yaroslavski, born Minei Izrailevich Gubelman, a national organization of atheists was created with the formation of a Society of Friends of the Newspaper *Bezbozhnik*, or "The Godless." In April 1925, a congress of *Bezbozhnik* correspondents and society members met in Moscow to establish the League of Militant Atheists. Aside from publishing newspapers and journals, the league funded museums of atheism, antireligious exhibitions, and radio lectures. Antireligious campaigns were carried out systematically and integrated within Soviet institutions, with antireligious corners appearing in every school and antireligious wall newspapers adorning the walls of every factory.

In mid-1926, an article in a wall newspaper from one of the factories in the city of Barysaw, in Belorussia, recorded a Party meeting organized for women.[82] Written by one Dina, the account of the Party meeting focused primarily on the ritual of circumcision. The practice was discussed in detail and criticized in a very simplistic and didactic fashion so as to be accessible to all the Jewish women workers in the factory, with the assumption that they were not as educated as men and were more likely to be under the spell of religious observance: "'Why are communists against circumcision?' asked the wife of comrade Dinershtein. 'Because many years ago Jews and Muslims lived in very warm countries.'" Someone then proceeded to give a medical explanation linked to hygiene to explain the practice and continued by stating, "Now that Jews live in less warm countries, circumcision is a purely religious ritual. . . . [Moreover] it is unhealthy to draw so much blood from the newborn baby." The edifying conclusion noted, "if circumcision was indeed necessary, then not only Jews would perform it but other nationalities as well."[83]

Despite a nominal membership of thousands, the League of Militant Atheists, which promoted the creation of antireligious displays and wall newspapers in the second part of the 1920s, was "largely a house of cards—a nationwide Potemkin village of atheism."[84] Moreover, its campaigns concentrated mostly on criticizing and attacking the institutions of belief, the clergy, and religious holidays, instead of really engaging with the promotion of atheism. In other words, it was more about destroying, closing down, persecuting, and abolishing rather than any successful persuasion of the masses. Finally, although in the beginning many experienced activists participated in the campaigns, by the mid-1920s few "godless cadres" had the appropriate training to lead such campaigns. Most of them became involved in the campaigns as a gateway to socioeconomic and political mobility. In the city of Berdychiv, for example, at the time of Easter and Passover, a "godless activist" delivered his antireligious lecture "trying to prove that Jews really use Christian blood for Passover."[85] He presented ritual murder as a fact. In other words, the activist, who was supposed to enlighten the backward religious masses, actually believed that Jews needed Christian blood for ritual purposes. For this very reason, he encouraged respectable Soviet citizens to reject both Easter and Passover.[86]

Cultural Wars and the Soviet Jewish Woman

One Soviet publication boasted the success of the antireligious campaigns through arrogating holy spaces and creating young "godless citizens" as follows: "Most Jews prefer attending performances and events organized in clubs, rather than attend synagogue; most do not follow dietary rules and other rituals like circumcision; and most Jewish boys marry non-Jewish women."[87] Not only was this triumph largely imagined, as most Jewish families, including those whose members belonged to the Communist Party, continued, for instance, to have their newborn sons circumcised during the 1920s.[88] But the progress made in the war against religion was also conceived as successful almost exclusively among Jewish men and not Jewish women. In other words, emancipation from Judaism was described as a highly gendered phenomenon. For this very reason, activists on the Jewish street launched a special kind of war to eradicate Judaism among women and to create the New Soviet Jewish Woman.

In 1924, *Bezbozhnik u stanka* (The godless at the workplace), the most widespread antireligious publication in the Soviet Union, included in its September issue an image portraying the dangers posed by the *mikveh*.[89] Traditionally used for the purpose of ritual ablutions of women as prescribed by Jewish law, in this Soviet reading, the *mikveh* did not grant ritual purity but, rather, through the presence of repulsive germs, spread illnesses and diseases. Forced into the soiled water by two fearsome-looking older women, the young women underwent a process of physical as well as moral contamination and corruption.

It is impossible to know how many Jewish women made use of the *mikveh* for ritual ablutions during the 1920s. Together with other buildings belonging to the Jewish communities located on the Eastern Front, many *mikvehs* had been destroyed at the time of World War I and the civil war. Rabbi Schneersohn actively sought funds from American philanthropic organizations to rebuild them. In a letter he sent to Cyrus Adler, he pleaded for a subvention of $37,500 to rebuild *mikvehs* in 108 localities of the Soviet Union. To support the request, he argued that many Jews had sent letters to rabbis in different localities pleading for assistance in rebuilding the *mikvehs* or in building new ones in the Agro-Joint-sponsored Jewish colonies.[90] But regardless of how many women still wished to use the *mikveh*, in the context of the antireligious campaigns and the general push to implement new hygienic rules in society, the ritual bath appeared as an ideal target. In the eyes of the "godless activists," it became one of the symbols of how unsanitary Judaism and its rituals were.

In attacking Judaism, Soviet antireligious propaganda often singled out Jewish women: because of their alleged backwardness and distinct traditionalism, they supposedly fell prey to male religious leaders and functionaries and became the favorite audience of the rabbi, the *mohel* (who performs the ritual of circumcision), and the *shochet* (who performs ritual slaughter). This assumed backwardness and innate religiosity made Jewish women more vulnerable than Jewish men to the threats of Judaism. Liberating women from the "dark forces" of religion, drawing them to the Party, and enticing them into playing an active role in the newly established Soviet institutions became priorities for the revolution on the Jewish street.

The question of whether women were indeed more committed than men to the Jewish tradition in the Soviet Union of the 1920s appears to be a key point in any exploration of the encounter between Jewish women and the Bolshevik project. The persecution of religious elites and the disruption of religious institutions under Bolshevik rule made ritual observance all the more connected to the private sphere of the home, possibly making it more central for ritual observance than in any other time in Jewish history, with the exception perhaps of the experience of the Marranos in medieval Iberia and of the Jews sealed in the ghettos of eastern Europe during World War II. Jewish women, who might have been generally more prone to abide by religious traditions because of their long-established focus on the home and their lower level of integration into the modern workforce, came to play a renewed assertive role in the Soviet context. In the absence of prerevolutionary religious infrastructure, largely destroyed or forced underground by the mid-1920s, folk practices gained the upper hand. Folk legitimacy refashioned religious practice, bringing changes to the rituals and customs and instilling in them a degree of creativity that appears surprising in the midst of an oppressive system like the one created by the Soviets. Many Jewish women were the key agents in this process. Rabbis were hounded, vilified, and marginalized. It was the women who did the real work of preserving as they countered the violent push for secularization that made its way through the heavily Jewish cities of the former Pale of Settlement.

This new assertive role appears clearly in two spheres of religious observance: the first one relating to the circumcision ritual, and the second to the consumption of kosher meat. In the Soviet context, circumcision—condemned by the Bolsheviks as a barbarian practice—became for the first time a women's domain and liability. Men, especially if they held key positions in Soviet society, would publicly blame their wives and mothers for having their sons circumcised, while privately entrusting them with the responsibility of arranging this "new Soviet Jewish ritual." Women, who in spite of Marxist theory on gender equality were often excluded from skilled or professional employment and had limited influence on the principal institutions in the Soviet life, especially the Communist Party, had no careers to lose and could risk making arrangements with the *mohel*, who, following the tradition, would usually perform the ritual in the private sphere of the home.[91]

While the *mohel* underwent constant harassment and lived in dire conditions, the service he performed was not formally outlawed by the Soviets. The Soviets never officially banned circumcision. There were of course numerous restrictions, which varied according to local ruling and were aimed primarily at the *mohelim*. From the Soviet vantage point, *mohelim* were not doctors and should not have been performing an unnecessary medical procedure supposedly detrimental to the infant's health. When a Soviet court found that a *mohel* failed to comply with sanitary rules while carrying out the ritual, it could sentence him to imprisonment. Of course, it was entirely up to the Soviet court to define what breaking sanitary rules meant.[92]

In this specific context, the *mohel*'s religious authority was challenged in the eyes of the average Jew. His function was seen principally as medical, with the religious aspect of the ritual downplayed and the ethnic one enhanced. According to Jewish law, the commandment to circumcise the newborn falls on the father. The father usually defers the commandment to the *mohel* but must be present and recite one of the blessings. In this new Soviet Jewish ritual, the father was largely absent. It was women—wives and mothers—who replaced husbands and fathers in this traditionally all-male Jewish covenant and thus came to play a crucial role in keeping, as well as in changing, the ritual that the majority of Soviet Jews abided by in the 1920s.[93] An image reproduced in *Bezbozhnik u stanka* captured this change, portraying a stern grandmother in distress as she warned probably her son or daughter, "My grandson must be circumcised." Another image portrayed naked Pioneers being chased by women and shouting at them, "We do not want to be circumcised!"[94]

Some attempts to do away with aspects of kosher slaughtering surfaced as early as 1920, promoted at the local level. In one of the earlier decrees on kosher slaughtering that we have, dated April 28, 1920, the Soviet authorities in charge of food supplies in the city of Poltava, in central Ukraine, outlawed the Jewish method of killing the animals "by cutting their throat."[95] A number of Jews disregarded the decree; they were arrested after the police discovered kosher meat being sold at their apartment (the harsh decision should also be seen in the broader context of the scarcity of food supplies during the civil war). But the arrest and the ban were temporary: the local Jewish community immediately petitioned Soviet central authorities, who annulled the decree. While Soviet law did not forbid ritual slaughtering (just as it did not forbid circumcision), it put many obstacles in its way. With kosher slaughtering perceived by the state as a threat to the rationality of production in the meat sector, the campaign against it persisted throughout the interwar period, across the Soviet Union.

In some cities and towns, kosher meat production continued throughout the 1920s. For instance, in 1928, in Minsk, local *shochtim* were such an integral part of the food industry that when the city administration decided to reduce their wages, they responded by going on strike. The Minsk city soviet explained that the wage cut was driven by fairness: *shochtim* in Vitsyebsk, Homyel, and other Belorussian cities received 60 percent of the Minsk ritual slaughterers' salary. While the strike did not succeed and the *shochtim* eventually accepted the wage cut, the incident suggests just how lively the phenomenon of kosher meat production could be in a Soviet capital in the late 1920s. When in response to the strike many Jews in Minsk stopped buying kosher meat, fearing that it was not slaughtered according to Jewish law, the authorities issued a statement reassuring the customers that other *shochtim* from other towns had been performing ritual slaughter in lieu of the strikers. In other words, Soviet authorities guaranteed the Jewish residents of a Soviet capital that there would be no shortage of kosher meat in the city.[96]

In a memorandum to Cyrus Adler, Rabbi Schneersohn acknowledged that the problem of accessibility of kosher meat for Soviet Jews did not depend on the shortage of *shochtim* but on the fact that ritual slaughterers were not given cattle to kill; from the vantage point of Soviet authorities, ritual slaughter, while not outlawed, defied the rationalization of meat production.[97] In most towns, especially by the late 1920s, cooperatives refused to sell kosher meat, but kosher poultry was easily accessible for those who sought to purchase and consume it. Cafeterias and kosher kitchens existed in many localities. As late as summer 1929, a small restaurant located on a busy street in Moscow served kosher food.[98] The future of kosher meat production in the Soviet Union seemed so uncertain that during that same summer, a close collaborator of Schneersohn recommended (rather naïvely) requesting funds from the JDC for the following plan: "Perhaps we should suggest that American Jews . . . establish a large production center for preserved meats (in the Ural region, for instance) where cattle is available in great quantity, and by means of the preserved food supply provide kosher meat to the thousands of Jews in the many communities. . . . And with the permission from the government, the production center could be established in accordance with the latest and most modern features and in strict accordance with Kashrut. Hundreds of thousands of Jews will find a solution to their problem."[99] Of course, this plan never came to fruition.

In many localities, ritual slaughter continued informally. In the shtetl of Sharhorod, where the *shochet* was not a functionary of the community or employed in a state facility, consumption of kosher meat depended on word of mouth: "If [the *shochet*] happened to be present when an animal was slaughtered, and you happened to know about it, then you could have kosher meat."[100] Kosher meat production continued throughout the 1920s, often in a "customized" Soviet fashion. It frequently became integrated into governmental structures and facilities, such as city cooperatives and slaughterhouses. The viability of kosher meat production in Ukraine, for example, was clearly stated in a resolution passed in 1924 by the NKVD (People's Commissariat for Internal Affairs), according to which the status of *shochtim*, who were employed in state facilities, was equaled to that of skilled laborers—hence the emergence of a "proletarian *shochet*," or a Soviet Jewish ritual slaughterer. In spite of occasional challenges to the official status of *shochtim*, possibly instigated by the members of the Evsektsiia, who, in their quest to create a New Soviet Jewish Man and Woman made it their aim to uproot also ritual slaughter, the NKVD confirmed the resolution about the *shochtim*'s rights as Soviet citizens and as Soviet butchers.[101]

As a result of the state's growing meddling in issues of kosher meat production, many *shochtim* came to forge a new social identity and presented themselves as members of the proletarian labor force. Traditionally part of the secondary religious elite after the rabbis, *shochtim* held status and power in the Jewish community and were well respected for their ritual function. Under the Soviets, many *shochtim* reinvented themselves as proletarian Jewish butchers: removed from rabbinic control, they shifted their allegiance to Soviet state authorities. In February 1927, a group of *shochtim* employed in the slaughterhouse in Odesa (not a very religious city) petitioned the City Voting Committee and complained for having been mistakenly classified as *sluzhiteli kulta* (religious functionaries), deprived of voting rights and branded *lishchentsy*. In their petition, the Jewish butchers stated that this classification was incorrect and emphasized their "proletarian social identity and function in society" over their religious role. "The work performed by Jewish butchers in the slaughterhouse," they argued, "has nothing to do with the administration of religious ceremonies. . . . The difference between the *shochet* and the regular butcher should not be sought in any specific religious function, but rather in their different ability to slaughter, abide by sanitary rules of cleanliness, and carry out a veterinary inspection," continued the petitioners.[102]

In this secular explanation of the method of Jewish slaughter, the *shochet* carried out a mere act of physical work through slaughtering, as well as a professional and medical examination of the killed animal to make sure that its consumption did not pose a threat to consumers' health. Technically speaking, the *shochtim* were explaining the religious prohibition to consume animals that, upon further inspection, are found to have blemishes or lesions.[103] "There is nothing religious in this," asserted the petitioners, as they played down the blessing traditionally pronounced by the *shochet* during the slaughtering process as devoid of any meaning, even reminding Soviet authorities that mute *shochtim*, who could not say the blessing, were nevertheless allowed to slaughter according to the Jewish method and finally that *shochtim* were usually secular and did not abide by ritual laws. "[The *shochet*] is seen as a layperson, alien to all rituals," contended the petitioners, who even stated, "The Jews who purchase our meat know very well that kashrut does not stem from God, nor from the holy person of the *shochet*, but it rather derives exclusively from his careful medical inspection of the animal."[104] While the main purpose of the petition was probably for the *shochtim* to be reinstated in their voting rights and escape social and legal stigma for themselves and their families, it is noteworthy that they conceptualized a new role for *shochtim* in Soviet society, entirely severing themselves from religion and religious authorities. They recognized the Soviet state as the only authority.

Most of these *shochtim* did not work under the supervision of the city's rabbi. While strictly Orthodox Jews could not accept as kosher the cattle and fowl slaughtered without rabbinical supervision and possibly without full compliance with the strict rules of kosher butchering, many consumers did: for them, such meat was sufficiently kosher, even without rabbinic certification. Whether they purchased the meat because of its lower price or because of their poor knowledge of the complicated laws of kosher butchering, their action represented an important step toward the emergence of a new kind of folk kashrut (or popular interpretation of Jewish dietary laws), based on traditional slaughtering practices and food habits rather than on religious authority. Not unlike other religious practices that were no longer monitored by the religious elites—such as birth rituals—kosher meat production in Soviet society did not depend on the rabbis, who ultimately failed; neither did it depend on the *shochtim*, who negotiated with the Soviet state mainly for professional reasons.

The production and consequently consumption of kosher meat in the Soviet Union largely depended on Jewish women. In spite of the revolutionary rhetoric about gender equality, embraced by Soviet authorities, mostly women bought food and brought it to the table. Jewish women, who never served as kosher butchers or as religious leaders and who, because of their gender, were rarely active in the administrative bodies that ran Soviet cities, played an important role in the preservation of kosher meat consumption under the Soviets. In one instance, in the city of Kremenchuk, Jewish housewives petitioned the central food cooperative in the city not to discontinue the sale of kosher meat to its members and threatened to launch a strike, by which they meant "abstain from cooking dinners for their husbands, unless kosher meat is provided."[105]

The extreme modernization process in Soviet society not only saw the emergence of a staunchly traditional Jewish woman, who came to play a crucial role in the preservation of tradition within the family and in the perpetuation of folk religion, but also saw the appearance of the fundamentally different and sharply dichotomous category of the radical Jewish woman, who rebelled against the ways of her mother, entered the mainstream of Soviet economic and political life, and often intermarried. Two images from *Bezbozhnik u stanka* capture these changes. In the first one, two young Jewish women state that in the absence of "the Jewish God overseeing their actions," they "will be having lunch at the cafeteria."[106] This, of course, implied that they would be eating nonkosher food. The second image portrays Sara, a mother who is in the process of blessing the candles to mark the beginning of the Sabbath, while her daughter is having fun in the Communist Youth League ("Sara molitsia a dochka komsomolitsia!")[107]

While the modernization of Jewish women took place in prerevolutionary times, the Soviet regime's insistence on equality accelerated changes to a dizzying speed. Some women took on leading roles in the Jewish cultural revolution of the late 1920s and actively participated in the 1930 gold campaign to support industrialization and collectivization, showing their commitment to the fulfillment of the First Five-Year Plan to modernize the Soviet economy in the shortest possible time. Brigades of women seized—presumably from their own mothers and grandmothers—Sabbath silver candlesticks and kiddush goblets to donate to the revolution. The Soviet Yiddish poet Sore Kahan called the Jewish woman to action: "Earrings and rings, candlesticks, samovars, the Kiddush goblet and the fish pan, take them, remove them, comrades, may it be a contribution to brace our country."[108]

The Jewish women's encounter with the campaign against Judaism resulted in the emergence of two different and fundamentally opposed women—one staunchly traditional, one surprisingly radical. For Jewish women, Sovietization elicited a schizophrenic model of acculturation. This tension, not devoid of a generational aspect, expressed itself largely as a cultural disconnect between mothers and daughters, rather than between fathers and daughters, as in the Yiddish writer Sholem Aleichem's Tevye the Dairyman stories. They were really Golde's daughters, not Tevye's. This sharp dichotomy and real division seems to be more unambiguous than among the surrounding non-Jewish population largely because of the advanced state of literacy and urbanization among Jewish women compared to their non-Jewish counterparts.

"Antisemitism Is a Greater Evil than Religion!"

Soviet activists involved in the antireligious campaigns on the Jewish street, as careful as they might have been, were ultimately playing with fire. Some tried hard to walk the fine line between attacking Judaism and avoiding eliciting antipathy toward Jews among non-Jews. Some Jews may have even construed an affinity between communism and tsarism, perceiving the attack on Judaism as analogous to the antisemitism of late imperial Russia. The literature attacking Judaism, especially in the Russian language, included a unique feature that was missing from the propaganda texts condemning Orthodoxy and Islam: it always comprised some reference to anti-Jewish prejudice and discrimination and to the fact that the Soviets would not tolerate it. "First of all, it is clear that the rabbis lie when they say that in the USSR the Jewish faith is persecuted. Here," wrote the author of a brochure against religion, "there is no persecution of Jews." "In fact," reassured and warned the author, "the antireligious propaganda targets all faiths equally, as the godless activists carry out propaganda against religion and not nationality. . . . It is the counterrevolution in fact—supported by the rabbis—that spreads antisemitism. . . . The Soviet state rejects it."[109] Antireligious propaganda literature also had to clarify, mostly for the non-Jewish audience, that the argument made by the Orthodox priest that "Jews are responsible for spreading atheism and that Christianity is being singled out in the war against religion" was indeed false.[110]

And yet, the antireligious campaigns that targeted Judaism inadvertently promoted hostility against Jews. The problem lay with the propaganda carried out in Russian (or in other non-Jewish languages): if Jewish rituals were depicted as barbarian in Yiddish, a language accessible almost exclusively to Jews, the attack was harmless for Jews (although very harmful for Judaism). But *Bezbozhnik u stanka* was read in Soviet classrooms, factories, and clubs and unintentionally sustained certain ideas of Jews as hostile others (its circulation reached as much as two hundred thousand in 1932). It also offered a new modern imagery of the other.[111]

Images of Jewish religious leaders, who were always male, included the daunting one-eyed Jehova; the rabbis depicted as NEPmen or capitalists in top hat and suits holding a Talmud; the abusive *melamdim* who tortured children in the heder; and the demonized *shochtim*, who in some cases were depicted with blood dripping from theirs mouth and hands.[112] And while Islam and Orthodoxy were also connected to the evils of capitalism, this link elicited a less obvious reaction compared to Judaism because of the deeply embedded anti-Jewish stereotypes connected to capital.[113] Moreover, those who resented the Bolshevik experiment could be easily swayed toward anti-Jewish hostility by the antireligious propaganda. For example, when they were reading about the blood libel and the fact that "Jews are not *krovopivtsy* [bloodsuckers] and do not use human blood in their bread" and that "the Jewish religion forbids them from consuming blood," they might have come to believe the exact opposite.[114]

A new stage in the war against religion, with rhetoric and actions reminiscent of the violence of War Communism, coincided with Stalin's Great Turn. The beginning of the great economic goals of the First Five-Year Plan, 1928–1932, with the purpose of strengthening the country's economy and guaranteeing its independence from capitalist countries, dealt a real blow to the relatively diverse religious life that had endured until then. During Passover of 1929, all five matzah-baking machines in Fastiv, a town in central Ukraine, were confiscated to serve the Soviet state's rush to industrialize. Prayer shawls, tefillin, and religious books were collected in cities and towns across the Soviet Union and donated as junk or scrap metal for the industrialization fund, eventually to be used to purchase tractors. The main Yiddish newspaper in Ukraine, *Shtern*, disseminated the slogan "convert prayer shawls and tefillin into tractors," as brigades of Jewish children conducted house-to-house searches, collecting ritual objects and removing prayer books from the synagogues.[115]

The year 1929 marked a new phase in the campaigns against religion. The decisive stage in the legislation on religion began on April 8, 1929, with a law (which remained in force until 1975, when it was amended) that further restricted religious activities, cracking down in particular on religious associations. Launched in the midst of Stalin's revolution, the persecution of religious life became more extreme, comprehensive, and unyielding. With the goal of breaking off all forms of resistance to the atheistic propaganda promoted by the state, the new laws further enforced the separation of church and state, increased the taxation on religious buildings and their employees, and further limited religious activities by supervising all religious associations.[116]

While synagogues were never entirely outlawed and continued to exist, although with restricted functions, a new wave to requisition religious buildings and turn them into factories or apartments for non-Jewish families began in 1929.[117] The involvement with the trade and distribution of matzah imported from Warsaw and Riga into Soviet cities could trigger accusations of spying on behalf of foreign powers; suspicion of being at the service of counterrevolutionary and imperialist forces became very plausible at the time, especially in light of the growing tensions between the Soviet state, Germany, and Great Britain. The neutral attitude toward religious holidays and rituals, typical among those Soviet Jewish citizens who acted in a "gray zone" between indifference to religion and a fanatic drive to uproot it, was in theory no longer an option. An antireligious behavior, as opposed to a nonreligious behavior, was expected in particular by a younger generation of Communist Party members at the time of Jewish religious holidays. But in many cases, the confrontation remained notional, as religious practice was too deeply entrenched in family relations.

When during Passover of 1929 a group of Jewish Komsomol members in Berdychiv criticized their peer for dressing up elegantly on the first day of the holiday, he retorted by stating, "Don't you understand that I want to give my parents some happiness? What's the big deal if I eat some *kneydlekh* with them, and I dress up nicely? I just want to live in peace with my parents; no one has the right to get involved in my private life; the revolution will not suffer from that!" Another one echoed, "Who will suffer if because of my old mother I eat some matzah? . . . Is it a sin to eat a good dinner?"[118] The pressure from family members and the persistence of an allegiance to the family could shape the attitudes toward religious customs and holidays.[119]

Whether the young "godless activists" participated in the new wave of antireligious campaigns out of peer pressure, because of idealism, or simply because they were lured by the prospect of earning some money, their effectiveness in carrying out the war against religion depended largely on where they lived. Many activists were sent to different localities, far away from their birth towns and cities. Being geographically removed from their families made countering religious practice easier, as they did not have to face their mothers and fathers in a personal war. Young Jews who migrated to the large city and left their family in the shtetl did not have to confront the Pesach issue with their parents.

Even in 1929, the state's antireligious campaigns could inadvertently trigger anti-Jewish hostility. Ironically, this new wave of antireligious campaigns contributed to the ballooning of animosity against Jews, a social problem that the system was committed to solve. In April 1929, on the eve of Easter, members of the Komsomol and of the League of the Godless organized antireligious carnivals throughout the cities of Ukraine, including Kyiv, Dnipropetrovsk, and Kharkiv, to counter the Orthodox Easter midnight processions. Violent clashes erupted between the participants in the antireligious carnival and the city residents, or the "believers," with Komsomol members storming the churches and refusing demonstratively to take their caps off in a sign of respect. The young communists also intimidated the crowds leaving the church by surrounding them with trucks, by throwing small grenades at the "believers," and by organizing dances on the churches' premises. The believers responded by throwing stones at, verbally abusing, and physically attacking the participants in the carnival. Red Army soldiers and police officers intervened to restore order and arrest the culprits: in one instance, an activist who was arrested committed suicide and left a note claiming that he was not guilty.[120]

One of the complaints recorded in the secret police reports mentioned the fact that participation in the carnival of Jewish members of the Komsomol could lead to an outburst of violence against Jews on the part of the believers: the assumption was that Jews were working on behalf of the Soviet state to sabotage Easter. One is left puzzled as to why the authorities did not rely exclusively on non-Jewish activists for the anti-Christian carnivals (as they usually did in the Jewish context, when young Jews only attacked Judaism). On the other hand, this might have been the deliberate decision of some member of the local authorities who ultimately preferred to see Jews blamed rather than the Soviet state.

One comment included in the OGPU report noted, "The Soviet state openly patronizes the 'hooliganism' of the atheists [here used as a synonym for Jews]: during their Easter [Passover], they did not organize any carnivals. They insult the believers." In other words, the participation of Jewish communists in the general antireligious campaigns triggered a backlash against Jews, or the Soviet state inadvertently sparked the attitudes that it officially condemned.[121] The Jewish response to these clashes was also spurred by memories of anti-Jewish violence, specifically of the pogroms that had taken place some ten years earlier in the context of the civil war. According to the OGPU report, the Jews in the city of Kyiv reacted negatively to the carnival not only because it was an open attack on religion but also because they feared that the rising violence, the excesses, and clashes at the time of the demonstrations and processions could degenerate into a pogrom.[122]

Place mattered and shaped the way in which Jews responded to these campaigns. On May 2, 1929, in the small town of Vinohrad, in the Uman province of Ukraine, local party activists met to discuss the closing down of the local synagogue (they might have been Jewish; we are not told). That same evening, the "believers" dispatched some guards to stand by the synagogue entrance and ward off the activists. The town's local authorities intervened; they inquired about the reason for the guards' presence and ultimately decided to ask them to leave; they were committed to maintaining order in the town. Someone even fired a gun in protest. Local Jews, unable to protect their building from the impending attack, stormed the homes of those who were in favor of confiscating the synagogue and physically attacked them. This kind of miniature civil war between neighbors, this kind of defiant resilience in 1929, could have taken place only in a shtetl, where Jews owned the urban space, disregarded the clear message from the local authorities, and attempted to challenge the antireligious campaigns.[123]

Rabbis were caught up in a new wave of arrests. Soviet authorities arrested them in connection with the radical changes in the economic policy introduced by Stalin's Great Turn and the abolishment of the NEP.[124] In some cases, Evsektsiia activists exploited the new policies to invigorate the persecution of the rabbis, arguing that all religious leaders were supporters of capitalism and the counterrevolution. But in some cases, the accusations were not entirely concocted. Disenfranchised by the state and forced to pay exorbitant taxes and even higher rent, religious leaders actually turned to speculation and private trade in the desperate hope to provide for themselves and their families. In early 1930, the secret police arrested Rabbi Menachem Gluskin of Minsk along with thirteen other religious leaders. They were charged with counterrevolutionary activity for corresponding with foreign Jewish organizations. Although they were subsequently released, the incident led to the JDC's discontinuation of support of religious life and institutions, which effectively put an end to the activities of the Committee of Rabbis.[125]

Under the Soviets, Jewish religious practice became less and less public and was increasingly reconfigured as a private affair. After a synagogue was closed down, prayer groups met in the private sphere of someone's home; after the heder was closed down, it was possible, though more and more difficult, to hire a *melamed* to teach in the home; when consuming kosher food outside the home became almost impossible, it could still be served at the family's table. If the family unit helped preserve religious practice, the opposite is also true. In fact, the demise of religion took place also as a result of the conflicted and ambivalent attempt on the part of parents to encourage their children's success and in some cases to rescue them from extraordinary poverty, especially when the parents, because of their alleged "bourgeois" background, had been disenfranchised and had become social outcasts, with restricted access to employment and housing. They encouraged their children to distance themselves from them, from their way of life, from the Jewish way of life. They encouraged their sons, and also their daughters, to join the workforce, join the Party—even though they viewed the movement as corrupt and ideologically false. Membership in communist organizations provided privileges and represented the gateway to socioeconomic success and upward mobility. Parents put their children's success and future happiness above all else, even above the preservation of Jewish religious life.

OLD WORLDS, NEW WORLDS

Jewish Cultures and Languages of the 1920s

Creating a new Bolshevik society out of the ruins of the civil war was no easy task. Devastation, displacement, and starvation plagued the cities and towns of the former Russian Empire long after 1921. Famine ravished the impoverished villages and weighed on the thousands of soldiers and peasants who poured into the cities searching for bread, housing, and livelihood. Even under these extreme conditions, the new Soviet leaders never lost sight of their political priorities. Fending off real (or imagined) enemies disguised as Ukrainian nationalists, bourgeois counterrevolutionary businessmen, or Russian Orthodox priests remained of utmost urgency: their existence threatened the very survival of the new system.

In the midst of the unprecedented social and political crisis, Lenin confronted, perhaps for the first time, the troubling reality of heading a country with a largely uneducated and illiterate population. Until the revolution, the Bolsheviks had paid little attention to the question of popular education and culture and to the fact that before World War I, the Russian Empire constituted the least literate state in Europe.[1] The notion that, for instance, at the end of the nineteenth century only 13.7 percent of women in European Russia, 6 percent in the Caucasus, and 2 percent in Central Asia were literate seemed of little political relevance.[2] But in the wake of the civil war, after the Red Army claimed victory and the Soviet Union was established, overcoming cultural backwardness became a vital task for the masters of the first socialist society.[3] In 1923, Lenin, on the eve of his death, explained this shift in priorities and described the dawn of a cultural revolution as follows: "We have to admit that there has been a radical modification in our whole outlook on socialism. The radical modification is this; formerly we placed, and had to place, the main emphasis on the political struggle, on revolution, on winning political power, etc. Now the emphasis is changing and shifting to peaceful, organizational, 'cultural' work. . . . [The] emphasis is shifting to educational work."[4]

The first step in this revolution was to control the production and circulation of culture and use it as a weapon of class struggle to spread socialism among the masses. The new authorities rushed to monopolize all means of cultural production and its producers. They confiscated cultural institutions and artistic organizations, including presses, theaters, and museums. At the same time, they began to train and closely supervise the political views of teachers, journalists, movie directors, exhibition curators, and belletrists. But the Bolsheviks soon came to realize that building a new culture from scratch posed huge challenges and produced intrinsic inconsistencies. Forging a new Soviet culture ex nihilo, by burning all bridges to preexisting spaces, people, languages, books, artifacts, and ideas, which had been deemed inherently backward and thus deplorable, was extremely arduous. Lenin himself eventually acknowledged the need to "build communism through noncommunist hands" and thus to adopt a softer line vis-à-vis prerevolutionary culture and cultural producers.[5] This compromise allowed many intellectuals who were neither Bolsheviks nor Marxists to continue to populate and contribute to the cultural, academic, and scientific communities in Soviet cities throughout the 1920s.[6] And even though this concession was expected to be short-lived, in the early 1930s Soviet academic institutions still employed numerous bourgeois academics who were not Party members.[7]

On the Jewish street too, the new ideal of a Bolshevik culture of the future, one imbued with the ethos of the revolutionary working class, emerged alongside what communist activists called the old bourgeois Jewish culture of the past, permeated by the hedonistic standards and conventions of the middle class. In the European regions of the new empire, throughout the 1920s, the state funded an extraordinary array of new publications and institutions with the goal of yielding a new communist culture for the Jewish masses. In order to reach them and to inculcate among them this new culture, as a matter of course, the state chose Yiddish, the language spoken by the large majority of the Jews in the region. In other words, having recognized the existence of a Jewish nationality endowed with a national language spoken by its masses, the state began to establish organizations and institutions that operated in that very language. And in June 1919, Soviet authorities issued a decree sanctioning Yiddish, and not the "clerical" Hebrew or the "bourgeois" Russian, as the language of instruction in Jewish schools as well as the preferred instrument of propaganda to enlighten the adult Jewish population and to create scholarly enterprises. Although at a slower pace, this same process, but in the different languages of the non-Ashkenazi communities, took hold in Crimea, the Caucasus, and Central Asia, areas that were somewhat removed from the more intense politics of Sovietization of the 1920s. Two reasons, then, drove the state's decision to support Yiddish (or other national languages like Judeo-Tajik, the language of Bukharan Jews) and not Hebrew or Russian. The first reason was pragmatic: the only way to successfully Sovietize Jews was to employ the language known by the Jewish masses—insisting on Russification would have hampered the state's effort to spread communism. The second reason was a matter of principle, namely, that all nationalities in the Soviet Union had the right to use their own national languages.

Whether produced in Yiddish or in Judeo-Tajik, the culture of the new world coexisted, intersected, and crossed paths with the cultures of the "old Jewish world," which were articulated through the languages of the Jewish past, mostly Hebrew and, to some extent, Russian (considered by the new regime as the language of the Jewish bourgeoisie). The cultural production of the "old Jewish world" endured with little or no state funding until the end of the decade. If many Jewish activists dashed to produce a new Bolshevik culture that would fit the state guidelines, many Jewish cultural figures and intellectuals who had been active before the revolution continued to produce, write, sing, and perform a "bourgeois" culture, in Russian and even in Hebrew, more connected to the past. Thus, in the 1920s Soviet Jewish culture unfolded through waves of ruptures and continuities.

Old Centers and New Centers: The Realignment of Jewish Cultural Geographies

The two most apparent spheres of change in Jewish cultural production pertained to language and geography. With regard to language dynamics, like other ethnic minorities, Jews in the Russian Empire had been subjected to Russifying pressures for several decades before the revolution. As a result, the Soviet effort to use Yiddish (or the different languages of the non-Ashkenazi communities) as the primary vehicle for Jewish cultural change represented something of a reversal of state policy. Yet, the tsarist state's Russifying pressures influenced the Jewish community's attitude toward Yiddish in a significant way and into the Soviet era.

Despite the widespread knowledge that most Jews living in the Pale of Settlement had of Yiddish, with the exception of the literary work of the pioneers of modern Yiddish literature (including writers like Mendele Mocher Seforim, Sholem Aleichem, Y. L. Peretz, and Sholem Asch), the language was generally not considered fit for high culture and was not used for modern school instruction prior to World War I. The Haskalah project, which had promoted Jewish acculturation to Russian along with the retention of Hebrew as a literary language, deemed Yiddish a jargon, a transitory tool devoid of status and future. Russian became the mandatory language of instruction in all modern elementary schools across the empire. At the same time, the pressure to embrace Russian in lieu of Hebrew among the Jewish middle class and intellectual elites especially continued apace during the second half of the nineteenth century. Well into the 1900s, Russian constituted the language of Jewish high culture and was the preferred means for historical, philosophical, or essayistic writings. Arguably, even following the February Revolution, when the end of legal restrictions on Jewish life triggered an unprecedented revival in Hebrew and Yiddish publications and cultural activities, decentering Russian on the Jewish street remained challenging. Russian represented the language of politics, scholarship, and economic mobility.

Besides the language of cultural production, the other most noticeable transformation pertained to the changing geography of Jewish cultural production. The sea change unleashed by World War I and the end of the civil war not only altered the content and means of production of Jewish culture in the former tsarist empire but also impinged on geography, rupturing some of the continuities of the past. The cities of Vilna and Warsaw, for instance, which during the nineteenth century had represented the most prominent centers for Hebrew and Yiddish printing and publishing, as well as for Jewish educational and literary activities in the Russian Empire, became part of independent Poland and were thus severed from the political and cultural map of the Soviet Union. Besides Vilna and Warsaw, the two key Jewish intellectual and cultural hubs before the revolution were the port metropolis of Odesa and the imperial city of Saint Petersburg. Odesa's strong economy, its growing Jewish population (it was the largest Jewish community in the Pale), its numerous literary and philanthropic organizations, and its well-established network of modern Jewish schools made the city an alluring place for leading intellectuals. Writers, poets, and thinkers like Ahad Ha-Am, Mendele Mocher Seforim, and Chaim Nahman Bialik moved to the city during the second part of the nineteenth century. War and revolution did not affect the city's status as a formidable cultural center in Jewish life. The cultural renaissance that enveloped the Jewish world after 1917 turned Odesa into the most important center for Hebrew book publishing in Russia and Ukraine.[8] Under the Soviets, Odesa continued to play a vibrant role in the realm of Jewish cultural production and activities, albeit not as conspicuously as it had before the revolution.

While the tsarist legal restrictions on Jewish settlement never allowed Saint Petersburg to develop into a prominent Jewish demographic center, its status of political, economic, and intellectual capital of the Russian Empire made it a preferred destination for many Jewish students, writers, and thinkers. Over the course of the nineteenth century, with numerous organizations for the study of Jewish ethnography, history, music, folk art, and Hebrew literature, the city grew into the most prolific center of high Jewish culture in late imperial Russia.[9] The Society for the Promotion of Culture among Jews (OPE), which was established in the city in 1863 and which advocated acculturation and civic emancipation for Jews, served as an umbrella organization for a variety of organizations devoted to culture and pedagogy.[10] In turn, OPE, alongside the many institutions it oversaw, attracted to the city a small but self-selecting group of Jewish intellectuals and cultural activists who published, read, or otherwise contributed to an impressive range of periodicals in Russian but also in Yiddish and

Hebrew. The future dean of Russian Jewish history, Simon Dubnov, who moved to Saint Petersburg is 1882 and who applied to prolong his residence permit every year until 1917, "chose his profession, taught his best students, and wrote his most important work" in the city.[11] Like Odesa, Saint Petersburg—renamed Petrograd after World War I and then, in 1924, renamed Leningrad following Lenin's death—continued to be a thriving Jewish cultural center after the revolution, with numerous "bourgeois" institutions and organizations that continued to operate under the Soviets.

But the geopolitical changes set off by the end of World War I and the civil war also brought to the horizon new Jewish centers, putting on the map places that had played little to no role in prerevolutionary Jewish cultural and scholarly life. Two intertwined circumstances triggered the new phenomenon: first, thousands of Jews—including writers and cultural activists—rushed from their towns and villages struck by war and revolution to the nearby larger cities; second, the new political system turned these same cities into new capitals of bureaucratic power, which accordingly offered new opportunities for Jewish cultural production and employment in new (and old) institutions and organizations.[12]

Moscow, the archetypal Russian city and new Soviet capital, became for the first time a center for Yiddish intellectuals and cultural activists. Writing about the immediate postrevolutionary years, the poet and journalist Daniel Charney recalled, "In the years 1918–1922, Bolshevized Moscow also became the capital of Soviet Yiddish literature. In those days not a single Yiddish writer in Russia did not pass through Moscow."[13] Of course, most aspiring cultural and political activists gravitated toward the political heart of the new regime. In the midst of the massive influx of newcomers pouring into the capital and the ensuing shortage of buildings available for cultural work, even the ostensibly most bitter of enemies sometimes shared the same spaces to strategize about the role they would play in the future of Jewish life. In these early years, thus, it could happen that activists who were committed to developing a new culture in Yiddish and activists who were more connected to prerevolutionary values and devoted to Hebrew language and culture would carry on with their cultural and political priorities in the same premises of the Evsektsiia building: while young Zionists studied the Balfour Declaration upstairs, young communists studied Bukharin's words downstairs.[14]

The new role that Yiddish was encouraged to play in Jewish cultural life echoed early on through the activities of the Moscow branch of the Jewish People's University, a short-lived institution of higher learning founded in Petrograd in 1918, which offered courses in Jewish studies. The 1918 branch's first meeting protocols, which included the historian Sofia R. Kotsyna's report on the university's mission to "disseminate knowledge among the masses," were written in Russian, but by 1919, most official documents were drafted in Yiddish only.[15] In the official correspondence, the institution's name began to appear in Yiddish (Yidisher folks universitet) in lieu of Russian (Evreiskii narodnyi universitet).[16] And different courses and seminars, including for instance "Economic Materialism" and "Karl Marx and the Jewish Question," were taught in Yiddish.[17]

The Moscow branch was eventually closed down in the early 1920s: one of the possible reasons was the failed attempt to replace Russian with Yiddish as the language of instruction, in a city in which the overwhelming majority of Jews spoke Russian. However, its brief existence and the experiment in linguistic shift attests to the projected new role that Yiddish was meant to play in Jewish cultural work, even in a city like Moscow. It was also an indication of the first steps taken to produce a new kind of Jewish pedagogy and scholarship in Yiddish.[18] While this initial experiment partly failed, Moscow would eventually develop into a major center of Soviet Jewish cultural and social activity. In fact, many institutions and organizations in the city would operate at least partly in Yiddish throughout the interwar period.

Minsk was another place that had offered meager contributions to Jewish cultural life before the revolution but that grew rapidly into one of the key centers of Soviet Jewish cultural work and education. A historic Jewish city since the late sixteenth century, Minsk had played an important role in Jewish religious life and culture, as well as in modern Jewish politics during the nineteenth and early twentieth centuries. But it had remained a largely provincial city. Things changed after the end of the civil war, when Minsk was crowned the capital of a Soviet republic (the Belorussian Soviet Socialist Republic), and the city moved from the margins to the center of Jewish cultural life. Unlike Moscow—where by the 1910s most Jews in the city were literate in Russian—in Minsk the overwhelming majority of the Jewish population spoke Yiddish. The unparalleled state support for institutions and agencies operating in Yiddish in the Belorussian Soviet capital brought the Jewish language to the forefront of cultural work with a new unprecedented intensity.

Minsk became a major center of cultural production in Yiddish thanks to the combination of a number of factors. The influx of thousands of newcomers from the surrounding Belorussian small towns and shtetls who searched for employment and better life conditions constantly replenished the city with Yiddish speakers. This ongoing inflow, combined with the fact that the Belarusian language never truly competed with Yiddish in establishing itself as a real alternative for the Jewish residents of the city (as Russian did for Jews in Moscow and Leningrad or as Ukrainian did for at least a number of Jews living in Kyiv or Kharkiv), turned Minsk into one of the most remarkable examples of the cultural revolution on the Jewish street. Visitors from neighboring Poland noticed with great surprise how Yiddish appeared in public spaces of importance, including, for instance, the building of the central train station (the name of the city appeared not only in Belarusian, Russian, and Polish but also in Yiddish) or the main campus of Belorussian State University (which displayed the institution's name in Belarusian and Yiddish). Traveling from Warsaw to Minsk in the late 1920s, the Yiddish writer I. J. Singer was startled: "These four languages, Belarusian, Russian, Polish, and Yiddish, meet me at the train station. . . . I come across them at every step, in every commissariat, office, everywhere there are signs in the four languages."[19] In the Belorussian Soviet Socialist Republic, Yiddish was granted the same official status of state language as Russian, Belarusian, and Polish.

The transformation of Jewish cultural life in Kyiv was akin to that of Minsk in some aspects but very dissimilar in others. Despite living within the confines of the Pale of Settlement, Kyiv Jews faced residence restrictions since the reign of Nicholas I, who expelled them from the city in 1827 and eventually excluded the city itself from the Pale in 1835. The restrictions on Jewish residence abated a bit—at least for some categories of Jews who were deemed "useful"—under Alexander II. A growing number of certified artisans, who could, though with limitations, settle outside the Pale, moved to the city. By the end of the nineteenth century, the city's Jewish population reached 13 percent, with wealthy Jewish merchants and entrepreneurs taking up residence in Kyiv, alongside significant numbers of youngsters who were attracted by the city's institutions of higher learning, in particular by St. Vladimir University.[20] The February Revolution marked a turning point in the history of Jewish Kyiv, insofar as it put an end to anti-Jewish legislation and lifted all residence restrictions. At the same time, war and revolution triggered an impressive influx into the city of Jews who fled the surrounding shtetls and towns torn by violence. The Jewish population swelled significantly, and by 1923, it made up for one-third of the four hundred thousand city inhabitants.

During the years that led up to 1917 and in the early 1920s, Yehupets (as the city was nicknamed in the literary masterworks of the Yiddish writer Sholem Aleichem, who moved there in 1887) became one of the most important Soviet Jewish cultural hubs attracting writers, educators, publishers, and literary critics. While Kharkiv was the political capital of the newly formed Ukrainian Soviet Socialist Republic until 1934, Kyiv became the de facto capital of the Soviet Yiddish Republic of Letters, setting the tone in Yiddish literature. In 1917–1921, 40 percent of all Soviet Yiddish titles were published in the city, and an entirely new generation of Yiddish cultural activists came together in the city.[21] While the members of the prerevolutionary Kyiv Group of Yiddish writers, which included renowned authors like Dovid Bergelson and Der Nister (Pinkhes Kahanovitsh), left the city, Kyiv emerged as the heart of Yiddish culture in the early Soviet period also thanks to the multifaceted activities organized by the avant-garde artistic and literary association Kultur-lige, the Cultural League.[22] Founded in the city in 1918, Kultur-lige promoted the development of Yiddish culture broadly defined, with a focus on Yiddish education, theater, art, music, and literature.[23] Even after the Evsektsiia clamped down on its autonomy, the Kultur-lige continued to exist and promote activities in the form of artistic and music production, as well as through a publishing house. By the time it was fully Sovietized, the Kultur-lige had spread throughout Ukraine and boasted ninety-nine branches with schools, libraries, children's clubs, orphanages, and children's homes. All these institutions inadvertently created the basis for Soviet Yiddish cultural programs throughout the 1920s.[24] Under the veneer of a cooperative enterprise, the Kultur-lige press remained the main producer of Yiddish books in the Soviet Union until 1931.[25]

The diverse non-Ashkenazi Jewish communities that came under the Bolsheviks experienced some of the same dynamics at play in the European regions of the Soviet Union, witnessing the rise of new centers of cultural production. In general, the Sovietization process was enforced at a very different tempo and with some softness and caution in the so-called Oriental areas of the Soviet Union, which included Crimea, the Caucasus, and Central Asia. As suggested in 1920 by Stalin, who served then as people's commissar for nationalities, the Party should be mindful "of nationalism and religious life" when enforcing Sovietization, especially in these regions.[26] To take a single but striking example, the students enrolled in the most prominent state-funded Jewish pedagogical institutions for teachers in Tashkent had to be members of the Komsomol but were served kosher food during the 1920s.[27] This same permissive attitude toward religion was displayed in the Orthodox Church in Georgia and in Islamic institutions in Crimea, Dagestan, Azerbaijan, and Central Asia.

Even in these regions of the Soviet Union, the establishment of the new political system led to the rise of new centers of Jewish cultural life. The cultures and language of the Jews of the Crimean Peninsula, of Georgian Jews, of Mountain Jews in the Caucasus, and of Bukharan Jews in Central Asia received official legal standing from the Soviet state, which entailed funding for cultural institutions and organizations and especially for a network of schools. As for Yiddish elsewhere in the Soviet Union, the official rationale justifying state support for these new cultural and educational endeavors was primarily functional: the support for national languages and cultures would help forge loyal Soviet citizens by spreading Marxist ideology among these communities, in their mother tongues.

With the 1921 establishment of the Soviet Autonomous Crimean Republic, many Krymchaks (members of the ancient Jewish community that had lived in Crimea for hundreds of years) resettled from smaller towns to the new political centers of the region, first in Simferopol, which saw the emergence of cultural and educational institutions, some of which operated in the Judeo-Crimean Tatar language.[28] The tendency among most peoples in the Soviet Union to prefer Russian due to its perceived higher literary status and a better guarantee for employment certainly affected the Krymchaks as well. The process of cultural assimilation into Russian, which started before the revolution, was in full swing during the 1920s, especially among the younger generations, who, in growing numbers, chose Russian over Judeo-Crimean Tatar.[29] Those Krymchaks who moved to the agricultural settlements established in Crimea in the 1920s to productivize and Sovietize Jews adopted Russian also because it served as the only common language with the many Ashkenazi Jews who joined them to toil the fertile land.

The Bukharan Jewish communities, as well as the Jews of Georgia and the Caucasus, had been historically less exposed to Russian than had the Krymchaks and with some exceptions had very low literacy rates in Russian.[30] Bukharan Jews, who were concentrated primarily in the cities of Samarkand, Bukhara, Dushanbe—located in the Uzbek Soviet Socialist Republic, established in 1924—and in the autonomous republic of Tajikistan, which was turned into a republic in 1929, spoke Judeo-Tajik among themselves and were more likely to speak Uzbek or Tajik with the surrounding Muslim population. Mountain Jews were concentrated primarily in the Dagestan Autonomous Soviet Socialist Republic, established in 1921, and in Azerbaijan, which became a Soviet republic in 1922, and they spoke predominantly Judeo-Tat.

Unlike other non-Ashkenazi communities, Georgian Jews, who resided mostly within the territory of the Georgian Soviet Socialist Republic, established in 1921, and who lived primarily in the cities of Sachkhere, Sukhumi, Kutaisi, and Tbilisi, generally shared the same language spoken by their non-Jewish neighbors: according to the 1926 Soviet census, almost 97 percent of Georgian Jews declared Georgian their mother tongue (many apparently resorted to a mixed form of Georgian and Hebrew only when they sought not to be understood by non-Jews).[31] Because of the relatively slower tempo with which Sovietization was implemented in so-called Oriental areas of the country, state authorities generally did not impinge as much on the traditional religious and cultural life of Georgian Jews—so much so that the Georgian Jewish communities emerged as cultural and social centers of Chabad Hasidism during the mid-1920s.[32] Rabbi Joseph Yitskhak Schneersohn, leader of the Chabad movement in the Soviet Union, recorded the flourishing of religious and cultural life among Georgian Jews at the time, emphasizing the growing number of heders and yeshivas, which attracted hundreds of students both in the larger and smaller cities of Georgia. An attempt to systematically promote Soviet cultural activities among Georgian Jews was undertaken in earnest only in the latter part of the 1920s.

During the 1920s, Jewish cultural projects emerged in different places across the Soviet Union. Some locations had a long-standing tradition of Jewish cultural production; others emerged almost ex novo as new centers following the general geopolitical transformation and the specific Jewish demographic revolution unleashed by the civil war. In some places, cultural activists worked under the auspices of the Soviet state; in another places, "bourgeois" organizations like the JDC sponsored noncommunist cultural institutions and activities. Some cultural projects were short-lived: they either ran out of funding or were closed down by Soviet authorities as unbecoming of a Bolshevik state. Others renewed and blossomed and endured well into the early 1930s. Most cultural projects resulted from a combination of tradition and innovation, with cycles of continuity and rupture in languages, content, and people.

The Politics of Nativization on the Jewish Street

Heir to the Russian multiethnic state, the new Bolshevik regime tried to accommodate the nationalism and national consciousness of its many ethnic minorities by becoming the world's first affirmative-action empire.[33] With the establishment of state-funded institutions and organizations throughout the union republics and autonomous regions, from Bashkiria to Belorussia, Ukraine, Armenia, Georgia, and Azerbaijan, the Soviet system deliberately promoted the national identity of national minorities. Stalin had first announced the Soviet policy of *korenizatsiia*, or nativization, in the fall of 1920. Nativization entailed that "all Soviet organs in the borderlands—the courts, the administration, the economic organs, organs of local power (as well as Party organs)—be composed to the greatest possible degree of people who know the customs, habits, and the language of the local population."[34] In other words, the nativization policy was a way to establish national elites who would work with the system in fostering national languages. The new national elites not only would teach communism to the masses, in their mother tongue, but would also instill in them the new system's values and thus fashion trustworthy Soviet citizens.

Officially launched in 1923, the nativization policy had an impact on Jewish culture and identity throughout the territories of the Soviet Union. The most articulate and sophisticated attempt to indigenize the Jewish street materialized in the European regions of the Soviet Union, in Ukraine, Belorussia, and areas of Russia, where the large majority of Jews lived. As part of the *korenizatsiia* policy, the state provided financial support to establish institutions and organizations that would produce a Soviet culture in Yiddish. Yiddish newspapers, journals, magazines, publishing houses, kindergartens, elementary schools, institutions of higher learning, literacy points, and theaters sprung up everywhere across the European regions of the Soviet Union and were funded by the state. Some Yiddish writers and poets who lived outside the borders of the Soviet Union even chose to move to Soviet cities: especially in interwar Poland, where Yiddish had no official status and where cultural and literary activists struggled to make ends meet, the prospect of becoming state employees and gaining public standing became attractive to many.

The support of a national language through *korenizatsiia* did not necessarily operate along purely ethnic lines. An original development in the nativization project in the Ukrainian and Belorussian republics in particular included Jewish intellectuals becoming actors and movers in the Ukrainian and Belarusian national cultural awakening of the 1920s, as they undoubtedly found inspiration in the fact that these languages had been elevated to the status of state languages after centuries of being treated as "barbarian dialects." These writers and poets chose to write in Ukrainian and Belarusian instead of in Yiddish or Russian. While Jewish Ukrainian and Belarusian literary creativity was not entirely new and included instances of Jews identifying with Ukrainian or Belarusian as oppressed and "backward languages" in the Russian imperial context, the Soviet state's commitment to *korenizatsiia* further reinforced this phenomenon. After 1917, and despite the ethnic tensions that had raged through the civil war, a noticeable cultural rapprochement transpired between a number of Jewish and Ukrainian intellectuals—as artists, writers, and painters integrated each other's national and cultural motifs in their work. In Kyiv and Kharkiv, which emerged as centers of experimentation in the arts and cultural productivity in Ukrainian and Yiddish, many Jews joined Ukrainian literary and artistic groups and movements.[35] Young writers and poets like Leonid Pervomaisky, who was born Ilia Hurevitch in Konstantinohrad, Kharkiv, in 1908 and who was one of the founders of the literary organization Molodniak, wrote in Ukrainian only. In the Belarusian context, some Jewish writers emerged as crucial creative voices in the flourishing of Belarusian literature of the 1920s. Among them, the poet Shmuel Plaunik (1886–1941), who started out his literary career as a Hebrew and Yiddish writer, eventually switched to Belarusian, choosing for himself the Belarusian pen name Zmitrok Biadulia. He became one of the founders of modern Belarusian literature and continued to write and publish in Belarusian throughout the 1920s and into the 1930s.[36]

From afar, the Soviet Union could appear as a haven for Yiddish. In 1928, Moshe Kulbak, a popular figure in Yiddish cultural life in interwar Poland, decided to leave Vilna and move to Minsk. He moved to the Belorussian capital, where members of his family lived, not only because of some ideological romanticism but also because of the economic prospects that the new system offered to Yiddish cultural activists and literati, especially compared to what seemed to him the oppressive atmosphere that reigned in Poland at the time. The American Yiddish writer Moshe Nadir, who traveled from Poland to the Soviet Union in 1926 as part of a bourgeoning political tourism toward the first socialist country, captured the great expectations tied to the new system in contrast to the independent Polish state when he wrote, "Crossing the Polish border into Russia is like leaving a stuffy room full of medicinal odors for the bright outdoors. For the time being I am a bit blinded and can't see a thing."[37] The literary historian Zalmen Rejzen, who in 1927 traveled from Vilna to the Soviet Union, where he "visited academic institutions and libraries to collect materials for his monumental Biographical Dictionary of Yiddish Literature, Press, and Philology" in Minsk, Leningrad, and Kyiv, was impressed with the fact that he could lecture about YIVO in Moscow in an auditorium packed with students.[38] Unlike Rejzen and Nadir, who after a romantic visit to the Soviet Union returned to Poland and the United States, respectively, Kulbak remained in Soviet Minsk. And in the late 1930s, together with many others who moved to the "Red Land of opportunity," he was arrested and killed by the Soviet state as a bourgeois nationalist.

Even some of those writers who at first condemned the Soviet system eventually reconsidered their position. In 1921, Dovid Bergelson, who had played a key role in the renaissance of modern Yiddish culture in Kyiv, fled Soviet power as part of a large emigrant wave of anti-Bolshevik intellectuals and settled in Berlin. From his exile in Germany, he bitterly criticized the new system—and the Evsektsiia's bigotry in particular. But he eventually retraced his steps. From afar, Bergelson reconsidered Jewish life in the Soviet Union through the lens of Yiddish culture, and in 1926 he even argued that compared to Poland and the United States, the Soviet center offered the best prospects for a flourishing modern Yiddish culture and literature.[39] Bergelson eventually moved to the Soviet Union in 1934 and settled in Moscow, where he became one of the preeminent figures in Soviet cultural and literary life. But like Kulbak years before, in the late 1940s Bergelson too would be arrested and shortly thereafter sentenced to death by the state, which accused him of Jewish nationalism and anti-Soviet activities.

In the 1920s, however, writers and poets who produced in Yiddish received support and official recognition from that same state, sometimes in the form of a salary and access to better housings. Being a Yiddish writer came with literary evenings, funding for publications, and even banquets. It also came with an income, something that enticed a young generation of novice writers but also provided some support for the older generation. In 1927, the People's Commissariat for Education of Belorussia issued a monthly salary of fifty rubles (approximately $25, which was equal in value to more than $400 today) to Yiddish poets in Belorussia, including the young writers Zelig Akselrod and Moyshe Teyf, both born in 1904.[40] That same year, the Council of People's Commissars of the BSSR ratified allocation of a monthly pension of fifty rubles to the older Yiddish writer David Marshak.[41] In 1928, the Central Commission for Pensions at the Commissariat of Education apportioned a monthly pension to the poet Moyshe Taytsh, to mark his twenty-five years of cultural work in Yiddish.[42] Soviet authorities even offered to pay travel expenses and a monthly stipend to some foreign Yiddish writers, trying to entice them to relocate to Russia.[43] As state employees, Yiddish writers were expected to promote the Sovietization of the Jewish street through their work. Among other things, this entailed celebrating the antireligious campaigns against Judaism, the establishment of a proletarian education in Yiddish and not in Russian or Hebrew, and the productivization of the Jewish population via resettlement on land. It was not unusual, then, for well-known Soviet Jewish writers to lead, on behalf of local Jewish cultural organizations, excursions through older and newer Jewish colonies in southern Ukraine and show firsthand the advantages of agricultural work for Jews.[44]

Yiddish Schools or Russian Schools?

A graduate of Warsaw University, Ester Rozental-Shnayderman was a committed Yiddish pedagogue working in the Polish Yiddish school system (TSYSHO, Central Yiddish School Organization) in the early 1920s. Like many other left-leaning young Polish Jews at the time, she looked eastward with great hope and romanticized a political system that not only was sympathetic toward Yiddish culture but actually invested state funds to support its flourishing. Rozental noticed the stark difference between the status of Yiddish culture in the Soviet context and the Yiddish schools in Poland: in Warsaw, TSYSHO schools faced ongoing financial difficulties—they often met in private homes and struggled to pay rent—and were occasionally closed down by Polish authorities on account of the real or imagined political views of staff and parents.[45] As Rozental aptly remarked, the more the Polish government intimidated and silenced young Jewish socialists, the more they idealized the Soviet Union and Soviet Yiddish culture. Young teachers like herself devoured the Yiddish pedagogical literature published in Moscow, Kyiv, and Minsk. As Rozental noted in her memoirs, "For us, Jewish teachers of Poland, used to constant evil decrees against the secular school system, it is new and joyful (and at times almost unbelievable) that *there* [in the Soviet Union] Yiddish culture not only experienced no persecution but was actually an official government concern. We literally devour the news about how the Soviet state itself takes care of Jewish cultural institutions equally as it does of all others. . . . No other state has ever undertaken such an enterprise since the Jews have been living in *goles* [diaspora]."[46]

Primary and secondary Yiddish-language educational institutions were established in larger cities as well as in smaller settlements throughout the European regions of the Soviet empire. If we focus on Ukraine alone, by 1927, at the height of the nativization project, 502 Yiddish primary schools existed for the approximately eighty thousand Jewish students in the territory of the republic. A growing number of educational institutions operated primarily in Yiddish. These included sixteen vocational schools (two of which focused on agricultural training); fourteen trade and industrial schools; five pedagogical colleges (one of which was agricultural); a Jewish section at the Odesa Institute for National Education; a Jewish Rabfak, which prepared Jewish workers to enter institutions of higher learning; a Jewish Department in the Ukrainian Academy of Science in Kyiv; an art school and a music school; and 518 Yiddish centers for the liquidation of illiteracy.[47] At the local level, in the Odesa province, for instance, twenty-four Yiddish schools were opened from 1925 to 1927, with four Yiddish kindergartens in the city and four more in the countryside.[48] In smaller places like Polonnoe, a town in the Shepetivka region of Ukraine, there were two Yiddish schools (and only one Ukrainian). In the small shtetl of Ruzhin, in Berdychiv district, one school operated in Yiddish; by 1929, by one assessment, it had successfully eradicated illiteracy in that language.[49]

The future of Soviet Yiddish schools hinged on several key factors. First, it was contingent on the existence of a sufficient number of pedagogues and teachers who could have access to training courses and pedagogical literature in Yiddish and thus would be able to supply the growing number of schools. The fact that all subjects needed to be taught in Yiddish posed some new challenges: gymnastics instructors, for instance, who were expected to coach students in Yiddish kindergartens and elementary schools, had themselves to learn how to teach human anatomy, physiology, and physical training in Yiddish.[50] In general, aspiring Yiddish instructors—many of whom were driven by economic need and searched for employment opportunities in the new Yiddish school system—received training in the educational facilities established in the larger cities of Ukraine and Belorussia. After graduation, they were usually dispatched back to the provinces and employed in the local Yiddish schools. In 1928, for instance, the three pedagogical colleges in Minsk, Vitsyebsk, and Homyel, as well as the Jewish Pedagogical Department at Belorussian State University in the capital, produced altogether a cadre of 180 pedagogues; trained to teach history, literature, math, and science in Yiddish, 165 graduates would be employed in educational institutions throughout the Belorussian republic, while the remaining fifteen would work in Yiddish-language institutions in Russia.[51]

The popularity of Yiddish schools among Jewish parents and the subsequent trends in student enrollment was the second factor determining the success of the Soviet Jewish educational project. A multitude of regional circumstances were at play in shaping the fluctuation in popularity and enrollment dynamics over the course of the 1920s. The statistical data collected in the 1927 Soviet school census reveal some local variations: In Odesa, for instance, where Jews constituted 36.4 percent of the population, 9 percent of all school-aged children attended Yiddish-language schools. In Kyiv, where Jews made up 27.3 percent of the population, the proportion of school-aged children attending Yiddish schools was 8 percent. In Kharkiv, where the Jews were 19.4 percent of the population, this proportion was 2.9 percent.[52] In Minsk, where Jews constituted 40.8 percent of the city population, the proportion of all school-aged children attending Yiddish-language schools was 55.3 percent for elementary school and 28.2 percent for middle school.[53] The fact that Minsk, despite its status as a capital city, was a much smaller and more provincial city compared to Odesa, Kyiv, and Kharkiv and that Belarusian never achieved there the same status that Ukrainian did for many Jews living in Ukrainian cities may help explain the noteworthy difference in the popularity of Yiddish education. The following figures confirm the relatively significant support for Yiddish education among Jewish families in the Belorussian capital: during the academic year 1927–1928, 3,859 Jewish students attended Yiddish-language schools, and 2,816 attended Russian- or Belarusian-language schools; during 1928–1929, the number of Jewish students enrolled in Yiddish-language schools increased to 4,042, while the number of Jewish students in Russian- and Belarusian-language schools decreased to 2,718.[54]

Needless to say, even in those areas where Yiddish enjoyed more support because of economic, political, or demographic reasons, the success of the *korenizatsiia* project on the Jewish street could be at most moderate. As in previous decades, Yiddish could never truly compete with Russian, which remained the all-Soviet language of power, politics, and upward mobility; nor could it effectively contend with the languages of the various Soviet republics spoken by the bulk of the residents. Most Soviet Jews, regardless of their political and religious views, encouraged their children to attend a Russian-language school instead of a Yiddish one, hoping that the younger generation would gain access to a better life and a remunerating job through

Russian—and not Yiddish—literacy. The fragility of the project lay in the fact that teachers and educational activists themselves often preferred to send their children to Russian schools: the preferred language spoken in the home of the communist intelligentsia (regardless of nationality) remained Russian, and in the absence of a full-fledged higher education in Yiddish, knowledge of Russian was a sine qua non to perform well in certain university entrance exams, including physics and math.[55] One notable exception was the Jewish section of the Rabfak, at Belorussian State University in Minsk, where in order to be accepted the applicant had to pass not only the general exams but also an additional exam in the Yiddish language.[56]

In spite of families' predilection for Russian as a gateway to upward mobility, with the support of the state, Jewish activists strove to impose on Jewish children a Yiddish-language education. In the mid-1920s, for instance, in Belorussia, Jewish activists advocated to turn all Belarusian- and Russian-language schools with a majority of Jewish children into Yiddish-language schools; to regroup smaller percentages of Jewish children who attended Belarusian- or Russian-language schools into Yiddish-language schools; to move Jewish teachers employed in Russian-language schools to Yiddish schools; and to regroup into Yiddish-language orphanages and kindergartens all Jewish children whose mother tongue was Yiddish.[57] But enforcement from above, which would have guaranteed that all Jewish children attend Yiddish schools, was never implemented. Some exasperated activists acknowledged the downside of the lack of compulsoriness for Yiddish education: "The principle of not forcing at the moment of enrollment has essentially turned into the slogan 'enroll your child wherever you want.'"[58]

But the biggest thorn in the side of the new Jewish political elite stemmed from the quixotic attempt to find a midway, a sustainable compromise, between the practical determination to forge a universal Soviet culture and identity, on the one hand, and the commitment to preserve a particular ethnic culture and identity, on the other hand. Owing to this tension, Jewish activists were not always in agreement about their vision for the future of Jewish culture and identity. In the context of the widespread chaos and experimental tendencies of the NEP years, when everything seemed possible, different understandings of the Communist Party line on the nationality question easily materialized. Evsektsiia members often went to battle over their juxtaposing views regarding the future of Soviet Jewish identity and culture. Should their priority be to accept the prospect of an eventual loss of national culture, endorse the progressive assimilation and divestiture of national identity among the Jews living in Soviet territories, and thus discontinue devoting time to the creation of a new secular Soviet Jewish culture? Or should they rather work to retain the Jewish identity of the younger generations, by establishing a new culture—socialist, secular, and Soviet—in the national language of the Jews? These debates were reminiscent of deliberations about culture that Jewish activists (Bundists in particular) had handled decades before the revolution. Should the leaders of the Jewish socialist party insist that the working class commit to Yiddish, or should they rather accept the Jewish workers' choice to give in to the natural forces of assimilation?

In the Soviet context, even once activists settled on the commitment to foster new forms of Jewish culture through the establishment of new organizations and institutions—including Yiddish schools—tensions persisted regarding whether this project should be regarded as a long-lasting one or a short-lived one. Should this culture merely constitute a temporary instrument to spread communism among the Jewish masses, or should it persist even after Marxist ideology touched the hearts and minds of Jewish youth? In 1924, Jewish cultural workers in Moscow cautiously defined their mission as provisional: "Our goal is to create a culture, one that is not nationalist or spiritual, Hebrew or Yiddish, not even Jewish, but our own culture that is harmonized with the needs of the current moment, the everyday life of the Jewish proletariat. When the Jewish proletariat internationalizes, our culture will have fulfilled its mission."[59] Soviet Jewish culture should continue to exist only for as long as Jewish workers retained their linguistic and cultural specificity; thereafter, it should retain the Sovietness only and forsake the Jewishness.

Ester Frumkin, one of the most passionate advocates for the use of Yiddish among the Jewish working class, a pioneering Yiddish pedagogue, and a staunch opponent of the neutralist laissez-faire approach to national culture, reconsidered (at least publicly) her position after the revolution. In the summer of 1922, Frumkin acknowledged the great difficulties that the Evsektsiia faced while carrying out cultural work in Ukraine, especially in those areas most affected by the pogroms. While she welcomed the plans to organize theatrical productions and Party schools and to publish dictionaries and grammars in Yiddish, she also warned against supporting Yiddish for its own sake: "Work in Yiddish does not constitute Yiddishism. . . . The Central Bureau is not involved in cultivating Yiddishism. We do communist work in Yiddish because the Jewish masses speak Yiddish. It is natural that the work be done in the language spoken by the masses."[60] Yiddish should thus become a mere instrument for cultural work and not be hailed as an independent value. When a few months later Frumkin commented on the role that the Russian language should play in the education of young Jews, she reiterated her condemnation of Yiddishism in the Soviet Jewish schools: "Using pupils' mother tongues at all levels is best, so the Yiddish facilities must be improved. [At the same time] Jewish workers in Russia must know Russian, the lingua franca here, so it must be taught in Yiddish schools at all levels. Continuing their studies in Russian will not hurt pupils. . . . The failure to teach Russian is partly due to Yiddishism even in the best schools."[61] The universal values of Soviet culture took precedence over the national values of Yiddish culture, even for someone like Ester Frumkin.

In the Soviet Union, the nation-building process was rooted in the development of a standardized national language for the officially recognized national minority, which was complemented by wide-ranging cultural and educational programs in that language. Soviet schools lay at the very heart of the process. As in any other European nation-state-building process, schools served as the incubator for citizenship and as channels to convey Soviet culture and identity to the younger generation. The most effective way to instill Soviet identity and ideology was in the children's mother tongue. Hence, Stalin's popular formula of "proletarian in content and national in form" became the way to describe Soviet culture: the different minority languages, alongside the customs and traditions of their corresponding nationality, conveyed the same socialist content. Whether the national language of instruction was Yiddish, Polish, Belarusian, or Tajik, the program of studies was almost identical and was centered on Marxism, atheism, and the refutation of bourgeois nationalist culture, including the national history of the minority group.

It was the proletarian content of the Soviet educational experiment in particular that caused uneasiness among many Soviet Jews. "Hundreds of complaint letters were sent to communist newspapers in America voicing their opposition to this experiment in Ukraine and Belorussia: not so much to the language [Yiddish] but rather to the content," reported a Polish Yiddish newspaper in 1925. According to the same report, Jewish artisans and store keepers resisted enrolling their children in the Jewish schools because "Soviet teachers encouraged their students to challenge their parents' authority, worldview, and culture, and condemned religion." Indeed, many chose to enroll their children in Russian- (and even Ukrainian- or Belarusian-) language schools because there Christianity, and not Judaism, was denigrated and put in the dock.[62] For Jewish children, the peer pressure to reject any residue of Jewish religious education was far greater in the Yiddish schools than it was in the Russian-language schools; after-school semilegal private tutoring with a *melamed* was more acceptable for children attending Russian-language schools, who did not have to endure their peers' mockery. It was easier to refrain from writing on the Sabbath—which was a school day—in a Russian-language school than it was in a Yiddish one.[63] Ironically, then, if just a few decades earlier religious Jews had hesitated to enroll their children in Russian-language schools, which they viewed as an evil source of assimilation, under the Soviets they came to favor Russian-language schools over the Jewish ones.

Despite the fluctuation in popularity, the intermittent criticism, and the lack of prestige, Soviet Yiddish schools did foster a sense of Jewish ethnic distinctiveness among the younger generation. This represented the unintended consequence of the Soviet nationality policy. While deprived of most subjects with Jewish content—including the study of Jewish history, the Bible, Hebrew, and Zionism—and despite the ongoing attack on Judaism, Yiddish schools inevitably sustained Jewish ethnic identity: the interactions between Jewish students and teachers, and the ensuing friendship networks that emerged, promoted a sense of ethnic distinctiveness within the Jewish space of the school. In addition to the social component, some works of Yiddish literature that students read in class also promoted a positive sense of Jewishness. For instance, students read the classic works of Y. L. Peretz, Mendele Mocher Seforim, and Sholem Aleichem, who, while critical of certain aspects of traditional shtetl life, also communicated some constructive features of Jewish ethnic identity.[64]

A sense of ethnic belonging and cohesiveness was forged in the Soviet Jewish schools also with regard to perceived antisemitism. For instance, in the shtetl of Dunaivtsi, in Kamianets-Podilskiy region, which had a population of six thousand, two seven-year schools operated, one in Yiddish and one in Ukrainian. A report that appeared in the late 1920s in the Yiddish-language Komsomol publication of Ukraine, the *Young Guard*, noted that nationalism (and chauvinism) was widespread among students in both schools: fistfights and quarrels often broke out between Jewish and Ukrainian students in the shtetl. In 1929, at the time of a literary anniversary celebrating the Ukrainian national poet Taras Shevchenko, the Dunaivtsi Yiddish school organized an evening in his honor. The Jewish students, however, complained: not only did they insinuate that Shevchenko might have been an antisemite since he used the term *zhid* in his work, but they also protested what they considered to be unfair: "Why did the Jewish school organize a Shevchenko evening, while the Ukrainian one did not organize a Mendele evening?" Two years after the event, Jewish students in the shtetl's Yiddish school still held a grudge against the Ukrainian school, which, despite the directive from the People's Commissariat for Education of Ukraine, failed to organize a Mendele evening in 1927 marking ten years since the death of the grandfather of Yiddish literature.[65]

New (and Old) Jewish Cultural Heroes

All ethnic minorities in the Soviet Union were entitled to have their own national cultural heroes, who were usually writers whose work did not clash with or, better yet, was in harmony with the socialist worldview. Their work was celebrated through art and music, issued by the state press, read in the classroom, or declaimed in the local theater. In the case of the Jewish nationality, the classical authors of Yiddish literature lent themselves particularly well to play the role of new Soviet Jewish heroes: insofar as they had written for the Jewish masses, not the elites, in the language of the Jewish proletariat, not of the religious leadership (Hebrew) or of the Jewish bourgeoisie (Russian), and had described everyday life for the average Jew in the shtetl, they could be reimagined as suitable Soviet Jewish national-cultural heroes, politically innocuous. The attempt to integrate a Jewish national hero within the Soviet narrative played out rather successfully in the case of Mendele Mocher Seforim.

Cultural events to mark the birth or death anniversary of Mendele Mocher Seforim (the pen name of Sholom Yakov Abramovitsch, 1836–1917), widely known as the grandfather of modern Yiddish literature, were organized throughout the towns and cities of Ukraine and Belorussia in particular. Festive celebrations in Jewish and non-Jewish schools were organized, while the writer's portraits were hung on the walls of cultural institutions. According to one source, in September 1927, on the occasion of the tenth anniversary of Mendele's death, the inspector for Jewish culture of the BSSR suggested to rename Mendele's native town Kapulye (Kopil) "Mendele-shtot."[66] The People's Commissariat for Education of Ukraine established a central commission to organize a series of events to celebrate Mendele's death anniversary, including lecture series in Yiddish and Ukrainian schools, literary evenings in workers' clubs, and performances of his work by drama studios, a new edition of his work in the Yiddish original (and some works in Ukrainian translation), as well as a pension for his relatives, a scholarship in his name for two students enrolled in institutions of higher learning in Ukraine, and a yearly prize of one thousand rubles for the best new literary work in Yiddish.[67] Soviet Jewish schools and colonies, as well as streets in different cities in Ukraine, including Kamianets-Podilskiy, Berdychiv, Zhytomyr, and Odesa, were renamed after the Yiddish writer. Odesa in particular, the city in which Mendele lived, wrote most of his literary gems, and died, was supposed to play a key role in immortalizing the cultural hero and his deeds: the Regional Executive Committee resolved to tidy up the writer's grave and erect a memorial by his burial site as well as to put up a plaque with his name on the building where he had lived.[68] A large crowd of Jewish men, women, and children gathered in front of Mendele's home on the occasion of the inauguration of the memorial plaque, which was crafted in Yiddish and in Ukrainian and framed the entrance to the building.[69] In Odesa alone, reported the local press, more than forty evening events were organized during "Mendele's week," in almost every club and Jewish school and even in Russian-language schools with a small number of Jewish children.[70] Perhaps the flagship event in the construction of a Soviet Jewish cultural hero was the decision of the People's Commissariat for Education in Ukraine to establish the Mendele Mocher Seforim

Jewish museum of Odesa, which was also the first Jewish museum in the Soviet Union, as an attempt to preserve the city's Jewish cultural excellency from the prerevolutionary years into the Soviet period.

Inaugurated on November 7, 1927, the Mendele Mocher Seforim Museum of Jewish Culture was located in downtown Odesa, in the city's historic Jewish quarter, on Bebel Street. The museum was conceived as a memorial to the culture, everyday life (*byt*), and history of Ukrainian Jewry. Its different rooms celebrated the Jewish workers' movement and the history of material culture, literature, theater, printing, and Jewish agricultural settlements, and it memorialized the history of the pogroms in Ukraine.[71] But it also put on display the pride of Jewish Odesa: Mendele and his work. It preserved his manuscripts, his library, his archive, his desk and velvet armchair, and even a yarmulka belonging to the great Yiddish writer.[72] It was a perfect coincidence that Mendele's death anniversary overlapped with the ten-year anniversary of the 1917 October Revolution, something that the Yiddish press in Odesa exploited, calling on local Jews to donate artifacts on the history, folklore, and art of Ukrainian Jewry.[73]

The phenomenon of establishing Jewish cultural heroes who took up public spaces was, at the time, unique to the Soviet experiment. The fact, for instance, that in 1927 in Melnik, in Vinnytsia district, a street was renamed after the Yiddish writer Sholem Aleichem was mostly unthinkable in other Jewish demographic centers like Vilna or Warsaw, where public spaces would rarely, if ever, carry the name of a Jewish writer or political activist. Although the essence and identity of these heroes was circumscribed to the political dictates of the new system, in Soviet society, Jews and their heroes could be seen, read, and heard in public spaces.[74]

One case in point was the creation of a Jewish cultural hero in Minsk, as opposed to in its Bundist twin-sister city, Vilna, where the hero was born. The legendary hero Hirsh Lekert—a young Jewish shoemaker who carried out an assassination attempt of the governor Viktor von Wahl and was sentenced to death by hanging in 1902—was rescued from the negative Bundist legacy via Sovietization. In a number of plays, poems, and songs written or performed in Soviet cities and towns of Belorussia, his connection to the Bund was downplayed, or even erased, and he was refashioned in Soviet mold as a new hero, as a fighter for the freedom of Jewish proletariat, but severed from the Bund. In Minsk in particular, which together with Vilna represented one of the key centers of the Bund in tsarist Russia, Lekert became a cultural phenomenon: during cultural events, Yiddish popular songs about Lekert were occasionally performed, and the play *Hirsh Lekert*, with a strong anti-Bundist narrative, was staged in Yiddish by the Belorussian State Jewish Theater in 1928, attracting large audiences.[75] Jewish students in the Soviet Yiddish schools read about the deeds of the twenty-year-old Jewish worker who fearlessly faced the tsarist authorities, and we can imagine that at least some of them must have felt some pride reading about the Jewish hero.[76] Jewish and non-Jewish residents of the Belorussian capital could also view a monument to Hirsh Lekert: erected in Freedom Square, on June 11, 1922, it was placed on top of the foundation of the statue of Tsar Alexander II, which was destroyed after the revolution, as a clear political statement of rejection of the loathed past.[77] In the beginning, the monument was an extension of the old monument to Alexander II, as a large plate with "Lekert" in Hebrew golden letters replaced the tsar's head; later on, the prominent Soviet Jewish sculptor Abram Brazer, who had taught painting and sculpture at the Vitsyebsk People's Art School and participated in many exhibits in Minsk and Moscow, crafted a separate bust of Lekert.[78] The existence of a statue dedicated to a Jewish figure occupying a public square in other cities of eastern Europe in the 1920s was highly improbable.

Yiddish in Action in a Revolutionary Society: High Culture and Low Culture

In the eyes of some Jewish cultural activists from abroad who visited the towns and cities of the Soviet Union in the 1920s, the country appeared as an "entirely new universe, in which the laws of physics had been rewritten." Born in a Belorussian shtetl in 1893 and emigrating from Kyiv to the United States before World War I, the Yiddish writer Borekh Glazman paid a visit to the Soviet Union in 1925 and described the country in awe: "[This is] not only . . . a new country, but actually . . . a new world—a new world just born, standing for the time being alone in the cosmos, surrounded by watery wilderness."[79] For Glazman as well as for many other Jewish cultural activists, the perception of the Soviet Union as a different planet stemmed not only from the extraordinariness of the social engineering project in human history but also from the new spaces in which Yiddish came to be heard and seen. Within the context of the nativization campaign, a new Soviet cosmos in Yiddish took on a life of its own, engulfing both popular culture and official high culture.

In the Belorussian Soviet Socialist Republic, for instance, Yiddish enjoyed the official status of a state language, a status that was enshrined in law—something that did not exist in other key Jewish centers like Odesa and Kyiv or in large cities with major concentrations of Jews like Moscow and Leningrad. According to the law in the BSSR, Yiddish was an official state language. This entailed its full legal equality "with respect to government agencies and in organizations and institutions of public education and socialist culture."[80] In other words, throughout the cities and towns of the BSSR, any Jew had "the right and the actual possibility to use his mother tongue in dealing with any kind of organ and institution in the Republic." This, in turn, meant that every public agency or organization should have the "appropriate number" of Yiddish-speaking employees.[81]

While Yiddish enjoyed the official status of a state language only in the Belorussian republic, the right to conduct all activities in the Jewish mother tongue existed elsewhere in the Soviet Union. According to Soviet law, any town in which at least five hundred of its inhabitants belonged to the same nationality had the right to establish a national council, in which all activities should be conducted in the mother tongue of that same nationality. Additionally, whenever several adjacent national councils existed in the same geographical area, its inhabitants were entitled to establish an autonomous district. If Jewish national councils were fewer in number and distant from each other in Belorussia and Russia, that was not the case in certain areas of Ukraine and Crimea, where the state established five autonomous districts.[82] Besides these five autonomous districts, which included Kalinindorf, Nay-Zlatopol, and Stalindorf in Ukraine and Fraydorf and Larindorf in Crimea, more than one hundred Jewish rural councils (*selsovety*) were organized in small settlements throughout Ukraine and Belorussia. Yiddish constituted the official language here, at least on paper. Needless to say, the actual implementation of this cultural autonomy depended both on local authorities and on the commitment on the part of Jewish citizens and activists.

What did Yiddish sound and look like on the ground, even in those cities and towns of Ukraine or Russia where the language did not enjoy the official status of state language? For the first time, the sound of spoken Yiddish and the sight of Yiddish letters took over public places and institutions, especially those located in densely populated Jewish cities. The spaces in which Yiddish was heard and seen ranged from the post office and the envelopes on which Soviet citizens penned the recipients' addresses in Yiddish to public buildings, squares, and streets, from university classrooms to Red Army detachments, police stations, local circuses, theaters, and cinema. In 1927, on the occasion of the tenth anniversary of the October Revolution, the state sponsored radio receivers with loudspeakers that broadcast programs in Yiddish in a number of districts in Ukraine, including Kherson, Kamianets, Proskuriv, Vinnytsia, Berdychiv, and Zaporizhzhia.[83]

For the first time, Yiddish became the language of legal and administrative culture. Unlike in the realm of literature and pedagogy, there was no preexisting tradition of Yiddish in these domains. In 1925, eight courts operated entirely in Yiddish in the Ukrainian cities of Proskuriv, Vinnytsia, Novo-Zhytomyr, Ekaterinoslav (renamed Dnipropetrovsk in 1926), Kyiv, Berdychiv, Kremenchuk, and Kamianets-Podilskiy. That same year, in different areas of Podilia province, the Financial Department and the People's Commissariat of Workers' and Peasants' Inspection, which supervised the execution of government decrees, hired a number of employees who were literate in Yiddish and could cater to the necessary services in that language.[84]

Fashioning from scratch a legal culture in Yiddish was no easy feat. Not only did lawyers, court clerks, and judges have to be able to speak and write in the language during the trial, but so did defendants and plaintiffs. The Prosecutors' Office of the BSSR regularly held sessions in Yiddish. Since the Central Jewish Courtroom in the city of Minsk served the Jewish population from neighboring towns and villages, court clerks and legal officers frequently traveled to the provinces to hold the trial. The more legal services became available in Yiddish, the more Jews—especially those with little knowledge of Russian—turned to the Jewish courts. From 1926 to 1927, the Minsk Central Courtroom increased the number of cases tried in Yiddish by 50 percent, reaching a total of sixteen hundred cases.[85] And yet the novelty of this cultural and political project inevitably yielded shades of artificiality and flaws. In the second half of the 1920s, the Yiddish writer Israel Singer visited the Minsk Jewish Courtroom during the hearing of a conflict over alimony. Coming from Poland, where this was not possible, he was interested in understanding how legal procedures could operate in Yiddish. He noticed that the lawyer representing the ex-husband, a well-known lawyer, "who knows the legal code as well as a religious Jew knows *ashrei* [one of the main prayers in Jewish liturgy], must now speak Yiddish and has trouble doing so." While the lawyer indeed began his speech in Yiddish, he then continued in a mixture of Yiddish and Russian for the rest of the trial.[86] Incidentally, Yiddish could be used not only in one of the Jewish courtrooms but also in the general Soviet court system, in particular when the victim or the defendant on trial could not speak Russian and as long as the trial took place in a Jewish demographic center. During a widely reported trial, which the Supreme Court of BSSR held in the main workers' club in Minsk in January 1929, the young Jewish woman who was the victim of assault had no knowledge of Belarusian or Russian, the languages in which the court conducted the proceedings. She still had the right to speak Yiddish during the trial, while an interpreter translated for her into Belarusian and Russian.[87]

Similarly, for the first time, Yiddish became the language of police culture. In 1925, with the approval of the Central Commission of National Minorities of Ukraine, Jewish police stations in different Ukrainian cities and towns began to operate exclusively in Yiddish to serve the local Jewish population. The first Yiddish police station was organized in Berdychiv.[88] The following year, police stations were operating in Yiddish in Odesa, Kyiv, and Bila Tserkva.[89] And in 1928, they were operating in Cherkasy too.[90] But again, incorporating Yiddish into the police culture, which had always been in Russian, posed some challenges. In May 1927, two years after the Yiddish police station was opened in Berdychiv, Soviet district authorities issued an order stating that all policemen in the city "must know Yiddish." Since Berdychiv was an overwhelmingly Jewish city—with more than 60 percent of the population being Jewish—it followed that every employee in the police department should have some knowledge of Yiddish. "Those who do not know Yiddish will lose their job."[91]

In mid-1928, the biweekly Yiddish publication *Der Odeser arbeter* (The Odesa worker), the organ of the Odesa regional communist organization, reproduced on its cover the photograph of the reception room of the Jewish police station in the city. Here, a young Jewish woman, seemingly the chief of the police station, interacts with two male police officers, who show her deference. Behind her desk appears a note in Yiddish that reads, "You and your question deserve to be treated with attentiveness and cordiality." The photograph of the Odesa Jewish police department interior projected the idea of a new customer service approach provided by police officers, as the complete opposite of what happened under the tsar. For Jews in particular, who had often been targeted for persecution by the (largely Russian-speaking) tsarist police forces, the existence of Yiddish-speaking police officers created a sense of trust and confidence in the new system.[92]

The introduction of Yiddish into new spheres entailed the creation of new terminology. In Minsk, for instance, as part of the Jewish Division of the scholarly Institute for Belorussian Culture, Jewish activists established a Language Commission with the goal of standardizing spelling and orthographic rules for Yiddish, as well as for creating a new Yiddish legal, military, chemistry, physics, and agricultural vocabulary when it did not exist.[93]

As in the case of the Soviet Jewish schools, the ups and downs of the nativization project in Yiddish were marked primarily by the tension between supply and demand. Interestingly, this was not a problem peculiar to Yiddish but plagued other Soviet national minorities and their languages during the 1920s. Not unlike Latvian, German, or Mordovian publications, the numerous Yiddish newspapers, journals, and books issued by state printing houses dealt with unreliable distribution networks, the inefficient postal system, and the low circulation. The average daily circulation of the central Party Yiddish-language newspaper *Der emes* reached the small number of three thousand, while between 1921 and 1924, Soviet publishers produced fewer Yiddish books than in 1919 alone.[94] The question of prestige and competition from Russian-language newspapers and books helps explain the low circulation of many Yiddish publications, especially in the realm of politics and propaganda—less so in the sphere of education, since the primary market for books were the Soviet Jewish schools.[95] By 1928, the total circulation of the three main Yiddish dailies (published in Moscow, Kharkiv, and Minsk) reached only thirty-two thousand; this number was extremely low compared to a potential readership in the hundreds of thousands.[96]

Soviet Yiddish publishing flourished in Ukraine and on a smaller scale in Belorussia. In Kyiv, the Kultur-lige publishing house enjoyed a de facto monopoly on Yiddish publishing, producing the highest number of Yiddish books in the Soviet Union of the early 1920s.[97] In addition to the Kultur-lige press (a de facto Soviet publishing house with an atavistic name), which remained committed to the centrality of literature and to the idea of high culture, even when it came under the leadership of some of the most politically radical activists at the time, the Bolsheviks established a Jewish division of the general Soviet publishing house. This division issued books almost exclusively in Yiddish and was mostly concerned with the production of a proletarian culture for the Jewish masses.

But Yiddish publishing efforts faced dire financial conditions during the NEP years, and in Belorussia in particular—despite the existence of one of the largest Yiddish-speaking communities in the world—the printing output was meager. This remained the case at least until the second half of the 1920s, when Yiddish newspaper printing in Belorussia went through a significant increase in circulation.[98] In general, all Soviet nationalities faced similar struggles. In the effort to obtain their own publishers and newspapers to enlighten the masses, Jewish but also Polish, German, and Latvian activists faced ongoing deficits in their cultural work; moreover, they were never fully autonomous in the choice of content. Jewish cultural production was centralized in Moscow and Kharkiv, the capital of Ukraine until 1934. This tension between the foci of Soviet political power and the traditional Jewish cultural centers reinforced the gap between the official suppliers of culture and the popular consumers of culture.[99] Furthermore, many Russified Jews, as well as former members of different Jewish parties who feared being branded by the authorities as Jewish nationalists purposefully eschewed all activities related to Yiddish culture and language.[100] The concern among many Jews that the Yiddish language smacked of Jewish separatism would only intensify in the late 1920s and into the early 1930s.

In responding to the cultural vision of "national in form and socialist in content," Jews living in other areas of the Soviet Union faced similar challenges as they experimented, moving through loops of continuity and rupture. Not unlike the Jews in Belorussia, Ukraine, and Russia, "Eastern Jews" attempted to retain or recast a new culture through "new and old languages." In 1927, a Soviet publication lamented the backwardness of the Mountain Jews of Dagestan, arguing that they remained largely uninvolved in the Soviet project. Since 1920, state propaganda authorities in the region had focused their efforts on the Jews of the Northern Caucasus, striving to engage Mountain Jews in the Soviet cultural construction project. In 1923, in Moscow, the People's Commissariat for Nationalities established a special commission for Mountain Jews, which also produced few results. School attendance was limited to the elementary school level and only in urban centers, while no institution of higher learning for Mountain Jews existed in the 1920s. Only one textbook had been hitherto issued in the native language of Judeo-Tat—a fact that could hardly satisfy the requirements of the Soviet schools.[101] On the other hand, most periodicals and the bulk of political and educational literature in the Caucasus appeared in Turkic and Russian, languages in which the masses of Mountain Jews were only partially literate. The only solution to the absence of a mature Soviet culture and to the deplorable socioeconomic conditions in which Mountain Jews lived—in particular in Magal, the Jewish quarter in the city of Derbent, where more than 50 percent of the Jewish population of Dagestan resided—led Soviet authorities to encourage resettlement on the land. Established in 1925, the OZET assigned to Mountain Jewish families from Dagestan land in the Kizlyar and Buikask districts, in the hope that there at last, under promising new socioeconomic conditions, they would be able to successfully "forge a new culture."[102]

Producing Soviet culture in the native language of the approximately forty-five thousand Bukharan Jews who lived in Uzbekistan and Tajikistan and who resided primarily in Bukhara, Andijan, and Samarkand also posed significant challenges. By 1928, several Soviet schools and workers' clubs operated in most urban centers. But the number of local cultural activists committed to the Soviet project, who could spread communism to the masses, remained small. In Tashkent, for instance, approximately one hundred teachers graduated from the Jewish Educational Institute in 1928. But the dearth of qualified cultural activists with pedagogical training remained an issue, as did the absence of textbooks in the native language, which made it nearly impossible to introduce the language in the schools. The Latinization of Bukharan Jews' native language—Judeo-Tajik, traditionally written in Hebrew letters—was suggested as the solution to the problem.[103]

The Moscow Jewish Theater: Art on Stage in the Time of Revolution

The state's support for Jewish scholarship and culture gave rise to high hopes that the Soviet Union would become the center of a new scholarship and culture in Yiddish.[104] One of the main challenges faced by Jewish cultural producers lay in the negotiation process between particular Jewish themes and motifs, on the one hand, and Soviet universal and proletarian ones, on the other. In the 1920s, most Jewish cultural producers strove to walk the fine line between imbuing culture and scholarship with a specific Jewish content, while making sure that their product also served the propaganda function of enlightening and Sovietizing the Jewish masses. This underlying tension between Jewish particularism and Soviet universalism, which characterized so much of the Evsektsiia's work, was more or less pronounced in most Soviet Jewish cultural and scholarly endeavors produced in the major Soviet Jewish cultural and scholarly centers of the 1920s. This tension became a common trait of the numerous literary publications and academic institutions that operated under the auspices of the Soviet state in Minsk, Kyiv, and Kharkiv. Traces of this tension cropped up in the work of the Jewish Department of the Institute for Belorussian Culture and its journal, *Tsaytshrift*, one of the finest academic publications in Yiddish to appear in the Soviet Union, issued in Minsk from 1926 to 1931; in the sophisticated journal *Shriftn*, which appeared in Kyiv in 1928; and in the performances of the Ukrainian and Belorussian divisions of the Soviet State Yiddish Theater, established in 1925 in Kharkiv and Minsk, respectively.[105] But this tension between art and propaganda, party control and freedom, Jewish themes and communist principles, became most noticeable in the crown jewel of Soviet Yiddish culture, namely, the Moscow State Jewish theater, or GOSET.[106]

As the hub of the most exciting cultural, scholarly, and political happenings of the 1920s, Moscow attracted intellectuals from all walks of life.

Jewish artists gravitated toward the capital, which became the heart of the Jewish art renaissance, holding exhibitions and other initiatives promoted by the local branch of the Kultur-lige Art Section. Jewish artists who moved to Moscow, included, for example, the brilliant El Lissitsky. Born in Pochinok, Russia, in 1890, Lissitsky joined the fine arts section of the Educational Commissariat of the Bolshevik government in 1918. Through the early 1920s, he became one of the most coveted illustrators for Jewish publications, which he adorned with motifs inspired by Jewish folk art. He would eventually become one of the most prominent expositors of Cubo-Futurism, Suprematism, and then Soviet Constructivism. Many professional and amateur actors and theater activists were drawn to the Soviet capital because of the State Jewish Theater, which arguably turned out to be the greatest accomplishment of Yiddish culture under the Soviets.[107]

From the moment of the theater's establishment as a studio in 1919 throughout the 1920s and 1930s, the many writers, actors, and artists involved were able to produce a particular national culture within the confines of Soviet nationality policies. The theater never served as a mere platform for Soviet propaganda but retained a distinctly Jewish focus, not only by virtue of the Jewish language—Yiddish—and the largely Jewish audience (although many non-Jewish theatergoers attended too) but also because of "overt and covert Jewish cultural contexts and signifiers."[108] The distinct Jewish identity of the theater was maintained by bringing to life onstage "shtetl fables, biblical heroes, Israelite lore, exilic laments." In the early part of the 1920s, the Jewish cultural context and signifiers were much more explicit and were conveyed to the audience by performing the work of or work based on Yiddish writers like Sholem Aleichem, Mendele Mocher Seforim, Y. L. Peretz, and Sholem Asch or the plays of the founding father of Yiddish theater, Abraham Goldfaden, through a modernist and avant-garde framework. Marc Chagall, who was born in the Belarusian shtetl Liozno in 1887, trained at the Y. Pen Vitsyebsk School of Drawing and Painting, then moved to Saint Petersburg, then to Paris, and then back to Moscow (where he briefly taught in a Jewish colony outside the capital for orphans of the pogroms of 1919) and who would eventually become one of the greatest avant-garde painters and graphic artist of the twentieth century, worked for GOSET in the early 1920s. He created panels, curtain decorations, and stage designs but also painted the costumes and the faces of the actors.[109] In front of an overwhelmingly Jewish audience—in 1924 the theater offered seventy-three performances to over ninety-one thousand spectators, and between 65 and 80 percent were Jewish—GOSET put onstage Sholem Aleichem's *Two Hundred Thousand*, *The Sorceress* and *Three Jewish Raisins* by Goldfaden, and *God of Vengeance* by Asch.[110] In the second part of the 1920s, the plays' Jewish content turned more and more covert and was expressed through the subversive use of Jewish symbols or subtexts.

The Moscow Yiddish Theater did not perform only in the Soviet capital but toured the cities and towns of the former Pale of Settlement. Heeding its "civilizing" mission of enlightening the masses in the provinces, the theater traveled almost every summer to the cities and towns of Ukraine and Belorussia, not without making some profit: in 1924, the Homyel State Theater invited GOSET to perform in the city, offering to pay twelve thousand rubles, while the Minsk theater offered fifteen thousand.[111] But the profit was always very unimpressive, insofar as students, workers, Party members, and soldiers had access to tickets at significantly reduced rates—and they constituted the ideal proletarian audience.

The theater also toured the capitals of western and central Europe. In 1927–1928, after performing in Odesa, Minsk, Uman, Kharkiv, Kyiv, and Berdychiv, the troupe left for a nine-month European tour that brought the Moscow Yiddish actors to Riga, Berlin, Leipzig, Breslau, Prague, Amsterdam, Brussels, Antwerp, Frankfurt, Vienna, and Paris.[112] In the summer of 1928, Chagall, who had settled in the French capital in 1923, invited the entire Moscow Jewish Theater's troupe, on a performance tour in Europe, to visit his home near Paris. During the European tour, Alexander Granovskii, under whose directorship the Moscow State Jewish Theater had reached its earlier successes putting onstage some spectacular productions of works by the founding fathers of Yiddish literature, defected to the West. He had grown frustrated over the way in which Soviet politics and Party bureaucracy encroached on the theater's artistic creativity.

Upon returning to Moscow, the troupe came under the artistic directorship of Solomon Mikholes, perhaps the greatest Yiddish actor of all time and a member of the troupe since the very beginning. Born in Dvinsk in 1890, in a large Orthodox Jewish family, Mikhoels joined Granovskii's first studio established in Petrograd in 1919, drawn by an unyielding passion and impressive talent for acting. Recalling his first encounter with Mikhoels in 1919, Chagall noticed the following: "That was young Mikhoels—strong though short, thin but sturdy, practical and dreamy; his logic merged with feeling, his Yiddish language sounded as if it came from Yiddish books. . . . Right at my first meeting with Mikhoels, I was amazed by that rare though still vague artistic striving and force, which one day will stumble onto logic and form, which—if you find them—take on various sounds, rhythms, and colors, although it all may look both illogical and unreal. Those are forms that break old artistic conventions and promise something important in life."[113] Under Mikhoels's leadership, the theater promoted the work of contemporary Yiddish writers such as Peretz Markish and Dovid Bergelson. But Stalin's cultural revolution of the First Five-Year Plan further constrained Yiddish cultural production, and circumventing the official political message by putting onstage performances rooted in Jewish themes and motifs became harder and harder. Following the new guidelines set by the state to produce a culture "national in form and socialist in content," the Moscow State Jewish Theater's performances drew more and more from Soviet playwrights, celebrating the great achievements of the Bolshevik Revolution and socialist construction.[114] The inherent tension between the theater's nationalist yearnings and its commitment to socialist principles continued to grow.

Sara Fibikh: The Star of Jewish Pop Music

Soviet Jewish activists strove to popularize revolutionary and antireligious songs and often did so by recycling old melodies to convey the new political message of anticapitalism and atheism. The Soviet parodies and remakes of traditional and religious folk songs were thus used to create an official proletarian canon of Yiddish songs, conceived as a powerful propaganda tool to reach and educate the masses.[115] These songs were widely published in newspapers and books and broadcast on national radio stations; and more than fifty collections of Yiddish folk songs appeared in the interwar period.[116] While not all songs and melodies managed to reach a mass audience, many were still popular in the late 1930s.

On the other hand, a largely apolitical song culture, often loathed by

Soviet Jewish activists, thrived in the 1920s. In mid-1929, at the height of Stalin's cultural revolution, an article in *Izvestiia*, the official organ of the Supreme Soviet of the USSR, panned the persistence of a "disgraceful bourgeois musical culture" tied to the past. The critical report denounced first of all Sarah Fibikh, the star of the Jewish estrada music (*estradnaia muzyka*) of the interwar period, describing her work as incompatible with Soviet art.[117] The annoyed author of the report noted that large posters advertising Fibikh's concerts of "vulgar tavern music, with synagogue tunes and Hasidic songs," appeared not only in the provinces, where she performed in the Jewish workers' clubs and was broadcast on the radio, but occasionally even in capital cities. This phenomenon, argued the author of the *Izvestiia* report, "was extremely dangerous from a political vantage point."[118]

Born in Warsaw in 1895, Sarah Fibikh began her career as an artist on the theater stage, when as a teenager, against her family's will, she performed operetta and drama in Lodz and Odesa. Before turning twenty, she studied literature and set out to translate into Yiddish the work of Carlo Goldoni and Shakespeare. In particular, her translation of *Hamlet* was used by all the Yiddish troupes. At the end of 1921, Fibikh moved to Moscow, where she established the theater studio Sholem Aleichem, attracting instructors and art directors from the prestigious Moscow Art Theater (MHAT), becoming a pioneering female theater entrepreneur. She performed on the stage of the Kharkiv Yiddish theater, Undzer vinkl (Our corner), established in the city in 1918, becoming its prima donna; and in 1924, by invitation of the Soviet cultural affairs department in the Kyiv region, she helped found the Kyiv Theater Bezker, which toured the cities and towns of Ukraine and Belorussia and performed short sketches of political content. Following one of the theater's first performances, which took place in February 1925 in a workers' club in Podil, the Jewish neighborhood of Kyiv, a rave review saluted the entertaining political satire against religion and alcoholism, hailing Sarah Fibikh as one of the best actors.[119] While these smaller theatrical ensembles and movable theater collectives received support from the state to engage the Jewish audiences in the provinces and spread communism in Yiddish, they would eventually be outmoded and superseded by the three Soviet state Yiddish theaters, namely, the GOSET in Moscow, the BELGoset in Minsk, and the UKRGoset in Kharkiv.[120]

Despite Fibikh's success on the stage and perhaps because of the growing pressure to politicize the content of theatrical performances, in the second part of the 1920s, she abandoned musical drama and theater and shifted to solo concert activity, dedicating her talent exclusively to the genre of Yiddish estrada, or popular show music. In 1928, she performed a concert titled "Evreiskie etnograficheskie pesni," Yiddish ethnographic songs, in the prestigious House of the Unions, the Dom Soiuz, in the Tverskoi district in central Moscow. Over the course of the late 1920s and early 1930s, Fibikh managed to put together a unique repertoire of little-known Jewish folk songs, which she helped collect and which were arranged by the Soviet Ukrainian composers Boris Lyatoshinkii and Levko Revutsky.[121] During the late 1920s and early 1930s, she toured with great success the towns and cities of Belorussia, Ukraine, Russia, and even Azerbaijan.

While the life and work of Sarah Fibikh demonstrate the great opportunities that the Soviet cultural scene offered to Jewish women, they also capture the seemingly intrinsic tension between tradition and revolution that existed in the Yiddish cultural project. In the mid-1920s, for instance, *Proletarskaia pravda* (The proletarian truth), the organ of the Kyiv oblast CP(b)U Committee, reveled over the establishment of two new Jewish musical ensembles in Moscow and in Kyiv. The publication hoped that the new vocal quartets would produce a new communist and politicized Jewish repertoire, completely severed from the tradition of the past.[122] In fact, this expectation never fully materialized. The 1920s allowed options for those citizens who remained indifferent to Soviet proletarian culture. If mass songs on the greatness of communism and its leader seemed dull to some, there were folk songs. The work of Sara Fibikh, who remained one of the most popular Jewish musical performers and a prominent cultural producer in the Soviet Union well into the 1930s, did not conform entirely with the optimistic view of a new communist Yiddish song disconnected from the prerevolutionary tradition. Her performance of "Forn forstu avek fun mir" (You are leaving, you are leaving me), a song about a Jewish recruit in tsarist Russia, and the love ballad "Dem fartekh farlorn" (I lost my apron), both of which had nothing to do with Stalin's cultural and political project but were deeply rooted in the Jewish folk-song tradition, were released in record form by the most popular record company in the Soviet Union of the 1930s. In general, folklore remained an acceptable genre even at the height of Stalin's cultural revolution.

How Hebrew, the Language of All Jews, Was Banned in the Soviet Union

The classification of certain languages like Yiddish or Judeo-Tajik as the only sanctioned languages for Jews living in different areas of the Soviet Union went hand in hand with the gradual banishment of Hebrew. The authorities branded Hebrew as the language of rabbis and Zionist foes. As such, the Hebrew language, which had historically served as a common denominator among different Jewish communities throughout the world, including Ukraine and Central Asia, could no longer be heard or seen in Soviet institutions and cultural life. The Evsektsiia, in particular, adopted a hostile, often destructive, approach to the Hebrew language and culture. The 1919 June decree that deemed Yiddish and not Hebrew the official Jewish language was for the Evsektsiia not only about setting the record straight and picking up the former battles against a long-standing Zionist adversary. The Evsektsiia's fraught relationship to Hebrew also stemmed from the allegedly "nationalist" role that its members had played on the Jewish street before the revolution via their affiliation with the Bund or the Poale-Tsiyon. In other words, in order to be taken seriously by Soviet authorities as trustworthy supporters of the Bolshevik cause, the Evsektsiia exaggerated the threat that other bourgeois Jewish organizations, personalities, and languages like Hebrew posed to the effective Sovietization of Jews. More than Soviet authorities, then, the Evsektsiia identified Hebrew, and by extension Judaism and Zionism, as the greatest menace to the future of Jewish life and culture in the new country. Putting an end to Hebrew killed two birds with one stone: it confirmed the Evsektsiia members' victory over old rivals and washed away the "original sin" of clashing with the Bolsheviks before the revolution.

Over the course of the 1920s, Hebrew-language instruction in both its religious and secular form was suppressed and essentially made illegal. Heders and Tarbut schools—Hebrew-language, Zionist-sponsored schools—were closed down. Not only Hebrew education was targeted. The future of Hebrew literature, publishing, and scholarship in the cities that had constituted the epicenter of Hebrew-language creativity outside of Palestine was also crippled. The Bolshevik regime put an end to the Moscow-based Hebrew weekly *Ha-Am*, established in 1916 by a group of Hebraist activists and Zionist leaders, and to its homonymous publishing house. The Odesa journals—including the last Hebrew publication to appear in the city, the weekly *Barkai* (The morning star)—were also suppressed.[123] The Evsektsiia took over Hebrew presses and printing shops and used them to issue Yiddish publications only. Many Hebrew writers and teachers were left with few options but to leave Soviet territories for Palestine at once.

From afar, the Hebrew poet Yitzhak Lamdan, who migrated to Mandatory Palestine from Ukraine in the wake of the civil war pogroms, bemoaned the Evsektsiia's attempt to erase Hebrew: "It is said that the Evsektsiia destroyed Hebrew vocalization—'the lead candle' in the candelabrum of the Hebrew alphabet in all the printing presses. In this way, they believe, they have torn out the tongue of Hebrew."[124] Lamdan referred here to the Sovietization of Yiddish spelling, namely, to the purging of the language's Hebrew components, including the removal of vowel signs and final Hebrew letters.[125] And yet, despite the growing hostility and active persecution promoted by Jewish communists in the 1920s, Hebrew did not disappear entirely from Jewish cultural life. Notably, the language became the medium for new exciting, even communist, cultural productions. Although Hebrew would eventually be silenced by the 1930s, the process did not take place overnight.

In the face of the Bolsheviks' intolerance for dissent, Hebrew culture found ways to persist against all odds. Some Hebrew cultural activists managed to carve out for themselves a semilegal or clandestine space on the Jewish street. For instance, the teaching of Hebrew language persevered mostly secretly, especially in larger cities, such as Kharkiv, Odesa, Moscow, and Leningrad. Here anonymity could keep the Evsektsiia at bay. In addition, the Joint Distribution Committee could rely on better networks to provide funding for underground cultural endeavors in larger urban setting.[126] In the mid-1920s, Hebrew language teachers—but also musicians and artists whose means of income had ended under the Soviets—pleaded with JDC delegates for more support. When confronted with the Evsektsiia's antagonism, which turned down all applications for Hebrew cultural activities, Zionist and Hebraist activists sought help elsewhere. Some turned to well-known Soviet Jewish intellectuals like the celebrated pianist David Shor, asking him to intercede with Soviet officials on behalf of Hebrew culture; others approached general Soviet authorities pleading for permission to organize Hebrew courses, evening lessons, or printing of anthologies.[127] Hundreds of Jewish children who attended Soviet schools petitioned the authorities, demanding that Hebrew be introduced in the curriculum.[128] As late as August 1928, Solomon Zeitlin, a scholar of ancient Judaism born in Belorussia who had emigrated to the United States in 1915, discussed with Anatoly Lunacharsky, responsible for the Soviet Ministry of Education at the time, the state of Hebrew in the Soviet Union and the possibility of establishing Hebrew-language schools.[129] This conversation indicates a degree of tolerance, or at least neutrality, on the part of Soviet authorities with regard to Hebrew. Needless to say, the schools were never established. In fact, the study of the Hebrew language, alongside the Bible and Hebrew literature, endured exclusively in a number of Soviet institutions of higher education. These included the Jewish division at Belorussian State University in Minsk, where courses in the Hebrew language were offered until the late 1920s.[130]

Initially, Hebrew may have held sway somewhat more successfully outside of the European regions of the Soviet Union. In Tashkent, Samarkand, and Kokand, the founders and directors of the Jewish schools clashed with local authorities over the use of Hebrew as the language of instruction. Beyond the reach of Moscow and the Evsektsiia, Hebrew remained an official language of instruction in the Soviet Jewish schools of Bukhara until 1923.[131] Along with Hebrew teachers and ordinary Jews, some local Jewish communists voiced their support for Hebrew as the language of school instruction in lieu of Tajik. In the words of a Jewish communist from Tashkent, "The Jews of Bukhara aspire to universal culture and there is only one path to this—Hebrew."[132] Only one Hebrew book appeared in the Soviet Union with an official state seal: it was a geography textbook for elementary schools issued in Tashkent by the Commissariat for People's Education of Turkmenistan.[133] And in Georgia, some form of officially sanctioned Hebrew education existed until the mid-1920s.[134]

If many Jews continued to secretly teach and study Hebrew, young writers from Kyiv, Babruysk, Uman, Kharkiv, and Moscow continued to write poetry in Hebrew. They met informally to read each other's work. They distributed their poetry in handwritten copies or included their work in the handwritten journals and anthologies produced in Kharkiv and Moscow. The Moscow group even managed to get a hold of a Hebrew typewriter and produce a monthly journal until the Soviet secret police discovered them. Two anthologies of Hebrew poetry prepared for publication in Leningrad and Moscow never saw the light of day.[135] One of them, titled *Bereshit* (In the beginning), was smuggled to Berlin in 1926 and published there in book form. Eventually a few copies of the published anthology were smuggled back across the border into the Soviet Union.

Given the adverse conditions in the Soviet Union, by the mid-1920s most Hebrew writers had left the country for Palestine. Only a small minority of them stayed and continued to write despite all. One of them was the Russian poet Elizaveta Zhirkova. Born in Ryazan in 1888, Zhirkova became interested in Jewish culture and Hebrew, inspired by a Jewish classmate. She moved to Moscow, enrolled in evening classes at the Society of Lovers of Hebrew, and on the eve of the revolution became enamored with the language.[136] Upon returning to Ryazan, where she celebrated the fall of tsarism walking down the city streets with local Jews and singing the popular Zionist song "Ha-Tivkah" (which would become the anthem of the Zionist movement in 1933), Zhirkova met a graduate of the Herzlia Hebrew gymnasium in Jaffa, who became her Hebrew teacher and later her husband. She began writing poetry in Russian and translated the work of Yiddish and Hebrew writers like Hersh Dovid Nomberg and Yosef Hayim Brenner into Russian. But in 1920, Zhirkova switched to Hebrew only and began to write under the nom de plume of Elisheva. Unable to satisfy her literary creativity in the Soviet Union, she moved in 1925 to Palestine, where she composed Hebrew prose and poetry on the bohemian life of Moscow and on the emergence of a new woman in the early Soviet years.[137]

Unlike Elisheva, some Hebrew poets at the time experimented with communism and strove to celebrate the revolution in the Hebrew language. Born in 1901 in Keplits, Belorussia, Yocheved Bat-Miriam (née Zhelezhiak) first moved to Kharkiv to study pedagogy and then to Odesa and Moscow, where she enrolled at university. In Moscow, she took up writing in Hebrew, joined the communist literary group known as "Hebrew Octobrists," which was active in the city until 1926, and eventually became an influential voice of Hebrew modernism. One of Yocheved Bat-Miriam's first poems, titled "Eretz" (Land), praised the new revolutionary society established in Russia and was included in the literary anthology *Bereshit*. But just like Elisheva, she too left the Soviet Union for Palestine, in 1928. Despite the emotional connection Yocheved Bat-Miriam nurtured for the Russian landscape and for communism, her writer's creativity was stifled by the impossibility of publishing in the Hebrew language.[138]

Other writers remained deeply committed to Hebrew, while successfully acculturating into the Soviet system. Born in Ukraine in 1900, Zvi Preigerzon secretly composed short stories and novels in Hebrew his entire life. At the same time, he worked as a Soviet mining engineer, adjusting to the new system, perhaps even accepting some of its tenets and ideals. Nevertheless, he remained deeply committed to a culture and language that was proscribed in the same society in which he lived. His poetry and short stories appeared in the late 1920s and 1930s in Hebrew-language periodicals that were published outside the Soviet Union.[139]

The oddest conundrum in the history of Hebrew culture in the early Soviet Union is represented by the existence of a Hebrew-language theater. The absence of institutions and publications, including schools, journals, newspapers, and books, is countered by the impressive success of the Habimah Theater, which staged public performances in Hebrew in the heart of Moscow until 1926. Established in 1918 in the Soviet capital, where it premiered on October 12 of that year, Habimah grew out of an amateur theater group that performed in Warsaw, Bialystok, and Vilna through World War I.[140] Soviet authorities disregarded the Evsektsiia's ongoing efforts to shut down the theater. In fact, throughout the early 1920s, one could meet leading figures of the Communist Party in the theater's hall entrance. In the words of the Zionist activist Benjamin West, who served as Habimah's secretary since its founding, "The Evsektsiia had to work extremely hard to bring down Habimah since it had supporters among the highest circles."[141] Communist leaders and activists were drawn to the Hebrew stage by the originality of Habimah's repertoire, which combined biblical and folkloric themes with the most innovative theatrical techniques of the Russian theater. The influential theater practitioner Konstantin Stanislavski, who served also as director of the prestigious Moscow Art Theater, commented on the skills of the Habimah actors as follows: "I was deeply impressed by the performance of plays, the language of which is unfamiliar to me. . . . The theater has its own special language. . . . [It is] the language of emotion and experience of genuine art."[142] The Russian writer Maxim Gorky, the voice and conscience of the Bolshevik Revolution, echoed Stanislavski's words about Habimah's artists and compared them to those of the Moscow Art Theater, noting, "Their art is not inferior. . . . They have more passion, more ecstasy. For them the Theatre is a rite. . . . A magnificent proof of magic force of Jewish art and talent has been created. Habima is a Theatre the Jews can be proud of."[143] One of Habimah's most successful early performances was S. An-sky's *The Dybbuk*. Steeped in eastern European Jewish folklore, the play was first staged in 1922 in Bialik's Hebrew translation. It played in Moscow three hundred times.[144] The modernist artist Natan Altman, who was born in Vinnytsia in 1889 and was considered by many people as Chagall's chief rival in the Jewish art renaissance, was hired by Habimah in 1921, after he moved to Moscow, where he worked as the stage designer for *The Dybbuk*.

The Evsektsiia appealed numerous times to the Central Committee of the People's Commissariat of Education, trying to bring Habimah's performances to a close. But while the Yiddish press continued to harshly criticize the Hebrew troupe, the reception in the Soviet press remained surprisingly positive. *Izvestiia* published encomiastic reviews of the "Biblical theater," as it was called. In the early years of its existence, the Soviet government even supported the theater, allocating to the troupe a small financial grant.[145] The existence of a Hebrew-language theater in the capital of Bolshevism, the very ideology that had de facto outlawed Hebrew, became a source of inspiration for the semilegal and underground Zionist youth groups that operated both within Moscow and outside the capital.

Amid international acclaim, in 1926, the theater left the Soviet Union for a tour across major cities in Latvia, Lithuania, Poland, Germany, France, and the United States. On December 12, the troupe performed a concert, organized by the Zionist Council of Greater New York, with dances and dramatic recitals from its well-known repertoire, and on December 13, it performed *The Dybbuk* at the newly opened Mansfield Theater in midtown Manhattan.[146] But during the tour, Habimah split, a development that led to the end of the Hebrew theatrical experiment in the Soviet Union. Of the troupe's thirty-two actors (fifteen women and eighteen men), some chose to stay in the United States, some returned to Moscow, but the majority made their way to Palestine, where Habimah would eventually become the national theater of Israel.

Despite the ongoing stifling of Hebrew culture, an enduring belief in Bolshevism continued to blind some Hebraists. In the late 1920s, for instance, the Hebrew writer and feuilletonist Reuben Brainin, then living in New York, embraced more and more the Soviet cause, siding with anti-Zionist Jewish activists and supporting the Birobidzhan project. At the height of the Soviet cultural revolution, Brainin celebrated the political system that was responsible for the devastation of Hebrew language and culture, emphasizing its impressive redefinition of time and space: "Contemporary physics is very concerned with the problem of time and space. There it is a matter of metaphysics. Here in the Soviet Union, these problems have a practical character. The Five-Year Plan in four years; a week in five days. I feel as if I have fallen onto a new planet. A new conception of time and space is being created."[147] Compared to the grandeur of the Stalinist path to communism, the disappearance of Hebrew language and culture seemed trivial.

Russian Language and Institutions: The Persistence of the Bourgeoisie

Ideological pressure on cultural activists, writers, and scholars, Jews and non-Jews alike, influenced what they produced as well as how and in which language they produced it. The culture of the "old" Jewish world, which was articulated through the languages of the Jewish past, mostly Russian, endured with little or no state funding until the end of the decade, primarily supported through private donations and institutions. It persisted thanks to the well-established tradition of Russian Jewish culture and scholarship that crystallized over the course of the late nineteenth century and flourished in the first decade of the twentieth century. Therefore, a new communist Jewish culture in Yiddish came into being alongside, and in competition with, the tenacity of a "bourgeois" Russian Jewish culture and its scholarly institutions. For some Jews who became committed to the Soviet cultural revolution on the Jewish street, using Yiddish remained taxing also because of the strong preexisting tradition of Russian-language Jewish culture and scholarship, especially in the fields of history and ethnography: not unlike the cultural producers of other "small" languages, such as Ukrainian, Jewish communists had to come to terms with the many Jewish organizations, institutions, and personalities that had promoted culture and scholarship among Jews in Russian before 1917.

The most important Jewish cultural institutions of the early 1920s, which produced both highbrow and popular culture in Russian, were located in Saint Petersburg–Petrograd–Leningrad. The city remained the undisputed center for Russian Jewish culture and scholarship until 1930. One of the key figures in the establishment of Saint Petersburg as the cradle of Jewish studies in Russian was Simon Dubnov, the dean of Russian Jewish history who, unable to adjust to Bolshevism, fled the new regime in 1922. His decision to leave the "Egyptian bondage," as he called the Soviet Union in his memoirs, came with a sense of tragedy and loss. At the event marking the fortieth anniversary of the beginning of his literary career, held on April 28, 1921, in the building of the Jewish People's University, established by the patron Baron David Ginzburg in February 1919, Dubnov spoke of a "solemn funeral." Addressing his students and colleagues, he referred to the burial of the "Jewish Russia of the past," of Russian Jewish literature, of the Jewish cultural center of Saint Petersburg, which he had so passionately contributed to fostering.[148] He voiced his grief over the twilight of Russian Jewish history writing and the dispersal of the Russian Jewish intelligentsia taking flight from Bolshevism.[149]

While the revolution engendered the twilight of Russian Jewish culture and scholarship, its demise did not happen suddenly. In effect, during the NEP years, Russian Jewish scholarly life in Petrograd even flourished.[150] The robust tradition of scholarship on the history of the Jewish communities in the Russian Empire allowed for some continuity in the midst of constraints and lack of funds. The three institutions that made Saint Petersburg so prominent on the map of Jewish culture and scholarship before the revolution continued to operate independently over the course of the 1920s, despite growing political pressure. These institutions included, first, the Society for the Promotion of Culture among Russian Jews (OPE), established to encourage Jewish acculturation and education; it continued to fund cultural endeavors and publications until it was closed down in 1929. The second major institution, which grew out of the Historical Ethnographic Committee of the OPE, founded in 1892 by Dubnov, was the Jewish Historical Ethnographic Society. It was established in 1908 as a scholarly society; after 1917, it continued to host lectures and academic seminars in Petrograd as well as in its different branches located in Odesa, Moscow, and Ekaterinoslav. The society also housed an impressive archival collection, a museum, and a notable library with sixty thousand published items and a unique collection of rare manuscripts, until the Bolsheviks closed it down in 1929.[151] Finally, the Jewish People's University, which was renamed the Institute for Jewish Studies (Institut vyshego evreiskogo znaniia), operated in the city as an institution of higher learning until 1925. Its faculty included Dubnov, until he fled Soviet Russia in 1922, and the renowned literary scholar Israel Zinberg (1873–1939), who served as the university's academic secretary and taught courses on Jewish literary history and Yiddish.[152]

The prestigious quarterly *Evreiskaia starina* (Jewish antiquity), founded and edited by Dubnov from 1909 until 1918, featured a first-rate collection of monographic studies, memoirs, and sources and was considered the embodiment of the efflorescence of Russian Jewish historical work. Despite the Evsektsiia's ongoing criticism of the "bourgeois-nationalist" scholarship, the journal continued to appear until 1930. Several major publications by Dubnov, including his books *The Jews under Tsar Nicholas II* (1922) and *The Jews in Russia and Western Europe at the Time of the Antisemitic Reaction* (1923), appeared in Petrograd after the historian left the Soviet Union. The work of other intellectuals and publicists appeared in Russian in Petrograd/Leningrad in the first half of the 1920s. These included a study on antisemitism by the historian and philologist Solomon Lurie; a collection of historical essays by Saul Ginzburg, a close friend and colleague of Dubnov's and a Zionist; a monograph on the Bund by the scholar Naum Bukhbinder; and a history of the Jewish people by the historian Yulii Gessen.[153]

Two new scholarly journals on Jewish studies appeared in Russian in the city: *Jewish Thought: A Scholarly and Literary Collection* (Evreiskaia mysl: Nauchno-literaturnyi sbornik) was published in Petrograd in 1922 by the OPE and edited by Saul Ginzburg; and *Evreiskaia letopis* (Jewish chronicle), a collection of publicist writing but also of sources and memoirs, appeared from 1923 to 1926, sponsored by the Jewish Historical Ethnographic Society. These efforts on the part of scholars, journalists, and literary critics, which were relatively successful in reaching a broader readership, represented a tribute to prerevolutionary Jewish Saint Petersburg.[154] But while these efforts were notable, not everything was rosy. The literary scholar Israel Zinberg's monumental study on the history of Jewish literature, the initial four volumes of which he wrote in Russian, never appeared in the Soviet Union but was published in Vilna from 1929 to 1937. And while Soviet authorities officially registered the OPE, they forbade the society from promoting cultural activities for the broader public.[155] Early on, Jewish activists in Moscow, a city that lacked the well-established Jewish scholarly tradition of Petrograd/Leningrad, supported centralizing, and hence exerting fuller control over, the scholarly and pedagogical institutions, commissions, universities, and societies operating in Petrograd.[156] Born in a traditional Jewish family in the Ukrainian city of Cherkasy in 1875, Moshe Litvakov turned to communism during the civil war and moved to Moscow, where he oversaw Soviet Yiddish culture and politics as editor in chief of the central Yiddish daily *Der emes*. About Jewish cultural and scholarly endeavors in Petrograd, Litvakov complained, "there are too many Jewish institutions, . . . some [of which] have an exotic character, with amateur people working in them." He possibly referred to the bourgeois organizations that evaded the Evsektsiia's control, in particular OPE and the Historical Ethnographic Society.[157]

At the same time, however, the new Soviet system made research on certain topics in Jewish history, which had been off-limits under the tsar, open to scholars. Thus, new opportunities, often sponsored by preexisting institutions, materialized. In 1919, for instance, three commissions to study different aspects of Jewish life were established in Petrograd. Under the patronage of the Historical Ethnographic Society, the Commission to Study the History of Anti-Jewish Pogroms existed until 1923 and produced two volumes on the origins of the pogroms of 1881 and 1903 in Russia. The study of anti-Jewish violence constituted a sensitive topic in prerevolutionary times, and tsarist authorities had restricted the access to many archival materials related to the pogroms. For the first time in Dubnov's long career, he gained access to some collections from the state archives, and as one of the commission's members, he wrote the foreword to the volumes.[158]

The second commission, also established in 1919, was called the Commission for the Scholarly Description of Jewish Questions of the Former Ministry of Public Education; under the direction of the historian and publicist Samuil G. Lozinskii—a professor at Petrograd University and the rector of the Jewish People's University until 1925—and with the support of the People's Commissariat of Education, the commission published a volume of documents related to the Jewish state schools (Kazennye evreiskie uchilishe). A third commission—short-lived but just as important as the other two scholarly endeavors—was the Commission for Investigating Blood Libel Trial Materials in Russia. Established in late 1919 and supported by the Commissariat of Education, it grew out of the reality of a system that officially condemned antisemitism, including the blood libel accusations against Jews that had taken place in nineteenth-century Russia. For the first time, thus, primary documents on the blood libel, most of which were housed in the Senate Archives, would be made available to the public.[159] Regrettably, the result of the commission's scholarly labor never saw the light.[160] Due to technical and financial difficulties, as well as the departure from Soviet territories of a number of scholars involved in the project, the ritual murder commission was liquidated at the end of 1920.[161]

It is difficult to pinpoint the exact reasons why Russian Jewish intellectuals and cultural activists who opposed Bolshevism decided to stay in the Soviet Union and participate in these cultural activities. Besides the personal dimension of their lives, which may have induced them to stay, the hope of working independently within the context of the moderately liberal NEP and its mixed economy may also have contributed to the decision. They wrote and researched on behalf of non-Bolshevik organizations, many of which had existed before the revolution, and hoped to be able to pursue their work without the state's interference. However, regardless of the tolerance of the NEP years, the Ministry of Education and the People's Commissariat for Nationalities supervised and even constrained their scholarship especially when it intersected with the field of history.

From the Soviet vantage point, more than any other discipline, historical writing was subordinate to politics. Over the course of the 1920s, the quality of Jewish historical writing declined steadily. Even the most original researchers in the field, most of whose work appeared in Yiddish and generally incorporated a sociological slant to the study of the Jewish past, did not succeed in establishing a real school of Soviet Jewish history writing. Both Tevye Heilikman (1873–1948), who taught Jewish history in Moscow and was the author of *History of the Social Movement among Jews in Poland and Russia*, and Israel Sosis (1878–1967), who taught at Belorussian State University and headed the Historical Department of the Jewish section of the Institute for Belorussian Culture in Minsk and was the author of *The History of Jewish Social Trends in Russia in the Nineteenth Century*, condemned as ontologically corrupt the "bourgeois-nationalist" narrative created by Dubnov. Their Marxist reading of the past replaced the idealization of the Jewish communal organs with class conflict as the driving force in Jewish history. Asher L. Margolis (1891–1976), who taught Jewish history first at the Jewish pedagogical college in Kyiv in the early 1920s and then at the Moscow-based Communist University of the Peoples of the West (called Mayrevke in Yiddish), published in 1930 *History of the Jews in Russia: Studies and Documents*. Not unlike his colleagues Heilikman and Sosis, Margolis too (who in the late 1920s served as head of the historical section of the Institute of Jewish Proletarian Culture in Kyiv) strove to denigrate the nationalist reading of Jewish history by creating an alternative one rooted in Marxism.[162] However, between the shrinking community of students interested in the study of Jewish history and the growing restrictions on the topic, Soviet Jewish historiography never reached the same stature of its imperial Russian predecessor. In the cultural and scholarly institutions in Minsk, Kyiv, and Moscow, the field of Jewish history just about disappeared. No matter how much Soviet Jewish scholars separated their work from that of previous Jewish historians, they were continuously reminded of the inherently nationalist and anti-Soviet nature of the study of Jewish history.

In the Soviet Union, museums not only became sites of collection, preservation, and display of artifacts, visual arts, and cultural heritage but also constituted significant conduits to indoctrinate the masses in the spirit of communism. Jewish museums, or Jewish sections of state or local museums, were established throughout the cities and towns of the Soviet Union during the 1920s and early 1930s. Besides the Mendele Museum in Odesa, Jewish museums and Jewish sections of regional museums opened in Poltava, Berdychiv, Mykolaiv, Vinnytsia, Minsk, and Samarkand. As with other cultural endeavors of the 1920s, Jewish museums too emerged from the support of the Bolshevik state, alongside a well-established tradition of collecting, preserving, and putting Jewish life on display, which had crystallized among the Jewish intelligentsia in the beginning of the twentieth century.

Established in 1908 by the writer and revolutionary activist An-sky (Shloyme Zaynvl Rapoport), the Jewish museum in Saint Petersburg deeply influenced the activists involved in the creation of most Soviet Jewish museums or sections of local museums. Born in the Belarusian shtetl Chashniki in 1863, after a political career as a populist and Bundist, An-sky turned to literature and ethnography, moved to Saint Petersburg, and joined the Russian Jewish intelligentsia. The ethnographic expeditions he led during the summers of 1912–1914 through the Jewish towns of the Pale of Settlement constituted one of his greatest achievements. With a team of Jewish intellectuals, musicologists, and ethnographers, An-sky traveled through Volhynia and Podilia, collecting thousands of photographs, folktales, folk songs, historical documents, manuscripts, and sacred objects. The ethnographic impulse that inspired his work stemmed from a growing sense that modernization and urbanization, but also the looming war and the pogroms, jeopardized the creativity and ingenuity of the Jewish people, which were on the verge of disappearing.[163]

The ethnographic treasures collected by An-sky in the heart of the Pale of Settlement were first put on display in the Museum of the Jewish Historical and Ethnographical Society (EIEO) in Saint Petersburg in 1908. During World War I, the exhibition grew in size, adding new artifacts and relics to the collection. The museum briefly opened to the public in 1917 but closed down again during the civil war. It finally reopened as the Jewish Museum in Petrograd in the summer of 1923, when the Jewish Historical and Ethnographic Society renewed its activities. The fact that several museum employees in the Jewish museum in Petrograd-Leningrad—and in other museums too—had worked closely with An-sky, sharing his understanding of Jewish ethnography, fostered a sense of continuity with prerevolutionary Jewish culture. The same fear of imminent loss experienced by Jewish intellectuals who traveled with An-sky through the shtetls of eastern Europe in 1914 was at play under the Soviets. It fueled the urgency to collect the folklore and ethnographic treasures of traditional Jewish life and to organize museum exhibits.

Soviet Jewish activists led expeditions to collect folklore in the shtetl; they not only conceived of the Jewish town as a site of warped socioeconomic and religious life but also saw it as the repository of an authentic culture on the brink of passing. In this respect, they were the heirs of An-sky's mission. During the 1920s, scholars and cultural activists in the Jewish section of the Institute for Belorussian Culture in Minsk and in the Jewish department at the Ukrainian Academy of Science in Kyiv organized ethnographic expeditions throughout the shtetls in the former Pale of Settlement.[164] Their goal was to produce an accurate portrayal of the shtetl, capture its everyday life and culture, and record the language and folklore of its inhabitants, before it vanished.[165]

The year 1929 marked a turning point in all spheres of Soviet life, including culture. The end of private funding to support independent non-communist organizations, together with the growing political pressure to conform, made the liquidation of the Jewish Historical and Ethnographic Society and its museum unavoidable. The authorities deemed both dangerous centers of "bourgeois nationalism" that were unable to produce proletarian culture. They expropriated the OPE property, including the organization's famous library.[166] In a harsh attack against the OPE and the institutions it supported, which appeared in the Soviet Jewish publication *Tribuna evreiskoi sovetskoi obshchestvennosti* (Tribune of the Soviet Jewish community), a cultural and political Russian-language journal published since 1927 by OZET in support of the resettlement of Jews on land, the journalist Solomon Nepomniashii called for the end of the "hotbed of corrupt Peterburgshina."[167] The great turn in Stalin's cultural revolution marked the end of Saint Petersburg–Leningrad as the remarkable center of Russian Jewish culture and scholarship.

Yet, some shades of continuity persisted. The OPE's museum and archives were transferred to the Jewish cultural institutes in Kyiv and Minsk. Several collections of artifacts were transferred from Leningrad to Odesa and put on display in the Mendele Museum of Jewish Culture, which existed until 1941, as well as in other museums and archives. The directors of the Jewish museums in both Odesa and Samarkand, who had closely collaborated with An-sky, remained committed, at least in part, to his vision.[168]

An-sky's work remained a reference point for Jewish museums and exhibits throughout the 1920s and 1930s, guiding even those activists who strove to distance themselves from him, his work, and the legacy of prerevolutionary Jewish studies.[169]

Whether as a result of intimidation or true belief in the new ways of communist life, younger Soviet Jewish producers of culture and scholarship rebelled against the previous generation and rejected their work, as pupils occasionally do with their mentors when searching for their own place in the world of ideas. Some, however, never rejected the work of the past entirely and unconditionally but rather attempted to weave through threads of the future communist culture and scholarship. Some intellectuals from the older guard, such as Israel Zinberg, remained anchored to the bourgeois remnants of pre-1917 Russian scholarship, never attempting to cross into the realm of communist *Wissenschaft*.[170] Others, like Shmuel Agursky (1884–1947), embraced the new Soviet scholarship uncompromisingly and without remorse, in Yiddish though not in Russian. Others yet were unable to severe all links with the past and attempted instead to produce a synthetic path between the Soviet proletarian culture and scholarship of the future and the bourgeois Jewish culture and scholarship of the past. The search for a path made of continuities through ruptures remained possible only during the 1920s. By the early 1930s, it was all but anachronistic.

The Pale of Settlement according to the boundaries established in 1835 and legally in effect until 1917. (NYU)

A propaganda poster depicting the pogroms carried out by the Polish army at the time of the Polish-Soviet War, 1919–1921. The text in Yiddish reads, "The smoldering ashes and blood of Jewish workers cover the path of the Polish *szlachta* [nobility]." (Courtesy of Blavatnik Archive Foundation)

Residents of Kyiv in front of the Demiev Synagogue, following the May 1920 pogrom. (Courtesy of JDC Archives)

Men inside the damaged Demiev Synagogue, following the May 1920 pogrom in Kyiv. (Courtesy of JDC Archives)

Jewish writers and cultural activists and artists, together with JDC representatives in uniform, posing for a group portrait, Kyiv, 1920. Standing and leaning left to right are Isidor Eliashev (an influential literary critic, pen name Baal-Makhshoves), Elias Tcherikower (the great historian of Ukrainian Jewry), Captain and Rabbi Elkan Voorsanger, Nokhem Shtif (a linguist and literary historian), Charles D. Spivak (a humanitarian and physician), Zelig Kalmanovich (a Yiddish linguist and community activist), and Dovid Bergelson (a Yiddish writer), Wolf Latsky-Bartoldy (a Jewish socialist activist). Sitting on the ground, left to right, are the artist Mark Epstein, the Yiddish writer Leyb Kvitko, and the artists Issachar Ber Rybak, Boris Aronson, and Josif Chaikov. (Courtesy of JDC Archives)

Corpses of adults and children tortured and murdered during the pogrom of May 1922, in the village of Zagore, Chechersk county (present-day Belarus), and local residents and family members saying farewell to the departed. (Courtesy of USHMM/Centropa Collection)

The tombstone of a pogrom victim, murdered in 1922, after the end of the civil war. Crimea, 1924. Inscribed on the tombstone in Hebrew, it says, "Here lies the young martyr who was killed in the month of Iyar 5682 [1922], Moyshe Dukhovniy." Inscribed in Russian, it says, "Rest in peace. . . . He met an untimely and harsh death at the hands of the bandits." (Courtesy of JDC Archives)

Jewish orphans, mostly refugees from small towns, displaced during the violence of the civil war, together with medical staff and caretakers, in a children's home in Kyiv, May 1920. (Courtesy of JDC Archives)

Jewish children and their caretakers of the orphanage named after the Yiddish writer Sholem-Aleichem, in Moscow, 1920s. In the upper left-hand corner, a banner in Yiddish reads, "Proletarians of all countries unite! Sholem-Aleichem children home. Children's administration." (Courtesy of JDC Archives)

A settlers' group portrait with propaganda posters and banners in Yiddish and Russian, from the Zaria (Dawn) cooperative, Alchin Jewish colony, Yevpatoria district, Crimea, 1920s. (Courtesy of JDC Archives)

A group of shoemakers holding shoes and working tools, Mykolaiv, 1928–1929. (Courtesy of JDC Archives)

Members of the Jewish agricultural commune "Unity," established in spring 1921 in the city Starodub. The commune spread across the farmstead Belovshchina in the Starodub region, Russia. The photograph was taken in 1924 to mark the third anniversary since the establishment of the Jewish commune. (Courtesy of USHMM/Centropa Collection)

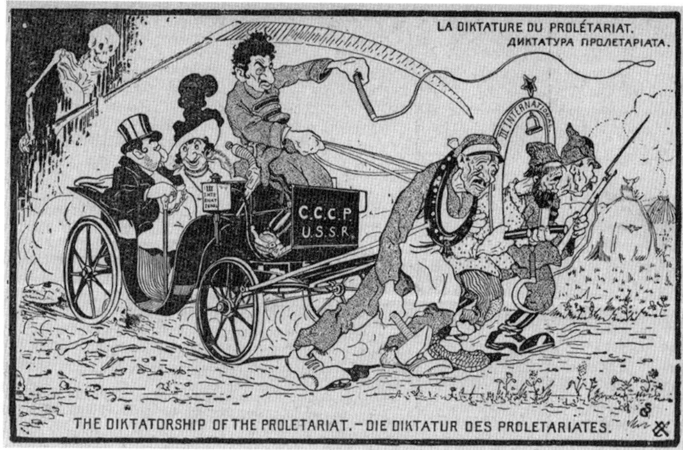

An antisemitic postcard, produced shortly after World War I and titled "The Dictatorship of the Proletariat," in which the Soviet Union appears as a haven for Jewish power. Two stereotypical Jewish capitalists, a man and his wife, ride in a carriage, which symbolizes the new regime and is driven by Leon Trotsky. The USSR carriage proceeds in the shadow of the Grim Reaper, sowing death and destruction everywhere. (Courtesy of Blavatnik Archive Foundation)

An antisemitic postcard, produced shortly after World War I and titled "There . . . the USSR." (Courtesy of Blavatnik Archive Foundation)

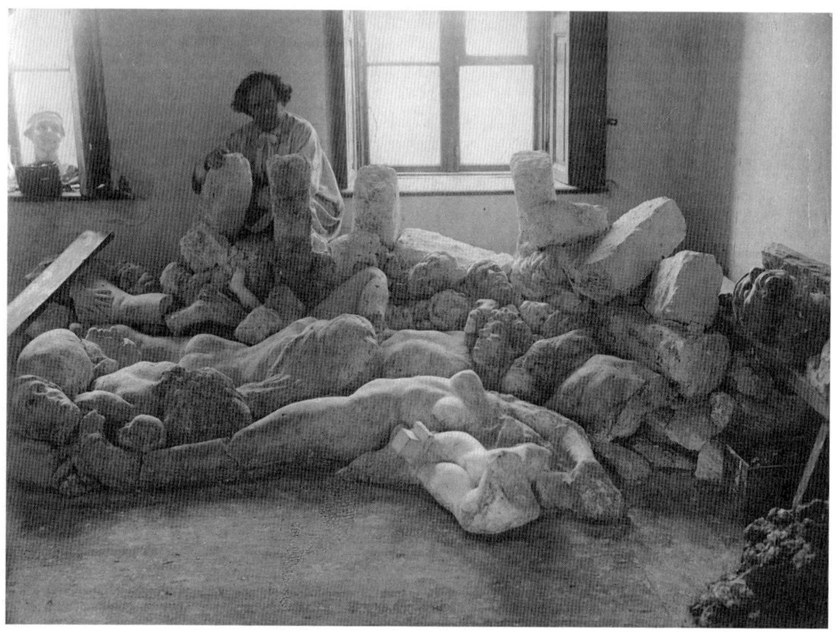

Pogrom by the remarkable Soviet Jewish sculptor Isaac Itkind. The sculpture is made of a tangle of bodies and body parts. Moscow, 1924. (Courtesy of JDC Archives)

A vinyl gramophone record of Vladimir Lenin's speech held in Moscow on March 23, 1919, titled "On Pogrom Persecution against Jews," in which the Bolshevik leader condemned the anti-Jewish violence of the civil war. Issued by the Music Section of the People's Commissariat for Education, the record was part of a series of thirteen speeches by Lenin recorded from 1919 to 1921 that addressed significant political questions and were disseminated through propaganda trains. The Russian text is the Soviet slogan "Proletarians of the world unite!"

Right: Jewish settlers farming the land of the Jewish colony of Sede Menuha, Kherson district, 1925. (Courtesy of JDC Archives)

Below: Settlers at the Jewish colony Tel Hai (Hills of Life) in the Dzhankoy district of Crimea, 1925. A man and a boy (wearing a white apron) display cheeses and the cheese-making equipment. (Courtesy of JDC Archives)

Settlers at the Jewish colony Tel Hai in Dzhankoy district, Crimea, 1925. (Courtesy of JDC Archives)

Young female settlers at the Jewish colony Avoda (Work), near the city of Kurman (Krasnohvardiiske), Crimea, 1925. (Courtesy of JDC Archives)

The Jewish trade school building in Kakhivka, a port city on the Dnipro River, in the Kherson district, 1928–1929. Located on Lenin street, the building was probably a former Jewish religious institution that was Sovietized after the revolution. The school's name appears in Yiddish and Ukrainian: "Kakhivka Handicraft School Woodworking Workshop." (Courtesy of JDC Archives)

Family members from different generations from the renowned and wealthy Davidoff family that settled in Tashkent in the nineteenth century, 1926. The women sitting in the first row are wearing sumptuous traditional Bukharan dresses and head coverings and are surrounded by their children and grandchildren, who are dressed according to the general fashion of the time. (Courtesy of Yad Izhak Ben-Zvi Photo Archive)

A propaganda poster from the 1920s in Yiddish that says, "Subscribe to *Der emes*," the social and political newspaper published in Petrograd and then in Moscow from 1918 until 1938. It was the Yiddish equivalent of *Pravda*, the central organ of the Communist Party. The poster promoted a subscription campaign for the Yiddish newspaper. (Courtesy of Blavatnik Archive Foundation)

A propaganda poster in Yiddish from the 1920s advertising a new series issued by the Kyiv publishing house Kultur-lige (Culture league). It says, "The 'Yiddish Writer' library—1,000 folios, 75 volumes of works by Yiddish classics, Soviet writers and authors from abroad. Yiddish reader! Subscribe to the 'Yiddish Writer' library." (Courtesy of Blavatnik Archive Foundation)

A propaganda poster from the 1920s that says, in Yiddish, "Read and Subscribe!" It promotes the subscription campaign of Yiddish newspapers and periodicals issued in the Soviet Socialist Ukrainian Republic by the Soviet Ukrainian Bolshevik Party and the Young Communist League. The designer is unknown. It was printed by the Ukrainian publishing house named after comrade Dzierżyński in Kharkiv, at the time the capital of the Ukrainian republic. (Courtesy of Blavatnik Archive Foundation)

Black and white photograph of fifth-grade students at a Soviet Russian school in Odesa, 1927. In the second row, at the bottom, second from the right, is Victor Feldman, born in Odesa in 1915. While there were a number of Soviet Yiddish schools in Odesa and Jewish communist activists tried to convince his mother to enroll him in a Yiddish-language school, she refused and enrolled her son in a Russian-language school in 1921. (Courtesy of USHMM/Centropa Collection)

The GOSET troupe (Moscow State Jewish Theater), together with the students of the theater's Jewish school of acting (Evreiskii teatralnyi tekhikum), in Moscow, second half of the 1920s. Sitting in the front row are some future celebrity actors, including, second from left, Solomon Zilberblat; fourth from left, Iustina Minkova (the stage name of Yokheved-Yudes Minkova); fifth from left, Lev Pulver (author of the theater's most famous musical compositions); and sixth from left, one of the GOSET's leading actors, Veniamin Zuskin (who had a walking stick due an injury he incurred during the performance tour in Odesa of 1924). (Courtesy of Blavatnik Archive Foundation)

The entire GOSET troupe at the home of Marc Chagall, who had left Russia for Paris in 1910 and invited the troupe, on a performance tour in Europe, to visit him near Paris in June–July 1928. In the front row (sitting), from left to right, are Evgenia B. Epshteyn, B. Rainer, Aleksei Granovskii (the theater's director, holding a vinyl record), Marc Chagall, Lev Pulver, Mariia Askinazi (one of the troupe's star dancer), Eda Berkovskaia, N. Kruglikova; in back row (standing), from left to righht, are the great actor Solomon Mikhoels, Sara Rotbaum, Ester Karchmer, Rakhel Imenitova, B. Krashinskii, Liubov (Leah) Rom (one of the theater's star dancer), Iakov Gertner, Iosif Shidlo, Mikhail Shteiman, Iustina Minkova, and Veniamin Zuskin. (Courtesy of Blavatnik Archive Foundation)

The first meeting of Soviet Yiddish writers, held in 1929 in Moscow and presided by the Soviet writer and cofounder of the Union of Soviet Writers Alexander Fadeyev. Sitting in the bottom row, from right to left, are Yasha Bronshtein, Peretz Markish, Alexander Fadeyev, Izi Kharik, and Itzik Feffer. Standing in the top row, from right to left, are Moishe Kulbak, Arn (Arka) Kushnirov, Meyer Daniel, Moishe Litvakov, Note Lurye, and Shmuel Godiner. Notably, there are no women writers in the photograph. Most of the men pictured here were arrested and executed in 1937 or in 1952. (Courtesy of Blavatnik Archive Foundation)

Children voting at the Jewish Children's Home No. 40, Kharkiv, September 1922. The meeting's agenda is written out in Yiddish on the blackboard. Below the blackboard, two young boys take the protocols and voting results. The banner above the children reads in Yiddish, "Jewish Children Home. The home of communist culture." (Courtesy of JDC Archives)

A propaganda poster from the 1920s, in Yiddish, titled "Old schools, Soviet schools," advocating for the Soviet education system. At the center of the poster, a Yiddish inscription explains how "the old religious school" (heder) produces enslaved people, while the new Soviet school produces healthy citizens, fit to work and ready for the socialist order. The poster depicts two routes, representing two possible paths in life: the red Soviet path begins with studying in a Soviet school, continues with working in the factory and agricultural work, and leads eventually to the "brotherhood of peoples." The blue path begins with studying in the "heder" and leads to working in a small store, praying in the synagogue, and hatred among the peoples.

Ethel Levit, mother of Asya Matveyuk, who died after having an abortion, in 1924. Because she died at the same time as Lenin did, her burial in a Jewish cemetery was, like all funerals, put on hold. The photo was taken in Mykolaiv in 1923. (Courtesy of USHMM/Centropa Collection)

Young Jewish students in a Rabfak, a Soviet educational institution that prepared workers to enter institutions of higher education, in Korsun, Ukraine, 1923. Second from the top left is Manya Karmazin, born in the shtetl Medvin in 1904, who, after attending the Rabfak, enrolled in and graduated from university in Kyiv. (Courtesy of USHMM/Centropa Collection)

Students in a Soviet Yiddish school in Rahachow (or Rogachev), present-day Belarus, 1921. Second to the left in the second row is seventeen-year-old Rosalia Khlevner (née Goldin), with a bow on her dress. To her right is the class teacher, wearing glasses and looking strict. A second teacher, also with glasses, is sitting fifth to the left in the second row. (Courtesy of USHMM/Centropa Collection)

Students at one of the professional technical schools for children of workers and peasants in Kyiv, 1926. On the right is Buzia Aloets, who moved from a Jewish children home in Uman to Kyiv in 1925, at the age of sixteen. Like many other young Jews from the provinces, she too moved to larger cities in search for employment and education and inspired by the ideals of the revolution. (Courtesy of USHMM/Centropa Collection)

Anna Vaisman, Kazan, Russia, 1925. She worked for the Zhenotdel, the Women's Department of the Communist Party, conducting ideological work among women workers and peasants. Specifically, Vaisman worked with Tatar women with the goal of eradicating their illiteracy in Russian. (Courtesy of USHMM/Centropa Collection)

Ballet students at the Choreographic College of the Kyiv Opera Theater, Kyiv, Ukraine, 1929. The well-known theater director Alexander Tairov (born Korenblit) is standing at the top, wearing a tie and a colored skull cap. Anna Ulik (first on the right in the upper row) was born in Zhytomyr in January 1925 and grew up in a highly educated Jewish family. Tairov personally admitted her to the college, after examining her feet and discussing them with her father, who at the time was vice director of the Kyiv Opera Theater. (Courtesy of USHMM/Centropa Collection)

7

THE FAMILY, THE BODY, AND THE SELF

Soviet (Jewish) Everyday Life in the 1920s

Born in 1919 in the Jewish colony of Novopoltavka, in the Mykolaiv region of southern Ukraine, Asia Matveyuk spent many days of her childhood at her grandparents' home. The home smelled of glue and paint from her grandfather's tools—he was a poor shoemaker. On Fridays, while Asia enjoyed watching her grandmother get ready for the Sabbath, polishing the floor and covering the table with a white tablecloth, the home smelled of freshly baked challah. On Saturday mornings, Asia's grandparents took her to the local synagogue, which "was big and beautiful and seemed like a palace" to her. There she sat with her grandmother in the women's gallery, on the second floor. But Asia's father was not pleased with this. A farmer and a winemaker who had served in the Russian Army during World War I, Asia's father embraced communism after the civil war. He became a village activist and a member of the Komsomol, and in 1927 he joined the Communist Party. While he relied on his parents for day care—his wife had died shortly after Asia's birth—he resented them for sharing their lifestyle with his daughter; he heatedly argued with them, forbidding them from taking Asia to synagogue. After all, on one occasion, he was nearly expelled from the Party because his grandparents attended synagogue. The clash between her grandparents' old *byt* (everyday life), which Asia remembered with nostalgia, and her father's new *byt*, which she would eventually live by, persisted throughout the 1920s, only to intensify at the end of the decade. If Asia's grandparents ignored her father's imperative to change their behavior, they could do very little when the state intervened to settle the score: in 1930, Soviet authorities closed down the synagogue in Novopoltavka where they used to take their granddaughter and turned the building into a school.[1]

Generational clashes between parents and children over changing worldviews and life styles is of course a rather typical phenomenon in every modernizing society. Ivan Turgenev first captured the cultural schism between generations in nineteenth-century Russia in his 1862 novel *Fathers and Sons*, in which he described the unsolvable rift between the fathers, who were the liberals of the 1830s and 1840s, and their sons, the Bazarovs, or the nihilists of the 1860s, who rejected everything about the established social order. In the Jewish context of imperial Russia of the 1860s and 1870s, many sons (more than daughters) embraced the ideals of the Haskalah, or Jewish Enlightenment. By doing so, they challenged their parents in the realm of language, education, fashion, and political allegiances. The 1880s then saw the rise of secular nationalist and socialist movements, which captured the hearts and minds of thousands of young Jewish men and women; these movements expected from them a revolutionary break from the old world of mothers and fathers. This had been the experience of Hodl, the middle daughter of Tevye, the main character in Sholem Aleichem's Yiddish short stories that would make up his *Gants Tevye der milkhiker* (The complete Tevye the dairyman) on the generational rift that tore apart a Jewish family in the Russian Empire; not only did Hodl reject an arranged match and chose to marry the poor student Perchik, but together with him, she also embraced socialism.

The generational clash in Soviet society therefore was exacerbated by Bolshevik ideology. The rejection of the old values of mothers and fathers was also an integral aspect of the modern welfare state's project, which promoted urbanization, secularization, increasing literacy, and education. The call for the establishment of a new Soviet everyday life, or *novyi byt*, of the early 1920s clearly intersected with the welfare state's modernization agenda. Creating new living arrangements, promoting new leisure activities, setting new rules for health and hygiene, monitoring family and friendship relationships and personal appearance were to a degree shared objectives of most modern European states.[2] The Bolshevik project differed insofar as the Soviet state forced its citizens to engage in a war against the old lifestyle and to create a new *byt* by internalizing the ideas of communism, which should reign unchallenged in both the public and private spheres of their lives. Building the revolution not only was a public endeavor but also entailed an internal transformation, the creation of a new Soviet self, by bringing ideology into every aspect of life and consciousness. Private life thus turned into a sort of homework assignment, which "was undertaken with great confidence in the 1920s, spurred by the certainty that with sufficient effort and commitment the ideological transformation was imminent and inevitable."[3]

The intimate sphere of family and friends, of the home, of the mind, were no longer sites of private and individual experiences that existed outside the reaches of the state. Rather, because these spheres came within the reach of the state, parents and children clashed over most aspects of daily life. Yet, as we will see, the Bolshevik confidence that everyday life and the individual subject could be merged with the public goal of communism did not always come to full fruition, at least during the 1920s, as family networks and personal interests and gain turned out to be more resilient than the Party and the state had hoped they would among Jews and non-Jews alike.

Bourgeois Institutions under Fire: Chuppah or Red Marriage?

Unlike other modernizing societies, the family and the state were no longer interdependent and mutually reinforcing entities in the Soviet case. Rather, the clash between the state, which upheld the values of the Party, and the family, which represented the old *byt*, became inevitable: every young member of the new society was pressured into taking an oppositionist stance and even to disparage blood ties whenever they stood in the way of the Party. And because one's communist identity and allegiance to the Party were measured against one's family and friendship networks too, the social and political pressure could drive the individual to give in to the rule of the Party and the state and to reject blood ties. On the other hand, for younger people in particular, the revolution meant liberation from the bourgeois conventions of the old *byt*, from the oppressive burden of the family and from everything that marriage stood for. Amid excitement and fury, they were eager to rebel against the past, to build a new society.

As a public statement of independence and autonomy from the oppressive bourgeois order, many young revolutionaries adopted the practice of a "free union," scoffing at the marriage institution and, at least initially, rejecting it altogether. Perl Karpovskaia, who was born in 1897 in a small shtetl in Zaporizhzhia oblast, Ukraine, before she became one of the most powerful women in pre–World War II Soviet society, worked first in a cigarette factory and then as a pharmacy cashier. In 1918, she joined the Communist Party, changed her name to Polina Zhemchuzhina (adopting, for her Bolshevik pseudonym, the Russian translation of her Yiddish name, Pearl), and became active as an instructor for women in the Central Committee of the Communist Party of Ukraine. As a delegate from Ukraine to the International Women's Congress in Moscow, in 1921 she met Vyacheslav Molotov, one of the conference's organizers, who would rise to power as Stalin's protégé and become one of the most influential Soviet politicians from the 1920s through the early 1950s. Within months after they met, Zhemchuzhina and Molotov were "married" in de facto Bolshevik fashion.[4]

Fruma Treivas was born in a small shtetl near Polotsk in a religious family—her father was a *shochet* and a *melamed*—and after the revolution, she joined her brother, who was a Komsomol official, in Petrograd.[5] After moving to Moscow in 1922, she enrolled in a Rabfak and eventually started working at the newspaper *Iunosheskaia pravda* (which later became *Moskovskii komsomolets*); she was in charge of the newspaper's subscriptions.[6] There she met her future husband, the newspaper's editor, Grigorii Waltenberg (Vasilkovsky). As she recalled, "we did not get married officially, but I moved to his place on Polianka and considered myself his wife."[7] Only later did Fruma Treivas marry Waltenberg, with the intention of starting a family with him.

So what should the family look like in Bolshevik society? Should it continue to exist or "whither away," as suggested by some leading Russian communists like Alexandra Kollontai or like the radical legal theoretician of free love Alexander Goikhbarg?[8] Born into a Jewish family from Kamianets-Podilskiy, Goikhbarg had converted to Russian Orthodoxy in order to dodge the Jewish quotas on admissions to institutions of higher learning in late imperial Russia and undertake a successful academic career; he was the first to argue that the family as a juridical entity would disappear, that the abolition of marriage would not be a matter of decree, and that in time, it would become a matter of reality.[9] But before it disappeared, as Goikhbarg had hoped it would, who should administer the wedding if the Soviet state had put an end to the legal recognition of religious marriage by declaring as lawfully binding only civil marriages?

According to the 1918 Family Code, which introduced some sweeping changes in the areas of marriage, divorce, and women's rights, the civil wedding replaced the religious one. Sometimes called "Red Wedding," the Soviet civil marriage was devoid of all religious and family connotation: it was performed in the presence of the two spouses only, sometimes with the International playing in the background, and administered by a Soviet clerk.[10] This was very different from prerevolutionary family laws. Under the imperial Russian Code of Laws, both marriage and divorce were within the exclusive jurisdiction of the ecclesiastical courts of the various religious confessions; furthermore, diversity of faith constituted a marriage impediment.[11] The Red Wedding, on the other hand, was a contract with the state, and the couple had no obligation to the divine or to the family. Notwithstanding their religious background, the couple simply registered the marriage in the civil registry offices, or ZAGS (Zapis aktov grazhdanskogo sostoianiia), the same offices responsible for the registration of other life-cycle events such as divorce, birth, and death, all of which were no longer a function of religious authorities.

Most young people, if they married at all, usually chose Soviet-style civil registration, as Fruma Treivas eventually did: they adjusted to the legal shift and opted to register their marriage through ZAGS, snubbing the religious ceremony. When Asia's communist father remarried in 1925, he did not even consider a religious wedding: he and his new wife, Frida, only registered their union in the local ZAGS office. But many others, especially in the smaller towns across the Soviet Union, organized a Jewish wedding canopy on the side, often to fulfill the expectations of family members and the social pressure from the community of friends and acquaintances.[12] In a place like Novopoltavka, which counted approximately twenty-five hundred inhabitants, most of them Jewish, the old *byt* held its sway more than it did in Moscow, and not everyone forsook a traditional Jewish wedding as Asia's father did. During the 1920s, all three of Asia's aunts had a traditional

Jewish marriage ceremony under the chuppah (canopy). Asia remembered how "the bride and bridegroom were taken to the synagogue separately" and how surprised she was "that the bride was crying," until "somebody explained to [her] that it was a ritual." After the chuppah ceremony took place in the synagogue courtyard, and a Jewish marriage contract (*ketuba*) was signed, a two-day festivity followed "with wine and sweets, . . . gefilte fish, meat, and chicken on the table." But the couples were Soviet enough to choose to also register the marriage through ZAGS: to make their union legally binding, they added a Red Wedding to the chuppah.[13]

The official rhetoric about marriage and family matters optimistically declared that the old ways of family life were dying off among Soviet citizens. In the Jewish context, the process of creating a family came to exclude matchmakers and even weddings altogether.[14] Yet, the realities of everyday life revealed something quite different, especially in those areas where the state's reach was more tenuous and where it faced some resistance from the deeply entrenched religious and family authority: in many places, religious weddings continued to be the accepted social norm for family members, relatives, and friends of the spouses. Anonymous complaints about Jewish religious weddings still taking place at the end of the 1920s appeared in the press. One of these appeared in mid-1927 in the Ukrainian Yiddish newspaper *Shtern*. The author criticized the former head of the Jewish loan fund in the shtetl of Stavishtsh (Stavyshche, in Bila Tserkva district), one Tetievski, because his sister got married with a religious ceremony. Guests from the surrounding area attended, and *klezmorim* from Uman performed at the wedding.[15] A photographer took pictures of the guests in the synagogue courtyard. Among them, reported the horrified observer, were members of the local Soviet administration, including the plenipotentiary of the People's Commissariat for Foreign Affairs and a teacher in the Soviet Yiddish school.[16]

The clash between new and old *byt* became particularly intense outside the European regions of the Soviet Union, in the areas where non-Ashkenazi Jews lived, including Central Asia and the Caucasus. There, the Jewish community battled the Soviet administration with great vigor over the role of women in family life and marriage. Specific points of contention included women's agency in choosing a husband or requesting a divorce and the bride's marriageable age, which according to local tradition—both

Jewish and non-Jewish alike—was significantly lower compared to elsewhere in the Soviet Union. Clashes between the Soviet administration and the Jewish population over the prohibition on marrying off minors were not uncommon during the 1920s in the Caucasus.[17] In order to ease acculturation in Central Asia and the Caucasus, the state was more careful in forcing change and at least initially deemed that secular institutions such as the registry offices should be incorporated into the Jewish community and controlled by community leaders.

But if the opening of a ZAGS office was meant to undermine and serve as an alternative to the religious institutions, in practice it came to boost them and reinforce their authority, at least during the 1920s. In the Bukharan Jewish communities of Samarkand, Kokand, and other cities, for instance, the Soviets de facto "legitimized the traditional-religious authority labeling it as part of the 'socialist' framework."[18] In these communities, Jewish women could marry and divorce only according to religious law, while being issued Soviet documentation for doing so.[19] In the process of imposing change and Sovietizing everyday life in places like Bukhara and Turkestan, the state attempted to ease the transition to communism also by relying on other Jews and using them as transmitters of communism in the hope that, as Jews, they would foster the change. The outcome was that new tensions emerged between local Jews and the "Jewish communists from Berdychiv" who became identified with the oppressive economic and cultural measures enforced from Moscow.[20]

Traditional peasant communities in the rural areas of Ukraine, Belorussia, and Russia also resisted the Sovietization of marriage and family life: arranged marriages survived long after the establishment of the Soviet Union, and choosing one's life partner continued to depend heavily on tradition, one's parents, and on the social networks in one's village.[21] Similar dynamics persisted, albeit with less tenacity, among Jews who lived in shtetls or small agricultural settlements in the European areas of the Soviet Union. In the wake of the changes introduced by the state, it is not surprising that confusion often stirred up the hearts of both those who supported and those who resisted the Sovietization of everyday life, particularly over whether secular or religious authority should prevail.

In 1924, in the shtetl of Poddobryanka, Mahilyow province, a local Yiddish amateur troupe put onstage a play titled *Forced Marriage*. The play exposed the evils of the Jewish traditional wedding, which the bride's parents arranged without regard for her will; the main character coerced the young bride into marrying him. As soon as the shtetl's rabbi found out about the play's plot, he intervened at once: he publicly declared from the synagogue's pulpit that from the vantage point of Jewish law, the actors should be officially considered husband and wife. After all, even though the wedding had been performed onstage, the couple had fulfilled all the rituals required by Jewish law in order to be considered a married couple. The rabbi also contended that if the couple refused to live together, a religious divorce would be necessary. Surprisingly, in the context of the new Soviet *byt*, the rabbi's opinion still mattered. The young female actress, who was presumably positively inclined toward communism and the Bolshevik project, still felt uncomfortable to go outside and walk through the town's streets following the rabbi's verdict, according to which, until proven otherwise, she was married. The rabbi's words may have weighed negatively on her, her family, or her social network. And for her at least, the blemish could be removed only with the intervention of the city soviet and the public dismissal of the rabbi's authority: no wedding had taken place onstage, and no divorce was necessary.[22]

There were other motivations to register the marriage through ZAGS besides love, sex, or the desire to have a family. In the early 1920s, for example, a number of Soviet citizens who wished to leave the Soviet territories but could not because of legal restrictions on movement arranged a fictitious marriage with foreigners. They essentially got married "until the border" but parted ways once they entered Poland or Romania.[23] Short-term marriages as a border-crossing strategy became common. In general, the restrictions on movement throughout the Soviet Union became more and more stringent. Although movement regulations in the 1920s were not as strict as they would become in the 1930s, obtaining an official pass (*propusk*) was required in order to change the place of residence, with additional obstacles and caveats for individuals with a suspicious political past. In such cases, an arranged marriage became useful in securing a residence permit and even in bypassing the housing crisis. As a contemporary put it, while "one can find a wife in Moscow very easily," and thus obtain a residence permit and a place to live via marriage, it was otherwise almost impossible to obtain these commodities in the city, except for an exorbitant price.[24] In the mid-1920s, many young Jews who moved to Moscow and could not rely on preexisting family networks married in order to obtain housing and reside there legally. In exchange for residence in the big city, a prominent member of the Zionist organization He-halutz married a young woman who belonged to a local trade union; he apparently even took her family name. The case was so well-known in the underground Zionist circles of Moscow that a member of the group wrote a parody about it by the title of "Fishl vil zikh legalizirn," or "Fishl wants to become legalized."[25]

While the 1918 family code attempted to solve the gender inequalities of everyday life and promote women's emancipation, in reality it triggered new social problems. At a public discussion about marriage and family life held in mid-1926 in Kharkiv, at the local state theater, the activists who took to the stage in front of hundreds of residents criticized the old ways of family life and noted that "the October Revolution had disrupted the bourgeois foundation of family life." But they also acknowledged that thousands of citizens were still not registering their marriage in the Soviet civil registry offices. The activists warned that failing to register the marriage, which made the union void of civil or legal value, led to countless social problems: the state, which was committed to fighting against women's enslavement and to protecting mother and child, could do nothing to contain the widespread phenomenon of polygamy and desertion of children if the marriage was not registered.[26] By 1926, as many as 7 percent of all women in the Soviet Union found themselves in unregistered marriages, with no rights to alimony payments and no protection under the law. This affected primarily women from lower social classes. The majority of those affected were poor women from the rural areas of the Soviet Union, most of them illiterate, who did not understand or ideologically resisted the reasons for registering through ZAGS. Taking seasonal wives or cohabiting with women during the harvesting season and then leaving the family once the harvest was over became a widespread problem in the 1920s.[27] As a *Pravda* journalist remarked in 1926, conceding the tensions between real life and early Bolshevik legislation, "the new family has not yet fully emerged from under the rubble of the old one and it is women, as well as children, who are paying the heaviest price."[28]

Divorce: A Room of Tears

The social setback in the family code became apparent in particular in the sphere of divorce. From the beginning, Soviet legislation had made divorce very easy. It could be settled in ZAGS without going to court, and while generally both spouses should be present, in fact the marriage could be terminated in the absence of one spouse, who would be informed by mail through a postcard.[29] The postcard instructed the newly divorced person to go to the people's court to solve any issues concerning child support and property. Anyone could afford the legal expenses, which amounted to three rubles only.[30]

These changes had some real bearing on the Jewish street as well, with cases of Jewish husbands deserting their wives, leaving them desperate without any legal rights, to fend for themselves and their children. With a mixture of shock and derision, the Yiddish press in the United States reported about the lenience with which, at the appearance of the first small argument, either side could approach a judge, sign a piece of paper, and be free without even letting the other side know. Some publications, to show their condemnation of the Soviet family legislation, exaggerated the situation and reported the existence of an alleged "woman's week," during which each man "in Russia can choose a woman of his liking, forcing her to live with him," and then leave her.[31] The Polish Yiddish press echoed the criticism, ridiculing the state of Soviet family life and the informality with which marriage and divorce could take place compared to in Poland. The Moscow correspondent for *Der moment*, one of the most widely read Yiddish publications in Poland at the time, who noted that "changing a wife is easier than changing a name," described the ZAGS divorce department with the label used by women at the time: "the room of tears." He reproached the careless state of divorce affairs in Soviet society, noting both the frivolity and the personal tragedies behind the choices made: too much love, too little love, jealousy, unfaithfulness, stinginess, profligacy, sexual looseness, illness, difficult character, poverty. The journalist aptly summarized the situation as follows: "Someone wants a divorce because his wife is unfaithful; another wants a divorce because her husband has a venereal disease; a third one wants a divorce because his wife tricked him: she promised him a dowry, while in fact she is utterly destitute; a man divorces his wife because he does not want her to perform in the theater; a woman divorces her husband because he plays cards; a young wife leaves her husband because she thought that married life would be easy and happy, while in fact she's been working as hard as before."[32] Many women faced the misery and anguish of being without work and without a home: as much as 70 percent of the initial job cutbacks that occurred during the NEP period affected women.[33] Furthermore, thousands of women in "free unions" had no financial security and legal protection that might have rescued them with registered marriage.[34]

The leniency over divorce in the Soviet Union compared to the United States and Poland encouraged some people to fictitiously end the marriage to circumvent part of the economic hardship and the housing restrictions of the New Economic Policy years. In the context of the NEP's mixed economy, when entrepreneurship was allowed but required paying heavy taxes, some Jewish businessmen got divorced in order to leave the city, to avoid paying high tariffs to the state, or as a cover-up for bankruptcy. Similarly, housing regulations in overcrowded cities like Moscow and Leningrad allowed husband and wife to live in one room only; but if the couple had two rooms before getting married, to circumvent the law and prevent the housing department from confiscating the other room, they immediately divorced, fictitiously.

A worrisome social issue that plagued the Jewish street in the early 1920s was the status of *agunot*, Jewish women who were separated from their husbands but were unable to obtain from them a legal bill of divorce (*get*) and consequently could not remarry according to Jewish law. In the wake of displacement, war, and terror at the time of the pogroms of the civil war, many husbands perished or were unable or unwilling to reunite with their families. While this did not represent a concern for the Soviet state, which dismissed Jewish religious law altogether, it remained a pressing matter for many Jewish women and the rabbis they turned to for help. In general, it seems that rabbis tended to opt for leniency in order to alleviate the predicament of the *agunot*.[35]

In 1926, a new family code replaced the 1918 one and marked a clear retreat from free love, free unions, and easy divorce. The new Code on Marriage, Family, and Guardianship was issued in response to the many social issues that plagued Soviet society in the early 1920s, particularly the vulnerability of women after divorce, the large number of orphans and street children (*bezprizorniki*, literally "unattended"), the uncertainty about questions of property rights, and whether there were any legal obligations of unmarried partners who cohabited. Heeding the despair of Soviet women, the 1926 code recognized de facto marriages, giving them equal status to registered marriages. If a woman and man had cohabited, shared a household, and raised children, then the de facto marriage was legally binding under the law, which meant that women had the right to alimony and child protection.[36] Trials to guarantee the protection of women and children took place in the Yiddish courts as well. In mid-1926, the Yiddish court in Ukraine tried a case involving a young couple: a nineteen-year-old father of a seven-week-old child refused to support the newborn's fifteen-year-old mother. Following the new Soviet laws to protect mother and child, the court required the father, who tried to evade his responsibility, to pay alimony, 25 percent of his salary, to support his son.[37]

But in some cases, the legal changes came too late. In a sensational trial that took place on Sunday, April 18, 1926, and that like so many others served as both propaganda and entertainment, the young worker Rosa Blayvays was accused of murdering her son. The Zhytomyr District Court held the trial in the shtetl of Baranovka, where the young Blayvays had become pregnant after a love affair with a Christian neighbor, one Sirota. He had apparently lured her into having a sexual relationship with the promise of marrying her but then abandoned her after she became pregnant. Risking unemployment because of the pregnancy, possibly facing the resentment from her family because of the spouse's identity, and without any help from the state and local authorities, the young Blayvays murdered her son out of despair.[38]

The new family code inevitably triggered confusion and anxiety. It could happen, for example, that a marriage registered in ZAGS and a de facto marriage were both legally recognized at the same time, which meant that there were two wives for one husband, who became responsible for alimony and child support, escalating family drama. The Yiddish court tried a case about property rights in the city of Poltava, where, after seventeen years, a butcher and his wife had dissolved their marriage. The husband argued that the wife was to blame because she fell in love with a young teacher (the daughter's tutor), while the wife retorted that this happened because he had a "second wife." The wife demanded in court that the husband pay thirty rubles a month for child support and that he leave the house property in their name as inheritance. The father initially rejected the solution outright, probably in light of his "other wife," but he was in the end forced to comply with the new law and leave to his children two-thirds of the property in inheritance.[39]

It seems likely that casual relations between husband and wife, separation, divorce, or even polygamy negatively affected lower-class women who financially depended on their husbands and less so those who succeeded in rising to the top of the Communist Party local, regional, or central institutions. One Ulyanova (née Buber), who grew up in the shtetl of Bogachevka in Odesa province and who had worked as a maid and then as a Jewish teacher until the revolution, joined the party in 1920. In a remarkable case of upward mobility, Ulyanova worked for the Cheka for two years, then joined the Party Committee of Odesa province and later the Stalin District Committee, eventually becoming Party secretary of the Odesa Housing Union and Party secretary of the Odesa Candy Factory. Ulyanova separated from her Jewish husband, a Party member and a prosecutor in Tula, but never got divorced. The husband left her in the mid-1920s when he got transferred to another town, where he worked for one year, and then they "lived together for a while, but then he left again, to work in Novosibirsk." There he married somebody else and had a child, but then he left the other wife as well. As Ulyanova pointed out, "My husband and I never got officially divorced. . . . He comes to visit sometimes, but we don't live together. He might come and then leave again. That's just the way he is. . . . I don't know how to judge." It is clear that for Ulyanova, who in her own words scoffed at "the Jewish way" of maintaining a family life (and by that she meant living together with her husband), career was the priority.[40] Thanks to her financial independence and her success in the local and regional Party structure, Ulyanova felt no resentment toward her husband.

For those Jewish women who prospered in Soviet society, pursuing a political career took precedence over marriage. Born in a shtetl in the Minsk province, in a destitute family, Rebecca Gimmelshtein joined the Communist Party after 1920. When her husband tried to dissuade her from being politically active, she left him and left for the Western Front as a special mission agent. In 1921, upon completing a degree the local institute of economics, Gimmelshtein was hired in the statistics bureau of the Belorussian Council of National Economy in Minsk and served as the chair of its Communist Party-cell. She later became the director of one of the largest stores in the newly established Minsk Central Workers' Cooperative.[41] What is noteworthy in her short autobiography, besides her exceptional career and economic independence apart from marriage, is the sense of pride with which Gimmelshtein stated that she abandoned her husband because he prevented her involvement in public life. She presumably did not remarry.

Toward the Brotherhood of Peoples: Intermarriage

The Soviet celebration of "brotherhood of peoples," which represented one of the founding blocks of a utopian equal new society, also entailed the celebration of intermarriage. Intermarriage favored intraethnic assimilation, a sought-after goal in the new Marxist society, where nationalities should wither away. Unlike in prerevolutionary times, the Soviet family codes had made differences in nationality and religious identity irrelevant and no longer an obstacle to family life. Among the proposed methods to fight against antisemitism in Ukraine in 1928, for instance, the Party strongly recommended non-Jewish Party members and young Komsomol members not only to strike up close friendships with Jews but to marry as well.[42] Intermarriage among Soviet Jews rose constantly during the 1920s and proceeded together with the urbanization process; but it also varied greatly from place to place. According to one demographic study that focused on different cities and towns in Ukraine, of 10,806 Jewish men, 490 married non-Jewish women in 1924; that same year and in the same localities under research, 593 out of 10,909 Jewish women married non-Jewish men. In the areas of the former Pale of Settlement in particular, more Jewish women than men married non-Jewish partners. The main explanation for this gender imbalance lies in the demographic changes that followed the violence and terror of World War I and the civil war. Emigration, war, and pogroms affected Jewish men in particular, who were targeted for murder, yielding a surplus of women in the small market towns of Ukraine and Belorussia. It seems that leaving the shtetls in search for employment was mostly a male phenomenon.[43] In turn, the reduced number of Jewish men made it somewhat more probable for Jewish women who looked to build a family to marry their non-Jewish neighbors.

The same study also highlighted some regional differences in intermarriage rates within the Ukrainian republic: in 1924, the highest percentage of intermarriage occurred in Zinovyevsk, where it reached 10 percent; while in Berdychiv and Bila Tserkva, cities with large Jewish populations, not a single case of intermarriage was recorded that year.[44] Without including any gender breakdown, the 1926 Soviet census revealed that approximately 5 percent of Jewish men and women intermarried in Ukraine and only 3.2 percent in Belorussia; on the other hand, as many as 21 percent of Jews intermarried in Russia.[45] Overall, despite the staggering increase in intermarriage rates, the likelihood for Jews to intermarry in the cities and towns of Ukraine and even more so Belorussia remained relatively insignificant compared to in Moscow and Leningrad during the 1920s.[46] In the two metropolises, the intermarriage rate reached analogous proportions to rates of Jews in Weimar Germany.[47] According to one concerned source, in Leningrad during the first year following the Bolshevik Revolution, one-third of Jews intermarried; by 1924, the rate had declined to 15 percent but would rise again.[48]

Of course, resistance to intermarriage was greater among the Jews of Central Asia and the Caucasus and their Muslim neighbors. As an expression of and a means for upward mobility, intermarriage also paved the way for assimilation. A number of social phenomena, which were largely missing in Central Asia and the Caucasus, fostered intermarriage in the European regions of the Soviet Union. First of all, geographic mobility for the thousands of Jews who moved from the small market towns to the larger Soviet cities entailed the beginning of a new life that was largely devoid of traditional authority figures, including family members. Mixed marriages became more likely in the absence of parents and religious leaders, who might have condemned the children's decision. Moreover, the revolution, which expected youth to break away from the old *byt*, deemed parents and rabbis irrelevant. Most importantly, parents were physically absent, geographically far away, still living in the towns and cities of the former Pale of Settlement, while their sons and daughters had left for the capitals of the Soviet republics. The combination of young Jews who wanted to reject everything from their Jewish past to succeed in the new society and who therefore strove to blend in by marrying non-Jews, together with the exotic novelty and the attractiveness represented by Jews in many Soviet political and cultural circles, contributed to the fertile soil for intermarriage, especially in larger urban centers.[49]

Presumably, the higher one climbed the Red ladder during the 1920s, the harder it became to marry within the Jewish fold: in a balance between Jewishness and Sovietness, the Jewish moment came to matter less, while the Soviet one came to matter more, both ideologically and pragmatically. The overwhelming majority of Jews who assimilated into the higher echelons of the Soviet cultural and political elites, and who had married before the revolution, usually chose a Jewish partner. This was the case, for example, of future members of the Soviet literary establishment like Ilya Erhenburg (in the 1920s, author of short stories and the picaresque novel *The Extraordinary Adventures of Julio Jurenito and His Disciples*), Boris Pasternak (mostly known for his poetry and work of translation during the 1920s), and Osip Mandelshtam (in the early Soviet years, known primarily for two collections of poetry and the memoir *The Noise of Time*, published in 1925) or of members of the new Soviet political leadership, including Lazar Kaganovich (from 1925 to 1928, first secretary of the Communist Party of Ukraine and in 1930 member of the Soviet Politburo), Maxim Litvinov (appointed first deputy people's commissar of foreign affair in the early 1920s and in 1930 people's commissar for foreign affairs), and Yona Yakir (a Red Army military commander and a member of the Party Central Committee in Moscow and of the Politburo of the Communist Party of Ukraine). With some exceptions, Jewish women remained strikingly absent from these elites primarily because, despite the gender-equality rhetoric and the real opportunities that the new system offered women, Bolshevik society was the product of an overwhelmingly male project.

During the 1920s, communist institutions active on the Jewish street did not encourage Jews to marry non-Jews and generally refrained from celebrating intermarriage; publicly rejoicing over intermarriage in literature and film became a much more common phenomenon in the 1930s. For example, while reporting about intermarriage, the Soviet Yiddish press of the 1920s did not promote it and certainly avoided condemning it, as it did instead with Jewish religious weddings or divorces. Similarly, propaganda posters from the 1920s promoted progressive and peaceful interethnic relations but did not celebrate intermarriage. In one such case, a poster proclaiming the benefits of the Soviet Yiddish school system, and recalling the shortcomings of the traditional Jewish education of the heder, reminded the observer that the Soviet school uprooted hatred between different nationalities and led to cooperation between peoples.[50]

Another poster, part of the OZET propaganda machine to promote the settlement of Jews on land, emphasized the economic shortcomings of prerevolutionary Jewish life and depicted a harmonious future in the farming colonies, in which "all nationalities of the Soviet Union stretch out their brotherly hand to the Jew."[51] In both cases, the promotion of intermarriage could only be inferred, between the lines. There were very few expressions of popular culture celebrating intermarriage. In one such case, a Russian song titled "Daughter of the Rabbi" advocated intermarriage and criticized the Jewish tradition. After the song's hero, a young woman by the name of Enta, dismisses all her suitors—the Jewish Yashas and Abrashas—she ends up marrying the chairman of a Soviet organization, one Ivan Ivanovich, to her father's dismay.[52]

Intermarriage marked the beginning of a new trend, which became more common in the late 1920s and escalated in the 1930s, reaching in the Russian republic the formidable rate of more than one-third of Soviet Jews marrying non-Jews in 1939. The Soviet city became the ideal place of intermarriage and therefore of assimilation. Mikhail Kalinin, the official head of the Soviet state and member of the Central Committee of the Communist Party and Politburo, while acknowledging this process, even deplored assimilation and intermarriage among Jews. He did so in November 1926, in Moscow, at the first OZET congress, in front of almost 270 delegates and fourteen delegations from abroad: emphasizing the three-way connection between urbanization, assimilation, and intermarriage, Kalinin exploited this warning to encourage Jews to settle on land and to productivize by toiling the land in the Jewish agricultural colonies. The main reasoning for the so-called Kalinin declaration was not so much the condemnation of assimilation and intermarriage as such but rather the support for the creation of Jewish collective farms and perhaps even a Jewish autonomous territory; the speech unleashed some contentious discussion of ethnically Jewish agricultural settlements, which ran counter to the principle of brotherhood of peoples.[53] On the other side of the spectrum, however, Commissar of

Enlightenment Anatoly Lunacharskii, who in the early 1920s left his wife to marry the Jewish actress Natalya Rozenel, commented enthusiastically about the rise in intermarriage rates between Jews and Russians: "With great happiness we take note of the increase in the number of Russo-Jewish marriages. This is the right path. Our Slavic blood still has a lot of peasant malt; it is thick and plentiful, but it flows a little slowly. . . . On the other hand, the blood of our Jewish comrades is very fast flowing. So let us mix our blood and, in this fruitful mixture, find the human type that will include the blood of the Jewish people like delicious, thousand-year-old human wine."[54]

Sex and Prostitution at the Time of Revolution

The revolution forged new relations between men and women, creating new notions of sexual habits. The yearning to experiment and get rid of the old *byt*, which was so intense during the 1920s, also set off a new desire to explore the realm of sexual morality, for men and women alike. The early Bolshevik push to reject entirely marriage as a bourgeois institution, a symbol of the patriarchy and enslavement of women, favored the sexual liberation and promiscuity of men and women.[55] Writing to a friend in Moscow in 1926, the Soviet Yiddish author and literary critic Nokhem Oyslender informed him nonchalantly about a threesome between his wife (the Yiddish poet Mira Khenkina), a young female student enrolled in the Minsk Musical College, and himself. He mentioned the relationship in passing, with great ease, without expressing any judgment on the laxity of his wife and the young female student involved with the couple. After all, this was the outcome of common sexual behavior at the time.[56] Experiments in "Red love," particularly in the fashion of ménage à trois, became rather common at the time, especially in intellectual milieus among members of the literary and artistic elites.

Lilia Kagan was born in 1891 in Moscow, where her father, Uri Kagan, practiced law defending the legal rights of Jews and her mother taught music. Lilia first married a young law student, Osip Brik, who later became a literary critic and a poet. They were married in a religious ceremony—the only option they both had in imperial Russia—presumably by the (Crown) rabbi of Moscow, Jacob Mazeh.[57] Lili Brik eventually became the muse of the Russian literary avant-garde and the beloved *salonnière* of Moscow writers and poets. While she remained married to Osip, she became publicly involved with poet Vladimir Mayakovsky, who dedicated much of his work to her. In the early Soviet years in particular, the socially emancipated Jewish woman, who moved through literary and political circles, became an exotic phenomenon that captivated the interest of the members of the intelligentsia. In Soviet society, Jewish women could be described and imagined as exotic beauties, passionate, promiscuous, and overly sexual. Not unlike the German lands more than a century before, when Jewish women established literary salons and became the symbol of emancipation attracting non-Jewish intellectuals who courted them and married them after they converted to Christianity, in the Soviet Union the socially emancipated Jewish woman became the quintessential symbol of excitement and freshness.[58] It was only after Mayakovsky's suicide in 1930 that Lili Brik divorced her husband, to marry the Soviet general Vitaly Primakov. Times had changed so significantly that in 1930, to be in a public relationship with a Soviet general without divorcing one's husband would have been unthinkable.

Infatuated with the grand social experimentation of the 1920s, many youngsters chose free love and free unions in lieu of legal marriages. By the mid-1920s, sexual libertinism came under the radar of Bolshevik morality, and campaigns to promote healthy sexual *byt* and spread sex education were launched by the state. In mid-1926, speaking in front of a full audience in the Ukrainian state theater in Kharkiv, Emilyan Yaroslavski preached about sex in everyday life. Born Minei Izrailevich Gubelman, Yaroslavski, who like so many other Jews who joined the Bolsheviks early on changed his name, criticized in particular the carefree relation that the youth showed too often to sex. In his disapproving words, which reflect the change in the culture of sex, he noted, "our youth starts to have a sex life too early in life, something that runs counter to the opinion of Comrade Lenin, and something that will hamper their chance of becoming tough fighters for socialism."[59] And indeed, for most people, sex came before the Party. In 1924, *Pravda* reprimanded Party members who engaged in sexual habits unbecoming a communist. The author of the report, himself a member of the Moscow control committee of the Communist Party, condemned the laxity of sexual habits of Communist Party members and brought as an example the case of a communist Don Juan who had married five times and abandoned two wives in the last months of their pregnancy.[60]

Beyond the intellectual and political elite circles, Communist Party leaders drew a clear divide between working-class men and women with regard to what was considered acceptable sexual behavior, expressing a double standard akin to conservative and antifeminist attitudes. Female promiscuity was perceived as dangerous and condemnable; male promiscuity, on the other hand, was of no concern at all. In March 1926, for example, the Construction Workers' Party-cell in Minsk debated the following issue: When a worker was informed by a Party member that comrade Vasserman was living with the worker's wife (the Russian verb for "living," *zhit*, was used here as a euphemism), the worker openly confronted Vasserman and accused him of acting immorally. The Party member who made the allegations, however, defended himself, asserting that he did not say that Vasserman did such a thing but rather that he presumed Vasserman could do such a thing. While it is unclear whether Vasserman did in fact sleep with the worker's wife, the image of women that emerges from the document is in tune with traditional gender notions. In the ensuing discussion, Party-cell members seemed to be much more concerned with the way in which the case would affect female Party-cell members than with Vasserman's behavior. As one comrade anxiously noted, "[This] may influence women. Rumors about this [case] are already circulating among them."[61] Women appear as susceptible and easily swayed into acting in a sexually improper fashion. Party-cell members, who should have been at the vanguard of supporting female liberation and equality, feared women's promiscuity, which would upset the traditional wife-husband relationship and disrupt the family. On the other hand, Party-cell members expressed no concern about the possible effect that the case might have on men's conduct. On the contrary, the double-standard message conveyed by the Party-cell was that men could freely experience love even outside the marital bond and that, just like Vasserman, they were not expected to conform to the traditional husband-wife relation.

Peretz Hirschbein, an American Yiddish writer who lived in a Crimean Jewish agricultural colony in 1928–1929, captured in his work the different sexual behavior tolerated in the city and in the village: one of the characters in Hirschbein's novel *Royte felder* (Red fields), Lana, a committed communist, dispatched her sister Beyla to Moscow, because she had become pregnant from a premarital relation and in the village she would have been branded as a woman of ill repute.[62] Fleeing the village or small town where everyone knew you for the metropolis because of a pregnancy out of wedlock must have been rather common despite premarital relations being so widespread in Soviet society at the time.

The modern Soviet city became a place of encounters, love, and sin. But behind the façade of possibility and excitement, it also hid despair and prostitution. In fact, the harsh conditions of the NEP years led to a growth in prostitution. When in 1920 the former anarchist, now communist Shmuel Agursky accompanied a *Forverts* correspondent on a stroll through Moscow, he proudly noted how much the city had changed under the Bolsheviks. He made it a point to also show the former "red-light district." Agursky compared the pre-1917 Moscow "red-light district," which he recalled "saw thousands of women who sold their bodies each evening," who made it impossible to pass through the street, to the same area in New York, on Broadway and Forty-Second Street. Agursky boasted the Soviet state's accomplishment of turning the neighborhood into a "clean and tranquil" area. And when the journalist inquired about the prostitutes' whereabouts, Agursky stated with pride that all former prostitutes were currently employed and "if they did not want to give up a life of sin they were arrested." In general, noted Agursky with his usual sexist flare, few women engaged in prostitution after the revolution: "those who do so are forced to because of economic reasons and unemployment" and do not do it out of "passion like before," or "because they wish to wear beautiful dresses like aristocrats once did. . . . There are no longer elegant ladies to be jealous of." In his exaggeratedly optimistic assessment, Agursky admitted that the social issue of prostitution had not disappeared entirely but noted that the Soviet state had done much more than France, England, or the United States had in solving the issue.[63]

The revolutionary upheaval led to changes in the family structure and made women inevitably more susceptible to crisis and violence. The state intervened but was not always successful. Leah Botnik hailed from a wealthy family, her house being nicknamed in the town in which she lived "House of Romanovs," but war and revolution changed all that. After the Bolsheviks came to power, her husband, who was a wealthy flour merchant, deserted her and fled to Germany. She was left in utter misery and destitution. She found some relief in the collective farm she joined, which allowed her to gain new footing in society. Yet the sense of abandonment was real, and not all women were as fortunate or as skilled to avoid disaster by taking advantage of the support provided by the Soviet state.[64]

Young women who moved to the city from the surrounding economically devastated shtetls in search of employment were often recruited by pimps, usually posted at the railway station, who lured them into prostitution. Internal migration from the towns and cities of the former Pale of Settlement to the large metropolises rendered young Jewish women particularly vulnerable. Because more men than women departed for the metropolis, women had fewer prospects of marriage in the small towns. Troubled by financial want and dire poverty, parents allowed their daughters to move to the cities with the promise of well-paid work. Vulnerable to sexual exploitation and assault, they were forced into—or they chose—prostitution. The Zhenotdel, or Women's Department of the Communist Party, treated sexual exploitation of young women as a social issue and organized lectures that addressed not only literacy and female unemployment but also prostitution. In larger Jewish demographic centers like Minsk, some of these events were conducted in Yiddish.

Occasionally, prostitution afflicted shtetls and other smaller Jewish settlements as well. An ethnographic study of the Jewish (and partly German) agricultural colony Novozlatopol, which during the 1920s became a destination for unemployed shtetl Jews from Ukraine, reported, "There is no prostitution here and never has been. Not a single Jewish girl is 'paid' or 'free of charge.'" But the author of the report also admitted, "In recent years there did appear one, a young lady of seventeen. According to the stories, she services the 'afflicted' portion of the youth. In this she is assisted by two German women, young widows."[65]

The First Country in the World to Legalize Abortion

In the wake of the terror of the civil war, Jewish women became targeted for sexual violence to an extreme degree. The extraordinary refugee crisis and population movements at the time of war and terror boosted the likelihood of women being victims of rape as civil society and safety networks in their destroyed communities collapsed. Rape marked the female experience of the pogroms and produced long-term consequences for the Jewish population as a whole. According to some studies, one in twelve Jewish women and girls in Ukraine—which became the epicenter of violence—experienced rape.[66] Available medical records gathered in the wake of the violence describe extensive cases of pregnancies, venereal disease, and abortion. Abortions were often carried out in the absence of medical care, which increased women's mortality rate. A gynecologist at the Jewish hospital in Cherkasy, Kyiv province, for example, recorded that following the pogroms in the area, at least half of the victims of sexual violence had become pregnant. As the doctor soberly noted, "There were very many abortions. Doctors facilitate them. Unfortunately, some sought a doctor's aid too late, while others, being too self-conscious, did it at home (using all sorts of methods) or with help from midwives, healer women, and so on. In the latter case, there were fatalities."[67] The situation was particularly hopeless in and around Kyiv, the heart of the health and social crisis, with more than twenty-five thousand desperate refugees streaming in from the surrounding shtetls. In 1921, the health-care department in Kyiv ordered to arrange for medical help, ambulatories, and health-care providers who spoke Yiddish.[68]

Soviet Russia was the first country in the world to legalize abortion, in October 1920. Although the liberal legislation fit in nicely with the rhetoric about women's emancipation, the legalization of abortion had little to do with women's freedom of choice and was mostly a way to curb high mortality rates due to illegal abortions, especially in the wake of the civil war. The number of abortions, or of women who sought an abortion, grew also as a result of the changes in family law. The world of illegal abortion clinics grew, as did the vulnerability of domestic servants and factory workers who experienced sexual assault, harassment, and "seduction" based on the promises of marriage. Designed to destroy the old social order and liberate women, the explosion of free unions (couples living together without a formal marriage) and the new family legislation backfired: in combination with the legalization of abortion, it yielded a recipe for disaster. Until 1936, when the new family code rejected a pro choice approach to abortion and made it illegal and unpatriotic, abortions were performed in medical clinics as a matter of choice.[69]

Of course, the legalization of abortion triggered resentment, fear, and anxiety among the members of the more traditional communities in the Soviet Union, Jews and non-Jews alike. Even though it was legal, young women tried to hide from their families their decision to have an abortion. In 1926, in the town of Kaniv, in central Ukraine, a young Ukrainian woman disappeared suddenly, seeking to keep from her parents that she was going to have an abortion. Her disappearance triggered an accusation of ritual murder against her Jewish neighbors, with the allegation almost unleashing a pogrom: local Jews hid in the synagogue, while the police and Party leaders from Kharkiv intervened; the turmoil subsided only once the father located his daughter in a nearby hospital, where she had secretly planned the abortion.[70]

Yiddish writers chronicled the reality of abortion in the 1920s. Khana Levin, active in Kharkiv literary circles and hailed as one of the first female poetic voices in Soviet Yiddish literature, wrote extensively about Soviet women's lives and the way they were affected by the new legislation. She went from celebrating female independence to criticizing free unions that caused more abortions. In a poem titled "Woman," Levin vividly captured the brutality and emotional pain that women endured, possibly because the social realities forced them to have abortions:

> Women are thrown about on the tables.
> A stranger's hand moved apart their bent knees
> People bring to rubbish dumps pailfuls
> Of pieces of kids' bodies, of women's horror and shame.[71]

When Asia Matveyuk's mother, Ethel Levit, got pregnant in 1924 for the third time, she decided, perhaps out of economic necessity, to have an abortion. From the small agricultural settlement of Novopoltavka, she went to the Red Cross hospital in nearby Mykolaiv. But the medical procedure did not go well. Upon returning home, she contracted an infection and became severely ill and eventually developed a brain inflammation; she was eventually taken back to a hospital in Mykolaiv, where she died. Asia's father, a Communist Party member who had often challenged the religious rituals and old worldview of his own parents and in-laws, could not allow himself not to bury his wife in a Jewish cemetery; in fact, he even bribed the morgue attendant to take Asia's mother's body away without autopsy, to avoid cremation, something not allowed by Jewish law. However, his compromise between Party-mindedness and Judaism did not lead to the results he hoped. Because Ethel had died approximately at the same time as Lenin did (January 21, 1924), funerals were put on hold. No burial was allowed during the mourning period for Lenin's passing. Therefore, the family had to wait a few days to inter Asia's mother's body, which again was in full contravention of Jewish law.[72] As Matveyuk later recalled, "Our relatives blamed my father that he gave his consent to my mother to have this abortion, forbidden by the Jewish religion. Grandfather Solomon didn't even want to talk to my father for many years."[73] What stands out, besides the ongoing tensions between family and party allegiance, is the fact that Asia's father, a committed communist who had made it a priority to carry out the revolution of the body and the mind, elected to bury his wife in a Jewish cemetery. Why did he choose a Jewish cemetery and not a Soviet one?

Soviet Death in the Jewish Cemetery

Like every other aspect of society and identity, funerals and death rituals too came under the scrupulous eye of the Soviets as part of their mission to radically and thoroughly reform everyday life. With the Decree on Funerals and Cemeteries, issued in December 1918, the Soviet state aspired first to revise and distance itself from the Christian Orthodox ritual, replacing it with a secular practice devoid of religious content. Cremation, which was forbidden in the Orthodox tradition, became the ideal and the symbol of a new Soviet burial.[74] The decree also proclaimed equal burial procedures for all citizens, who, regardless of ethnicity and religious identity, could be buried for free in any cemetery.

In light of the new decree, two major issues pertaining to Jewish cemeteries and burial customs arose on the Soviet horizon. First, Jewish burial grounds, without which a Jewish community could not exist and which were considered sacred sites in perpetuity, were considered, by both Jewish and state authorities, for Jews only. This, of course, defied the attempt to internationalize death in harmony with the Soviet ideal of brotherhood of peoples. The Soviet civil cemetery, on the other hand, was for everyone, with no distinction of ethnicity or religion. Second, every Jewish cemetery functioned through a burial society, or Chevrah-Kadisha (The holy society), which ensured that each member of the community received a proper funeral in agreement with the requirements of Jewish law; observing Jewish burial customs meant, among other things, avoiding cremation and allowing the body to decompose naturally. Every Jewish community in prerevolutionary Russia, regardless of its size, relied on the Chevrah-Kadisha to ensure that the burial strictly followed the meticulous regulations dictated by Jewish law. Belonging to the Chevrah-Kadisha therefore entailed privileges, power, and a visible communal and socioeconomic status. The burial society held sway over the Jewish cemetery and could even refuse burial services to a member of the community whose behavior was deemed undeserving or to one who failed to pay the sliding-scale fee determined by the society.

During the 1920s and probably into the 1930s, the custom of burying Jews in Jewish cemeteries as opposed to Soviet ones "was observed even by the most fanatically anti-religious Evsektsiia members."[75] That is why Asia's father buried his wife in a Jewish cemetery. This practice had in fact very little to do with religion. Death and burial customs, like birth rituals, are once-in-a-lifetime ceremonials, and as such, they carry much more weight even for those Jews who do not publicly identify as Jews. Not unlike the widespread practice of circumcision on the part of Jewish communists during the 1920s, burial in a Jewish cemetery was not an indication of religious behavior but grew out of family loyalty or perhaps out of a Jewish *mentalité* or an expression of Jewish identification that was privately retained. Like the birth ritual of circumcision, the power of burial customs lay in "a ritual instinct in the human psyche [which] predisposes us to attribute more importance to once-in-a-lifetime rituals than to repetitive rituals"; this instinctual response guaranteed the persistence of death customs over other rituals that were performed daily, weekly, or yearly.[76] Both birth and death rituals thus became indispensable markers of Jewish identity and family loyalty.

Despite the 1918 law, Jewish cemeteries remained the only, or at least the most, "Jewish space" in the Soviet Union, one that was largely left untouched by the state despite Bolshevik ideology.[77] But while the space of the cemetery remained Jewish, it also changed and underwent a process of

Sovietization. First, clashes between the Chevrah-Kadisha, local authorities, and the Jewish residents of towns and cities across the Soviet lands became inevitable during the 1920s. These clashes escalated especially in 1922, when the campaign to debunk the old culture of death was put on hold: in the confusion of the mixed economy of the NEP years, the control over graveyards was temporarily suspended and returned to the religious communities.[78] While many Jews like Asia's father wished to bury their dear ones in a Jewish cemetery, they no longer accepted the cemetery's authorities. Many defied the members of the Chevrah-Kadisha for ideological reasons, others for financial ones, preferring to dodge any existing burial fee. Unlike most other traditional Jewish societies (such as the ones that provided lodging for poor visitors or assistance to the sick or those that provided help to purchase holy books or to study the Mishnah), which were closed down in the early Soviet period, the Chevrah-Kadisha continued to exist. It remained a necessary body to guarantee the functioning of the cemetery, but at the same time, its authority was being challenged. With the interference of the state in matters of death, the Chevrah-Kadisha's influence began to decline. In some cases, it survived in a new secular and bureaucratic guise, as a "cemetery committee" or a "burial cooperative," but even then, it had to struggle to retain some control over the Jewish cemetery and the burial process.[79]

In the confusion about authority that emerged in Soviet society of the 1920s, new syncretistic rituals were born. These combined together aspects of the Jewish ritual—such as the reciting by a member of the Chevrah-Kadisha of the funeral prayer *el malei rachamim* or of the mourning prayer, kaddish—with features from the new Soviet funeral, such as the orchestra playing Chopin and the eulogy for the departed delivered by the head of the workers' union.[80] Not unlike the late nineteenth and early twentieth centuries, tensions between the "owners of the Jewish cemetery" and its patrons were not uncommon. Clashes over the territorial boundaries of the Jewish cemetery had occurred in Russia before the revolution and were still a common occurrence in the Jewish communities of Europe and the United States during the 1920s.[81] The Soviet state's struggle against the old *byt* enhanced these tensions after 1917. For instance, while many Jews were committed to burying their relatives in a Jewish cemetery, many refused to pay the fee to the Chevrah-Kadisha or cemetery committee for its services, which included the recital of the kaddish on the *yortsayt*—anniversary of death—of the deceased. In some cases, clashes erupted over the right to bury a family member in a Jewish cemetery without following the religious ritual, including, for example, the wrapping of the body of the deceased in the customary shrouds (*tachrichim*) for the burial. But in some instances, Jews had to give in to the authority of the Soviet Chevrah-Kadisha, as in the case of a staunch communist who reluctantly paid the fee to the cemetery committee to guarantee that his deceased father have a Jewish burial.[82] In mid-1926, Jewish communists who did not wish to have their family members buried in a cemetery controlled by the Chevrah-Kadisha discussed the possibility of establishing separate Jewish cemeteries in towns with large Jewish demographic concentrations. The complaint was about the way Jewish cemetery administrators handled the burial of Jewish communists. In one instance, the body of a Jewish communist was brought to the cemetery already in a coffin; the Chevrah-Kadisha refused to inter the body until it was removed from the coffin and dressed in the traditional burial shrouds, according to the Jewish ritual. In another instance, the body of a two-year-old boy—the son of a Jewish communist—was brought to the Jewish cemetery; again, Chevrah-Kadisha officers refused to inter the body because the corpse had not been circumcised. According to the child's father, permission for burial was withheld until the boy had been circumcised.[83]

The Sovietization of everyday life also entailed rethinking and reshaping the places and spaces inhabited by Soviet citizens. In this spirit, the grounds of the Jewish cemetery, usually located in the oldest sections of a city or town, often came under scrutiny and even attack. In many places, the existence of the Jewish cemetery represented an obstacle to the Soviet urban planning of the 1920s, the goal of which was to rebuild cities and towns following rational and modern blueprints or to make room for the real or perceived needs of their residents. Many Jews were concerned about the future of the burial grounds of Jewish cemeteries, and they had good reasons to be. In 1923, the Land Commission of the City Executive Committee in Minsk requisitioned the Jewish cemetery on University Street and turned it into a grazing field for goats. The local Yiddish press observed, "All Minsk residents who live in the center of town and own goats must obtain the permission from the city and pay a ruble and 50 kopecks a year per goat to have access to the field."[84] In 1926, the president of the district council in the town of Luhiny, in Zhytomyr oblast, ordered the closing down of the local Jewish cemetery.[85] When in the summer of 1927 the Soviet government granted permission to convene the first conference of Jewish religious representatives and communities, one of the main questions on the agenda of the 179 delegates representing 110 Jewish religious communities related to the purchase and care of cemeteries.[86] Arguing that Jewish religious needs were different from those of other faiths because Judaism pertained to all aspects of everyday life, the Jewish religious community of Leningrad asked Soviet authorities that Jewish cemeteries be under the jurisdiction of the Jewish communities and not of the city councils.[87] These concerns were real and echoed the unfolding events, as more and more Jewish cemeteries were partially or entirely destroyed. In 1927, in Homyel, local Jews petitioned Soviet authorities, protesting because the Red Army built horse stables and a timber yard over the city's old Jewish cemetery.[88] In 1928, the chairman of the district soviet in Vitsyebsk was dismissed from his position not only because he apparently fired all Jewish officials under his jurisdiction but also because he ordered that all the trees in the local Jewish cemetery be destroyed.[89]

Despite the petitions and the hope to preserve control over Jewish cemeteries, the 1922 law that had temporarily given religious bodies the right to supervise or control burial grounds was revoked in 1929. All cemeteries came under the jurisdiction of local authorities only. New rules accompanied the making of a Soviet burial, including provisions that affected the Jewish funeral, such as one that forbade the interment of the body before forty hours after death.[90] As with other changes introduced in 1928 at the onset of the cultural revolution, confusion regarding what was allowed and what was no longer allowed ensued. In some places, for example, following the prohibition on burying in the old Jewish cemeteries, Jews collected funds to purchase new lots or fences to close off new burial grounds. However, in an ever-changing Soviet reality, by doing so, they could face arrest. Their action in fact defied the new regulations on cemeteries as institutions that were exclusively controlled by the state.

The decisions regarding Jewish cemeteries did not necessarily grow out of ill will toward Jews. Non-Jewish cemeteries too faced the threat of destruction in the midst of the Soviet drive to renew and modernize urban spaces. In Homyel, for example, the local Catholic cemetery was destroyed before the old Jewish cemetery was.[91] But in other cases, the combination of anti-Jewish prejudice and the culture of modernization became the driving force to reform the old Jewish *byt*. A case in point was the decision to convert the two-hundred-year-old Jewish cemetery located in the center of Berdychiv—a city with one of the largest Jewish populations in Ukraine—into a public park. The decision spurred a clash between local Jews and the workers employed to excavate the burial ground and turn it into a park. The police intervened. According to one account, Jews attacked the workers with stones (some of whom may also have been Jewish), demanding that the excavation cease. One policeman and a few workers were wounded in the clash.[92] Berdychiv rabbis called for a protest demonstration to take place at the site of the reburial of the remains unearthed during the excavations. And as much as the rabbis argued that those remains were human, local authorities retorted that the bones belonged to horses dug up during the excavations. The authorities also claimed that the cemetery had been destroyed long before, and, making some hostile allusions, they justified their decision by arguing that the cemetery spread infectious diseases, threatening the health of the city's residents. To further exacerbate the commotion, rumors spread about workers suffering paralysis while digging at the excavation site; some refused to continue the work, fearing that God's wrath would strike them because they exhumed the bodies of holy rabbis.[93] The decision to destroy the cemetery caused an uproar not only among Jews but also among employees at the city museum, who petitioned local and regional authorities, requesting the preservation of the cemetery. They even turned to the All-Ukrainian Archeological Committee and the People's Commissariat of Education. Some called for the oldest tombstones to be relocated to the Jewish section of the city museum. But apparently, local authorities remained unaffected: the plan to build a park persisted, and ancient tombstones were damaged.[94] While one is left to wonder whether local authorities would have behaved differently had the cemetery been Catholic or Russian Orthodox, the fact remains that there was no room for an old Jewish cemetery in a Jewish city like Berdychiv under Soviet rule.

Into the Quotidian: Names, People, Places, and Spaces

Renaming seems to have been key to the early Soviet project, a symbolic act, almost a first step in the purifying process of reforming the self and everyday life. Renaming was embedded in the iconoclastic thrust of the early Soviet years, which "helped erase reminders of previous holders of power and majesty, and made way for the refashioning of new symbols and emblems of the revolutionary order."[95] Renaming places, streets, squares, memorials, towns, and also people became an attempt to eradicate the old *byt* and envelop the new one in the spirit of communism. As in the wake of the French Revolution, renaming provided a new set of symbols to replace those of the past: it was about honoring new heroes, commemorating the dead ones, and most importantly getting rid of any association with the loathsome past.[96] Mothers and fathers renamed their children. Naming a child after a revolutionary personality became very widespread among Jews (as well as non-Jews). The name of a child became the symbol of the extent to which Jewish parents were willing to reject the old ways of their family or to continue instead along the path of tradition. When Fruma Treivas gave birth in Moscow, in Hospital No. 1, and the members of the editorial office of the communist newspaper she worked for came to offer their congratulations, she declared that she would name her son Engel, after a Polish Komsomol member who had been hanged for killing an agent provocateur.[97] In the Russian Jewish writer Isaac Babel's brilliant satire of Jewish life at the time of the NEP years, he mocks the circumcision ritual, after which the baby boy is usually named in the Jewish tradition. Titled "Karl-Yankl," Babel's short story depicts a family conspiracy in the suburbs of Odesa against a good communist father, who opposes the old Jewish *byt* but who is duped by his wife and mother-in-law. The father takes revenge by bringing the guilty ones to court but also publicly shames them by naming the baby Karl, in honor of Karl Marx, and rejecting the traditional Jewish name of Yankl that the grandmother and mother opted for during the clandestine ceremony.[98] The same theme appears in the family saga *Zelmenyaner* by the Yiddish writer Moshe Kulbak. By focusing on the name controversy, Kulbak captures the generational struggles between the old uncles and aunts and the young nieces and nephews of a Minsk family: the older generation watches with disbelief as the younger one embraces communism, celebrates electricity and literacy, intermarries, and even names the newborn member of the family with the revolutionary name Marat, after the hero and martyr of the French Revolution Jean-Paul Marat, instead of Zalmen, after the family's patriarch, Reb Zelmele.[99]

It happened that adults too changed their names. After all, the 1917 Soviet law allowed all citizens to change their names after turning eighteen. Some adults opted for names that captured the great undertakings of the Soviet project: these included the productivization of unemployed or disenfranchised Jews via resettlement on land; hence, new names appeared like Traktorina (a feminine version of the term "tractor"); Dzhan, after the Jewish collective farm near the Crimean town of Dzhankoy, a symbol of the success of the collectivization drive of the late 1920s that transformed bourgeois Jews into farmers; or Bire, after the Yiddish name of the Bira River, which flows through the city of Birobidzhan, the main city of the Jewish Autonomous Region (the first group of Jewish settlers arrived in Birobidzhan in May 1928). Other names of revolutionary heroes like Vladlen, Vladlenina, Ilich (and any other variant for Lenin), of revolutionary concepts like Oktiabrina or Ateist, and of industrial imagery like Industriia or Elektrifikatsiia (electrification) became a new fad in the 1920s.[100] In other instances, name changing was less about ideology and more about the effort to blend in, assimilate, and cast off all elements of Jewish identity. If not through marriage to Russians, Ukrainians, or Uzbeks, Jews could try to pass as ethnically Russian, Ukrainian, or Uzbek by changing their names or at least by having their children assume non-Jewish names.

But not everyone was committed to name changing. After the future Soviet literary star Vasily Grossman's graduation from university in 1929, both of his parents encouraged him to officially change his name. They suggested that life would be much easier for Vasily Semyonovich than it would be for someone with such a Jewish-sounding name as Iosif Solomonovich, his birth name. But Grossman refused to "suddenly become transformed." While he did change his first name and patronymic, he did not change his last name.[101]

Getting rid of suspicious namesakes, because they could be perceived as shameful traces of a bourgeois or anti-Bolshevik past, became a priority across the towns and cities of the Soviet Union. In the midst of complaints from local authorities, institutions that by 1925–1926 still retained a problematic prerevolutionary name, which could be imagined as hampering the Sovietization process of the Jewish masses, were renamed to embody the spirit of Bolshevism. For instance, the two most well-known Bundist institutions in the city of Minsk—the Bronislaw Grosser Workers' Club and the Yiddish newspaper *Veker*, which evoked salient moments in the history of the Bund, were renamed the Lenin Club and *Oktyabr* (October), the quintessence of the Bolshevik Revolution.[102] Political and cultural changes echoed through the new names chosen for cities and towns. Names of major Soviet cities were changed to Ulyanovsk, Sverdlovsk, Leningrad, Uritski, and Trotsk, all echoing the names of the great leaders of the Bolshevik old guard. The names of Jewish agricultural settlements and colonies were also changed: "Veker" collective farms that existed in different part of Belorussia changed their name to "Oktyabr." Over the course of the 1920s, the revolutionary Jewish hero Hirsh Lekert, despite his Bundist past, was considered universal enough and enough of a member of the general proletariat to fit in harmoniously with the ideal of Soviet universalism. Streets and colonies and a variety of institutions and organizations were renamed after him, especially in Belorussia, including a hospital, a professional school, a collective farm in the shtetl Liadi, the children's home in Mahilyow, and the Soviet Jewish school in Homiel.[103]

One Day in the Life of . . .

Over the course of the 1920s, the Soviet state strove to normalize and stabilize diplomatic relations with Western countries. Following the excesses of "War Communism," in the midst of the liberal NEP years, the priorities of Soviet foreign policy, galvanized especially by First Deputy People's Commissar of Foreign Affairs Maxim Litvinov, included the establishment of trade relations and a commitment to conform to the norms of diplomatic society.[104] Playing by the rules of diplomacy and adhering to diplomatic protocols meant also allowing visitors to enter the country, interact with its citizens, and visit its cities, all the more so as the presence of Western travelers to the Soviet Union had the potential not only of bringing in foreign currency but also of improving the country's image in the West.

The Soviet state prevented foreigners from having unlimited access to information about the country's real socioeconomic conditions and from gathering evidence about the full extent of political repression and arrests. Viewing travel to the Soviet Union as educational and aimed primarily at cultivating support for the new system, state authorities monitored closely the opportunities that foreigners had to meet up with Soviet citizens. Obtaining a visa to enter the Soviet Union was not always easy. In 1924, the People's Commissariat of Foreign Affairs denied entry visas to citizens of states that did not recognize the Soviet Union. Germany, Great Britain, and France established diplomatic relations with the Soviet state beginning in 1923 or 1924, but the United States did so only in 1933. Yet, Americans who traveled to the Soviet Union mostly, but not exclusively, on business were usually never denied a visa.[105] On the other hand, those writers and intellectuals who were known for their critical views of the new Bolshevik state, as was the case, for instance, of journalists at the *Chicago Tribune*, were refused entry visas.[106]

Despite the Soviets' efforts, however, they could not always prevent real-life encounters between locals and foreigners. Many visitors may have actually been able to gaze through the drawn curtain and capture some aspects of everyday life that were inconsistent with the ideological principles of the new system and, while criticizing the new country, grasp the inherent tensions between theory and practice in the implementation of communism.

In 1926, the prolific travel writer, biographer, and photographer Ethel Brilliana Tweedie was among those foreigners who arrived on Soviet soil to see the revolution with their own eyes. She spent one month in Moscow and Siberia capturing what she described as the brutal essence of the new Soviet system. She wrote,

> Yes—I've seen this Soviet Russia and spent a month lately in Moscow and Siberia. . . . The bulk of the people of Russia are more or less starving under the Soviets. They are overworked and underfed, and terror is on their faces. I never saw anyone smile. It is almost impossible to get a passport either in or out. Russia is a veritable hell of misery, and the Soviets wisely allow no one to see its workings except at their own invitation and after they have prepared the scene for view, and carefully organized escorts. . . . Never, never in all my world travels have I seen such heart-rending sights as I saw in those hideous days in

> Moscow. . . . In Russia no one lives any longer in his own house. Everything is shared from houses, to wives, to families. Houses are communal property. . . . Boys of adolescence and girl-children encouraged in free love, rudeness and disobedience. They had had babies born to them like rats or rabbits. . . . On the other hand, Vodka had been stopped by the Tzar, cash was wanted—Vodka brought cash, so back came Vodka under the Soviet regime. . . . Nothing that ever happened to the Jews of yore in Russia, which so horrified the world, can exceed the corruption, starvation, dislocation, cruelty, neglect of children, plundered homes and decimation, of the population today. Russia—as it is—is the most cruel, the most demoralized death trap the world has ever seen.[107]

Tweedie's bleak assessment of everyday life in the Soviet Union was one example of the many reportages produced by visitors from across Europe and the United States. Visitors included newspaper correspondents, trade unionists, fellow travelers, businessmen, filmmakers, engineers, workers' football teams, and women delegates to women's meetings who traveled to Soviet cities and towns during the 1920s.[108] Many wrote accounts about their experiences and impressions. Some were significantly less dreary and skeptical than Tweedie's. Some celebrated the new Soviet system and voiced their admiration for the state's great accomplishments in human history, hoping that the heroic future of socialist construction could one day belong to them too. Other travelers shared with the prolific English writer the same negative impressions. Depending on the place they traveled to, the people they met with, and their political assumptions, visitors saw and experienced the country's reality differently.

Through the pages of the diary the Yiddish writer Hersh Dovid Nomberg kept while visiting the Soviet Union, he captured the secrecy of the system: "About contemporary Russia, about the Soviet Union, we know everything and we know nothing. Russia has friends and enemies, passionate supporters, exasperated critics. Everything one reads sounds like propaganda."[109] Visitors with an interest in Jews and Jewish life would have traveled to one of the many shtetls in Belorussia or Ukraine. There, besides observing the economic devastation caused by World War I, the civil war, and War Communism, visitors would have noticed that despite the Soviet prohibition of black-marketing and petty trade, these means of subsistence remained a fixture in the everyday life of the small towns. They would also have noticed the specific shtetl architecture and spatial layouts, which continued to differentiate Jews from non-Jews in the public eye: compared to peasant dwellings, Jewish houses exhibited some peculiarities in the architecture and house building, as well as in the ethnocultural artifacts they contained, which were connected to Jewish customs and traditions.[110] Had they traveled to a shtetl like Sharhorod, they would have remarked that some Jewish families affixed mezuzot to the doorpost, not only in the interior but also to the home's entrance.[111] Of course, they would have traveled to Moscow, the political and cultural center of the new Bolshevik system but also one of the cities with the fastest-growing Jewish population in the Soviet Union, which eventually reached more than 250,000 on the eve of World War II. In Moscow, visitors might have gotten word of the existence of an underground yeshiva supported by Lubavitch or would take note that phone conversations between the Soviet capital and the Polish city Bialystok occurred daily, often in Yiddish.[112]

The travelers would have also observed that Jews engaged in different leisure activities depending on their place of residence. Many came together to hang out in the local Jewish workers' clubs. In urban centers with larger Jewish demographic concentrations, Jewish clubs hosted artistic, musical, and sports activities, including chess tournaments. If some hardcore Jewish communists complained about the fact that Jews preferred to gather in the Jewish club, while avoiding the non-Jewish clubs, foreign visitors might have heard a Jewish worker's retort to the criticism: "when you go . . . [to the Jewish] club you meet your usual circle of friends, with whom you can talk, [whereas] in . . . [the general communist club] there is no one to talk to."[113] After Puah Rakovsky, a leader of the Zionist movement and a committed feminist, submitted a request for an entry visa to the Soviet Union in 1928 to see her son, she left Poland for Moscow, where she spent some time. There, she visited the large building with the sign "Borochov Club." She attended lectures about Birobidzhan, noticing that the club's hall was always packed: the club's space represented a favorite meeting point for many young Jews, even though most of them had little to do with Borochov's Zionism.[114]

Visitors might have noticed that in many places, the synagogue still retained its prerevolutionary character as a social center and neighborhood institution. It remained a space where Jews, regardless of their views on religion, spent their leisure time in the company of other Jews. Some chose the synagogue over the club as a meeting point to discuss current events because of the proximity of the building to their home or because of their "nonproletarian" background, which prevented them from obtaining union membership and therefore attending cultural club activities; others preferred the club as a social venue to meet friends.

Especially those visitors to the Soviet Union who came from Poland would have been intrigued by the ways in which Jewish youth interacted daily with their non-Jewish peers and created strong social bonds. Had they met with Asia Matveyuk, they would have heard from her that in 1926 she attended a Soviet school in Novopoltavka: because of the colony's shrinking population and the fluency with which Ukrainian children spoke Yiddish and Jewish children spoke Ukrainian, the school was a mixed Ukrainian-Jewish one, with both as languages of instruction. Asia, who spoke Yiddish at home and Yiddish and Ukrainian with her Jewish, Ukrainian, and ethnic German friends, enjoyed "strolling through the Jewish, Ukrainian, and German parts of [her] village." The successful horizontal socialization among children took place beyond the walls of the Soviet school, as well as through the parades, parties, and meetings organized by the pioneer and Komsomol institutions to mark Soviet holidays and celebrate the new rituals of Soviet life.[115]

In light of Lenin's famous remark that "Cinema, for us, is the most important of the arts" and of Commissar of Enlightenment Anatoly Lunacharky's observation that "a socialist government must imbue even film shows with a socialist spirit," travelers to the Soviet Union with an interest in Jewish life might have been curious to know what movies Jews watched in the 1920s.[116] Like non-Jews, they paid to watch Soviet blockbusters like *Cement*, for example, a chronicle of post-civil-war reconstruction based on the best-selling novel by Fyodor Gladkov. But Jews (perhaps more than non-Jews) also paid to view one of the several 1920s silent movies based on Jewish themes, some of which were less politicized than others.[117] These included the 1925 Soviet adaptation of Sholem Aleichem's *Menachem Mendl the Matchmaker*, titled *Jewish Luck* (*Evreiskoe schast'e*), which starred the well known Yiddish theater actor Solomon Mikhoels. Set in Berdychiv and Odesa, the movie highlighted Jewish poverty but also presented a rather positive depiction of traditional Jewish life and culture, ending with an open-air wedding.[118] Others might have opted to see *Laughter through Tears* (*Smekh skvoz slezy*), also based on Sholem Aleichem's classic works *Motl Peisi the Cantor's Son* and *The Enchanted Tailor*: in it, shtetl life under the tsar was depicted as one of poverty and repression only. A 1928 movie titled *His Excellency* (*Zayn ekselents* in Yiddish and *Ego prevoskhoditelstvo* in Russian) was shown with intertitles in Yiddish and Russian in different movie theaters across the Soviet Union.[119] It focused on the participation of Jews in the revolutionary struggle and was one of the few Soviet film productions to portray the economic and cultural life of the Jewish working masses.

During Soviet citizens' free time, they filled up theaters as well. Many paid for a ticket for one of the five hundred seats of the Moscow Yiddish Theater, for a ticket to one of the plays put onstage in Minsk and in Kharkiv by the major state Yiddish theaters of the Belorussian Soviet Socialist Republic and the Ukrainian Soviet Socialist Republic, or for a ticket to one of the shows performed in smaller Jewish population centers by one of the many itinerant Jewish theaters and troupes. Travelers to the Soviet Union might have also noticed that, at least in theory, leisure time came under strict political supervision: a theatrical performance that was not political enough could face harsh criticism. Visitors may have wanted, for example, to attend a performance by the well-known Yiddish Traveling Folk Ensemble of Musical Comedy, founded by Yaakov Guzik. In the summer of 1929, the Evsektsiia, which had repeatedly tried to forbid the ensemble from staging its operettas in the Soviet Union since 1927, renewed its attacks, writing nasty reviews and disparaging the troupe's performances as vulgar and religious. The Evsektsiia submitted a formal complaint to the Moscow repertoire commission, but the commission ignored it and instead granted the Guzik ensemble the right to perform in the city, thus gratifying plenty of theatergoers who were eager to enjoy vulgar operettas devoid of political content.[120]

Visitors to the Soviet Union might have also attended public trials that showcased different aspects of everyday life. Used as entertaining propaganda, show trials of rabbis, ritual slaughterers, and *mohelim* marked the Soviet legal landscape on the Jewish street, attracting a diverse audience that included reporters from Poland, religious Jews, and workers. Public trials were organized in local clubs against wives who allegedly served as a corrupting force in the family, distorting the political beliefs of husband and children and persuading them not to attend Party meetings or participate in the club's activities. There were court cases against individuals who behaved in violation of Stalin's cultural revolution, namely, of the set of ideals, activities, and policies aimed at radically restructuring society: if visitors happened to travel through the Berdychiv region in March 1928, they could have attended a show trial against two Jewish Komsomol members who, because they consumed alcoholic drinks and played cards with some "bourgeois elements," were blamed for promoting anti-Soviet behavior. They were both kicked out of the communist youth organization.[121]

Besides attending movies and theater performances, taking strolls, or meeting with friends, Soviet citizens became keen on reading. Insofar as literacy was seen as a key to success in the new Soviet way of life, it was turned into a significant feature of urban leisure culture in Bolshevik society.[122] Daily papers played a crucial role in molding public opinion. It is not by chance that some of the most prominent revolutionaries, including Lenin himself, were also journalists, who used the press as an important vehicle to organize and draw to the cause those who were not yet committed. In the early 1920s, a chronic shortage of paper and machines affected production and paper quality and even contributed to a fall in circulation. In some of the largest urban railroad stations in the south of the country, there were no newspapers. The fall in circulation was also due to the way in which the Bolsheviks monopolized the written word: without apologizing for it, they erased most light fiction and entertaining news from their newspapers, leaving only serious information.[123] This influenced the readership too. Visitors to the Soviet Union may have agreed with some reports originating from neighboring Poland according to which everyone read in Moscow, in the kiosks, restaurants, at the theater; but they were not necessarily reading *Pravda* or *Der emes*, because of the dry and boring subject matter. They were more likely to be reading literature, not necessarily political in content, or leafing through the journal *Ogoniok*, "which contained less official protocols, more photographs, and short stories by Russian writers."[124] Some subscribed to Yiddish newspapers and magazines and sought out Yiddish translations of world classics, including Shakespeare, Cervantes, Goethe, Dostoevsky, and Victor Hugo. Yiddish translations could be found in the local libraries and schools of larger and smaller Jewish centers.[125]

On the other hand, not unlike in the cities of neighboring Poland and the United States, even in the European regions of the Soviet Union, most younger Jews preferred to read works of literature and the press in Russian, which was more authoritative, prestigious, and useful to find employment than that in Yiddish.

Visitors to the Soviet Union of the 1920s may have also noticed how the ideal of the New Soviet Jewish Man and Woman not only played out via the literary and cinematic representations produced at the time but also echoed through real life. Supposedly tough, strong, and serious, the New Soviet Jewish Man was imagined as the exact opposite of the shtetl *luftmentsh*, the impractical "air person" without business or income, or of the despicable Jewish NEPman, the exploiting entrepreneur who rejected the principles of communism. The new Soviet "muscle Jew" could be seen smelting the iron in a metallurgical plant in Homyel, ploughing the land and raising pigs in the early Jewish settlement Valdheym located in Birobidzhan, or graduating from the Jewish section of the Party School in Odesa. Asia Matveyuk's father matched this description:

> My father was a charming, handsome, and very strong man. There were circus wrestlers at the time traveling from one town to another and when they came to Novopoltavka, the villagers asked my father to wrestle with them. I remember a famous wrestler, huge, with his boots unpicked in the seams on his fat legs, came to the village. My father looked thin and short compared to him. My father grabbed him by his belt and threw him to the ground. The wrestler rose to his feet and shook my father's hand acknowledging his victory. Then some circus representatives came trying to convince my father to become a professional wrestler, but Frida [his second wife] was whining begging my father to refuse and never again take part in wrestling.[126]

In 1923, the writer Mikhail Zoshchenko captured the ideal of womanhood that took shape in Soviet society, celebrating the new taste in fashion: "Fellows, I don't like dames who wear hats. If a woman wears a hat, if her stockings are fuzzy, if she has a lap dog in her arms, or if she has a gold tooth, such a lady aristocrat, to my mind, is not a woman, but just a void."[127] Like Soviet women of all nationalities, the New Soviet Jewish Woman was supposed to be liberated, mannish, plain, unattractive, and even armed and eager to fight for her country. In addition, Soviet Jewish women were expected to shun the shame of the shtetl for the prestige of city life or work as a toiler of the land. They were imagined as the opposite of the traditional Jewish mother, who with devotion imparted the laws of Judaism to her children, or as the counterpart to the bourgeois woman, wife of the well-to-do Jewish merchant, who wore sophisticated clothes and makeup. Flipping through the pages of the Yiddish newspapers, visitors to the Soviet Union would have noticed photos of Jewish women workers attending a Rabfak, institutions that prepared them to enter institutions of higher learning; speakers and delegates at a Zhenotdel meeting; or tractor drivers in a Jewish colony in Crimea. But by the end of the 1920s, in combination with the strong revolutionary woman, who was dedicated to the cause, the ideal of a more maternal woman made its way, as the state began to introduce measures to encourage higher birthrates. Repressive pronatalism came together with a rhetorical celebration of women's liberation.

A keen observer at the time might have been interested in probing the real condition of women against the theory, language, and images of female emancipation. The visitors would have been surprised by the inequalities that persisted in the sphere of the home, as they listened to the grievances at a 1926 Zhenotdel meeting by Jewish women married to communist men. The women complained about their ten- to twelve-hour-long working day and protested the lack of spare time for themselves. Visitors might have also noticed with wonder the existing tension between the rhetoric of equality and the reality of women playing the typically "bourgeois role" of raising children, knitting, sewing, and cooking for their husbands who were Communist Party members. And some visitors would have been alarmed to hear that instances of exploitation of maids took place particularly within the walls of the most enlightened communist households: there were reports of prominent trade-union members who employed underaged girls who had recently moved to the city from the provinces as "house workers." The young women received a salary of three to five rubles a month, worked every day until midnight, had no leisure time (not even during the revolutionary holidays), and became the target of disreputable comments about their sexual behavior out of fear that they would bring home "infectious diseases from the square."[128] The domestic servant, a seemingly paradoxical legacy from prerevolutionary Russia, was in fact common, especially in the homes of privileged members of the communist elites; they faced the burdens of laundry, maybe sexual harassment, abuse, and crowded living conditions.[129]

Visitors to the Soviet Union noticed the food, of course, the quantity of which went in cycles of abundance and complete shortage, from the horrific years of the civil war to the relatively stable conditions of the mid-1920s. If visitors had traveled to Odesa, for example, in 1920, they would have learned that the widow of the great Yiddish writer Mendele Mocher Seforim had died that same year of hunger and hardship in the city. They also would have found out that the writer's sick daughter lived in the only heated room in the apartment, while other people had moved into the rest of the house, taking what they could.[130] A few years later, in 1925, the Yiddish poet H. Leyvik, who visited family members in the Minsk region, mentioned food and clothing: "Nobody suffers from hunger here, it is possible to eat and drink in abundance. . . . Food is very inexpensive. There are mountains of fruit, . . . meat and dairy products. The aspect of life where you notice poverty is clothing. But in fact the Minsk region and its shtetls have never been very fashionable—one family always shared one pair of boots."[131]

At the same time, the status of disenfranchised Jews—branded as *lishchentsy* because of their prerevolutionary bourgeois life—would have stood out to anyone traveling through the towns of Soviet Ukraine or Belorussia: they lacked food and housing (only trade-union members had access to co-op stores with food and housing allotment). Noticing the uncertainty and ambivalences of everyday life, visitors might have remarked that while *lishchentsy* had difficulties feeding their own families, Jewish women bought kosher meat at the meat stand, for as long as it was available in any given city or town; or if the housewives happened to know that a *shochet* happened to be present when an animal was slaughtered, then they could purchase a piece of kosher meat even after the Soviets significantly restricted its production.[132] And then the same visitors could have noticed young Jewish female students who, perhaps unbeknownst to their parents, went to the cafeteria to meet friends and eat nonkosher meat. Some Communist Party members did not turn away from a Sabbath meal with religious family members.[133] Yet others might have found a compromise, and while they could no longer follow the rules of kashrut outside the home, they refrained from eating pork or reinvented entirely their understanding of Jewish dietary laws.[134]

In the eyes of travelers to the Soviet Union, the foodscape on the Jewish street was further complicated by the fact that matzah remained available during Passover. As late as April 1929, after Stalin launched his crash collectivization, the American company Manischewitz sent wagons of matzah to major Soviet cities, including Leningrad and Moscow. Of course, the Evsektsiia complained about how quickly the matzah had arrived via Riga, in independent Latvia: "It flew! As opposed to everything else that is needed to build communism, like tractors, which take such a long time."[135] Who ate the matzah? Many who disassociated themselves from Judaism but who did not wish to renounce the traditional food customs and still craved matzah during Passover.[136] In some places, schoolchildren would visit other children's homes to check and see if they celebrated Passover and ate matzah, and if they did, they publicly condemned them; and even so, both "inspectors" and "inspected" enjoyed eating Jewish foods.[137] While the Soviet government limited the distribution of matzah during Passover and clamped down on kosher meat production, it could not monitor the preparation of ethnic foods, especially in the private sphere of the home.

In some cities, local eateries offered Jewish ethnic food like kugel. In one of the busy streets in Moscow, the entrance to a small restaurant read, "Jewish Cuisine" (*Evreiskoe pitanie*), a place that served Jewish dishes with one thousand flavors.[138] But the home in particular remained a space for Jewish ethnic food, Jewish-style latkes, blintzes, borsht, and even challahs and gefilte fish with horseradish. While food traditions endured more in the private kitchens than in public spaces, it was common to have Jewish dishes at wedding celebrations. By the 1930s, food too could become a site of ideology and come under attack. At the same time, however, food customs remained a central aspect of everyday life and a real marker for Jewish identity as other markers declined.[139]

The channels of communication between the Jews living within the borders of the new Soviet state that emerged out of the ruins of the civil war and other Jewish centers outside these borders did not collapse after 1921. Cultural, political, and economic exchanges between Soviet Jews and other

Jewish centers in North America, western and central Europe, and Palestine continued throughout the 1920s, in multifaceted forms, which included publications, tourism, immigration and emigration, economic transactions, journalism, and relief work. As a result of war and revolution, the Russian Jewish center collapsed, and the Jewish communities within the tsarist empire, spanning from Vilna to Riga, from Warsaw to Kyiv, from Chişinău to Saint Petersburg, were now separated by the new borders of the newly established nation-states. New political borders carved up the former Pale of Settlement. In the early 1920s, Bratslav Hasidim, who under the new geopolitical order lived in independent Poland, had to cross the border into Soviet territories in order to reach the city of Uman—now part of the Ukrainian Soviet Socialist Republic—to celebrate the Jewish holidays and pay a visit to the grave of Rabbi Nachman of Bratslav.[140] The movement across borders, which in one way or another continued throughout the 1920s, ensured that Soviet Jewries were not entirely cut off at first from the remnants of "Russian Jewries," now part of Poland, Romania, and the Baltic countries, or for that matter from world Jewry. This reality grew out of the general geopolitics of the post–World War I and civil war years.

The readiness to maintain a porousness of the Soviet borders stemmed from different factors, including the new state's uncertain international position. With a devastated economy and a weakened military and surrounded by hostile states, including Lithuania, Latvia, Estonia, Finland, Romania, and Poland, the Soviet Union was desperate for some kind of international recognition and acceptance. Furthermore, the Soviet Union's exclusion from the League of Nations and the failure of the revolution in countries like Germany and Hungary urgently drove the People's Commissariat for Foreign Affairs, headed from 1920 to 1930 by Georgy Chicherin, to seek diplomatic and economic relations with as many states as possible. Against the backdrop of this cautious but ongoing cultural, political, and economic exchange, made of press coverage, leisure travel, literati events, or commercial deals between the Soviet Union and other countries, Soviet Jewries remained connected to world Jewry. At this time, they were not alienated from the geocultural centers that had once constituted a whole. While communal and personal contacts and exchanges between the new Jewries that emerged out of the breakdown of the Russian Empire might have lessened and were indeed closely monitored by the new states, they did not halt.

Contacts between Jews living in the two sister cities of Minsk, now capital of the Belorussian Soviet Socialist Republic, and Vilna, now included in independent Poland, changed as a result of the new geopolitical order but did not subside. Yiddish writers and journalists crossed the borders back and forth, traveling to and from Poland, to and from Mandate Palestine, to and from North America. Nominally apolitical international organizations, such as ORT and the JDC mutual-aid and immigrant associations like the *landsmanshaftn* that raised funds for Jews from their same hometown now under Soviet rule, or spokespeople from different communist and socialist organizations all guaranteed a flow of information, opinions, knowledge, and funds. Over time, however, the balance between the integration and the separation of Soviet Jewries from the rest of world Jewry changed. By the early 1930s, Stalin's growing isolationist policy in foreign affairs, due also to the economic catastrophe in the West triggered by the Great Depression and to the rise of fascism in Europe, significantly curtailed the possibilities of any form of exchange with the outside world. This resulted in Soviet Jewries' mounting isolation from other Jewish centers. Breaching this isolation might lead to dire consequences.

Born in Trostianets in 1888, the Hebrew poet Abram Friman witnessed the brutal pogrom that took place in his hometown in May 1919. Like other writers, he too tried to make sense of the violence through his writing and produced a Hebrew novel titled *1919*. Friman published excerpts of the novel in British Mandatory Palestine, where they appeared, with his initials only, in the Hebrew-language journal *Ha-olam*, and in 1931 and 1935, respectively, he published in Berlin the first and the second part of the novel. *1919* remained unfinished. Yet, in 1935, while he was living in Odesa, Friman received notice that he had been awarded the Bialik Prize, the prestigious literary award for significant accomplishments in Hebrew literature. The prize was given from the municipality of Tel Aviv, in Mandate Palestine. But a literary recognition from outside Soviet borders did not sit well with the new isolationist climate. Perhaps for this very reason, the NKVD arrested Friman shortly thereafter.[141]

Conclusion: Successes and Limits of Ideology

Mark Derbaremdiker was born in Berdychiv in 1920, just a few days after the Red Army declared victory in the city. The Soviet success in the city included, among other things, shooting "the ten richest Jews in town, not because they were Jews, but because they were rich." Because his paternal home was destroyed during the civil war, Derbaremdiker moved with his family into the apartment that had previously belonged to Mendele Mocher Seforim, located on Zolotoy Lane, which was renamed Mendele Mocher Seforim Street in the mid-1920s. His mother baked challah to celebrate the Sabbath, used special dishes during Passover, which were stored away for the rest of the year, and made sure kashrut laws were strictly followed within the confines of the home. He attended heder, possibly an underground one, and then a Soviet Jewish school, called Grininke Boymelekh (Little green trees). Here, while studying arithmetic and poems about Lenin in Yiddish, he became a Pioneer, a member of the communist youth movement. He attended a Jewish club, situated in the former Choir Synagogue, and read books from its library. It seemed like Derbaremdiker accepted his father's approach to life under the Soviets, a choice that entailed more negotiation than rebuff: "My father believed that one shouldn't live in conflict with the authorities, but at home we could have our own way of life, observing our rules and traditions. . . . We were like *marranos*. . . . We were like this: we were pioneers at school, and at home we followed the rules of Judaism."[142]

As bearers of a revolutionary culture, the new revolutionary man and woman had to refashion language, gestures, dress, behavior, feelings, and mind. In doing so, they inevitably clashed with their parents and the old *byt*. With varying degrees of intensity, depending on whether they lived in a growing urban center, a small town, or a rural settlement, both the parents of the new revolutionary man and woman and the young revolutionaries themselves had to reach compromises while going about their everyday lives. Compromises could be painful and entail loss. Some parents accepted the new rules about Soviet quotidian existence, taking advantage of the opportunities offered by the new Soviet system, out of concern for their children's future and livelihood. Others resisted these rules and rejected the system, at the risk of turning themselves and their children into socially marginalized and economically ruined citizens of the Soviet Union.

Accepting the Sovietization of everyday life hinged more often on material need than on ideology. For instance, young Jews who were born into a family of poor artisans had no chance of getting an education or a job without joining a communist organization like the Komsomol. Becoming a member of the communist youth organization involved making a break from the family, its old *byt*, and its religious traditions. This break may have pained the individual and even stirred a sense of guilt, but most parents probably never reproached the choice. They rather accepted it, or even encouraged it, knowing that it was the only solution available.

This kind of harmonious negotiation proposed by Derbaremdiker's father was contingent on the strength of family and friendship networks, on personal ties, and on the economic realities of communist children living with "bourgeois" parents. These networks represented a bulwark to the Party's interference in everyday life and allowed for aspects of Jewish everyday life to survive despite the ongoing social and political pressure. While family allegiances continued to matter for many Jews, many more rejected them out of necessity more than conviction. If the socialist attempt to create alternative rites to mark life-cycle events met many hurdles in the 1920s, the titanic changes brought about by rapid industrialization and collectivization of the First Five-Year Plan quieted down these challenges and came to mark a real watershed in Soviet everyday life for decades to come.

CONCLUSION

It Was the Spring of Hope, It Was the Winter of Despair . . .

Over the course of the 1920s, the system born out of the Bolshevik coup of October 1917 produced some of the most sweeping changes in the cultural, religious, economic, and political life of the Jewish communities of the former Pale of Settlement. The new system proffered Jews exceptionally auspicious political conditions that until then could only have appeared implausible in the territories of the former Russian Empire, as well as in many other European states at the time. The first socialist country galvanized for Jews great hopes in a future rich in civil and political equality, unprecedented prospects of success and upward mobility, and, at least on paper, without antisemitism and popular anti-Jewish violence. Furthermore, the Soviet state of the 1920s seemed to be supportive of the Jewish population not only in its official rejection of tsarist anti-Jewish legislation and active expressions of hostility but also in its practically motivated compromise with prerevolutionary Marxist notions of the Jewish national question: Lenin and Stalin, revising their earlier statements about the nonexistence of a Jewish nation, acknowledged the presence of a Jewish nationality, which was ipso facto entitled to use its own national language in the myriad of cultural and educational institutions and organizations established during the 1920s in the Soviet state.

On the other hand, the new system imposed ruthless policies that restricted the lives of all Soviet citizens, including those of Jews. Even in the context of the relatively tolerant 1920s, these policies put an end to the wide range of cultural, religious, and political diversity that had marked prerevolutionary Jewish life. The state barred many manifestations of Jewish identity linked to socialist parties and youth groups, Zionist schools and cultural associations, and religious organizations throughout the republics of the Soviet Union, categorizing them as residues of Jewish bourgeois life. Although in hindsight, the 1920s appear as a feast of communist liberalism, the kernel of totalitarianism and brutality was in place and would further ripen by the end of the decade.

Like any other modern political system, the Bolshevik state set out to establish a new order. It did so by reshaping the behavior, the mentality, the beliefs, and the work habits of its citizens, managing their lives, disciplining and supervising them. What discriminated the Soviet state from other political systems at the time was the exceptional violence and the tempo with which it strove to implement the changes, attempting to create a new biopolitical order based on the transcendence of the old order and the construction of new forms of life.[1] For instance, the newly established Polish state and the Soviet Union—the geopolitical entities within the borders of which the two largest Jewish communities in Europe resided in the 1920s—yielded very different political and cultural constellations. If over the course of the 1920s Poland progressively grew into a more authoritarian state, it still retained a functioning public sphere, where different Jewish political groups interacted with each other, where Jewish party leaders held seats in the Parliament, where a diverse Jewish press, alongside theaters and schools, operated in different languages. On the other hand, as a one-party system, which had decimated its real or alleged enemies, the Bolsheviks suppressed opposition, retained power over the state's legislative and executive structures, and controlled the press, the culture, the everyday life of its citizens in a far more comprehensive way than did any other political system at the time. All this left a lasting impact on the ways in which Soviet Jewries developed.

The expressions of Jewishness in communist society and the support for communism in the Jewish towns and cities of the former Pale of Settlement took on different shades and nuances that build on many variables. The experience of communism and Jewishness in the system's capital of Moscow differed significantly from the experience of communism and Jewishness in a provincial city, in a small town, or in an agricultural colony.

Similarly, an older Jewish woman living in Kirghizia experienced Sovietization quite differently from the way in which a young Jewish man came to terms with the new system in Ukraine. Geography, age, and gender defined the ways in which Jews (and non-Jews) came to support the new system, resisted it, adjusted to it, or conformed to its ideals. Thus, geography, age, and gender determined the ways in which Jews became involved in the political life of the country, accepting positions in the general Soviet administration or Party institutions; the ways in which they attempted to retain Judaism, hiring a *melamed* to instruct their children or purchasing kosher meat for the family; the ways in which they supported the construction of a new Soviet Jewish identity, enrolling their children in a Yiddish school or performing in a Yiddish state choir; and the ways in which they challenged popular expressions of hostility, turning to the local police or to the regional courts to seek redress.

This volume is also a reminder of the complexities, messiness, and richness of the early Soviet Jewish experience that took shape within the leniency of the NEP years and despite the constraints of communist ideology. It is an experience that withstands both the "communalist" interpretation of the Jewish past and the "dispersionist" one: if the first revolves exclusively around the Jews active in and committed to Jewish institutions and organizations, the latter focuses primarily on the study of those men and women of Jewish ancestry who were not necessarily involved with Jewish institutions or committed to the preservation of Jewish life and identity.[2] The study of Soviet Jewish history, in which Jews chose to or were forced to recoil from preexisting notions of Jewish identity and continuity, blurs the boundaries between the "communalist" and the "dispersionist" experience. The emergence of new social networks as informal carriers of Jewish self-identification for those who were no longer able to or ceased to be affiliated with Jewish institutions, many of which were closed down by Soviet authorities, represents an interesting case in point. Jewish men and women cultivated informal social networks—often as a nonideological response to the alienation caused by urbanization and the novelty of forceful Sovietization. They did so by creating new ties or by reinforcing preexisting ones with other Jewish families, relatives, coworkers, or friends. In the midst of the extraordinary ruptures brought about by the revolution and its ideals, forging new social networks ensured the emergence of friendships that in turn nurtured a sense of ethnic self-identification and belonging, inadvertently creating a web of Jewishness that went well beyond the world of sanctioned politics and culture.

Similarly, official Soviet Yiddish culture, which flourished over the course of the 1920s via numerous state-funded institutions and publications and which promoted the faith in a communist identity and in the grand vision of Birobidzhan, was made likewise of informal everyday interactions and contacts. These exchanges produced, in turn, ethnic spaces, in the classroom, in the club, in the theater, or at the work plant, which preserved ethnic identity through less readily apparent markers of Jewishness.

Established by the new Bolshevik leadership to bring communism to the Jewish masses, the Evsektsiia effectively promoted the Sovietization of the Jewish street over the course of the 1920s, serving as an agent of change but also as one of destruction. The scale of wreckage perpetrated on prerevolutionary Jewish life and institutions, encouraged by the members of the Evsektsiia, was remarkable. This wreckage affected the identity, religion, culture, language, and political affiliation of one of the largest Jewish communities in prewar Europe.

Jewish life in the Soviet territories was therefore not only suppressed by the regime but quashed by fellow Jews, many of whom felt intoxicated by the possibility of rising up as the new trustworthy leadership on the Jewish street, destroying their adversaries, be they Zionists, Mensheviks, Hasidim, or wealthy Jewish factory owners, with impunity. In many places, the Evsektsiia spearheaded the requisition of Jewish property and buildings, the closing down of religious institutions, and the arrest of religious leaders, as well as the persecution of Hebrew-language and Zionist activists. And when in 1929 Stalin abandoned the NEP policy in favor of collectivization and industrialization and launched the Great Turn, the Evsektsiia bowed its head—as all other Jewish and non-Jewish organizations did—and renewed its commitment to liquidate "Jewish nationalism and counterrevolution." Calling for the transformation of the great Moscow synagogue into a workers' club, the Evsektsiia's official organ, *Der emes*, pledged to dismantle all bourgeois institutions that still existed in the capital of international communism as well as anywhere else in the Soviet Union.

Most memoir literature and witness accounts recorded both before and after the Holocaust identify the members of the Evsektsiia as the sole culprits for the brutality perpetrated against prerevolutionary Jewish life. The term "Evsek" became a code word for a traitor, oppressor, or tyrant. It elicited hatred, anger, or even disgust throughout the Jewish world, even among those activists and writers who had not observed the Evsektsiia in action from close up. In 1931, the Yiddish writer and educator Eliezer Shteynbarg, who played a leading role in the cultural life of Romanian Jewry, upon returning to Cernăuţi, Romania, from Rio de Janeiro, Brazil, where he lived for two years, described the Evsektsiia as follows: "Since the dawn of Jewish nose-blowing, one has never seen such a kind of snot (to put it mildly) as the one produced by the Evsektsiia. The consequences of its activities continue to be felt even now that it [the Evsektsiia] lies in the spittoon."[3] While Shteynbarg had not witnessed firsthand the work of the Evsektsiia, he blamed it for corrupting Jewish culture globally. Of course, the Evsektsiia was not alone in shoving communism onto Jewish life and culture. Jewish communists from different parts of the globe became infatuated with the appeal of building a better and more just world, an appeal that made them embrace with enthusiasm and devotion an ideology that did not shy away from violence. They were true believers.

In the Soviet context, many young Jews became the by-product of the experiment promoted by the Evsektsiia. They supported and benefited from the Evsektsiia's vision of a new, secular, urban, productive, and Yiddish-speaking Jewry. Born in 1908 in the shtetl Voskovichi, in Zhytomyr district, Ukraine, Elye Shekhtman grew up in a large, traditional, and very poor family. After moving to Odesa in 1926, where he studied Yiddish literature at the Jewish Pedagogical College, he met and married Sheindl Magazinnik, an actress in the Yiddish theater. In the 1930s, Shekhtman moved to Kharkiv and eventually to Kyiv. He started writing Yiddish poetry in 1928 but soon shifted to prose. He published his short stories and novels in the major Soviet Yiddish journals at the time and eventually composed some of the most significant work in the genre of socialist realism in Yiddish of the 1930s. Thus, he went from growing up in the provinces, in abject poverty, in a religious Jewish family, to joining the vanguard of the Yiddish cultural front and becoming a celebrated cultural figure. But Shekhtman not only lived through "the spring of hope" but also experienced "the winter of despair." After serving as an officer in the Red Army during World War II, he returned to Kyiv and was arrested as a "Jewish nationalist" with alleged ties to Zionism. He was released from prison after Stalin's death and ultimately moved to Israel, in 1972.

Writing several years after Stalin had died, Elye Shekhtman captured the irrational and irresistible power in the belief in communism that took hold of the hearts and minds of so many Jews, including himself. In a short story titled "The Golem's Punishment," he recast the folkloristic legend of the creature of clay—brought to life by the rabbi of Prague in the sixteenth century to protect the imperiled Jewish community—through the lens of communism. In Shekhtman's story, the Golem metaphorically stands for the revolution, which rises up to safeguard the Jews from the absolute destruction brought on by the danger of anti-Jewish violence and government repression. But like the revolution, the Golem too becomes an unstoppable, destructive, and brutal force, which remains enticing, irresistible, and blinding even when it brings about the devastation and rape of the ones it is supposed to protect.[4]

Jewish communists who made use of violence to bring the revolution to the Jewish street were so effective in facilitating the destruction of Jewish life that by the end of the 1920s, they themselves were no longer necessary to the state. Stalin's Great Turn, a "revolution from above" that sought to build socialism through forced industrialization and collectivization, also marked the beginning of the "liquidation of the liquidators." Those activists, intellectuals, cultural workers, and writers who had all dreamt—some with reason, some naïvely—of a better future, sooner or later had to come to terms with the fact that the revolution was willing to devour its own children, and the most faithful ones at that. The Evsektsiia was liquidated in January 1930, as part of a general decision to terminate the national sections in the Communist Party of the Soviet Union—and the state deemed the Jewish question solved once and for all.

Yet, the Evsektsiia's actions, which disrupted the relative ethnic solidarity that existed among Jews before the revolution, are yet another reminder that Jewish assimilation into the Soviet system was not only voluntary but also the product of unadulterated brutality. Cultures of violence are contagious and often circular. Those who embrace them are often swallowed up by them. The liquidators of Jewish life were themselves liquidated in the purges of 1937–1938, killed in prison or in the labor camps, with ruthless violence by the regime in the name of which they had suppressed fellow Jews and different expressions of Jewish identity. They were liquidated because by then, in the eyes of the regime, they were just as bourgeois and nationalist as those Jews whom they had helped to wipe out. These violent Jews wrote themselves into extinction, becoming the victims of Stalinist violence, instead of a mass pogrom.

But there was a new generation of Soviet Jews on the rise, for whom the work of the Evsektsiia could only have seemed utterly irrelevant and in contradiction with their cultural and social aspirations. Born right before the revolution or shortly thereafter, they matured into committed Soviet citizens, who eagerly rejected their parents' past and embraced the great hopes of the 1930s. Stalin's magic spell of "life has become better, life has become happier," which reverberated in the spirit of grandiose Soviet mythmaking through the press, radio, visual culture, and banners that plastered the cities and towns of the Soviet Union, would become even more credible when faced with the reality of growing fascism throughout Europe.

ACKNOWLEDGMENTS

This volume benefited significantly from the work of the scholars who came before me, in particular, the research of Mordechai Altshuler and Zvi Gitelman, who developed the field of Jewish history in the Soviet Union and lay the ground for the exciting work that has flourished over the course of the past three decades. Like so many others, I am indebted to their pioneering work. This volume has also benefited greatly from the generous feedback of the other colleagues involved in the Comprehensive History of Jews in the Soviet Union project, who took the time to read and engage with my work during our workshops in New York City and in Oxford. They include Oleg Budnitskii, David Engel, Gennady Estraikh, David Fishman, Zvi Gitelman, Zeev Levin, Ben Nathans, Anna Shternshis, Jeffrey Veidlinger, Debbie Yalen, and Arkadi Zeltser. I am grateful to the staff of the many archives and libraries where I conducted the research for this volume. I am thankful to the archivists in the Central State Archives and in the Regional Archives in Kyiv and Minsk; in New York, to the staff and archivists at the American Jewish Joint Distribution Committee, at the YIVO Institute for Jewish Research, and at the Blavatnik Archive; in Washington, DC, to the staff and archivists at the United States Holocaust Memorial Museum; and in Jerusalem, to the staff and archivists at the Central Archives for the History of the Jewish People, at the Central Zionist Archives, and at the Yad Izhak Ben Zvi Archives. In particular, I am thankful to Vadim Altskan, Julie Chervinsky, Misha Mitsel, and Edward Serotta for helping me locate key sources and images.

As always, I thank my friends (you know who you are) and my family for their endless support, for tolerating my workaholic moods, and for being patient with me. I dedicate this book to my son, Elia: may you always be able to find the best in all times, to smile in the face of adversities, and to find your own star among the stars.

NOTES

INTRODUCTION

1. For an overview of the evolution of the Soviet Union as a multiethnic empire and for an interpretation of ethnicity as central to the Soviet experience, see Brigid O'Keeffe, *The Multiethnic Soviet Union and Its Demise*, London: Bloomsbury Academic, 2022. On the Soviet nationality policies, see Terry Martin, *The Affirmative Action Empire: Nations and Nationalism in the Soviet Union, 1923–1939*, Ithaca, NY: Cornell University Press, 2001; Ronald Grigor Suny and Terry Martin, eds., *A State of Nations: Empire and Nation-Making in the Age of Lenin and Stalin*, Oxford: Oxford University Press, 2001; and Francine Hirsch, *Empire of Nations: Ethnographic Knowledge and the Making of the Soviet Union*, Ithaca, NY: Cornell University Press, 2014.
2. Martin, *Affirmative Action Empire*, 31–33.
3. *Naselenie SSSR*, Moscow: Izdatelstvo politicheskoi literatury, 1983, 8.
4. Technically, Congress Poland was separate from the Pale of Settlement, but both were areas in which Jews could reside without special permission.
5. While Catherine the Great set up the conditions for the establishment of the Pale, it was first instituted in law by Tsar Alexander I, who in 1804 passed the first statute delineating the provinces in which Jews were allowed to live. In 1897, the Jewish population of the Pale amounted to 5,189,401, or 4.13 percent of the population. Salo Baron, *The Russian Jew under Tsars and Soviets*, New York: Macmillan, 1964, 63–64.
6. From the vast literature on Jewish life, culture, and legal status in the Pale, see, for example, Steven J. Zipperstein, *The Jews of Odessa: A Cultural History, 1794–1881*, Stanford, CA: Stanford University Press, 1985; John Doyle Klier, *Imperial Russia's Jewish Question, 1855–1881*, Cambridge: Cambridge University Press, 2005; Jeffrey Veidlinger, *Jewish Public Culture in the Late Russian Empire*, Bloomington: Indiana University Press, 2009; ChaeRan Y. Freeze and Jay Michael Harris, eds., *Everyday Jewish Life in Imperial Russia: Select Documents,*

1772–1914, Waltham, MA: Brandeis University Press, 2013; ChaeRan Y. Freeze, *Jewish Marriage and Divorce in Imperial Russia*, Waltham, MA: Brandies University Press, 2002; Eli Lederhendler, *Road to Modern Jewish Politics: Political Tradition and Political Reconstruction in the Jewish Community of Tsarist Russia*, New York: Oxford Unviversity Press, 1989; Michael Stanislawski, *Tsar Nicholas I and the Jews: The Transformation of Jewish Society in Russia, 1825–1855*, Philadelphia: Jewish Publication Society, 1983; Nathan Cohen, *Yiddish Transformed: Reading Habits in the Russian Empire, 1860–1914*, New York: Berghahn Books, 2023; Michael Stanislawski, *For Whom Do I Toil? Judah Leib Gordon and the Crisis of Russian Jewry*, New York: Oxford University Press, 1988.

7. On the origin and growth of the Jewish community in St. Petersburg, see Valerii Gessen, *K istorii Sankt-Peterburgskoi evreiskoi religioznoi obshchiny: Ot pervykh evreev do XX veka*, Saint Petersburg: Tema, 2000; Saul Ginzburg, *Amolike Peterburg: Forshungen un zikhroynes vegn Yidishn lebn in der rezidents-shtot fun tsarishn Rusland*, New York: CYCO Bikher farlag, 1944; and Benjamin Nathans, *Beyond the Pale: The Jewish Encounter with Late Imperial Russia*, Berkeley: University of California Press, 2002.
8. Baron, *Russian Jew*, 65.
9. The Karaites, a Turkic-speaking community that traced its origin in the Crimean Peninsula back to the thirteenth century, practiced a kind of Judaism that was based on the Hebrew Bible but that rejected the Talmud and Rabbinic texts. Over time, the Karaites relinquished all Jewish elements from their heritage. The Russian state exempted them from most legal restrictions imposed on the Jewish population and in 1863 granted them equal status with the Christian residents of the empire. During the German occupation of World War II, Nazi authorities defined the Karaites as members of the Turkish-Tatar ethnic group and not as members of the Jewish "race."
10. As an ideology and a movement, Zionism emerged in central and eastern Europe in the late nineteenth century. Based on the belief that Jews constitute a nation and as such have the right to self-determination within historical Palestine, Zionism gave voice to but one form of Jewish nationalism; it developed in rivalry but also in conjunction with Diaspora nationalism, which pursued Jewish autonomy in eastern Europe, and Territorialism, which aimed to find a place anywhere in the world where Jews could establish a safe homeland. For a comprehensive portrait of Zionism, see Derek J. Penslar, *Zionism: An Emotional State*, New Brunswick, NJ: Rutgers University Press, 2023.
11. For studies on the Soviet Jewish experiences of the 1920s that favor a regional or local focus, see, for instance, Elissa Bemporad, *Becoming Soviet Jews: The Bolshevik Experiment in Minsk*, Bloomington: Indiana University Press, 2013; Arkadi Zeltser, *Evrei sovetskoi provintsii: Vitebsk i mestechki, 1917–1941*, Moscow: ROSSPEN, 2006; Andrew Sloin, *The Jewish Revolution in Belorussia: Economy, Race, and Bolshevik Power*, Bloomington: Indiana University Press, 2017; Jeffrey Veidlinger, *The Moscow Yiddish State Theater: Jewish Culture on the Soviet Stage*, Bloomington: Indiana University Press, 2000; Zeev Levin, *Collectivization and*

Social Engineering: Soviet Administration and the Jews of Uzbekistan, 1917–1939, Leiden: Brill, 2015; and Mordechai Altshuler, *Yehudei Mizrah Kavkaz: Toledot ha-yehudim hahareriim me-reshit ha-meah ha-teshah esreh*, Jerusalem: Mekhon Ben-Tsevi le-heker kehilot Yisrael ba-Mizrah; Makhon le-Yahadut zemanenu, ha-Universitah ha-Ivrit bi-Yerushalayim, 1990. For studies on Soviet Jewish life and culture of the 1920s through an all-Soviet lens, see, for instance, Zvi Gitelman, *A Century of Ambivalence: The Jews of Russia and the Soviet Union, 1881 to the Present*, Bloomington: Indiana University Press, 2001; Mordechai Altshuler, *Ha-yevseḳtsyah bi-Verit-ha-Mo'atsot (1918–1930): Ben le'umiyut le-ḳomunizm*, Jerusalem: Hebrew University, 1980; Anna Shternshis, *Soviet and Kosher: Jewish Popular Culture in the Soviet Union, 1923–1939*, Bloomington: Indiana University Press, 2006; and Sasha Senderovich, *How the Soviet Jew Was Made*, Cambridge, MA: Harvard University Press, 2022.

12. See, for example, Gennady Estraikh, *Transatlantic Russian Jewishness: Ideological Voyages of the Yiddish Daily Forverts in the First Half of the Twentieth Century*, Boston: Academic Studies Press, 2020.
13. On Jewish exceptionalism, see Yuri Slezkine, *The Jewish Century*, Princeton, NJ: Princeton University Press, 2019.
14. For the most authoritative studies on the Evsektsiia, see Altshuler, *Ha-yevsektsyah bi-Verit-ha-Mo'atsot*; and Zvi Gitelman, *Jewish Nationality and Soviet Politics: The Jewish Sections of the CPSU, 1917–1930*, Princeton, NJ: Princeton University Press, 1972.
15. This process was much more arduous and perhaps forceful when carried out among the Jews living in Central Asia and the Caucasus, who had been less exposed to modernization and secularization compared to the Jews living in the European regions of the tsarist empire and, for that ostensible reason, had to be reformed in new system.

1. THE JEWS IN REVOLUTION

1. On the shift to radicalism and the crisis of liberalism among the Jews of the Russian Empire, see Jonathan Frankel, *Prophesy and Politics: Socialism, Nationalism, and the Russian Jews, 1862–1917*, New York: Cambridge University Press, 1984.
2. On the Kishinev pogrom, see Steven J. Zipperstein, *Pogrom: Kishinev and the Tilt of History*, New York: Norton, 2018.
3. Quoted in Frankel, *Prophecy and Politics*, 143.
4. On the emergence of the new Russian-Jewish politics based on the notion of "self-emancipation" through socialism and/or nationalism, see ibid., in particular chapters 2 and 3.
5. On the rise of right-wing politics and the Jewish response, see Hans Rogger, *Jewish Policies and Right-Wing Politics in Imperial Russia*, Berkeley: University of California Press, 1986.
6. Quoted in Frankel, *Prophecy and Politics*, 150–151.

7. On acts of violence perpetrated by the Russian troops against Jews during World War I, see Eric Lohr, "The Russian Army and the Jews: Mass Deportation, Hostages, and Violence during World War I," *Russian Review*, vol. 60, no. 3, 2001, 404–419; and Semion Goldin, *The Russian Army and the Jewish Population, 1914–1917: Libel, Persecution, Reaction*, London: Palgrave Macmillan, 2022.
8. According to the Georgian calendar, the February Revolution occurred in March, but because Russia still followed the Julian calendar, it is known as the "February Revolution." Similarly, the October Revolution, which began on November 7 according to the Gregorian calendar, or New Style, is known as the "October Revolution" because it began on October 25 according to the Julian calendar, or Old Style. The Soviets dropped the Georgian calendar in favor of the Julian one on February 14, 1918.
9. Geoffrey Hosking, *The First Socialist Society: A History of the Soviet Union from Within*, Cambridge, MA: Harvard University Press, 1985, 34.
10. Quoted in Vivian Gornick, *Emma Goldman: Revolution as a Way of Life*, New Haven, CT: Yale University Press, 2011, 106.
11. *Forverts*, March 16, 1917, quoted in Seth Lipsky, *The Rise of Abraham Cahan*, New York: Schocken, 2013, 124.
12. In 1903, the Russian Social Democratic Workers' Party split into two factions: the Mensheviks, or "those of the minority," who opposed Lenin's view of a highly centralized party and favored a mass party similar to other European social democratic parties; and the Bolsheviks, "those of the majority," who called for a dictatorial role of a party led exclusively by professional revolutionaries. In the years that led up to the revolution, the ideological differences between the two factions continued to grow: the Bolsheviks rejected the Mensheviks' support of a collaboration with the middle class and the bourgeoisie to achieve the revolution. The Socialist Revolutionary Party, or SR, was founded in 1901 as an alternative to the Russian Social Democratic Workers' Party. It appealed largely to the peasantry; the party favored the socialization of the land and terrorist strategies, which it never completely abandoned. In 1918, Lenin was wounded in a political assassination attempt by an SR member. In 1917, the SR constituted the largest socialist group in Russia.
13. For the translation of the poem "Vek," see *The Penguin Book of Russian Verse*, ed. Dimitry Obolensky, London: Penguin, 1962, 361–362. Mandelshtam wrote the poem in 1923.
14. Maks Goldfarb, "Di rusishe frayhayt un di yidishe rekht," *Forverts*, March 18, 1917, 5, quoted in Joshua Meyers, "A Portrait of Transition: From the Bund to Bolshevism in the Russian Revolution." *Jewish Social Studies* 24, no. 2, Winter 2019, 107–134.
15. The Pale had already been abolished de facto when, during World War I, Jews were expelled from the border regions.
16. "The Abolition of Religious and National Restrictions," *Russkie vedomosti*, no. 65, March 22, 1917, 3, quoted in Robert Paul Browder and Alexander F.

Kerensky, *The Russian Provisional Government 1917: Documents*, vol. 1, Stanford, CA: Stanford University Press, 1961, 214.

17. Gitelman, *Century of Ambivalence*, 60. On the cultural responses to the Bolshevik Revolution and the different positions taken by Jewish writers and intellectuals, see Kenneth B. Moss, *Jewish Renaissance in the Russian Revolution*, Cambridge, MA: Harvard University Press, 2009.
18. Sh. Agursky, *Der yidisher arbeter in der komunistisher bavegung (1917–1921)*, Minsk: Melukhe farlag fun Vaysrusland, 1925, ix.
19. Ginzburg, *Amolike Peterburg*, 252.
20. Quoted in Mikhail Beizer, "Antisemitism in Petrograd/Leningrad, 1917–1930," *East European Jewish Affairs* 29, nos. 1–2, 2008, 6.
21. Max Sadikoff, *In yene teg: Zikhoynes vegn der rusisher revolutsye un di ukrayner pogromen*, New York, 1926, 15–17.
22. Moss, *Jewish Renaissance.*
23. Ibid., 15.
24. J. S. Hertz, *Di geshikhte fun Bund*, vol. 3, New York: Undzer tsayt, 1960, 139.
25. Sadikoff, *In yene teg*, 23–25.
26. Brendan McGeever, *Antisemitism and the Russian Revolution*, Cambridge: Cambridge University Press, 2019, 31. The All-Russian Constituent Assembly, which was convened in Russia after the February Revolution of 1917, was disbanded by the Bolsheviks following the meeting and elections held in January 1918 and was replaced with the Third All-Russian Congress of Soviets as the country's new governing body.
27. Joshua Rubenstein, *Leon Trotsky: A Revolutionary's Life*, New Haven, CT: Yale University Press, 2011, 76.
28. *Daily Trade Record*, according to *Yidishe gazeten*, March 30, 1917, 7, quoted in Zosa Szajkowski, *Jews, Wars, and Communism*, vol. 1, *The Attitude of American Jews in World War I, the Russian Revolutions of 1917, and Communism (1914–1945)*, New York: KTAV, 1971, 285.
29. Philip S. Foner, *The Bolshevik Revolution: Its Impact on American Radicals, Liberals, and Labour*, New York: International, 1967, 21.
30. Quoted in Brian Jackson, *The Black Flag: A Look Back at the Strange Case of Nicola Sacco and Bartolomeo Vanzetti*, London: Routledge, 1981, 153.
31. On the mutiny, see Israel Getzler, *Kronstadt 1917–1921: The Fate of Soviet Democracy*, Cambridge: Cambridge University Press, 1983.
32. Alexander Berkman, *The Bolshevik Myth*, London: Pluto, 1989, 318–319.
33. Quoted in Estraikh, *Transatlantic Russian-Jewishness*, 70–71.
34. Boris Kolonitsky, "Antibourgeois Propaganda and Anti-'Burzhui' Consciousness in 1917," *Russian Review*, 53, 1994, 183–196; Laura Engelstein, *Russia in Flames: War, Revolution, Civil War, 1914–1921*, New York: Oxford University Press, 2017.
35. In December 1925, the party adopted the name the All-Union Communist Party (Bolsheviks), reflecting the establishment of the Soviet Union in 1922.
36. Baruch Caro (Krupnik), "Yerushalaim de-Volin: Ha-sefer al berdichuv

sh-khorova," in *Yalkut Volin, osaf maamarim, reshimot, skirot, teudot ve-tsilumim*, Tel Aviv: Arkhion Volhin be-eretz Israel, 1951, 4.

37. E. I. Estraikh and G. Melamed, "'O pogrome v Berdicheve' (Novonaidennaia zapiska D. Lipetsa 1919)," in *Arkhiv evreiskoi istorii*, vol. 8, ed. O. V. Budnitskii, Moscow: ROSSPEN, 2016, 157.
38. Ibid., 159–160.
39. Zvi Kaminski, *Geven a mol a shtot Berdichev*, Paris: Kaminski, 1952, 83–84. After a detailed discussion of the city's prerevolutionary life, Kaminski moved on to chronicle the violence of the pogroms of the civil war, which erupted in the wake of the October Revolution in the territories of present-day Ukraine, but also of Belarus and southern Russia, between different armies and forces representing opposing geopolitical goals. During these years of war and violence, from 1918 to 1921, hundreds of Jewish communities—including Berdychiv—were caught up in the fire of destruction, some bearing the brunt of the conflict's violence, through despoliation, murder, and rape. The pogrom described in Zvi Kaminski's memoirs was perpetrated in early January 1919 by the forces of Symon Petliura, the leader of Ukraine's struggle for independence following the Russian Revolution. While Kaminski expressed his grief over the violence in Berdychiv, he also admitted that compared to other places, the city remained relatively undamaged by the pogroms. Interestingly, he explained this disparity by referring to the effectiveness of the local Jewish self-defense units, which managed to deter the attacking mobs and protect the community and its property. On the long tradition of Jewish self-defense in Berdychiv, see John Klier, *Russians, Jews, and the Pogroms of 1881–1882*, Cambridge: Cambridge University Press, 115.
40. Benjamin Pinkus, *The Jews of the Soviet Union: The History of a National Minority*, Cambridge: Cambridge University Press, 1988, 77–78.
41. Antony Polonsky, *The Jews in Russia and Poland: A Short History*, Liverpool: Liverpool University Press, 2020, 175.
42. Ibid.
43. When Trotsky was asked about his identity, he clearly stated, "I am not a Jew, I'm a Marxist internationalist." Quoted in Rubenstein, *Leon Trotsky*, 115. There is no evidence that either Kamenev or Zinoviev gave much thought to his Jewishness.
44. Quoted in Baron, *Russian Jew*, 230.
45. Simon Rabinovitch, "Russian Jewry Goes to the Polls: An Analysis of Jewish Voting in the All-Russian Constituent Assembly Elections of 1917," *East European Jewish Affairs* 39, no. 2, 2009, 205–225.
46. Zionist parties received all together two-thirds of the votes in the elections to the Constituent Assembly. See Gitelman, *Jewish Nationality and Soviet Politics*, 79–80; and Rabinovitch, "Russian Jewry Goes to the Polls."
47. Gitelman, *Jewish Nationality and Soviet Politics*, 78.
48. Arye Rafaeli (Zenzipper), *Ba-maavak li-geula: Sefer ha-tziyonut ha-rusit mi-mahapekhat 1917 ad yameinu*, Tel Aviv: Davar ve-ayanot, 1957, 29; Yitzchak

Maor, *Ha-tnua ha-tziyonit be-rusya me-reshita ve-ad yameinu*, Jerusalem: Hasifriya ha-tziyonit and Magnes, 1973, 460–489. It can be assumed that most of the three hundred thousand were politically inactive and that they obtained membership by paying a symbolic shekel that identified them as supporting the establishment of a Jewish state in Palestine.

49. Josef Stalin, *Marxism and the National and Colonial Question*, New York: International, 49.

50. Before the revolution, 74 percent of Jews were employed in trade and crafts fields, while 60 percent of them were independently employed. This meant that according to the Bolshevik definition, a very large proportion of Jews belonged to the bourgeoisie, which after 1917 became the class enemy and as such suffered confiscation of property and arrests. See Vladimir Levin, *Yehude Rusiya ba-me'ah ha-esrim*, vol. 1, Ra'anana: Open University of Israel, 2014, 34, citing Arcadius Kahan, *Essays in Jewish Social and Economic History*, Chicago: University of Chicago Press, 1986, 82–100, 159–160.

51. In the 1917 Russian Constituent Assembly elections, the Socialist-Revolutionaries emerged as the most popular party, with more than 37 percent of the votes, while the Bolsheviks received a little over 23 percent of the votes. See Oliver H. Radkey, *Russia Goes to the Polls: The Election to the All-Russian Constituent Assembly, 1917*, Ithaca, NY: Cornell University Press, 1990.

52. S. M. Dubnov, *Kniga zhizni: Vospominaniya i razmyshleniya: Materialy dlia istorii moego vremeni*, Saint Petersburg: Peterburgskoe vostokovedenie, 1998, 378.

53. On the Soviet Jewish alliance, see Elissa Bemporad, *Legacy of Blood: Jews, Pogroms, and Ritual Murder in the Lands of the Soviets*, New York: Oxford University Press, 2018, 13–34.

54. On the different roles Jews played in the civil war, see Oleg Budnitskii, *Russian Jews between the Reds and the Whites, 1917–1920*, Philadelphia: University of Pennsylvania Press, 2012.

55. On the various trends in the White movement, see Liudmila Novikova, *An Anti-Bolshevik Alternative: The White Movement and the Civil War in the Russian North*, trans. Seth Bernstein, Madison: University of Wisconsin Press, 2018; Jonathan D. Smele, *Civil War in Siberia: The Anti-Bolshevik Government of Admiral Kolchak, 1918–1920*, Cambridge: Cambridge University Press, 1996; Peter Kenez, *Civil War in South Russia*, 2 vols., Washington DC: New Academia, 2004 [1971–1977]. For a survey of the different sides and battlefields, see Jonathan D. Smele, *The "Russian" Civil Wars, 1916–1926: Ten Years That Shook the World*, New York: Oxford University Press, 2015.

56. Before the war, more than half a million Jews (or 66.8 percent of the total Jewish population in the area that would come under Soviet domination) lived in Ukraine. See Baron, *Russian Jew*, 182.

57. Jeffrey Veidlinger, *In the Midst of Civilized Europe: The Pogroms of 1918–1921 and the Onset of the Holocaust*, New York: Metropolitan Books, 2021, 50–51, 252, 268. The Cossacks, who traced their origin back to the late fifteenth century, when they began to establish self-governing military communities along

the Dnipro and Don Rivers, over the course of the seventeenth century fought against Polish rule to retain their political autonomy. They eventually established their own independent state, known as the Hetmanate. Following the abolishment of the Hetmanate by the Russian state, in the eighteenth century it was incorporated into the tsarist empire. The Cossacks were recruited by the tsar for their military services, which included the defense of the empire's frontier and its territorial expansion, as well as for the suppression of revolutionary activities in the early twentieth century. At the time of the civil war, the majority of Cossack military units fought with the White armies, but some joined the Red Army.

58. On the percentage of pogroms perpetrated by different troops, see Henry Abramson, *A Prayer for the Government: Ukrainians and Jews in Revolutionary Times, 1917–1920*, Cambridge, MA: Harvard University Press, 1999, 115; and Oleg Budnitskii, "Jews, Pogroms, and the White Movement: A Historiographical Critique," *Kritika: Explorations in Russian and Eurasian History* 2, no. 4, 2001. Approximately 25 percent of all the pogroms were perpetrated by different local peasant bands and anarchist gangs enticed into attacking the Jewish community by the possibility of looting.
59. There is no agreement on the number of Jews who perished during the pogroms. For a discussion about the estimate number of victims, see, for example, Budnitskii, "Jews, Pogroms, and the White Movement," 1. According to the Russian writer S. I. Gusev-Orenburgskii, the number of Jewish victims reached 100,000. See his *Kniga o evreskikh pogromakh na Ukraine v 1919: Sostavlena po ofitsialnym dokumentam, dokladam s mest i oprosam postradavshchikh*, Petrograd: Ispolneno izd-vom Z.I. Grzhebina, n.d. [192?], 14. According to the Soviet economist Yurii Larin, the number was 200,000. See his *Evrei i antisemitizm v SSSR*, Moscow: Gosudarstvennoe izd-vo, 1929, 55. This number was also reported in 1932 in the *Great Soviet Encyclopedia*. See S. Dimanshtein, "Evreiskie pogromy v Rossii," in *Bolshaia Sovetskaia entsiklopedia*, vol. 24, Moscow: Sovetskaia entsiklopedia, 1932, 148. In one of the earlier publications of documents about the pogroms of the civil war, Elias Heifetz argued that 120,000 Jews in Ukraine alone were killed during the violence. See E. G. Elias Heifetz, *The Slaughter of the Jews in the Ukraine in 1919*, New York: Thomas Seltzer, 1921, 180. The data collected by the Evobshchestkom, the Soviet Jewish aid organization established in the summer of 1920, confirmed the number 200,000 but added that this number did not include the thousands who perished as a result of wounds, venereal disease, typhus, and cholera. See Z. S. Ostrovskii, *Evreiskie pogromy, 1918–1921*, Moscow: Shkola i kniga, 1926, 74–76. For more figures, see David Engel, ed., *The Assassination of Symon Petliura and the Trial of Sholem Schwarzbard 1926–1927: A Selection of Documents*, Archiv Judischer Geschichte Und Kultur / Archive of Jewish History and Culture, Göttingen: V&R Academic, 2016, 58–59.
60. Thomas Chopard, "Ukrainian Neighbors: Pogroms and Extermination in Ukraine 1919–1920," in "The Pogroms of the Russian Civil War at 100: New

Trends, New Sources," ed. Elissa Bemporad and Thomas Chopard, *Quest. Issues in Contemporary Jewish History*, 15, August 2019, 150.

61. Malka Lee, *Durkh kindershe oygn* (Buenos Aires: Yidbukh, 1955), 17.
62. "Anecdotes," in *Mass Culture in Soviet Russia: Tales, Poems, Songs, Movies, Plays and Folklore, 1917–1953*, ed. James von Geldkern and Richard Stites, Bloomington: Indiana University Press, 1995, 119.
63. See William Hagen, *Anti-Jewish Violence in Poland, 1914–1920*, New York: Cambridge University Press, 2018, 66, 100. Hagen describes an anti-Jewish theater: "deep-rooted and often subconscious socially shared visions of the world, and especially its dangers and menaces, found expression and channeled—at the cost of Jewish suffering—recuperative, even redemptive action" (66).
64. According to Thomas Chopard, most men in the period between the Great War and the civil war served in some capacity in the military, and the "meaning of 'civilian' had become relative as neighbors easily switched from bystander to partisan or armed pogromist" ("Ukrainian Neighbors," 152).
65. On the concept of exclusionary violence in the long nineteenth century, see Christhard Hoffmann, Werner Bergmann, and Helmut Walser Smith, eds., *Exclusionary Violence: Antisemitic Riots in Modern German History*, Ann Arbor: University of Michigan Press, 2002; and Helmut Walser Smith, *The Continuities of German History: Nation, Religion, and Race across the Long Nineteenth Century*, Cambridge: Cambridge University Press, 2008, 115–166.
66. In the words of Eugene M. Avrutin, "Governed by unwritten rules, the rioting probably bore some resemblance, as well, to the modern exclusionary outbursts that erupted from time to time in nineteenth century Russia and Germany." Avrutin, "The End of Everything? Pogroms in Wars and Revolution," *Journal of Modern History* 95, no. 3, September 2023, 672.
67. Chopard, "Ukrainian Neighbors," 159.
68. On pogroms in 1917–1918, see Vladimir P. Buldakov, "Freedom, Shortages, Violence: The Origins of the 'Revolutionary Anti-Jewish Pogrom' in Russia, 1917–1918," in *Anti-Jewish Violence: Rethinking the Pogrom in East European History*, ed. Jonathan Dekel-Chen, David Gaunt, and Nathan M. Meier, Bloomington: Indiana University Press, 2011, 74–91; McGeever, *Antisemitism and the Russian Revolution*; and Bemporad and Chopard, "Pogroms of the Russian Civil War at 100." On anti-Jewish violence during the civil war, see Budnitskii, *Russian Jews*; Bemporad, *Legacy of Blood*, in particular chapters 1, 3, 6; and Veidlinger, *In the Midst of Civilized Europe*.
69. "Pogromy," *Kratkaia evreiskaia entsiklopediia*, vol. 6, Jerusalem: Keter, 1976, 562–576.
70. Ibid., 569.
71. Rakhil Faygnberg, *Letopis mertvogo goroda*, Leningrad: Priboi, 1928, 20–21.
72. On relief work during World War I in the region, see Jaclyn Granick, *International Jewish Humanitarianism in the Age of the Great War*, Cambridge: Cambridge University Press, 2021.
73. Vladimir P. Buldakov, "Freedom, Shortages, Violence: The Origins of the

'Revolutionary Anti-Jewish Pogrom' in Russia, 1917–1918," in Dekel-Chen et al., *Anti-Jewish Violence*, 84. Brendan McGeever writes, "in the early months of the civil war, Bolshevik power was constituted *through* anti-Jewish violence" (*Antisemitism and the Russian Revolution*, 52).

74. On the role of the Jews and anti-Jewish violence in the civil war, see Budnitskii, *Russian Jews.*
75. Elias Tcherikower, *In der tkufe fun revolutsye: Memuarn, materyaln, dokumentn*, Berlin: Yidisher literarisher farlag, 1924, 382–383.
76. Some of the bloodiest instances of anti-Jewish violence in Belorussia took place in the context of the Polish-Soviet war. In the summer of 1920, in the process of taking over the northwestern region of the former empire, the Polish army carried out a number of pogroms throughout the cities and towns, including Minsk, Babruysk, Barysaw, Koidanov (Dzyarzhynsk), and Slutsk. For a description of Polish brutality in Minsk in July 1920, see Bemporad, *Becoming Soviet Jews*, 28. For a detailed account of a pogrom carried out in Vitsyebsk by the armed peasants of the Green Army and the ensuing investigation, arrest, and trial of the culprits, see *Evreiskii pogrom na zavode "Novki,"* Vitebsk: Izdanie Vitebskogo Gubvoenrevkoma, 1920. For evidence of the violence perpetrated in Belorussia by the Polish army, the White Guards, and the troops of Stanislav Bulak-Balakhovich, see also Ostrovskii, *Evreiskie pogromy*, 22–27, 41, 48, 53–55, 58–63; and L. B. Miliakova, *Kniga pogromov: Pogromy na Ukraine, v Belorussii i Evropeiskoi chasti Rossii v period grazhdanskoi voiny: 1918–1922: Sbornik dokumentov*, Moscow: ROSSPEN, 2007, 539–743.
77. See Jeffrey Veidlinger, "Anti-Jewish Violence in the Russian Civil War," in *Pogroms: A Documentary History*, ed. Eugene Avrutin and Elissa Bemporad, New York: Oxford University Press, 2021, 133–138.
78. Veidlinger, *In the Midst of Civilized Europe*, 150.
79. Ibid.
80. Ostrovskii, *Evreiskie pogromy*, 84.
81. Gosudarstvennyi arkhiv rossiiskoi federatsii (GARF), f. R-1339, op. 1, d. 438, ll. 25–26, "Looting and Rape in Smila, 1919."
82. Several scholars have reached this conclusion, including Hagen, *Anti-Jewish Violence in Poland*, 379–388, 416, 418, 433, and 461; Bemporad, *Legacy of Blood*, introduction; Veidlinger, *In the Midst of Civilized Europe*, 9–10; and Robert Blobaum, *A Minor Apocalypse during the First World War*, Ithaca, NY: Cornell University Press, 2017, 63–64.
83. Institute for Jewish Research Archives (YIVO), Tcherikower Archive, RG 80, folder 235, ll. 21708–21801 (Rokhl Faygnberg, *Khurbn Dubove, a pinkes fun a toyter shtot*).
84. Rokhl Faygnberg, "Spektor der privat mentsh," in *Spektor-bukh*, ed. D. Kassel, Warsaw: Akhisefer, 1929, 132.
85. Faygnberg, *Letopis mertvogo goroda*, 133.
86. YIVO, Tcherikower Archive, RG 80, folder 235, ll. 21708–21801 (Rokhl Faygnberg, *Khurbn Dubove, a pinkes fun a toyter shtot*, 1922).

87. "Reznia v Proskurove," *Kommunist*, March 7, 1919, 1.
88. YIVO, Tcherikower Archive, RG 80, folder 360, 32863 ("Memorandum about the pogrom in Kytaihorod, June 19, 1919").
89. Ibid., 32864–32865.
90. On rape during the civil war, see Irina Astashkevich, *Gendered Violence: Jewish Women in the Pogroms of 1917 to 1921*, Boston: Academic Studies Press, 2018; and Thomas Chopard, "La guerre aux civils. Les violences contre les populations juives d'Ukraine, 1917–1924," PhD diss., EHESS, 2015, in particular chapter 4, 309–326.
91. Astashkevich, *Gendered Violence.*
92. GARF, f. R-1339, op. 1, d. 438, ll. 81–82ob., "Doctors' reports, 1919."
93. Budnitskii, *Russian Jews.*
94. See, for example, State Archives of Zhytomyr Oblast, f. 1820, op. 5, d. 97, ll. 3–5 ("Court case against Sura (Sonya) Margulian, 1919").
95. On the case of a Jewish male bandit who, in a shtetl in Cherkasy, killed a young woman and helped murder a member of the local Jewish self-defense unit, see, for example, DAKO, f. 3050, op. 1, d. 128, l. 34.
96. L. Shapiro, *Bakalakhat ha-rusit: Pirkei zikhronot*, Jerusalem: Lustigman, 160, quoted in Gitelman, *Jewish Nationality and Soviet Politics*, 166.
97. YIVO, Tcherikower Archive, RG 80, folder 64, 4970-1 (A. Chomskii, "My Trial"). Petliura called his soldiers "Haidamaks" after the eighteenth-century Cossack insurgents who fought for their freedom and autonomous status.
98. Both Bundist leaders Ester Frumkin and Moyshe Rafes began to advocate for a closer relationship with the Bolsheviks in the wake of the revolutionary events in Germany. However, it was the pogrom violence carried out primarily by anti-Bolshevik forces that forced them to reconsider their strong anti-Bolshevik position and eventually to support a Ukrainian Bund pro-Bolshevik faction. On Rafes's shifting political views in the midst of the years 1918–1919, see Gitelman, *Jewish Nationality and Soviet Politics*, 168, 172–174. On Ester Frumkin's reconciliation with the Bolsheviks, see, for example, E. Folkovich, "Ester, der lebnsveg fun der groyser revolutsyonerin," *Folkshtime*, May 24, 1965.
99. McGeever, *Antisemitism and the Russian Revolution*, in particular 53–87.
100. Hyman Lumer, *Lenin on the Jewish Question*, New York: International, 1974, 142. See also "Vnimanie borbe s antisemitizmom," *Pravda*, no. 41, February 19, 1929, 1.
101. Meyers, "Portrait of Transition," 113.
102. Elias Tcherikower, *Di ukrainer pogromen in yor 1919*, New York: YIVO, 1965, 83–84.
103. For a detailed account of the pogroms carried out by the troops of General Stanislav Bulak-Balakhovich in Belorussia, in particular in the Mazyr region, see YIVO, Tcherikower Archive, RG 80, folder 99, 8107–8161 ("Balakhovich in Belorussia"). On the pogroms perpetrated in Belorussia by the Polish army, the White Guards, and Bulak-Balakhovich's troops, see also Ostrovskii, *Evreiskie pogromy*, 22–27, 41, 48, 53–55, 58–63.

104. Tsentralniy Nauchnyi Arkhiv Natsionalnoi Akademii Nauk Belarusi (TsNANANB), f. 72, op. 1, d. 4, l. 67–67ob (Report by Yechezkel Abramski, "They are not to blame if they do not believe," Minsk, Sunday, July 11, 1920).
105. *Komune*, no. 26, September 17, 1920, 1.
106. Sore Rejzen, "Nu, oyb krig, to zol zayn krig," *Komune*, no. 24, September 13, 1920, 2.
107. Bemporad, *Legacy of Blood*, 62–75.
108. On the relations between the majority group (usually a higher-ranking ethnic or religious group) and the minority group (whose members are usually considered a lower-ranking or subaltern group) as a background for the eruption of ethnic violence, see David Engel, "What's in a Pogrom? European Jews in the Age of Violence," in Dekel-Chen et al., *Anti-Jewish Violence*, 24.
109. Elias Heifetz, *The Slaughter of the Jews in the Ukraine in 1919*, New York: Thomas Seltzer, 1921, 130.
110. "Evrei Dagestana," *Tribuna evreiskoi sovetskoi obshchestvennosti* (hereafter *Tribuna*), nos. 4–5, 1927, 9–10.
111. For the most comprehensive study of Jewish self-defense and fighting units' formation in the twentieth century, see Mihaly Kalman, "Hero Shtetls: Jewish Armed Self-Defense from the Pale to Palestine, 1917–1970," PhD diss., Harvard University, 2017.
112. Beizer, "Antisemitism in Petrograd/Leningrad," 5–28.
113. Kalman, "Hero Shtetls," 234–309. Kalman's work also discusses how Soviet authorities, struggling to reestablish state power in the countryside, heavily relied on the Jewish paramilitaries.
114. Zusia Val, "Tsum yortsayt fun Proskurover pogrom," *Di yidishe tsaytung*, February 20, 1924, in YIVO, Tcherikower Archive, RG 80, folder 521, 43248.
115. Miliakova, "From the Report of the Plenipotentiary in the Uman Region, about the Pogroms in the City, 5 July, 1919," in *Kniga pogromov*, 125.
116. See Elissa Bemporad, "The Rape of the Jewish Home: Violating the Domestic at the Time of the Pogroms," in *The Jewish Home*, ed. Leora Auslander, Federica Francesconi, and Joshua Teplitsky, Philadelphia: Pennsylvania University Press, forthcoming.
117. For new scholarship on the ways in which Yiddish poets confronted the violence of the civil war, see Harriet Murav, *A Dust of the Earth: The Literature of Abandonment in Revolutionary Russia and Ukraine*, Bloomington: Indiana University Press, 2024; and Sasha Senderovich, *How the Soviet Jew Was Made*, Cambridge, MA: Harvard University Press, 2022, in particular chapter 1. On protests, strikes, and demonstrations against the violence, see YIVO, Tcherikower Archive, RG 80, file 136, 11119, and file 540, 46376; "As an Expression of Grief and Protest," *Forverts*, November 22, 1919, 9; and "Veyst un dresmeyker troyer parad," *Forverts*, November 23, 1919, 9.
118. On the conditions of Jewish victims of violence, see Granick, *International Jewish Humanitarianism*, in particular 72–108 and 150–196. On the health conditions of Jewish women, which led to migration and prostitution, see Elissa Bemporad,

"The Female Dimension of Pogrom Violence, 1917–1921," in *Pogroms: A Documentary History*, ed. Eugene Avrutin and Elissa Bemporad, New York: Oxford University Press, 2021, 162–169. On destruction and loss of property, see Joint Distribution Committee Archives (JDC), Collection 21/32, folder 496 (Report on Fastov), 1–3.

119. DAKO, f. R-3050, op. 1, d. 162, ll. 7–7ob. These numbers were also used by the Jewish Section of the People's Commissariat for Nationalities; see Miliakova, *Kniga pogromov*, 807–808, 817–819.
120. Hersh Smoliar, *Vu bistu khaver Sidorov?*, Tel Aviv: Farlag I. L. Peretz, 1975, 30, 50.
121. On the role of state authorities in addressing the issue of Jewish property restitution, see DAKO, f. 3050, op. 1, d. 522, l. 119 ("Memorandum, May 15, 1923").
122. DAKO, f. 3050, op. 1, d. 246, l. 52ob ("Program to collect materials on the pogroms").
123. For more on the ways in which the memory of violence played out in Jewish life in Trostianets in the interwar period, see Bemporad, *Legacy of Blood*, 57–62.
124. Asia Matveyuk, interview by Zhanna Litinskaya, Kherson, 2003, "Asia Matveyuk," Centropa (E), Interviews, www.centropa.org.
125. YIVO, Tcherikower Archive, RG 80, folder 587, 50992 ("The Exhibition"). Pogrom memorials erected by the sites of mass graves existed in places like Skvira, Bohuslav, Proskuriv, Cherkasy, Fastiv, Chernihiv, Bratslav, Trudoliubovka, Kyiv, Zhytomyr, Horodyshche, and many others. A pogrom memorial was erected in 1924 in the city of Proskuriv, site of one of the bloodiest pogroms of the civil war. The memorial survived World War II and was renovated after the collapse of the Soviet Union.
126. Matveyuk interview.
127. D. Kh. Nomberg, "Rayze fun Moskve keyn Kharkov," *Forverts*, June 3, 1927.
128. Tsentralnyi derzhavniy arkhyv gromadskikh obednan Ukrainy (TsDAGO), f. 1, op. 20, d. 2785, ll. 4, 5, 6 (Materials about the question of studying the problem of the shtetl population in the district of Proskuriv, 1928).
129. Sh. E-d., "Vi zet oys di Yidishe Moskve," *Dos naye lebn*, July 24, 1925, 9.
130. Lawrence A. Coben, *Anna's Shtetl*, Tuscaloosa: University of Alabama Press, 2007, xi, 7–8.

2. A SOVIET STORY OF ACCULTURATION

1. Pinkus, *Jews of the Soviet Union*, 55. For the census report, see Tsentralnoe statisticheskoe upravlenie, *Vsesoiuznaia perepis naselenia 17 dekabria 1926 g., kratkie svodki*, Vypusk 4, Narodnost i rodnoy iazyk naselenia SSSR, Moscow: Izdanie TsSU SSSR, 1928.
2. Slezkine, *Jewish Century*, 206.
3. Pinkus, *Jews of the Soviet Union*, 78.
4. In 1926, there were 141,703,000 people living in the Soviet Union. Ronald Wixman, *Peoples of the USSR: An Ethnographic Handbook*, London: Routledge, 1984, 124.

5. Pinkus, *Jews of the Soviet Union*, 78–80. In 1926, there were 1,238,000 ethnic Germans, 782,344 Poles, and more than two and a half million Jews living in the Soviet Union. Benjamin Pinkus, "The Extra-territorial National Minorities Living in the Soviet Union, 1917–1939: Jews, Germans, and Poles," in *Jews and Other Ethnic Groups in a Multi-ethnic World*, ed. Ezra Mendelsohn, Studies in Contemporary Jewry 3, Jerusalem: Hebrew University of Jerusalem, 1987, 85. Pinkus also reminds us that in 1927 in Ukraine, there were twenty thousand Jewish Communist Party members, or 12 percent of all Party members, while in Belorussia, there were 6,012 Jews in the Party, or 24 percent of the party membership. While the number of Jews in the Party rank and file in the two republics was significant, their share in the party echelons there was rather trivial. TsDAGO, f. 413, op. 1, d. 10, l. 89 ("Otchet Tsentralnyi komissi natsionalnikh menshentsv pri VuTsike, October 1, 1924 through April 1, 1925"): the number of Jews living in the Ukrainian Soviet Republic amounted to 1,554,376; ethnic Germans were 362,000, Poles 239,000, and Tatars 9,779.
6. Pinkus, *Jews of the Soviet Union*, 81. The number of Jews on the Central Executive Committee in Belorussia was significant, especially when compared to that of Ukraine. In 1924–1925, for instance, 22.6 percent of all the delegates were Jewish.
7. Lev Iu. Krichevsky, "Razvenchanie mifa: Evrei v apparate VChK-OGPU v 1920-e gody," *Vestnik evreiskogo universiteta*, no. 1 (8), 1995, table 4.
8. Ibid., table 5.
9. Ibid., table 9, 10, and 13.
10. Ethnic Germans constituted between a minimum of 18 percent and a maximum of over one-third of the tsarist administrative elite. John Alexander Armstrong, *The European Administrative Elite*, Princeton, NJ: Princeton University Press, 1973, 31.
11. Pinkus, *Jews of the Soviet Union*, 96.
12. Ibid., 83–84.
13. Slezkine, *Jewish Century*, 225.
14. Pinkus, *Jews of the Soviet Union*, 98.
15. Slezkine, *Jewish Century*, 236.
16. Ibid., 222.
17. All-Union organizations, such as the All-Union Leninist Young Communist League, usually known as Komsomol, and the All-Union Communist Party (Bolsheviks), were national, with purview throughout the entire territory of the Soviet Union.
18. Aleksandr Bezymenskii, *Izbrannoe proizvedeniia v dvukh tomakh*, vol. 1, Moscow: khudozhestvennaia literature, 1989, 35, 53, quoted in Slezkine, *Jewish Century*, 228. By Bezymensky, see, for example, *Komsomolia: Stranitsy epopei*, Moscow: Gos. izd-vo, 1927. For more on Bezymensky's life and work, see *Russkaia literatura XX veka. Prozaiki, poety, dramaturgi*, vol. 1, Moscow: Olma Press Invest, 2005, 183–184.
19. See Brigid O'Keeffe, "The Woman Always Pays: The Lives of Ivy Litvinov,"

Slavonic and East European Review 97, no. 3, July 2019, 501–528; and Brigid O'Keeffe, "The People's Ambassadress: The Forgotten Diplomacy of Ivy Litvinov," *Aeon*, March 29, 2021, https://aeon.co. As O'Keeffe writes, "For any Anglophone dignitary, celebrity, artist or journalist who visited the Soviet Union in the late 1920s and '30s, tea with Madame Litvinoff was de rigueur."

20. Lenin appointed Leon Trotsky as people's commissar for foreign affairs to lead, together with Adolph Joffe, the peace negotiations in Brest-Litovsk, from November 8, 1917, through March 13, 1918. Trotsky stepped down from this position once he became head of the Red Army, while Adolph Joffe was made ambassador to Germany and in 1920 led the Soviet delegation at the peace talks with the Baltic republics and Poland, signing the Peace of Riga, which ended the Polish-Soviet War. But Trotsky and Joffe served far shorter terms as foreign diplomats than did Litvinov. In general, there were only two other Jews who had served as foreign ministers in the rest of prewar Europe: Luigi Luzzatti in Italy and Walther Rathenau in Germany. And both of them held this position for far less time than did Litvinov. On Litvinov's early life and career, see Hugh Phillips, "From a Bolshevik to a British Subject: The Early Years of Maxim Litvinov," *Slavic Review*, 48, no. 3, Autumn 1989, 388–398.
21. Gosudarstvennyi arkhiv Minskoi oblasti (GAMO), f, 12, op. 1, d. 758, ll. 537a, 537 b, "Moia biografiia, 10/1/1928."
22. Mark Mazower, *What You Did Not Tell: A Russian Past and the Journey Home*, London: Penguin Books, 2018, 203.
23. D. A. Petrovsky, *Voennaia shkola v godi revoliutsii (1917–1924gg)*, Moscow: Vysshii voennyi redaktsionniy sovet, 1924, 8; Mark Von Hagen, *Soldiers in the Proletarian Dictatorship: The Red Army and the Soviet Socialist State, 1917–1930*, Ithaca, NY: Cornell University Press, 1990, 24, 94. The Communist International, or Comintern, which was also known as the Third International, was founded in 1919 to advocate for world communism. Although it operated as an international organization, it was controlled by the Communist Party of the Soviet Union.
24. Meyers, "Portrait of Transition," 107–134.
25. Lipets did retain some connections to his Jewish past. See, for example, Gennady Estraikh, "Mnogolikii David Lipets. Evrei v russkoi revoliutsii," in *Arkhiv evreiskoi istorii*, vol. 7, ed. Oleg Budnitskii, Moscow: ROSSPEN, 2012, 225–241.
26. *Getselt* in Yiddish is translated into Russian as *shalash*, a cabin made of branches and straw, which refers to a temporary structure in which Lenin hid in 1917 before the revolution. Ester Frumkin, *Gey mit Lenins veg!*, Moscow: Farlag 'Yunge gvardye,' 1925, quoted in Suzanne Faigan, "An Annotated Bibliography of Maria Yakovlevna Frumkina (Esther)," PhD diss., Australian National University, June 2018, 249–253. On Ester Frumkin's life and work, see Naomi Shepherd, *A Price below Rubies: Jewish Women as Rebels and Radicals*, Cambridge, MA: Harvard University Press, 1998.
27. "Court Record of the Military Collegium of the USSR Supreme Court, May 8–July 18, 1952," in *Stalin's Secret Pogrom: The Postwar Inquisition of the Jewish*

Anti-Fascist Committee, ed. Joshua Rubenstein and Vladimir Pavlovich Naumov, New Haven, CT: Yale University Press, 2001, 109. On Markish's life and work, see Joseph Sherman, Gennady Estraikh, David Shneer, and Jordan Finkin, eds., *A Captive of the Dawn: The Life and Work of Peretz Markish*, London: Routledge, 2020.

28. Jews became prominent in the world of Soviet culture and the arts. Such prominent figures included, for example, the brother and sister ballet dancers Asaf and Sulamith Messerer, who joined the Bolshoi in the 1920s as ballet dancers and choreographers; Leopold Averbach, who headed the Russian Association of Proletarian Writers (RAPP); the painter Isaak Brodsky; and the extraordinary violinists Natan Milstein and David Oistrakh.
29. Slezkine, *Jewish Century*, 217; Sh. E-d., "Vi zet oys di Yidishe Moskve," *Dos naye lebn*, July 24, 1925, 9.
30. Sh. E-d., "Vi zet oys di yidishe Moskve," 9.
31. David L. Hoffmann, "Moving to Moscow: Patterns of Peasant In-Migration during the First Five-Year Plan," *Slavic Review* 50, no. 4, 1991, 847.
32. Baron, *Russian Jew*.
33. Diane Koenker, "Urbanization and Deurbanization in the Russian Revolution and Civil War," *Journal of Modern History* 57, no. 3, September 1985, 424–450.
34. Faygnberg, "Spektor der privat mentsh," 134–135.
35. Ibid. The term "ataman" designates a Cossack military leader.
36. Up to 15 percent of those who left Russia following the revolution and the civil war were Jewish: "as many as 120,000 Jewish Russian exiles lived in Europe between the two world wars." See Maxin Shrayer, introduction to "Emigrations: 1917–1967," in *An Anthology of Jewish-Russian Literature, 1801–1953: Two Centuries of Dual Identity in Prose and Poetry*, ed. Maxim Shrayer, vol. 1, New York: M. E. Sharpe, 2007, 419.
37. Faygnberg, "Spektor der privat mentsh," 138–139.
38. TsDAGO, f. 413, op. 1, d. 10, ll. 65–76 ("Rabota Komissia nats.men. pri VUTsIK [All-Ukrainian Central Executive Committee] v otnoshenii evreiskogo naselenia").
39. "Rusishe nayes," *Forverts*, September 9, 1921. On war relief work in eastern Europe in the wake of World War I, see Granick, *International Jewish Humanitarianism*.
40. GAMO, f. 12, op. 1, d. 758, l. 225 (Autobiography of Chaim Davidovich Zaretskii, March 30, 1928).
41. By the end of the 1920s, Jews constituted 4 percent of the Komsomol total membership. Pinkus, *Jews of the Soviet Union*, 81.
42. Aino Kuusinen, *Gospod' nizvergaet svoikh angelov: Vospominaniya, 1919–1965*, Petrozavodsk: Kareliia, 1991, 128.
43. "Text of Kalinin Statement on the Jewish Question," Jewish Telegraphic Agency, July 30, 1926.
44. Central Archives for the History of the Jewish People (CAHJP), MMF, 1058 A/B, letter dated May 12, 1924, author Yudl (no last name).

45. CAHJP, MMF, 1058 A/B, letter dated February 1, 1925, author unknown.
46. CAHJP, MMF, 1058 A/B, letter dated March 3, 1925, author Lev Fridliand.
47. CAHJP, MMF, 1058 A/B, letter dated March 3, 1925, author Rakhmiel Zinger.
48. On the NEP era and its impact on Soviet economy and society, see Sheila Fitzpatrick, Alexander Rabinowitch, Richard Stites, eds., *Russia in the Era of NEP: Explorations in Soviet Society and Culture*, Bloomington: Indiana University Press, 1991; and R. W. Davies, ed., *From Tsarism to the New Economic Policy: Continuity and Change in the Economy of the U.S.S.R.*, London: Palgrave Macmillan, 1990.
49. Smoliar, *Vu bistu khaver Sidorov?*, 41.
50. Zeltser, *Evrei sovetskoi provintsii*, 97–98, 258.
51. Arkadi Zeltser, "Artel," in *The YIVO Encyclopedia of Jews in Eastern Europe*, ed. Gershon David Hundert, vol. 1, New Haven, CT: Yale University Press, 2008, column 2, 73.
52. Polonsky, *Jews in Poland and Russia.*
53. Iryna Skubii, "Wealth in Soviet Times: The Material World of the Ukrainian Economic Elite, 1920s–1930s," *Res Historica* 48, 2019, 202.
54. Ibid., 203.
55. On the ruble's purchasing power at the time, see Yurii Goland, "Currency Regulation in the NEP Period," *Europe-Asia Studies* 46, no. 8, 1994, 1251–96; and Paul Ashin, "Wage Policy in the Transition to NEP," *Russian Review* 47, no. 3, 1988, 293–313.
56. Skubii, "Wealth in Soviet Times," 200.
57. "Yidishe parnoses in Moskve," *Di yidishe tsaytung*, April 30, 1926.
58. Pinkus, *Jews of the Soviet Union*, 93.
59. Ibid., 93.
60. See JDC, Collection 21/32, file 565, "Statement of Industrial Activities of the JDC in Russia," August 1, 1930.
61. Gennady Estraikh, *In Harness: Yiddish Writers' Romance with Communism*, Syracuse, NY: Syracuse University Press, 2005, 151.
62. Yuri Slezkine, *The House of Government: A Saga of the Russian Revolution*, Princeton, NJ: Princeton University Press, 2017). See Eileen Kane, "The Revolution Failed Promise to Women," *Public Books*, June 26, 2018, www.publicbooks.org.
63. Tatiana Varsher, "Things Seen and Suffered," in *In the Shadow of Revolution: Life Stories of Russian Women from 1917 to the Second World War*, ed. Sheila Fitzpatrick and Yuri Slezkine, Princeton, NJ: Princeton University Press, 2000, 113.
64. On the politicization of women in prerevolutionary Russia, see Deborah Hertz, "Dangerous Politics, Dangerous Liaisons: Love and Terror among Jewish Women Radicals in Czarist Russia," *Histoire, économie & société* 33, no. 4, 2014, 94 109; and Barbara Alpern Engel, *Mothers and Daughters: Women of the Intelligentsia in Nineteenth-Century Russia*, Cambridge: Cambridge University Press, 1985. See also Elissa Bemporad, "Issues of Gender, Sovietization and Modernization in the Jewish Metropolis of Minsk," in "Modernity and the Cities of the

Jews," ed. Cristiana Facchini, *Quest. Issues in Contemporary Jewish History*, 2, October 2011.

65. Paula E. Hyman, "Two Models of Modernization: Jewish Women in the German and the Russian Empires," in *Jews and Gender: The Challenge to Hierarchy*, ed. Jonathan Frankel, Studies in Contemporary Jewry 16, New York: Oxford University Press, 2000, 48; and J. S. Hertz, ed., *Doyres Bundistn*, New York: Farlag Unser Tsayt, 1956.
66. Oleg Kozerod, *Jewish Women in Ukraine: Writers, Zionists, Leaders in the 1920s*, Warsaw: European World, 2019, 54.
67. On women delegates, see Bemporad, *Becoming Soviet Jews*, 149–154.
68. Bemporad, "Issues of Gender."
69. See Bemporad, *Becoming Soviet Jews*, 152–153.
70. On the dissolution of the Zhenotdel, see Richard Stites, *The Women's Liberation Movement in Russia*, Princeton, NJ, Princeton University Press, 1978, 341–345.
71. "Vsesoiuznyi sezd rabotnits i krestnianok," *Tribuna*, no. 8, October 1927, 22.
72. Ibid.
73. Alex Marshall, *The Caucasus under Soviet Rule*, London: Routledge, 2010.
74. Barbara Alpern Engel, "New Directions in Russian and Soviet Women's History," in *Making Women's Histories: Beyond National Perspectives*, ed. Pamela Susan Nadell and Kate Haulman, New York: New York University Press 2013, 54.
75. Zeev Levin, "The Khujum Campaign in Uzbekistan and the Bukharan Jewish Women," in *Gender Politics in Central Asia: Historical Perspectives and Current Living Conditions of Women*, ed. Christa Ehrmann-Hammerle, Koln: Böhlau-Verlag, 2008, 102.
76. Michael Zand, "Notes on the Culture of the Non-Ashkenazi Jewish Communities under Soviet Rule," in *Jewish Culture and Identity in the Soviet Union*, ed. Yaakov Ro'i and Avi Beker, New York: New York University Press, 1991, 411.
77. On options for former Bundists, see Meyers, "Portrait of Transition," 107–134.
78. Gitelman, *Jewish Nationality and Soviet Politics*, 122. For more on the complicated relationship between EVKOM and the Evsektsiia, see ibid., 122–126, 130–135, and 244–246.
79. Ibid., 122.
80. Zand, "Notes on the Culture of the Non-Ashkenazi Jewish Communities," 400.
81. For the most comprehensive study on the relationship between the Bund and the Evsektsiia, see Gitelman, *Jewish Nationality and Soviet Politics*. See also Altshuler, *Ha-yevsektsyah bi-Verit-ha-Mo'atsot*. For a local study of the relationship between the Bund and the Evsektsiia, see Bemporad, *Becoming Soviet Jews*, in particular chapter 3.
82. Frankel, *Prophecy and Politics*, 185.
83. Gitelman, *Jewish Nationality and Soviet Politics*, 11.
84. Ibid., 26.
85. Ibid., 373.

86. David Shneer, *Yiddish and the Creation of Soviet Yiddish Culture*, Cambridge: Cambridge University Press, 2004, 27.
87. On Sara Mariasina, see Bemporad, *Becoming Soviet Jews*, 168. See also Sara Mariasina, *Di alte un di naye shul (a bikhl farn masn-leyener)*, Minsk: Folkombild fun Vaysrusland tsentral yidish bildung-biuro, 1929.
88. On the Haskalah and the goal of regenerating Jews through productive labor, see Mordechai Levin, *Erchei hevrah ve-kalkalah be-ideologiah shel tkufat ha-haskalah*, Jerusalem: Bialik Institute, 1975; and Shmuel Feiner, *The Jewish Enlightenment*, Philadelphia: University of Pennsylvania Press, 2002.
89. Nokhem Khanin, *Soviet Rusland: Vi ikh hob ir gezen*, New York: Farlag Veker, 1929, 9, 11, 30–31, 51–53.
90. See, for example, Berl Nakhamkin, "A rov zogt az men tor nit ganvenen," *Der veker*, no. 126, June 1, 1925, 3; and V.D., "Peklekh far zikh," *Oktyabr*, no. 23, January 2, 1928, 4.
91. Gitelman, *Jewish Nationality and Soviet Politics*, 380.
92. Ibid., 358.
93. JDC, Collection 21/32, folder 526 ("The Forward, To the Soil Movement of Jews in Soviet Russia," report by Louis Fischer), 1.
94. Pinkus, *Jews of the Soviet Union*, 91.
95. "Evrei Dagestana," *Tribuna*, nos. 4–5, 1927, 11.
96. Gitelman, *Jewish Nationality and Soviet Politics*, 383.
97. Pinkus, *Jews of the Soviet Union*, 65.
98. On the Agro-Joint's successes and failures, see Jonathan Dekel-Chen, *Farming the Red Land: Jewish Agricultural Colonization and Local Soviet Power, 1924–1941*, New Haven, CT: Yale University Press, 2005; and Misha Mitsel, *Posledniaia glava: Agro-Joint v gody Bolshogo terrora*, Kyiv: Dukh i litera, 2012. On American Jewish relief in Ukraine, see Jaclyn Granick, "The First American Organization in Soviet Russia: JDC and Relief in the Ukraine, 1920–1923," in *The JDC at 100: A Century of Humanitarianism*, ed. Avinoam Patt, Atina Grossman, Linda G. Levin, and Maud S. Mandel, Detroit: Wayne State University Press, 2019, 61–93; and Estraikh, *Transatlantic Russian Jewishness*, 178–181.
99. Quoted in Estraikh, *In Harness*, 84.
100. Moshe Litvakov's titles and roles as one of the leaders of the Soviet Yiddish intelligentsia multiplied over the course of the 1920s and 1930s. After joining the Communist Party in early 1921, besides serving as a Yiddish literary and theater critic and an instructor in different Soviet Jewish institutions, he became editor of *Der emes* and of the School and Book Publishing House, thus controlling the two primary sites of Yiddish cultural and political production in the Soviet Union of the 1920s. In 1923, he became the Jewish censor for the Main Administration for Literature, or Glavlit, the state censorship agency. See Shneer, *Yiddish and the Creation of Modern Yiddish Culture*, 28. For more on Litvakov, see Mikhail Krutikov, "Soviet Literary Theory in the Search for a Yiddish Canon: The Case of Moshe Litvakov," in *Yiddish and the Left*, ed. Gennady Estraikh and Mikhail Krutikov, Oxford, UK: Legenda, 2001, 226–241.

101. Quoted in Estraikh, *In Harness*, 84.
102. YIVO, Joseph Rosen Papers, RG 358, J. C. Hyman, "Statement of Russian Activities," March 16, 1934.
103. Ibid.
104. Dekel-Chen, *Farming the Red Land*, 40–41, 44.
105. JDC, Collection 21/32, folder 526 ("The Forward, To the Soil Movement of Jews in Soviet Russia," report by Louis Fischer). The JDC often sponsored communist cultural activities for Jews in order to cover up the funding of illegal activities. For instance, as late as July 1930, a cable from Rosen to New York reported about the monthly support that the JDC provided for non-Agro-Joint-related purposes, which included funding for medical supplies, trade schools, factory shops, and cultural training for young Zionists. See JDC, Collection 21/32, folder 565 (Cable from Joseph Rosen to Joint New York, July 1, 1930).
106. See Dekel-Chen, *Farming the Red Land*, in particular 21–26, 86–93.
107. JDC, Collection 21/32, folder 526 ("The Forward, To the Soil Movement of Jews in Soviet Russia," report by Louis Fischer).
108. "Additional $1,100,000 Will Be Expended in Russia, Joint Distribution Committee Announces," Jewish Telegraphic Agency, March 15, 1926.
109. JDC, Collection 21/32, folder 526 ("The Forward, To the Soil Movement of Jews in Soviet Russia," report by Louis Fischer).
110. Dekel-Chen, *Farming the Red Land*, 92, 105.
111. "Kino-film *Evrei na zemle* v letnikh rabochikh klubakh," in *Tribuna*, nos. 4–5, 1927, 34.
112. Gitelman, *Jewish Nationality and Soviet Politics*, 385.
113. Valery Dymshits, *Facing West: Oriental Jews of Central Asia and the Caucasus*, Amsterdam: Rossisskii etnograficheskii muzei / Joods Historisch Museum, 1998.
114. Gitelman, *Jewish Nationality and Soviet Politics*, 386–387.
115. Szajkowski, *Jews, Wars, and Communism*, vol. 1, 428.
116. JDC, Collection 21/32, folder 565 (Copy of letter sent by Rosenberg to Rosen, on December 18, 1929).
117. Nora Levin, *The Jews of the Soviet Union: A Paradox of Survival*, vol. 1, New York: New York University Press, 1990, 230.
118. "Zemledelie," in *Kratkaia evreiskaia entsiklopedia*, vol. 2, Jerusalem: Keter, 1982, column 554.
119. TsDAGO, f. 1, op. 20, d. 2800 ("OGPU, Summary of the most important manifestations in workers' mood, GPU Ukraine, 20/1/1928"), l. 15.
120. Gitelman, *Jewish Nationality and Soviet Politics*, 431.
121. Quoted in Robert Weinberg, "Jews into Peasants? Solving the Jewish Question in Birobidzhan," in *Jews and Jewish Life in Russia and the Soviet Union*, ed. Yaakov Ro'i, New York: Routledge, 1995, 100n13.
122. Pinkus, *Jews of the Soviet Union* 75. In 1931, 3,250 Jews moved to Birobidzhan.
123. Weinberg, "Jews into Peasants?," 98.
124. Robert Weinberg, *Stalin's Forgotten Zion: Birobidzhan and the Making of a Soviet*

Jewish Homeland, an Illustrated History, 1928–1996, Berkeley: University of California Press, 1998, 28.

3. THE SOVIET STATE, THE JEWISH QUESTION, AND RETHINKING ANTISEMITISM IN SOVIET SOCIETY

Epigraphs: TsDAGO, f. 1, op. 20, del. 3192, l. 27 ("Special summary of workers' conversations in the factories in Dnipropetrovsk and Odesa, 1926"); H. D. Nomberg, *Mayn rayze iber rusland*, Warsaw: Kultur-lige, 1928, 105.

1. TsDAGO, f. 1, op. 20, d. 2314, l. 1 ("GPU Summary of the most important workers' events, August 15–27, 1926, Kharkov").
2. TsDAGO, f. 1, op. 20, d. 2314, ll. 1, 11 ("GPU Summary of the most important workers' events, August 15–27, 1926, Kahrkov").
3. TsDAGO, f. 1, op. 20, d. 2314, l. 124ob ("GPU Report on the most prominent manifestations in the mood of the unemployed, November 15 through December 1, 1926, Kiev").
4. TsDAGO, f. 1, op. 20, d. 2314, l. 25 ("OGPU Summary of the most important events in the workers' mood for the period of November 8–14, 1926").
5. TsDAGO, f. 1, op. 20, d. 2314, ll. 57–58 ("OGPU Summary n. 9 of the most important events in the workers' mood from December 23 to January 9, 1926").
6. TsDAGO, f. 1, op. 20, d. 2314, l. 124ob ("OGPU Report on the most prominent manifestations in the mood of the unemployed, November 15 through December 1, 1926").
7. TsDAGO, f. 1, op. 20, d. 2314, l. 38 ("OGPU Report on the most prominent manifestations in the workers' mood, August 15–23, 1926").
8. TsDAGO, f. 1, op. 20, d. 2314, l. 25 ("OGPU Summary of the most important events in the workers' mood for the period November 8–14, 1926").
9. For an analysis of the relationship between the Russian Revolution and the Jewish question through the lens of the sociology of racism, see McGeever, *Antisemitism and the Russian Revolution*, in particular, 111, 124.
10. Reinhard Rürup, "A Success Story and Its Limits: European Jewish Social History in the Nineteenth and Early Twentieth Centuries," *Jewish Social Studies* 11, no. 1, 2004, 3–15.
11. Paul Hanebrink, *A Specter Haunting Europe: The Myth of Judeo-Bolshevism*, Cambridge, MA: Harvard University Press, 2018, 33–34.
12. Archivio Segreto Vaticano, L'archivio di mons. Achille Ratti visitatore apostolico e nunzio a Varsavia (1918–1921), 148–150 (Titolo 1, 191, Carteggio di Mon. Ratti Visitatore Apostolico della Polonia, 1918–1919).
13. See Beizer, "Antisemitism in Petrograd/Leningrad," 8–10; and McGeever, *Antisemitism and the Russian Revolution*, 20, 23–24.
14. Yurii Sandomirskii, *Puti antisemitizma v Rossii*, Moscow-Leningrad: Gosudarstvennoe izdatelstvo, 1928, 49.
15. Z. Vendrof, "Antisemitizm in sovet-rusland un tsi iz er geferlekh far yidn?," *Der moment*, May 28, 1925.

16. TsDAGO, f. 1, op. 20, d. 1920, ll. 54–55 ("Personal secret letter, March 30, 1924").
17. TsDAGO, f. 1, op. 20, d. 1920, l. 84 ("Flier: Ne pozvolim vyvozit' khleb za granitsu").
18. "Anti-semitism in Soviet Factories Due to Peasant Element Now in Cities," Jewish Telegraphic Agency, December 27, 1928.
19. Pinkus, *Jew of the Soviet Union*, 85.
20. Ibid., 85–86. Trotsky himself would later refer to Stalin's use of antisemitism. One of the consequences was the appearance in the Party press of antisemitic caricatures of the Jewish leaders of the Opposition. Leon Trotsky, *Stalin: The Revolutionary in Power*, vol. 2, London: Panther History, 1969, 224, quoted in Pinkus, *Jew of the Soviet Union*, 335n80.
21. TsDAGO, f. 1, op. 20, d. 2314, l.109ob ("GPU Summary n. 13, December 1, through December 12, 1926").
22. TsDAGO, f. 1, op. 20, d. 2314, ll. 57–58 ("GPU Summary n. 9 on the most important manifestations in the workers' mood, September 1 through October, 1926").
23. See, for example, Annie Gérin, "Caricature as a Weapon in Class Struggle: Early Soviet Graphic Satire," in *The Languages of Humor: Verbal, Visual, and Physical Humor*, ed. Arie Sover, New York: Bloomsbury, 2018, 140.
24. TsDAGO, f. 1, op. 20, d. 2314, l. 109 ob. ("Summary, Information department, December 1926").
25. Quoted in Iakov Etinger, "The Doctors' Plot: Stalin's Solution to the Jewish Question," in *Jews and Jewish Life in Russia and the Soviet Union*, ed. Yaakov Ro'i, 2nd ed., London: Routledge, 2016, 103. See also Sloin, *Jewish Revolution in Belorussia*, 209–210.
26. Pinkus, *Jew of the Soviet Union*. 86.
27. See Randi Cox, "NEP without Nepmen! Soviet Advertising and the Transition to Socialism," in *Everyday Life in Early Soviet Russia: Taking the Revolution Inside*, ed. Eric Naiman and Christina Kiaer, Bloomington: Indiana University Press, 2006, in particular 128–135.
28. A number of tsarist decrees issued over the course of the nineteenth century were intended to protect the peasantry from the alleged exploitation of the Jewish middle class. This condemnation of trade practices in the context of an economy that was largely based on agriculture and peasant labor was not unique to Russia. To be sure, this same dynamic that fueled antisemitism emerged in early modern Catholic Poland, perhaps the most anticommercial country in Europe at the time. In both Poland and Russia, where Jews were indeed largely concentrated in the trade economy as "minority entrepreneurs who mediate between the dominant and subordinate group," antisemitism was further promoted by Enlightenment discourse. Enlightenment thinkers—Jews and non-Jews alike—promoted the idea of modernization through productivization. In light of this new ethos, criticism of Jews for being associated with trade and not participating in agricultural production mushroomed, further

exacerbating antisemitism. See, for example, Adam Teller, *Money, Power, and Influence in Eighteenth-Century Lithuania: The Jews on the Radziwill Estates*, Stanford, CA: Stanford University Press, 2016.

29. McGeever, *Antisemitism and the Russian Revolution*, 185, 202–205.
30. Ibid., 32. On silence and denial in the Soviet press on antisemitism in the Red Army, see also ibid., 130–137.
31. Andrew Sloin, "Speculators, Swindlers, and Other Jews: Regulating Trade in Revolutionary White Russia," *East European Jewish Affairs* 40, no. 2, 2010, 112.
32. Sandomirskii, *Puti antisemitizma*, 32; L. Liadov, *O vrazhde k evreiam*, Moscow-Leningrad: Mosskovskii rabochii, 1927, 16.
33. Sandomirskii, *Puti antisemitizma*, 38, 40.
34. Isaac Babel, *Benja Krik (kinopovest)*, Moscow: Artel pisatelei "Krug," 1926.
35. Jarrod Tanny, *City of Rogues and Schnorrers: Russia's Jews and the Myth of Old Odessa*, Bloomington: Indiana University Press, 2011, 91, 114–115.
36. "Soviet Officials Make New Arrests on Charges of Speculation Activities," Jewish Telegraphic Agency, July 13, 1928.
37. "Says Ruthless Procedure of Soviet Officials Affects Large Number of Jews," Jewish Telegraphic Agency, October 28, 1928.
38. G. L. Zhigalin, *Prokliatoe nasledie (ob antisemitisme)*, Moscow-Leningrad: Molodaia Gvardia, 1927, 83.
39. Commissioned by the Jewish philanthropist Baron Horace De Gunzburg, the Russian novelist Nikolai Leskov in 1883 wrote a moving plea for religious tolerance and equal rights for Russian Jews: *The Jews in Russia: Some Notes of the Jewish Question*, trans. Harold Klassel Schefski, Princeton, NJ: Kingston, 1986. Leskov's defense was supposed to convince Russian authorities to underwrite Jewish emancipation.
40. Amelia Glaser, "Maxim Gorky's 'Pogrom': Jewish Victimhood and Russian Revolutionary Thought," *Shofar: An Interdisciplinary Journal of Jewish Studies* 37, no. 2, 2019, 166–190.
41. Elias Tcherikower, *Istoriia pogromnogo dvizheniia na Ukraine 1917–1921*, Berlin: Ostjudisches Historisches Arkhiv, 1923, 287.
42. On the committee, see McGeever, *Antisemitism and the Russian Revolution*, 179–177.
43. G. V. Kostyrchenko, *Tainaia politika Stalina: Vlast' i antisemitizm*, Moscow: Mezhdunarodnie otnosheniia, 2001, 63; and McGeever, *Antisemitism and the Russian Revolution*, 193.
44. On the press discussion of instances in which pogromists were punished and on open calls to combat antisemitism in the cities and towns of the former Pale of Settlement, see, for example, YIVO, Tcherikower Archive, RG 80, folder 540, 46374, 46392, and 46398.
45. Bemporad, *Legacy of Blood*, 62–66.
46. For examples of materials collected by the Jewish Committee and sent to Paris as evidence for the Schwartzbard trial, see YIVO, Tcherikower Archive, RG 80, folder 641, 54842–54844.

47. See YIVO, Tcherikower Archive, RG 80, folder 357, 32621–32691. See also "Ukrainian Pogrom Archives Sent to Paris by Soviet Embassy," Jewish Telegraphic Agency, September 14, 1926.
48. On the diplomatic incident known as the Arcos affair and the break of the Anglo-Soviet deal, see Harriette Flory, "The Arcos Raid and the Rupture of Anglo-Soviet Relations, 1927," *Journal of Contemporary History* 12, no. 4, 1977, 707–23.
49. TsDAGO, f. 7, op. 1, d. 165, l. 1 ("Memorandum, December 8, 1926").
50. B. Pinkus and A. A. Greenbaum, comps., *Pirsumim rusiim al yehudim veyahadut bi-vrit ha-moatsot 1917–1967*, ed. Mordechai Altshuler, Jerusalem: Historical Society of Israel, 1970, 51–56.
51. The crux of the ambivalence is captured in the tension between the early condemnation of antisemitism on the part of the Bolshevik leadership and the fact that no explicit ban on antisemitism and on anything that might be considered manifestation of it ever appeared in the Codes of Criminal Law, which were adopted after 1922 in all Soviet republics. Absence of criminal sanctions surely made it more difficult to deter public anti-Jewish behavior; under certain circumstances, it may even have encouraged it. See Pinkus, *Jews of the Soviet Union*, 85.
52. Tsentralnyi derzhavnyi arkhyv vishikh organiv vladi ta upravlinnia Ukrainy (TsDAVO), f. 2708, op. 2, d. 362, ll. 66–68, "Protocol."
53. Larin, *Evrei i antisemitizm*, 127.
54. Ibid., 130–133. See Bemporad, *Legacy of Blood*, 47–48.
55. For more on this case, see Bemporad, *Legacy of Blood*, 48–50.
56. See M. Gorev, *Protiv antisemitov: Ocherki i zarisovki*, Moscow-Leningrad: Gos. Izd-vo, 1928, 29.
57. Ibid.
58. Quoted in Kostyrchenko, *Tainaia politika Stalina*, 106.
59. Quoted in Slezkine, *Jewish Century*, 249.
60. "Na borbu s antisemitizmom," *Tribuna*, no. 9 (18), June 1, 1928, 25.
61. "Evreiskaia zhizn,'" *Tribuna*, May 15, 1929, 25.
62. "Moskovskii garnizon boretsia s antisemitizmom," *Tribuna*, no. 9, May 1, 1929, 27.
63. Slezkine, *Jewish Century*, 249.
64. APPO MK VKP(b), *Metodicheskie posobia dlia dokladchikov i gruppovykh agitatorov ob antisemitizme*, Moscow-Leningrad: Moskovskii rabochii, 1929.
65. TsDAVO, f. 2514, op. 1, d. 2, l. 24 ("Luganskaia Pravda," December 20, 1928).
66. Narkompros RSFSR, *O borbe s antisemitizmom v shkole*, Moscow: OGIZ, 1929.
67. "Uladovker antisemitn protses," *Der shtern*, January 10, 1929, 3.
68. L. Liadov, *O vrazhde k evreiam*, Moscow-Leningrad: Mosskovskii rabochii, 1927, 28–29.
69. "Evreiskaia zhizn,'" *Tribuna*, May 15, 1929, 25.
70. L. Kuchinki, "Antisemity poluchili po zaslugam," *Tribuna*, February 10, 1931, 22–23.

71. Larin, *Evrei i antisemitizm*, 124, 127. Cultural reasons may also have determined the convergence between accusations of ritual murder and violence in certain places instead of others.
72. N. Lagovier, *Antisemitizm i borba s nim*, Moscow: Gosudarstvennoe iuridicheskoe izdatelstvo, 1930, 30. See also "Soviet Russian Press Reports Anti-Jewish Pogrom in Russian Town," Jewish Telegraphic Agency, December 10, 1928.
73. "Soviet Embassy Denies Communist Paper's Report of Anti-Jewish Riots," Jewish Telegraphic Agency, August 21, 1928. For another example of pogrom, see "Anti-semitism in Soviet Factories Due to Peasant Element Now in Cities," Jewish Telegraphic Agency, December 27, 1928. The report discussed the case of a Jewish colony in Babruisk district, which came under attack; defendants included local authorities and policemen, who had failed to intervene to put an end to the violence.
74. "Moscow Hears of Anti-Jewish Acts in Several Russian Centers," Jewish Telegraphic Agency, December 4, 1928; M.S., "Mishpet iber di antisemitn," *Oktyabr*, February 23, 1929, 4. On Krasnoyarsk, see "Accuse Soviet Judges of Persecution of Their Jewish Associate," Jewish Telegraphic Agency, March 8, 1929: the assistant prosecutor in the District Court of Krasnoyarsk published in the press complaints about antisemitism in the court system, writing, "I cannot endure it any longer. The persecutions have becoming unbearable."
75. V. Glebov, *Sovremenniy antisemitizm i borba s nim*, Moscow-Leningrad: Molodaya gvardia, 1927, 42–44.
76. APPO Leningradskogo oblastkoma VK(b)B, *Na borbu s antisemitizmom: Materialy dlia agitatorov i besedchikov*, Leningrad: APPO Len. Obk., 1929, 19, 20–21.
77. Lagovier, *Antisemitizm i borba s nim*, 44.
78. "Soviet Authorities Investigate Anti-semitic Murder of Worker," Jewish Telegraphic Agency, February 24, 1929; "Anti-semitic Murderer's Trial in Pskov Attracts Wide Attention in Russia," Jewish Telegraphic Agency, April 8, 1929.
79. "Trofimov's Sentence Is Considered Mild in Soviet Russia," Jewish Telegraphic Agency, April 12, 1929.
80. See, for example, "Delo o zverskom izdevatelstve nad rabotnitsei na zavode Oktyabr," *Izvestiia*, November 23, 1928; "Vokrug dela rabotnitsi Barshai," *Izvestiia*, November 25, 1928.
81. "Zikh ongehoybn der protses iber di antisemitn-khuliganes," *Oktyabr*, January 16, 1929, 1; B. Alter, "Protses iber di khuliganes-antisemitn," *Oktyabr*, January 22, 1929, 4; "Barshay Trial Opens in Minsk, Attracts Wide Attention in Russia," Jewish Telegraphic Agency, January 20, 1929.
82. "Barshay Trial Staged as Object Lesson against Petty Anti-semitism," Jewish Telegraphic Agency, January 23, 1929.
83. "Novaia antisemitskaia vykhodka," *Izvestiia*, November 24, 1928; Lagovier, *Antisemitizm i borba s nim*, 18; APPO Leningradskogo oblastkoma VK(b)B, *Na borbu s antisemitizmom*, 16.
84. "Barshay Trial Turned into Anti-semitic Demonstration by Soviet Officials," Jewish Telegraphic Agency, January 21, 1929. For subsequent instances of

antisemitism and ensuing trials, see "Delo antisemitov," *Izvestiia*, April 21, 1929; and "Opiat' v Babruiske," *Izvestiia*, April 30, 1929.

85. "Sentence 8 for Persecuting Jewish Workers in Soviet Factory," Jewish Telegraphic Agency, October 27, 1929; "Try Two Assailants of Jewish Worker in Soviet Factory," Jewish Telegraphic Agency, August 25, 1929.
86. M. Semenov, "Ni odnogo beznakazannogo," *Tribuna*, no. 9, May 1, 1929, 9–10.
87. TsDAGO, f. 1, op. 20, d. 2800, ll. 11, 14–16 ("GPU Summary of the most important manifestations in workers' mood, Ukraine, December 1, 1928").
88. Liadov, *O vrazhde k evreiam*, 26.
89. Zhigalin, *Prokliatoe nasledie*, 72. Glebov, *Sovremennyi antisemitizm*, 18–21. See also Sandomirskii, *Puti antisemitizma.*
90. APPO Leningradskogo oblastkoma VK(b)P, *Na borbu s antisemitizmom: materialy dlia agitatorov i besedchikov*, Leningrad: APPO Len. Obk., 1929, 19.
91. Zhigalin, *Prokliatoe nasledie*, 83.
92. Mikhail Kalinin, "Evreiskii vopros i pereselenie evreev v Krym," *Izvestiia*, July 11, 1926, 3. See also "Text of Kalinin's Statement on Jewish Question in Russia," Jewish Telegraphic Agency, July 30, 1926.
93. The siege of Perekop was the final battle on the southern front and a key event in the civil war.
94. Kalinin, "Evreiskii vopros i pereselenie evreev v Krym," 3.
95. Glebov, *Sovremennyi antisemitizm*, 45–47.
96. On this canard in the Red Army, see Shternshis, *Soviet and Kosher*, 153–154.
97. Sandomirskii, *Puti antisemitizma*, 50–51.
98. See, for example, ibid., 49–50.
99. Larin, *Evrei i antisemitizm*, 7.
100. Ibid., 8.
101. Ibid., 19. The speech was reproduced also in Zhigalin, *Prokliatoe nasledie*, 91–92; Liadov, *O vrazhde k evreiam*, 39; Ef. Dobun, *Pravda o evreiakh*, Leningrad: Krasnaia Gazeta, 1928; and Sandomirskii, *Puti antisemitizma*, 49.
102. Born in Sebezh, Vitsyebsk *guberniia*, Dimanshtein received two rabbinical ordinations (one of the them from the leading rabbi of Lithuanian Orthodoxy, Chaim Ozer Grodzenski) but quickly embraced socialism, in 1904 joining the Russian Social Democratic Party in Vilna. Beginning with the October Revolution and throughout the 1920s and early 1930s, he served in different key positions in the Soviet government and Communist Party, including those of Jewish commissar of the Commissariat of Nationality Affairs, deputy head of the Department of Propaganda and Agitation of the Central Committee Secretariat of the Communist Party, head of the nationalities sector of the Central Committee, director of the Institute of Nationalities of the Central Executive Committee, chair of OZET (the Society for the Settlement of Jewish Toilers on Land), and editor of several Yiddish publications. Throughout his career, Dimanshtein remained committed to promoting and celebrating the Soviet aversion to antisemitism.
103. On collaboration between the local population in western Ukraine and Belorus-

sia and the German occupying forces during World War II, see, for example, Leonid Rein, *The Kings and the Pawns: Collaboration in Byelorussia during World War II*, New York: Berghahn Books, 2011; Martin Dean, *Collaboration in the Holocaust: Crimes of the Local Police in Belorussia and Ukraine, 1941–1944*, London: Palgrave Macmillan/USHMM, 2000; and Evan Mawdsley, *Thunder in the East: The Nazi-Soviet War 1941–1945*, London: Bloomsbury, 2005. For a discussion on this issue, see also Oleg Budnitskii, David Engel, Gennady Estraikh, and Anna Shternshis, eds., *Jews in the Soviet Union: A History*, vol. 3, *War, Conquest, and Catastrophe, 1939–1945*, New York: New York University Press, 2022.

104. Pinkus, *Jewish of the Soviet Union*, 87.
105. "V diskussionnom poriadke," *Tribuna*, no. 14 (23) August 15, 1928, 11.
106. TsDAVO, f. 2708, op. 2, d. 362, ll. 66–68, l. 130 ("Petition").
107. DAKO, f. 111, op. 1, d. 527 (September 15, 1923, Protest).
108. "Evreiskaia zhizn v SSSR," *Tribuna*, no. 16, 1928, 25.
109. YIVO, Joseph Rosen Papers, RG 358, folder 28A, 004 ("JTA Cable from Moscow, dated November 21, 1929").
110. M. Kiper, "Natsionale filbarkayt un oysgetrakhter antisemitizm," *Yunge gvardie*, March 29, 1929, 4.
111. See, for example, "Di partey bakemft dem antisemitizm un shovinizm," *Oktyabr*, December 28, 1928, 2; and Odeser krayz-partkom, "Antisemitizm un yidishe shovinizm: ideologyes fun der kontr-revolutsye," *Des emes*, March 16, 1929, 3.
112. M. Levitan, "Untern druk funem yidishn natsionalizm (tsu der frage vegn kamf kegn der rekhter gefar in der yidisher svive)," *Der shtern*, January 5, 1929, 2.
113. Sh. Murokh, "Far vos varft men op mayn forshlog," *Oktyabr*, March 26, 1928, 3.
114. APPO Leningradskogo oblastkoma VK(b)B, *Na borbu s antisemitizmom*, 17; and "Delo Beirakha," *Komsomolskaya pravda*, February 22, 1927.
115. See, for example, "Higher Court Annuls Sentence on First Jewish Kulaks Tried in Soviet Anti-kulak Fight," Jewish Telegraphic Agency, January 24, 1930.
116. Hersh Smoliar, *Fun ineveynik: Zikhroynes vegn der "Yevsektsye,"* Tel Aviv: Farlag Peretz, 1978.
117. In general, Soviet authorities were not consistent: at times, they used the term "antisemitism" in legal proceedings, and at other times, they did not.
118. Levitan, "Untern druk funem yidishn natsionalizm," 2.
119. Vendrof, "Antisemitizm in sovet-rusland un tsi iz er geferlekh far yidn?" On Vendrof, see G. Estraikh, "Zalman Wendroff: The Forverts Man in Moscow," in *Leket: Yidishe shtudyes haynt*, ed. Marion Aptroot, Efrat Gal-Ed, Roland Gruschka, and Simon Neuberg, Dusseldorf: Dusseldorf University Press, 2012, 509–528.

4. LONGING FOR ZION UNDER THE SOVIETS

1. Central Zionist Archives (CZA), F30, A. Rafaeli-Zenzipper Collection, file 1358/2, 3–4, "Nachum Goldin."

2. CZA, F30, A. Rafaeli-Zenzipper Collection, file 78, 1–2, "Secret Memorandum of the Belorussian Regional Committee, Ts. S.Y.F."
3. Ibid., 3.
4. See, for instance, Zvi Gitelman, ed., *The Emergence of Modern Jewish Politics: Bundism and Zionism in Eastern Europe*, Pittsburgh: University of Pittsburgh Press, 2003.
5. See J. B. Shechtman, "The USSR, Zionism, and Israel," in *The Jews in Soviet Russia since 1917*, ed. Lionel Kochan, London: Oxford University Press, 1970, 101. See also Vladimir Levin, *Mi-mahpekhah le-milhamah: Ha-politikah ha-Yehudit be-Rusyah, 1907–1914*, Jerusalem: Merkaz Zalman Shazar, 2016, 141. In May 1917, the All-Russian Zionist Congress in Petrograd included 522 delegates representing 140,000 shekel payers from 340 cities and towns.
6. J. B. Shechtman, "Sovetskaia Rossia, sionizm i Izrail," in *Kniga o russkom evreistve, 1917–1967*, ed. Yakov G. Frumkin, Grigoriy J. Aronson, and Aleksei A. Goldenveizer, New York: Soiuz russkikh evreev, 1968, 329.
7. "Israel Kargman," in *Beyn yeush le-tikvah: Mikhtavim shel asirei-tsyon be-rusyah ha-sovetit*, ed. Benjamin West, Tel Aviv: Arkhion ha-avodah, 1973, 199.
8. "Fanya Zubrin," ibid., 114–115.
9. On nineteenth-century Jewish colonies, see Saul Ia. Borovoi, *Evreiskaia zemledelcheskaia kolonizatsiia v staroi Rossii: Politika, ideologiia, khoziaistvo, byt*, Moscow: Sabashnikovy, 1928; and Zvi Livne-Liberman, *Ikarim yehudim be-Rusyah*, Tel Aviv: Aleph, 1967.
10. "Zerubavel Yevazrikhin," in West, *Beyn yeush le-tikvah*, 130.
11. Ziva Galili and Boris Morozov, *Exiled to Palestine: The Emigration of Zionist Convicts from the Soviet Union, 1924–1934*, London: Routledge, 2018, 4.
12. United States Holocaust Memorial Museum Archives (USHMM), RG 31.075, OGPU, Shepetovka department (original records in State Archives of the Vinnytsia region, Ukraine, f. R-196, op. 1, d. 2, ll. 0001–0008).
13. Quoted in Aharon Rozin, "Ha-yeshuv ha-yehudi," in *Minsk, ir va-em: Korot, maasim, ishim, havai*, ed. Sh. Even-Shoshan, Tel Aviv: Irgun yotse Minsk k u-venotecha be-Yisrael, 1985, 95.
14. Galili and Morozov, *Exiled to Palestine*, 7. See also Ziva Galili, "Zionism in the Early Soviet State: Between Legality and Persecution," in *Revolution, Repression, and Revival: The Soviet Jewish Experience*, ed. Zvi Gitelman and Yaacov Ro'i, Lanham, MD: Rowman and Littlefield, 2007, 38. On the Evsektsiia's role in promoting the persecution of Zionists, see Gitelman, *Jewish Nationality and Soviet Politics*, 270–277, 286–291.
15. CZA, F30, A. Rafaeli-Zenzipper Collection, files 30, 78, 1–3, "Secret memorandum of the Belorussian Regional Committee, Ts. S. Y. F."
16. Galili and Morozov, *Exiled to Palestine*, 14.
17. Mattityahu Mintz, "Illegal Zionist Organizations in Ukraine, 1924–1925," *Jews in Eastern Europe* 31, no. 3, Winter, 1996, 53.
18. Anita Shapira, "Labor Zionism and the October Revolution," *Journal of Contemporary History* 24, no. 4, October 1989, 623; Ezra Mendelshon, "Black

Night, White Snow," in *The Jews and the European Crisis, 1914–21*, ed. Jonathan Frankel, Studies in Contemporary Jewry 4, New York: Oxford University Press, 1988, 155.

19. Galili and Morozov, *Exiled to Palestine*, 5. The heading for this section comes from "From a Secret Memorandum by Eduard Karlson, Deputy Chairman of the Ukrainian OGPU 1925," trans. Mattityahu Mintz, in "Illegal Zionist Organizations in Ukraine, 1924–1925," *Jews in Eastern Europe* 31, no. 3 (Winter 1996): 46–66.
20. Rafaeli, *Ba-maavak li-geulah*, 127.
21. Galili and Morozov, *Exiled to Palestine*, 5.
22. Ibid., 6.
23. USHMM, RG 31.075, 163–164, "Thesis of T. Daniel on the question of the *Ha-shomer ha-tsair* movement and our immediate goals" (original in the State Archive of the Khmielnitsky Province, Derzhavniy arkhiv Khmielnitskoy oblasti, f. R-6193, op. 12, d. 27360, ll. 79–80, 81.)
24. Galili and Morozov, *Exiled to Palestine*, 6, 11–12n14.
25. USHMM, RG 31.075, 194–195, "Untitled and undated handwritten news sheet" (original in the State Archive of the Khmielnitsky Province Derzhavniy arkhiv Khmielnitskoy oblasti, f. R-6193, op. 12, d. 27360, ll. 91–92).
26. Larin, *Evrei i antisemitizm*, 16.
27. Hadad, *Der tsionizm vi er iz*, Moscow: Farlag shul un bukh, 1925.
28. Aharon Rozin, *Mayn veg aheym: Memuarn fun an asir-tsiyon in Ratn-Farband*, Jerusalem: Yiddish Culture Association, 1981, 106.
29. Ibid., 49–50.
30. "Eliezer Isakin," in West, *Beyn yeush le-tikvah*, 29.
31. Because of some organizations' positive approach to Marxism, in many cities, Soviet authorities allowed organizations like Kadimah (and other, similar left-leaning Zionist youth groups like Hitpathut [Development]) to secure a meeting space for their members, with theater, music, or sport activities. See CZA, F30, A. Rafaeli-Zenzipper Collection, file 82, 1.
32. CZA, F30, A. Rafaeli-Zenzipper Collection, file 1358/2, 1, 2.
33. Ibid., 3–6.
34. Leah Rafaeli (Zenzipper), *Shiroi makhtorot (Umlegale lider): Parodiyot al nasiim me-khaiei ha-makhteret shel ha-noar ha-tsioni be-Rusiah*, Tel Aviv, n.p., 1971, 5.
35. Ibid., 5–6. The Moscow Sholem Aleichem Drama Studio was directed by the writer and cultural activist David Hofshteyn, whose support for Hebrew led to his yearlong emigration, first to Berlin and then to Tel Aviv, where he wrote poems in Hebrew. The Soviet government ostracized him in 1924 for signing a memorandum backing the teaching of Hebrew in the Soviet Union.
36. Ibid., 18–20.
37. Ibid., 12–14.
38. Ibid., 16.
39. Ibid., 11. Chertok was the chief OGPU agent for questions related to Zionism

in Moscow. On a similar but politically opposite phenomenon of Yiddish buffooneries that targeted Zionism, see Shternshis, *Soviet and Kosher*, 91–92.

40. Mintz, "Illegal Zionist Organizations in Ukraine," 53.
41. USHMM, RG 31.075, OGPU, Shepetovka department (State Archives of the Vinnytsia region), ll. 012, 049.
42. USHMM, RG 31.075, "Excerpts from protocol number 66," ll. 058, 059.
43. USHMM, RG-31.075, "Excerpts from protocol, 18 November 1927," l. 060.
44. See Benyamin West, *He-Halutz be-Rusyah: Le-toldot He-Halutz ha-bilti-legali (Ha-le'umi-amlani)*, Tel Aviv: Mishlahat shel He-Halutz ha-bilti-legali be-Rusyah, 1932.
45. Galili and Morozov, *Exiled to Palestine*, 5.
46. On the shifting centers of Labor Zionism, see R. Yona, "From Russia to Palestine via Poland: The Shifting Centre of Interwar Labour Zionism," *Contemporary European History* 30, no. 4, 2021, 513–527; and Jeffrey Koerber, *Borderland Generation: Soviet and Polish Jews under Hitler*, Syracuse, NY: Syracuse University Press, 2020.
47. Rafaeli, *Ba-maavak li-geula*, 141.
48. Vera Kaplan, *K tebe dusha izdaleka: Po vospominaniiam Racheli Blekhman*, Tel Aviv: Piles Studio, 2000, 92.
49. The Committee for the Settlement of Jewish Laborers on the Land (KOMZET in Russian; KOMERD in Yiddish). On similarities between Soviet-era Jewish colonization and prerevolutionary Jewish colonies, see Jonathan Dekel-Chen, "Jewish Agricultural Settlement in the Interwar Period: A Balance Sheet," in Gitelman and Ro'i, *Revolution, Repression, and Revival*, 72.
50. Headed by Yuri Larin, OZET accepted as members individuals without a criminal record and without affiliation to religious associations and political parties, in particular Zionism. See Dekel-Chen, *Farming the Red Land*, 237n82.
51. In 1926, there were nine thousand members in the illegal He-halutz and seven thousand in the legal faction of He-halutz. See Benjamin West, *Struggles of a Generation: The Jews under Soviet Rule*, Tel Aviv: Massada, 1959, 75–76, 180; and D. Pines, *Hehalutz be-kur ha-mahapekha: Korot ha-histadrut he-haluts be-Rusiya*, Tel Aviv: Davar, 1938, 199, 234.
52. On different aspects of the Soviet colonization project in Belorussia, see Khone Shmeruk, "Ha-kibbuts ha-yehudi veha-hityashvut ha-haklait ha-yehudit be-Bielorusiah ha-sovetit, 1918–1932," PhD diss., Hebrew University, 1961. See also Gennady Estraikh, "The Rise of Ilya Yegudin: An Exemplary Jew in Soviet Agriculture," *East European Jewish Affairs* 51, nos. 2–3, 2021, 249–265.
53. On Jewish migration from Belorussian shtetls to larger cities, see L. G. Zinger, "Chislennost i geograficheskoe razmeshenie evreiskogo naselenia SSSR," in *Materialy i issledovania*, vol. 4, *Evrei v SSSR*, Moscow: Pravlenie vserossiiskogo ORT, 1929, 51; and Mordechai Altshuler, *Soviet Jewry on the Eve of the Holocaust. A Social and Demographic Profile*, Jerusalem: Center for Research of East European Jewry, Hebrew University of Jerusalem, 1998, 13, 220.
54. Yehuda Bauer, *My Brother's Keeper: A History of the American Jewish Joint*

Distribution Committee, 1929–1939, Philadelphia: Jewish Publication Society of America, 1974, 62. On mechanization methods introduced by Agro-Joint and on the latter's relation with the Soviet government, see Dekel-Chen, *Farming the Red Land*, 41–42, 44, 64–65, 288n54.

55. Matthew Silver, *Louis Marshall and the Rise of Jewish Ethnicity in America: A Biography*, Syracuse, NY: Syracuse University Press, 2013, 501.
56. Matthew Silver, "Fighting for Palestine and Crimea: Two Jewish Friends from Philadelphia during the First World War and the 1920s," in *Jews and Violence: Images, Ideologies, Realities*, ed. Peter Y. Medding, Studies in Contemporary Jewry 18, Oxford: Oxford University Press, 2002, 210.
57. Silver, *Louis Marshall*, 501.
58. Estraikh, *Transatlantic Russian Jewishness*, 181.
59. Ibid., 180.
60. Chizuko Takao, "American Jews and the Zionist Movements in the Soviet Union: The Joint and He-Haluts in Crimea in the 1920s," in *From Europe's East to the Middle East: Israel's Russian and Polish Lineages*, ed. Kenneth B. Moss, Benjamin Nathans, and Taro Tsurumi, Philadelphia: University of Pennsylvania Press, 2021, 348.
61. Estraikh, *Transatlantic Russian Jewishness*, 196–197. After visiting the colonies, Cahan noted, "[My] heart was filled with great sympathy for the colonization work. If every American Jew could see the colonies there would then be no difficulty in getting the necessary funds for continuing and expanding the work." Abraham Cahan, "Jewish Colonization in Soviet Russia a Success," *Forverts*, November 6, 1927, English section, 2, quoted in Estraikh, *Transatlantic Russian Jewishness*, 196.
62. Bauer, *My Brother's Keeper*, 60–61.
63. In the JDC's philanthropic support, it also built on preexisting colonies and on the philanthropic help from Baron Maurice de Hirsh, who had founded the Jewish colonization society in 1891.
64. See David Ben-Gurion, *Igorot David Ben-Gurion*, vol. 2, ed. Yehuda Erez, Tel Aviv: Am Oved and Tel Aviv University, 1973, 166.
65. Elissa Bemporad, "JDC in Minsk: The Parameters and Predicaments of Aiding Soviet Jews in the Interwar Years," in Patt et al., *JDC at 100*, 40–59.
66. Estraikh, *Transatlantic Russian Jewishness*, 198–199.
67. Oral History Division, Hebrew University, Institute for Contemporary Jewry (OHD) (Interview with Shterna Ninburg, 12/20/1986), 1.
68. Ibid., 2.
69. Ibid., 3.
70. OHD (Interview with Benjamin Gorstein, 1986), 9; and West, *Struggles of a Generation*, 170.
71. OHD (Interview with Shterna Ninburg), 2.
72. See Isaakhar Ryback, *On the Jewish Field of the Ukraina*, Paris: A. Simon and Cie Editeurs, 1926, 15–16.
73. "Supreme Court of Crimea Sentences Chaluzim Colony to Prison," Jewish

Telegraphic Agency, January 18, 1928; "Russian Supreme Court Confirms Jail Sentence for Chaluzim Leaders," Jewish Telegraphic Agency, February 27, 1928. After a short period in exile in Kostroma, the He-Halutz leadership was allowed to resettle in Palestine; see "3 He-Chaluz Leaders Freed from Prison Go to Palestine," Jewish Telegraphic Agency, August 7, 1928.

74. Ryback, *On the Jewish Field*, 10–11.
75. Galili and Morozov, *Exiled to Palestine*, 89–90. See also "Entire Administration of Chalutz Colony in Russia Imprisoned," Jewish Telegraphic Agency, 6 July 1928; and Dekel-Chen, *Farming the Red Land*, 101–102.
76. OHD (Interview with Shterna Ninburg), 3–4.
77. Ninburg's parents might have opted to leave in 1933 also as a result of the Great Famine, or Holodomor, which resulted from the collectivization policy, took four million lives, and had a profound impact too on Jewish agricultural settlements in Ukraine.
78. Autonomous regions were administrative units established for a number of smaller peoples that were granted autonomy within the fifteen national republics in the Soviet Union. On the formation of Soviet autonomous regions and national republics, see Hirsch, *Empire of Nations*, 74–82.
79. Yad Vashem, "Kalinindorf," accessed October 1, 2023, https://collections.yadvashem.org. For information on the Jewish colonie, see also "Fraydorf," "Fraylebn," "Frayfeld," in *The Encyclopedia of Jewish Life before and during the Holocaust*, ed. Shmuel Spektor, vol. 1, New York: New York University Press, 2002, 401.
80. Galili and Morozov, *Exiled to Palestine*, 7.
81. "F. E. Dzerzhinskii to V. R. Menzhinskii," Rossiiskii gosudarstvenniy arkhiv sotsialno-politicheskoi istorii (RGASPI), f. 76, op. 3, d. 326, l. 4, quoted in Galili and Morozov, *Exiled to Palestine*, 94.
82. "F. E. Dzerzhinskii to his deputies V. R. Menzhinskii and G. G. Iagoda," RGASPI, f. 76, op. 3, d. 326, ll. 2–3, March 15, 1924," quoted in Galili and Morozov, *Exiled to Palestine*, 91.
83. On the fear that antisemitism, and in particular the blood libel, would encourage Zionism, see TsDAGO, f. 413, op. 1, del. 10, l. 8 (Activity report of the Central Commission of national minorities at the VUTsIK, 1925–26).
84. West, *Struggles of a Generation*, 40.
85. Galili and Morozov, *Exiled to Palestine*, 7.
86. USHMM, RG 31.075, 115 "Closing indictment" (original in the State Archive of the Khmielnitsky Province, Derzhavniy arkhiv Khmielnitskoy oblasti, f. p-6193, op. 12, d. 27360, l. 35).
87. See, for example, USHMM, RG 31.075, 021–022, GPU, Shepetovka Department, "Interrogation protocol" (original records are in the State Archives of the Vinnytsia region, f. R-196, op. 1).
88. USHMM, RG 31.075, 197 "Information leaflet of EVOMS" (original in the State Archive of the Khmielnitsky Province, Derzhavniy arkhiv Khmielnitskoy oblasti, f. R-6193, op. 12, d. 27360, l. 92).

89. USHMM, RG 31.075, 133 "Interrogation protocol" (original in the State Archive of the Khmielnitsky Province, Derzhavniy arkhiv Khmielnitskoy oblasti, f. R-6193, op. 12, d. 27360, l. 48).
90. Gitelman, *Jewish Nationality and Soviet Politics*, 286–291.
91. West, *Struggles of a Generation*, 142, 144.
92. Yitshak Rabinovich, *Me-moskva ad yerushalayim: Ha-maavak ha-yehudi ha-leumi bi-Verit ha-Mo'atsot*, Jerusalem, n.p., 1957.
93. West, *Struggles of a Generation*, 144.
94. Ibid., 144–145. West himself was arrested at the event.
95. Ibid., 140.
96. Ibid., 141.
97. CZA, F30, A. Rafaeli-Zenzipper Collection, file 1358, 2, 1, "Nahum Goldin."
98. Ibid., 1, 3, 5.
99. Ibid., 6–7. See also CZA, F30, A. Rafaeli-Zenzipper Collection, file 1358, 2, ll. 8–9 (EVOSM member Lev Tsvik questionnaire).
100. Galili and Morozov, *Exiled to Palestine*, 1. Minus towns were located far from the larger cities where Jews usually lived, excluding, among others, Moscow, Leningrad, Kyiv, and Kharkiv.
101. Substitution immigration had a precedent: in 1922, the Soviets forced imprisoned Mensheviks to leave the country, and in 1923, they did the same with intellectuals who criticized the regime. Approximately thirteen hundred Zionists received substitution for Palestine. But other Jews who were not Zionist activists reached Palestine during the 1920s, including families from Central Asia and the Caucasus and Chasidim.
102. "Ekaterina Peshkova," in West, *Beyn yeush le-tikvah*, 67, 95–97, 113, 165–166, 198, including reference to Zionist political prisoners who thanked Peshkova for advocating for them.
103. See, in particular, Ziva Galili, "The Soviet Experience of Zionism: Importing Soviet Political Culture to Palestine," *Journal of Israeli History, Politics, Society, Culture* 24, no. 1, 2005, 1–33. The JDC also contributed financially to support the Zionist political prisoners; see JDC, Collection 21/32, folder 565 (cable from Rosen July 1, 1930 to Joint NY).
104. West, *Struggles of a Generation*, 184–185.
105. Kozerod, *Jewish Women in Ukraine*, 55.
106. Galili and Morozov, *Exiled to Palestine*, 16–18.
107. Ibid., 78; West, *Beyn yeush le-tikvah*, 15.
108. Galili and Morozov, *Exiled to Palestine*, 79. See also "Eliezer Isakin," in West, *Beyn yeush le-tikvah*, 29.
109. On Shira Gorshman, see Faith Jones, "Borrowed Shoes: Shira Gorshman's Politics of Literature," in *Women Writers of Yiddish Literature: Critical Essays*, ed. Rosemary Horowitz, Jefferson, NC: McFarland, 2015, 71–74. Her memoirs, *In di shpurn fun Gdud Ha-avodah*, were published in 1998 in Israel.
110. "Memorandum of A. Merezhin, Central Bureau of the Evsektsiia to the Politburo," RGASPI, f, 445, op. 1, d. 119, ll. 120–121, quoted in Galili and Marozov,

Exiled to Palestine, 86–88. The Evsektsiia's fear of an alliance between anti-Soviet forces that could weaken its work on the Jewish street was not entirely unfounded. One case in point was the 1921 agreement between the Revisionist Zionist leader Vladimir Jabotinsky and the leader of the short-lived Ukrainian state, Symon Petliura: after the Red Army's victory in the civil war, united by their anticommunism, Jabotinsky and Petliura vowed to bring together an army of Ukrainian exiled expatriates and Jewish soldiers to fight against Bolshevik power in Ukraine.

111. Clubs and even streets named after Ber Borochov existed in several towns and cities in the Soviet Union, including Moscow and Kyiv.
112. Zand, "Notes on the Culture of the Non-Ashkenazi Jewish Communities," 408.
113. Bemporad, *Becoming Soviet Jews*, 47.
114. See Baruch Gurevitz, "The Liquidation of the Last Independent Party in the Soviet Union," *Canadian Slavonic Papers* 18, no. 2, 1976, 178–186.
115. Szajkowski, *Jews, Wars, and Communism*, vol. 1, 406.
116. Galili and Morozov, *Exiled to Palestine*, 9. The class wing of Ha-shomer ha-tsayr continued to operate for longer than any other youth group, with six thousand members by mid-1927.
117. See, for instance, Rozin, *Mayn veg aheym*, 96–97, 130–131, 133.
118. On the Birobidzhan project, see Weinberg, *Stalin's Forgotten Zion*; and Gennady Estraikh, *The History of Birobidzhan: Building a Soviet Jewish Homeland in Siberia*, London: Bloomsbury, 2023.
119. "Suppression of Judaism and Zionism in Russia Condemned and Plea Made to End Policy of Silence About," Jewish Telegraphic Agency, December 9–10, 1929.

5. "DOWN WITH THE SABBATH"

1. Ilia Ehrenburg, "Burnaia zhizn Lazika Roitshvanetsa," in *Neobychainye pokhozhdenia: Proza*, edited by B. Ia. Frezinskii, St. Petersburg: Kristall, 2001, 948.
2. Daniel Peris, *Storming the Heavens: The Soviet League of the Militant Godless*, Ithaca, NY: Cornell University Press, 1998.
3. Victoria Smolkin, *A Sacred Space Is Never Empty: A History of Soviet Atheism*, Princeton, NJ: Princeton University Press, 2018, 4.
4. On these and other strains within the Jewish communities of Russia, see, for example, Israel Sosis, *Di sotsial-ekonomishe lage fun di Ruslendishe yidn in der ershter helft fun 19tn yorhundert*, Petrograd: Hevrat mefitse haskalah be-Israel, 1919; *Di geshikhte fun di yidishe gezelshaftlekhe shtrebungen in Rusland in XIX y.h.*, Minsk: Folkombild fun Vaysrusland tsentral yidish bildung-biuro, 1929; Raphael Mahler, *Hasidism and the Jewish Enlightenment: Their Confrontation in Galicia and Poland in the First Half of the Nineteenth Century*, Philadelphia: Jewish Publication Society of America, 1985; Stanislawsky, *For Whom Do I Toil?*; and Olga Litvak, *Conscription and the Search for Modern Russian Jewry*, Bloomington: Indiana University Press, 2006.

5. Olga Sobolevskaia and Vladimir Gancharov, *Evrei Grodnenshchiny: Zhizn do katastrofy*, Donetsk: Nordpress, 2005, 233.
6. The tsarist regime operated as a confessional state until its demise, relying on religious affiliation as the main criterion to document individuals as part of a larger collective group. The religious category was used to draw up censuses, passports, and vital statistics records, as well as "to regulate morality and administer local organs of government, welfare, and education." Eugene M. Avrutin, *Jews and the Imperial State: Identification Politics in Tsarist Russia*, Ithaca, NY: Cornell University Press, 2010, 10. On religious categories and identification politics in the Russian state, see Robert Crews, "Empire and the Confessional State: Islam and Religious Politics in Nineteenth-Century Russia," *American Historical Review* 108, 2003, 50–83.
7. On the Bolsheviks' persecution of church leaders, bishops, and clergy, see Lev Regelson, *Tragediia Russkoi tservki, 1917–1945*, Paris: YMCA Press, 1977; and Anatoli Levitin and Vadim Shavrov, *Ocherki po istorii Russkoi tserkovnoy smuty*, 3 vols., Kusnacht: Institut Glaube in der 2 Welt, 1978. See also Gregory L. Freeze, *Gubitel'noe blagochestie: Rossiiskaia pravoslavnaia tserkov' i padenie imperii*, St. Petersburg: Izdatel'stvo Evropeiskogo Universiteta, 2019; and Gregory L. Freeze, "Churching Russian History: Orthodoxy in the Great War and Revolution," in *Religion and the Russian Revolution of 1917: Conflicts, Encounters, and Transformations*, ed. Nadia Kizenko and Francesca Silano, Bloomington: Indiana University Press, forthcoming.
8. Vladimir Lenin, "The Attitude of the Workers' Party to Religion," *Proletary*, no. 45, May 13, 1909. This article is also the source of the quotation in the section title.
9. Peris, *Storming the Heavens*, 25. For the full text of the decree, see James Bunyan and H. H. Fisher, *The Bolshevik Revolution, 1917–1918: Documents and Materials*, Stanford, CA: Stanford University Press; London: H. Milford, Oxford University Press, 1934, 590–591.
10. Peris, *Storming the Heavens*, 25.
11. Estimates of the number of clergy killed between 1918 and 1921 range between 1,434 and 9,000. Edward E. Roslof, *Red Priests: Renovationism, Russian Orthodoxy, and Revolution, 1905–1946*, Bloomington: Indiana University Press, 2002, 27.
12. Szajkowski, *Jews, Wars, and Communism*, vol. 1, 393.
13. Glennys Young, *Power and the Sacred in Revolutionary Russia: Religious Activists in the Village*, University Park: Penn State University Press, 2008, 96–99, 113–116.
14. Sean McMeekin, *History's Greatest Heist: The Looting of Russia by the Bolsheviks*, New Haven, CT: Yale University Press, 2009, 83. The heading for this section comes from The title is from the translation of the Russian title of M. (Ester) Frumkina's *Doloi ravvinov!*, Moscow: Krasnaia nov, 1923.
15. M. M. Sheinman, *O ravvinakh i sinagogakh*, Moscow: Bezbozhnik, 1927, 5–7. See also David Fishman, "'The Kingdom on Earth Is Like the Kingdom of

Heaven': Rabbinic Reactions to Jewish Radicalism in Russia," *Let the Old Make Way for the New: Studies in the Social and Cultural History of East European Jewry Presented to Immanuel Etkes*, ed. David Assaf and Ada Rapoport-Albert, vol. 2, Jerusalem: Shazar Center, 2009, 227–259.

16. Sheinman, *O ravvinakh i sinagogakh*, 8–9.
17. Ibid., 22–23.
18. Ibid., 13.
19. See Sholem Dovber Levin, *Toldot Chabad be-Rusiah ha-Soviyetit*, Brooklyn, NY: Kehot Publication Society, 1989.
20. Tcherikower, *In der tkufe fun revolutsye*, 346.
21. Gitelman, *Jewish Nationality and Soviet Politics*, 239–240; Oleksander Iakovich Naiman, *Evreiski partiy ta obednannia Ukrainy, 1917–1925*, Kyiv: Natsionalna akademia nauk Ukrainy, Institut politichnikh i etnonatsionalnikh doslidzhen, 1998, 171. See also A. I. Zhitnik, *Di yidn in Sovetn-Rusland*, Cleveland: Independent, 1925.
22. Gitelman, *Jewish Nationality and Soviet Politics*, 239.
23. Mordechai Altshuler, "The Rabbi of Homel's Trial in 1922," *Michael* 6, 1980, 12.
24. JDC, Collection 21/32, USSR Cultural and Religious 1921–1926, folder 472 (copy of the Soviet Constitution).
25. For an autobiographical memoir of the 1922 trial, see *Der morgen zhurnal*, November 19, 1923; and Altshuler, "Rabbi of Homel's Trial," 9–61.
26. Altshuler, "Rabbi of Homel's Trial," 28–29.
27. Ibid., 15.
28. Ibid., 17–18.
29. *Detroit Jewish Chronicle*, May 4, 1923; "Rabbi Eisenstadt under Arrest," Jewish Telegraphic Agency, April 27, 1923, www.jta.org; "Homel Rabbis to Face Soviet Justice," Jewish Telegraphic Agency, April 26, 1923.
30. On protests and clashes among Jews as result of the antireligious campaigns, see Bemporad, *Becoming Soviet Jews*, 112–113; and A. A. Gershuni, *Yahadut be-Rusiayh ha-Soviyetit: Le-korot redifot ha-daat*, Jerusalem: Mosad ha-Rav Kuk, 1961, 56–64.
31. See Zeltser, *Evrei sovetskoi provintsii*, 232–244.
32. GAMO, f. 37, op. 1, d. 224, ll. 97, 99 (Excerpts of meeting protocols, Evsektsiia, 1922). For more on the clash see, Bemporad, *Becoming Soviet Jews*, 112–113.
33. Natsionalnyi arkhiv Respubliki Belarus (NARB), f. 4, op. 1, d. 586, ll. 33–35 (Petition to the Central Executive Committee of the Communist Party of Belorussia, April 7, 1922). On recent scholarship on petitions in the context of totalitarian regimes, see, for example, Thomas Pegelow Kaplan, "Reinterpreting Jewish Petitioning Practices during the Shoah: Contestation, Transnational Space, and Survival," *Journal of Holocaust Research* 35, no. 4, 2021, 306–325.
34. Quoted in David E. Fishman, "Yiddish and the Formation of a Secular Jewish National Identity," in *Jews and Muslims in the Russian Empire and the Soviet Union*, ed. Franziska Davies, Martin Schulze Wessel, and Michael Brenner, Göttingen: Vandenhoeck and Ruprecht, 2015, 109.

35. See Elissa Bemporad, "Defying Authority in the Pale: The Making of Soviet Jewish Rituals and the Emergence of Folk Legitimacy," in *Reappraisals and New Studies of the Modern Jewish Experience: Essays in Honor of Robert M. Seltzer*, ed. Brian M. Smollett and Christian Wiese, Leiden: Brill, 2015, 67–68.
36. Ibid., 89. The shift to the Sunday rest was met with less opposition in those enterprises with a large proportion of workers who were members of the Communist Party.
37. GAMO, f. 37, op. 1, d. 307, l. 6 (Report, Workers' collective, city of Minsk, 1923).
38. GAMO, f. 37, op. 1, d. 308, l. 4 (Report, Workers in private enterprises, city of Minsk, 1923–1924).
39. *Arbeter shtime, Golos pratsi*, no. 1, January 1924, 1.
40. JDC, Collection 21/32, folder 526 ("The Forward, To the Soil Movement of Jews in Soviet Russia," report by Louis Fischer), 33–34. This report was published in the *Jewish Tribune and Hebrew Standard*, November 20, 1925, and the *American Jewish Weekly*, December 4, 1925.
41. Ryback, *On the Jewish Field of the Ukraina*, 21. A member of the Central Committee of the Kultur-lige in Kyiv after 1917, Rybak helped establish a formal department of art for the Kultur-lige; he was active in the Jewish Theater Studio in Kyiv, established in 1919, and later in Moscow and in Kharkiv, where in 1925 he designed stage sets for the Yiddish theater. For more on Rybak, see Seth L. Wolitz, "The Jewish National Art Renaissance in Russia," in *Tradition and Revolution: The Jewish Renaissance in Russian Avant-Garde Art, 1912–1928*, ed. Ruth Apter-Gabriel, Jerusalem: Israel Museum, 1987, 23–42; and Sabine Koller, "Anti-Jewish Violence, Jewish Art and Literature: The Pogroms of 1919 and the Kultur-lige," in *Building Modern Jewish Culture: The Yiddish Kultur-Lige*, ed. Harriet L. Murav, Gennady Estraikh, and Myroslav Shkandrij, Oxford, UK: Legenda, 2023, 122–140.
42. Gennady Estraikh, "From 'Green Fields' to 'Red Fields': Peretz Hirschbein's Soviet Sojourn, 1928–29," *Jews in Russia and Eastern Europe* 56, 2006, 69.
43. Charles E. Hoffman, *Red Shtetl: The Survival of a Jewish Town under Soviet Communism*, New York: American Jewish Joint Distribution Committee, 2002, 71.
44. Estraikh, "From 'Green Fields' to 'Red Fields,'" 69.
45. JDC, Collection 21/32, folder 475 ("Letter by Rabbi J. Schneersohn to Cyrus Adler from Riga, dated April 16, 1928"), 3.
46. NARB, f. 4, op. 1, d. 703, l. 80 (Resolution, Belorussian People's Commissariat of Labor, 1923). A second resolution passed by the Commissar of Labor in January 1928 reduced to seven the total number of official religious holidays (including Christian and Jewish holidays) that workers in the Belorussian SSR were allowed to observe. Besides the religious holidays (and Sundays), Soviet citizens did not work during the seven official revolutionary holidays. Those who did not wish to observe the religious holidays had the right to other days of rest in their lieu or could work and receive a bonus salary.

47. "Ale shuln in Moskve iberful Yom-Kiper," *Undzer ekspres*, October 2, 1928, 3.
48. "Der shvartser rov oder di helishe sreyfe," *Der apikoyres*, no. 1, 1923, 18–19. For a detailed discussion of this special issue and its use for the struggle against the celebration of Rosh Hashanah and Yom Kippur, see Shternshis, *Soviet and Kosher*, 20–26.
49. "Der shvartser rov oder di helishe sreyfe," 19.
50. Sheinman, *O ravvinakh i sinagogakh*, 2.
51. See David E. Fishman, "Rabbi Joseph Isaac Schneersohn: The Making of a Jewish Religious Leader in the USSR," in Kizenko and Silano, *Religion and the Russian Revolution of 1917*; and David E. Fishman, "Preserving Tradition in the Land of Revolution: The Religious Leadership of Soviet Jewry 1917–1930," in *The Uses of Tradition: Jewish Continuity in the Modern Era*, ed. Jack Wertheimer, New York: Jewish Theological Seminary of America, 1992, 85–118.
52. Fishman, "Rabbi Joseph Isaac Schneersohn."
53. Ibid.
54. See Ester Frumkina, *Doloi ravvinov!*, Moscow: Krasnaia nov, 1923, 29.
55. Fishman "To Our Brethren Abroad," 139–167.
56. Levin, *Toldot Chabad*, 66–70.
57. Zand, "Notes on the Culture of the Non-Ashkenazi Jewish Communities," 401.
58. S. Levin, *Toldot Chabad*, 66–70.
59. See *Shvut: Studies in Russian and East European Jewish History and Culture*, nos. 23–24, 2000, 134.
60. Fishman, "Rabbi Joseph Isaac Schneersohn."
61. Ibid.
62. Engelstein, *Russia in Flames*.
63. See Betsalel Shif, "Zabveniiu ne podlezhit," *Lechaim*, November 2004, https://lechaim.ru.
64. Frumkina, *Doloi ravvinov!*, 11–24.
65. Ibid., 24–41.
66. Bentsion Katz, "Di sore-bas-toyvim fun der rusishe revolutsye: Tsum shlus fun Ester Frumkins karyere," *Der morgen zhurnal*, February 13, 1931.
67. On the emergence of a "Judeo-Bolshevism" during the civil war, see Bemporad, *Legacy of Blood*, 5–12.
68. Gershuni, *Yahadut be-Rusiayh ha-Soviyetit*, 63.
69. On Frumkin's attack on religion, see Gitelman, *Jewish Nationality and Soviet Politics*, 309–312.
70. Peris, *Storming the Heavens*, 27.
71. Ibid., 125. By 1927, the number of synagogues in Ukraine had decreased by 23 percent; the number of Orthodox churches had also decreased by 23 percent. See Sheinman, *O ravvinakh i sinagogakh*, 3.
72. For a discussion of "speaking Bolshevik," see Stephen Kotkin, *Magnetic Mountain: Stalinism as a Civilization*, Berkeley: University of California Press, 1995, 198–237.

73. On the anti–Yom Kippur balls, see, for example, Rebecca E. Margolis, "A Tempest in Three Teapots: Yom Kippur Balls in London, New York and Montreal," *Canadian Jewish Studies / Études Juives Canadiennes*, 9, 2001, 38–84.
74. *Der apikoyres*, no. 1, 1923, 22.
75. This musical, by Yitskhok Nozhik, a Polish Yiddish playwright, was very popular in Vilna at the time. See "Fun Vilner yidishn teater," *Teater un kunst*, May 19, 1923, 28.
76. K. Bernard, "Reyzele dem rebns, Gorteater," *Rabochee ekho*, no. 10, 1923, 3.
77. On antireligious culture, see Shternshis, *Soviet and Kosher*, 1–43.
78. Gennady Estraikh, "Soviet Dreams of a Cultural Exile," in *Joseph Opatoshu: A Yiddish Writer between Europe and America*, ed. Sabine Koller, Gennady Estraikh, and Mikhail Krutikov, Oxford, UK: Legenda, 2017, 35–54.
79. See Bemporad, *Becoming Soviet Jews*, 119–123.
80. Estraikh, "Soviet Dreams of Cultural Exile," 42.
81. For a list of Minsk yeshivas and heders and the number of students, see JDC, Collection 21/32, file 476 ("Report of the Accomplishments of the Rabbinical Board in Russia during 5688").
82. GAMO, f. 37, op. 1, d. 307, l. 21 (Wall-newspaper: Circumcision). The exact date does not appear in the document.
83. Ibid.
84. Peris, *Storming the Heavens*, 9.
85. E. Yaroslavskii, *Razvernutym frontom: O zadachakh i metodakh antireligioznoy propagandy*. Moscow: Bezbozhnik, 1929, 35.
86. Ibid., 37.
87. Sheinman, *O ravvinakh i sinagogakh*, 13.
88. Bemporad, *Becoming Soviet Jews*, 133–143.
89. *Bezbozhnik u stanka*, no. 1, January 1933.
90. JDC, Collection 21/32, folder 475 ("Letter from Riga, dated September 10, 1928, to Cyrus Adler from Rabbi Schneersohn"), and folder 476 ("Memorandum of Interview with Rabbi Schneersohn and his secretary, Rabbi Gourary, by Dr. Adler and Mr. Wiernik, October 9, 1929").
91. On Jewish communists and circumcision, see Bemporad, *Becoming Soviet Jews*, 137–143; and Joshua Rothenberg, *The Jewish Religion in the Soviet Union*, New York: Ktav, 1971, 146–149. On the limits to women's upward mobility, see Bemporad, *Becoming Soviet Jews*, 154–158.
92. "The Soviet Court Sentences Mohel to Imprisonment," Jewish Telegraphic Agency, May 27, 1927. In this case, the midwife too was sentenced to prison.
93. According to one source, 60 percent of all Jewish children in Moscow underwent circumcision in the late 1920s. See Hersh David Nomberg, "Fun mayn rayze in Rusland: Notitsn fun a tog-bukh," *Der moment*, no. 104, May 6, 1927, 5.
94. *Bezbozhnik u stanka*, no. 1, 1926, 14. On punishment in the form of fines for family members who had a newborn baby circumcised unbeknownst to the parents, see, "Soviet Court Fines Grandparents for Circumcising Child Despite

Parents," Jewish Telegraphic Agency, November 7, 1927; and "Grandfather Fined for Circumcising Grandson in Russian Town," Jewish Telegraphic Agency, January 27, 1929.

95. Tcherikower, *In der tkufe fun revolutsye*, 391–392. See also YIVO, Tcherikower Archives, RG 80, folder 735, folios 62296–62297 (Decree by the GubProd-Kom, 1920).
96. "Acute Shechita Problem in White Russia's Capital," Jewish Telegraphic Agency, August 13, 1928.
97. JDC, Collection 21/32, folder 476 ("Memorandum of Interview with Rabbi Schneersohn and his secretary, Rabbi Gourary, by Dr. Adler and Mr. Wiernik, October 9, 1929"), 1–2.
98. "Vi azoy me makht koshere yidishe maykholim," *Der kustar*, June 15, 1929, 9.
99. JDC, Collection 21/32, folder 476 ("Memorandum of Interview with Rabbi Schneersohn and his secretary, Rabbi Gourary, by Dr. Adler and Mr. Wiernik, October 9, 1929") 1–2.
100. Hoffman, *Red Shtetl*, 71.
101. On the special license issued by Soviet authorities to the *shochtim* and on the reasons and excuses to rescind the license, including evasion of taxes, violation of sanitary regulations, and so on, see Leonid Smilovitsky, *Jewish Life in Belarus under Stalin: The Final Decade of the Stalin Regime (1944–1953)*, Budapest: Central European University Press, 2014, 160.
102. TsDAVO, f. 5, op. 3, d. 335, ll. 109–109ob (Complaint to the city election committee by Odesa shochtim, February 16, 1927).
103. See Robin Judd, "The Politics of Beef: Animal Advocacy and the Kosher Butchering Debates in Germany," *Jewish Social Studies* 10, no. 1, Fall 2003, 126–127.
104. TsDAVO, f. 5, op. 3, d. 335, ll. 109–109ob (Complaint to the city election committee by Odesa shochtim, February 16, 1927).
105. "Women Strike as Protest in Stop on Kosher Meat Sale," Jewish Telegraphic Agency, April 29, 1929.
106. *Bezbozhnik u stanka*, no. 2, 1926, 15.
107. *Bezbozhnik u stanka*, no. 12, 1925, 9.
108. Sore Kahan, "Tsum 8tn Mart," *Oktyabr*, no. 56, March 8, 1930, 4.
109. Sheinman, *O ravvinakh i synaogogakh*, 45. The section title is from Diana Dumitru, *The State, Antisemitism, and Collaboration in the Holocaust: The Borderlands of Romania and the Soviet Union*, New York: Cambridge University Press, 2016, 121.
110. Sheinman, *O ravvinakh i synaogogakh*, 20–21.
111. See Robert Weinberg, "Demonizing Judaism in the Soviet Union During the 1920s," *Slavic Review* 67, no. 1, Spring 2008, 120–153.
112. Bemporad, *Legacy of Blood*, 91–96. According to Weinberg ("Demonizing Judaism"), the Jewish god Jehova was depicted with inhuman, bizarre, and bestial features such as a single eye and a nose made out of a fist. While other deities, like Allah and the Holy Spirit, were all depicted somewhat comically, the Jewish

God had an inhuman physiognomy. This portrayal of Judaism drew on antisemitic tropes and motifs.

113. Weinberg, "Demonizing Judaism," 133–134.

114. Sheinman, *O ravvinakh i sinagogakh*, 21–22, 31.

115. "Soviets Confiscate Jewish Ritual Objects for Junk," Jewish Telegraphic Agency, February 18, 1930.

116. See Dimitry Pospielovsky, *A History of Soviet Atheism in Theory and Practice, and the Believer*, vol. 1, *A History of Marxist-Leninist Atheism and Soviet Anti-Religious Policies*, New York: St. Martin's, 1987.

117. "Synagogues Now Converted into Apartment Houses in Russian Towns," Jewish Telegraphic Agency, July 11, 1929.

118. "Odeser proletaryer in kultur-marsh kegn religye," *Shtern*, April 30, 1929, 3.

119. "Problem of Selling Kosher Products Bothers Ukraine Department of Commerce," Jewish Telegraphic Agency, December 18, 1929. According to the Department of Commerce in Ukraine, by December 1929, thirty-five million chickens were killed each year in the Ukrainian republic for kosher slaughtering. On family conflicts associated with Jewish dietary laws and kashrut, see Anna Shternshis, "Salo on Challah: Soviet Jews' Experience of Food in the 1920s–1950s,'" in *Jews and Their Foodways*, ed. Anat Helman, Studies in Contemporary Jewry 28, New York: Oxford University Press, 2016, 10–27.

120. TsDAGO, f. 1, op. 20, d. 2994, ll. 23–23ob ("Memorandum about the Easter Anti-Religious Carnival, April 1929)".

121. Ibid.

122. Ibid., l. 23ob.

123. The tensions among Jews under the Soviets may have also built on the tradition of intra-Jewish violence between various Hasidic groups (in particular against the Bratslav Hasidim), which was strong in this area. See David Assaf, *Untold Tales of the Hasidim: Crisis and Discontent in the History of Hasidism*, Waltham, MA: Brandeis University Press, 2010, especially chapter 4.

124. "Fun gerikht: Der rov yadakhas mit di spekuliantn," *Shtern*, September 14, 1928, 4.

125. On the pressure on Soviet authorities by foreign Jewish leaders to free the rabbis, see JDC, Collection 21/32, folder 477 (Cable from Vilna. February 17, 1930 to JDC NY; Telegram of February 21, 1930, signed by Schneersohn from Chicago to JDC; and Memorandum on requests to Dr. Rosen on behalf of Rabbis in Russia, August 20, 1930).

6. OLD WORLDS, NEW WORLDS

1. Robert J. Kaiser, *The Geography of Nationalism in Russia and the USSR*, Princeton, NJ: Princeton University Press, 1994, 67.

2. Marcelline J. Hutton, *Russian and West European Women, 1860–1939: Dreams, Struggles, and Nightmares*, Lanham, MD: Rowman and Littlefield, 2001, 49.

3. Peter Kenez, "Lenin's Concept of Culture," *History of European Ideas*, 11, 1989, 359–363.
4. Vladimir Lenin, "On Cooperation," *Pravda*, no. 115–116, May 26–27, 1923, www.marxists.org.
5. Robert F. Byrnes, "Creating the Soviet Historical Profession, 1917–1934," *Slavic Review* 50, no. 2, 1991, 299.
6. Sheila Fitzpatrick, "The 'Soft' Line on Culture and Its Enemies: Soviet Cultural Policy, 1922–1927," *Slavic Review* 33, no. 2, June 1974, 267.
7. John Barber, *Soviet Historians in Crisis, 1928–1932*, London: Palgrave Macmillan, 1981, 14.
8. From 1917 to 1919, the city produced 60 percent of all Hebrew books published in Russia and Ukraine. The loss of Vilna and Warsaw, which following World War I became part of Independent Poland, had an impact on Odesa's ascent as center of Hebrew book publishing. On Odesa as a Jewish cultural center during the nineteenth century, see Zipperstein, *Jews of Odessa.*
9. On the rise of Saint Petersburg as a center of Jewish culture, see Nathans, *Beyond the Pale*, in particular part 3.
10. OPE was founded in 1863 during a period of liberalization. It remained active until it was forced to close in 1929 under the Bolshevik government's program to abolish independent political and cultural institutions.
11. Mikhail Beizer, "Dubnov's St. Petersburg," in *A Missionary for History: Essays in Honor of Simon Dubnov*, ed. Kristi Groberg and Avraham Greenbaum, Minnesota: University of Minnesota, 1998, 83.
12. The new status of political capitals of Soviet republics turned cities like Kharkiv, capital of the Ukrainian Soviet Socialist Republic until 1934, into vibrant centers of Jewish culture also. Thousands of cultural activists, teachers, and writers moved from Kyiv to Kharkiv to join the city's growing Jewish population (which reached 115,800, or 17.7 percent of the total population, in 1933) and to contribute to the different spheres of Yiddish culture, including education, literature, theater, and art.
13. Danil Charny, *A yortsendlik aza, 1914–1924*, New York: CYCO Bikher farlag, 1943, 293–294.
14. Ibid., 213.
15. GARF, f. 9530, op. 1, d. 61, ll. 1–2 ("Jewish People's University, 1918–1922").
16. See, for example, ibid., ll. 2–3, 5, 8.
17. Ibid., l. 8.
18. Alfred A. Greenbaum, *Jewish Scholarship and Scholarly Institutions in Soviet Russia, 1918–1953*, Jerusalem: Hebrew University of Jerusalem, 1978, 10.
19. I. J. Singer, *Nay-Rusland: Bilder fun a rayze*, Vilna: Kletskin, 1928.
20. Natan Meir, *Kiev, Jewish Metropolis: A History, 1859–1914*, Bloomington: Indiana University Press, 2010, 222–223.
21. Gennady Estraikh, "From Yehupets Jargonists to Kiev Modernists: The Rise of a Yiddish Literary Centre, 1880s–1914," *East European Jewish Affairs* 30, no. 1, 2000, 17–38.

22. Dovid Bergelson and Der Nister left Kyiv for Moscow in 1920 and then moved abroad to Kaunas and then Berlin, before returning to the Soviet Union in 1926 and 1934, respectively.
23. On the Kultur-lige as a complex cultural phenomenon, see Moss, *Jewish Renaissance in the Russian Revolution.*
24. Harriet L. Murav, Gennady Estraikh, and Myroslav Shkandrij, introduction to *Building Modern Jewish Culture: The Yiddish Kultur-Lige*, ed. Harriet L. Murav, Gennady Estraikh, and Myroslav Shkandrij, Oxford, UK: Legenda, 2023, 6.
25. Gennady Estraikh, "The Yiddish Kultur-Lige," in *Modernism in Kyiv: Jubilant Experimentation*, ed. Irena Makaryk and Virlana Tkacz, Toronto: University of Toronto Press, 2010, 209.
26. Zand, "Notes on the Culture of the Non-Ashkenazi Jewish Communities," 391.
27. Ibid., 401.
28. Ibid., 392–394.
29. Ibid., 395.
30. Ibid., 385.
31. Ibid., 382.
32. Mordechai Altshuler, "Georgian Jewish Culture under the Soviet Regime," *East European Jewish Affairs* 5, no. 2, 1975, 22.
33. Martin, *Affirmative Action Empire.*
34. Quoted ibid., 75.
35. Belarusian, Ukrainian, and Yiddish languages and literatures all faced analogous problems of finding their voices and facing the dominant Russian and Polish literatures and languages, with their longer and established traditions. By embracing Ukrainian and Belarusian, some Jewish writers and poets made an anticolonial choice. See Yohanan Petrovsky-Shtern, *The Anti-Imperial Choice: The Making of the Ukrainian Jew*, New Haven, CT: Yale University Press, 2009.
36. Vital Zajka and Z. Gimpelevich, "Zmitrok Biadulia: A Belarusian Jewish Writer Who Was Loved by Many," *Tsaytshrift* 8, no. 3, 2013, 131–159.
37. Quoted in Daniel Soyer, "Back to the Future: American Jews Visit the Soviet Union in the 1920s and 1930s," *Jewish Social Studies* 6, no. 3, 2000, 132.
38. "Evreiskaia zhizn v SSSR," *Tribuna*, no. 9, 1927, 21.
39. Avraham Novershtern, "Hundert yor Dovid Bergelson: Materialn tsu zayn lebn un shafn," *Di goldene keyt* 115, 1985, 44–58. This same faith in the great potential of the Soviet center for the future of Yiddish literature was echoed by many who did not settle there, including, for instance, the Polish-born Yiddish novelist Joseph Opatoshu. After visiting the country in 1928, Opatoshu compared the Soviet Union to the United States (which had a shrinking Yiddish readership) and to Poland (which had readers but not enough Yiddish writers). Opatoshu agreed with Bergelson: "In no other country does Yiddish literature have such possibilities and prospects as in the Soviet Union. Here every stone works in favor of Yiddish literature." Quoted in Soyer, "Back to the Future," 139–140.
40. Z.B., "Evreiskaia zhizn v SSSR," *Tribuna*, nos. 4–5, 1927, 40.
41. "Evreiskaia zhizn v SSSR," *Tribuna*, no. 8, 1927, 24.

42. "Evreiskaia zhizn v SSSR," *Tribuna*, nos. 1–2, 1928, 36.
43. Soyer, "Back to the Future," 136. This was, for instance, the case of the veteran of the revolutionary movement in Russia the Yiddish writer Morris Winchevsky, who upon traveling to Moscow and other cities of Belorussia and Ukraine was welcomed with great fanfare by crowds of workers, students, party activists, and journalists; organizations were named after him, and his poems were published in different Soviet Yiddish publications.
44. "Evreiskaia zhizn v SSSR," *Tribuna*, nos. 1–2, 1928, 36.
45. Ester Rozental-Shnayderman, *Af vegn un umvegn: Zikhroynes, geshenishn, perzenlekhkaytn*, vol. 1, Tel Aviv: Havatselet, 1972, 354.
46. Ibid.
47. "Evreiskaia zhizn v SSSR," *Tribuna*, no. 9, 1927, 21.
48. Z.B., "Evreiskaia zhizn v SSSR," *Tribuna*, nos. 4–5, 1927, 40.
49. Shame Tsimring, "Git undz a verkshtat," *Yung gvardie*, April 12, 1929, 6.
50. NARB, f. 42, op. 1, d. 1132, ll. 39–42 (Yiddish schools in Minsk province, 1921–1922).
51. "Kulturnaia khronika," *Tribuna*, no. 12, 1928, 23. For example, in 1928, in the Russian city of Pskov, the seven-year Yiddish school was named after the Yiddish cultural activist Shimon Dimanshtein. See "Evreiskaia zhizn v SSSR," *Tribuna*, nos. 1–2, 1928, 35.
52. See Solomon Schwarz, *The Jews in the Soviet Union*, Syracuse, NY: Syracuse University Press, 1951, 136.
53. GAMO, f. 12, op. 1, d. 851, l. 4 (Report about education and cultural work among the Jewish population, 1927–1929).
54. See GAMO, f. 320, op. 1, d. 599, l. 18 (Enrollment figures, Yiddish schools, Minsk, 1927–1929).
55. "Dos yidishe lebn in soviet-rusland," *Haynt*, November 17, 1925, 4.
56. Z.B., "Evreiskaia zhizn v SSSR," *Tribuna*, nos. 4–5, 1927, 40.
57. NARB, f. 42, op. 1, d. 1632, ll. 57–58, 60 (Protocols of the meeting of the inspectors for Jewish culture BSSR, August 24–26, 1924).
58. GAMO, f. 12, op. 1, d. 562, l. 53, quoted in Bemporad, *Becoming Soviet Jews*, 93.
59. H. Kazakevich, "Der ershter alfarbandisher tsuzamenfor fun yidishe kulturtuers 25.11–2.12 1924," *Di royte velt* 1 (1925): 28–29, quoted in Shternshis, *Soviet and Kosher*, xvi.
60. Ester Frumkin, "Der ershter alukrainisher tsuzamenfor fun idishe kultur-tuer II," *Der emes*, no. 119, June 13, 1922, 2–3, quoted in Faigan, "Annotated Bibliography," 210–211.
61. Ester Frumkin, "Vegn ort fun rusish in der idisher shul," *Der emes*, no. 210, September 30, 1922, 1, quoted in Faigan, "Annotated Bibliography," 218.
62. "Dos yidishe lebn in soviet-rusland," 4.
63. Bemporad, *Becoming Soviet Jews*, 131.
64. G. Yabrov, *Di yidishe literatur in frages, ufgabes un temes, a hilfbukh far di eltere grupn fun tsveytn kontsenter, far lerer, student fun pedtekhnikum un far shuln fun*

hekhern tip, Minsk: Vaysruslendisher melukhe-farlag, 1928, 36–37; *Program fun yidish un literatur far zibnyoriker shul mit metodishe briv tsu der program*, Minsk: Folkombild fun Vaysrusland tsentral yidish bildung-biuro, 1927, 5–7.

65. Y. Vurhaft, "Shovinistishe shtimungen tsvishn di yidishe kinder," *Yung gvardie*, April 19, 1929, 4.
66. Bemporad, *Becoming Soviet Jews*, 65.
67. "Evreiskaia zhizn v SSSR," *Tribuna*, no. 3, 1928, 12.
68. "Pamiati Mendele Mocher Sforim," *Tribuna*, no. 9, 1927, 24.
69. "Vegn 'zogmuk' in melukhishn teater," *Der Odeser arbeter*, no. 15, February 5, 1928, 14.
70. Kh. Zilberman, "Di Mendele fayerung in Odes," *Der Odeser arbeter*, no. 14, January 21, 1928, 17–18.
71. While the Mendele museum was the first Jewish museum established in the Soviet Union, other Jewish museums existed elsewhere in the country. See "Evreiskaia zhizn v SSSR," *Tribuna*, nos. 1–2, 1928, 35.
72. E. Adasov, "Muzei imeni Mendele Mocher Seforim," *Tribuna*, no. 7, May 1, 1928, 24; "Muzei imeni Mendele," *Tribuna*, no. 9, November 1927, 24. The museum operated throughout the interwar period. Most of its collections were destroyed during the war. On the Mendele museum and its fate during the 1930s and 1940s, see Marina Shcherbakova, "K voprosu o kontseptualnom razvitii evreiskogo muzeia i etnografii evreev na territorii Ukrainy v 1917–1941gg," *Judaic-Slavic Journal*, no. 1 (2), 2019, 44–79.
73. "Helft mit boyen dem Yidishn muzei in Odes," *Der Odeser arbeter*, nos. 6–7, September 1, 1927, 17. Calls to send artifacts or writings about the history and culture of the Jews in Ukraine were issued regularly; see "Tsu di yidishe arbetndike masn," *Der Odeser arbeter*, no. 13, January 1, 1928, 20.
74. The editor of a textbook for Yiddish schools published in Moscow at the end of the decade lamented the weak connection between Jewish students and works of Yiddish literature and recommended organizing literary excursions to the Mendele Museum in Odesa, as well as to the statues dedicated to Yiddish writers. In the footnote to this call for rapprochement, the author decried, "it's time already that we should have statues and memorials to Peretz, Sholem Aleichem, and Mendele." Cf. A. R. Tsvayg, *Muter shprakh in shul fun der ershter shtufe, metodishe hantbukh*, Moscow: Folkskomissariat far bildung fun RSFSR, tsentrale felker farlag fun FSSR, 1929, 62.
75. See Shternshis, *Kosher and Soviet*, 80, 110. Based on the drama by the Soviet Yiddish writer Aron Kushnirov, specially written for Belgoset, the play opened in Minsk on March 23, 1928, and was performed eleven times from 1928 to 1929. See Avraham Greenbaum, "The Belorussian State Jewish Theater in the Interwar Period," *Jews in Eastern Europe* 2, no. 42, Fall 2000, 66–67.
76. A Yiddish textbook used in the Soviet Yiddish schools of the Belorussian Soviet Republic included a detailed account of the 1902 events that led to Lekert's execution. He was described as an ideal hero. See K. Hodoshevitsh, Sh. Yofe, and M. Mogilnitski, *Undzer royte heym: Arbet-bukh af gezelshaftkentenish farn*

4tn lernyor, Moscow-Kharkov-Minsk: Tsentraler felker farlag fun FSSR, 1931, 56–58.

77. Bemporad, *Becoming Soviet Jews*, 67–69. On the Sovietization of a Bundist hero and its remodeling into a Soviet Jewish cultural hero, see also M. Rafes, "Pochemu my chestvuem pamiat Lekerta," *Tribuna*, nos. 4–5, 1927, 12–13.
78. On Lekert's statue, see Leon Dennen, *Where the Ghetto Ends: Jews in Soviet Russia*, New York: A. H. King, 1934, 145; Yakov Basin, *Bolshevizm i evrei: Belorussia, 1920-e*, Minsk: Baraskin, 2008, 229; and Yakov Basin, "Delo Girsha Lekerta (1902) i ego interpretatsiia v filme Belgoskino *Ego prevoskhoditelstvo*, 1927," *Belarus y XX stagoddzi*, no. 3, 2004, 34–45. Brazer crafted a number of sculptural portraits of leading figures in Jewish culture and art, among them the artist Y. Pen (1921, 1926), the Jewish actor Solomon Mikhoels (1926), and the Yiddish poet Izzy Kharik (1932).
79. Quoted in Soyer, "Back to the Future," 134.
80. *Prakticheskoe razreshenie natsionalnogo voprosa v Belorusskoi SSR*, Minsk: Izdanie tsentralnoi natsionalnoi komissii TsIK BSSR, 1927, 120–123.
81. Ibid., 134–135.
82. J. Lezman, *Fun Seydemenukhe biz Kalinindorf*, Kharkiv-Kyiv: Melukhishe natsmindfarlag bam prezidium fun Vutsik, 1932.
83. "Evreiskaia zhizn v SSSR," *Tribuna*, no. 9, 1928, 20.
84. TsDAVO, f. 413, op. 1, d. 10, l. 97 (p. 10) (Report of the central commission of national minorities by the VUTsIK from December 1, 1924 through April 1, 1925).
85. "Khronika," *Tribuna*, no. 9, 1928, 18.
86. Singer, *Nay-Rusland*, 32.
87. "Barshay Trial Opens in Minsk, Attracts Wide Attention in Russia," Jewish Telegraphic Agency, January 20, 1929.
88. TsDAVO, f. 413, op. 1, d. 10, l. 7 (p. 7) (Report on the activity of the central commission of national minorities by the VUTsIK 1925–1926).
89. Ibid., l. 40.
90. "Evreiskaia zhizn v SSSR," *Tribuna*, no. 12, 1928, 23.
91. "Ale politseilayt fun Berdichev muzn kenen yidish, a bafel," *Forverts*, May 26, 1927.
92. *Der Odeser arbeter*, nos. 6–7, September 1927.
93. On the Language Commission, see Ber Orshansky, "Di Yidishe opteylung fun Invayskult," *Af di vegn tsu der nayer shul*, nos. 7–8, 1927. On the creation of a Belarusian military terminology, see also Per Anders Rudling, *The Rise and Fall of Belarusian Nationalism, 1906–1931*, Pittsburgh: University of Pittsburgh Press, 2014. Incidentally, the same concern for a standardized writing system in Yiddish was voiced by the Belarusian activists, who faced similar challenges and solutions, often turning to Ukrainian terminology when it was missing in Belarusian.
94. David Shneer, *Yiddish and the Creation of Soviet Jewish Culture, 1918–1930*, Cambridge: Cambridge University Press, 2004, 108.

95. Ibid., 109.
96. Gitelman, *Century of Ambivalence*, 89.
97. On the impressive achievements of the Kultur-lige, see Moss, *Jewish Renaissance*, in particular 53–57, 71–72; and Murav, Estraikh, and Shkandrij, *Building Modern Jewish Culture*. In a way, the legacy of the work of Kultur-lige dominated Soviet Yiddish cultural life well into the 1980s.
98. Shneer, *Yiddish and the Creation of Soviet Jewish Culture*, 123–124.
99. Ibid., 29.
100. Ibid.
101. Z. Ostrovskii, "Evrei Dagestana," *Tribuna*, nos. 4–5, 1927, 11.
102. Ibid.
103. R. Kalendarov, "Evrei v Uzbekistane," *Tribuna*, no. 12, 1928, 20–21; M. Yagudaev, "Evrei v sred.azii," *Tribuna*, no. 12, 1928, 21. On the Soviet Latinization campaign, see Martin, *Affirmative Action Empire*, 185–203.
104. On Yosef Liberberg, the energetic leader of the Kyiv Institute of Jewish Proletarian Culture, which acquired many of the libraries and archives of the old Saint Petersburg Jewish societies and institutions, see Efim Melamed, "The Fate of the Archives of the Kiev Institute of Jewish Proletarian Culture: Puzzles and Discoveries," *East European Jewish Affairs* 42, no. 2, August 2012, 99–110.
105. On Jewish theaters in the Soviet Union, see Mordechai Altshuler, ed., *Ha-Teatron ha-yehudi bi-Verit ha-Mo'atsot*, Jerusalem: Hebrew University, 1996. On the Belorussian Soviet Jewish Theater, or Belgoset, see Greenbaum, "Belorussian State Jewish Theater"; and Bemporad, *Becoming Soviet Jews*, 73–74, 182–183. On the Jewish theater in the Ukrainian Soviet Socialist Republic, see Irina Meleshkina, *Mandrivni zori v Ukraini: Storinki istorii evreiskogo teatru*, Kyiv: Dukh i litera, 2019.
106. For the comprehensive history of GOSET from its establishment through its demise, see Veidlinger, *Moscow State Yiddish Theater*. See also Benjamin Harshav, *The Moscow Yiddish Theater: Art on the Stage at the Time of Revolution*, New Haven, CT: Yale University Press, 2008.
107. Among other noteworthy cultural and scholarly endeavors in Moscow was *Shtrom: Khoydesh heftn* (Stream: Monthly notebooks). Published in Moscow and featuring writers of such caliber as David Hofshteyn and Arn Kushnirov, it was the most important literary journal of the 1920s.
108. Veidlinger, *Moscow State Yiddish Theater*, 3.
109. Harshav, *Moscow Yiddish Theater*, 36–54. From 1920 to 1922, Chagall actively participated in the activities promoted in Moscow by the Kultur-lige Art Section.
110. Veidlinger, *Moscow State Yiddish Theater*, 58–59.
111. Ibid., 58.
112. "Evreiskaia zhizn v SSSR," *Tribuna*, no. 8, 1927, 24.
113. Marc Chagall, "My First Meeting with Solomon Mikhoels," in Harshav, *Moscow Yiddish Theater*, 77–78.
114. Jeffrey Veidlinger, "How the Weasel and the Well Became the Heavens and the

Earth: Soviet Yiddish Drama in the 1930s," in *Enemies of the People: The Destruction of Soviet Literary, Theater, and Film Arts in the 1930s*, ed. Katherine Bliss Eaton, Evanston, IL: Northwestern University Press, 2002, 94.

115. Shternshis, *Soviet and Kosher*, 23–24.
116. Ibid., 106; on the old and new canon, see 107–108.
117. "Estrada," from the French for "stage," referred to a genre of popular show music, with a performer often accompanied by an orchestra. See, for example, Anastasia Gordienko, *Outlaw Music in Russia: The Rise of an Unlikely Genre*, Madison: University of Wisconsin Press, 2023, 196.
118. "Evreiskie vokalnie kvartety," *Izvestiia*, August 29, 1929.
119. G. Povkhovtsev, "Kultura i iskusstvo," *Proletarskaia pravda*, February 5, 1925, 5.
120. A Yiddish drama studio was established in Leningrad in 1928.
121. Ts. P., "Yubilei Sarry Fibikh," *Sovetskoe iskusstvo*, February 14, 1939, 4.
122. G. Povkhovtsev, "Kultura i iskusstvo," *Proletarskaia pravda*, February 5, 1925, 5.
123. Moss, *Jewish Renaissance*, 34; Patricia Herlihy, *Odessa Recollected: The Port and the People*, Boston: Academic Studies Press, 2019, see in particular chapter 4.
124. Yehoshua A. Gilboa, *A Language Silenced: The Suppression of Hebrew Language and Culture in the Soviet Union*, New York: Herzl, 1982, 109.
125. "Evreiskaia zhizn v SSSR," *Tribuna*, nos. 1–2, 1928, 35.
126. On the JDC's work in Soviet Russia during the initial years until the creation of the Agro-Joint in 1924, see Michael Beizer, *Relief in Time of Need: Russian Jewry and the Joint, 1914–1924*, Bloomington: Slavica, Indiana University, 2015. On the JDC's support of underground cultural activities in the 1920s, see Bemporad, "JDC in Minsk."
127. West, *Struggles of a Generation*, 148, 150.
128. Gilboa, *Language Silenced*, 42–44, 120.
129. JDC, Collection 21/32, folder 475 (copy of a letter from prof. Solomon Zeitlin to Cyrus Adler about his interview with Anatoly Lunacharsky).
130. See Bemporad, *Becoming Soviet Jews*, 45.
131. Benjamin Pinkus, *The Soviet Government and the Jews, 1948–1967: A Documented Study*, Cambridge: Cambridge University Press, 1984, 452. On the language dispute between Hebrew and Tajik as the language of instruction in the Jewish schools, see Gilboa, *Language Silenced*, 88–90; and West, *Struggles of a Generation*, 146–147.
132. Eyner, "Di opgeshtanene fun di opgeshtanene," *Der emes*, July 13, 1923, quoted in Gilboa, *Language Silenced*, 91.
133. Gilboa, *Language Silenced*, 191.
134. Ibid., 87.
135. Ibid., 109–110. On the 1924 anthology *Twilight*, see also West, *Struggles of a Generation* 151–153.
136. "Kak ia uchila ivrit," *Lekhaim*, 2007, www.lechaim.ru.
137. On the life and work of Elisheva, see Yaffah Berlovitz, "Elisheva Bichovsky," in *Shalvi/Hyman Encyclopedia of Jewish Women*, December 31, 1999, Jewish

Women's Archive, https://jwa.org; and see Elisheva, *From My Memoirs*, Elisheva Archives, Genazim (7863/5), Saul Tchernichowsky House, Tel Aviv.

138. On the life and work of Yocheved Bat-Miriam, see Wendy Zierler, "Yokheved Bat-Miriam (Zhelezhniak)," in *Shalvi/Hyman Encyclopedia of Jewish Women*, December 31, 1999, Jewish Women's Archive, https://jwa.org; and Wendy Zierler, "Chariot(ess) of Fire: Yokheved Bat-Miriam's Female Personifications of Erets Israel," *Prooftexts* 20, nos. 1–2, Winter–Spring 2000, 111–138.

139. On Zvi Preygerzon, see Yehoshua Gilboa, "Tzvi Preigerzon: A Hebrew Writer in the USSR," *Soviet Jewish Affairs* 7, no. 2, 1977, 62–68; Matthew Kupfer, "Zvi Preigerzon: The Soviet Union's Secret Hebrew Writer," *Odessa Review*, November 17, 2017; and Zvi Preigerzon, *Memoirs of a Jewish Prisoner of the Gulag*, Boston: Academic Studies Press, 2022.

140. West, *Struggles of a Generation*, 139–140.

141. Ibid., 142, 146.

142. Quoted in West, *Struggles of a Generation*, 160–161. According to West, in the beginning, the actors brawled over whether they should follow the Sephardi or the Ashkenazi pronunciation of Hebrew. They eventually settled for the former.

143. Maxim Gorky, *Teater i muzyka*, November 14, 1922, 1–7.

144. V. V. Ivanov, *Russkie sezony teatra Gabima*, Moscow: Artist-Rezhesser-Teatr, 1999.

145. This is according to West, *Struggles of a Generation*, 164.

146. "Habima Players Arrive in United States," Jewish Telegraphic Agency, December 7, 1926.

147. Reuben Brainin, "Di rede fun Reuvn Braynen af dem fareyniktn plenum fun 'Gezerd,'" in ICOR, September 1930, 10–11, quoted in Soyer, "Back to the Future," 134.

148. S. M. Dubnov, *Kniga zhizni:Vospominaniya i razmyshleniya*, Moscow-Jerusalem: Mosty Kul'tury, Gesharim, 2004, 459–460.

149. Dubnov, *Kniga zhizni*, 458. The grief grew out of the alleged collapse of the greatest center in the Diaspora (*raspad velichaishego tsentra Diaspory*), the Russian Jewish center, as Dubnov viewed its creativity and multifacetedness being swept away by the new regime. The collapse of the Russian Jewish center even led him, in the last months of 1921, to question his own use of Russian, the key language of his literary creativity. Why write *The Book of Life*—which he saw at the time as his most important legacy—in Russian, the language of the former center, Dubnov hesitated. He first considered Yiddish, soon to realize that the writing pace in that language was too slow for him. He then experimented with Hebrew, but after composing one chapter, he went back to his most intimate literary medium, albeit with some reluctance. See Elissa Bemporad, "Da letteratura del popolo a storia del popolo: Simon Dubnov e l'origine della storiografia russo-ebraica," *Annali di storia dell'esegesi* 18, no. 2, 2001, 533–557.

150. Michael Beizer, *Evrei Leningrada, 1917–1939: Natsional'naya zhizn' i sovietizatsia*, Jerusalem-Moscow: Gesharim, 1999, 311.

151. Ibid.

152. Viktor E. Kelner, "Dubnov, Platonov i drugie (Komissia dlia nauchnogo izdaniia dokumentov ritualnykh prozessov v Rossii. Petrograd, 1919–1920)," in *Ocherki po istorii russko-evreiskogo knizhnogo dela vo vtoroi polovine XIX—nachale XX v.*, Saint Petersburg: Rossiiskaia natsionalnaia biblioteka, 2003, 186–221.
153. Beizer, *Evrei Leningrada*, 312.
154. Ibid., 315.
155. Ibid., 312–313.
156. Kelner, "Dubnov, Platonov i drugie," 201.
157. YIVO, Tcherikower Archive, RG 89, folder 982, Listia 75354 (Meeting Transcripts, Commission for Investigating Blood Libel Materials, December 1919–December 1920).
158. Simon M. Dubnov and Grigory Ia. Krasnyi-Admony, eds., *Materialy dlia istorii antievreiskikh pogromov v Rossii*, vol. 1, Petrograd: Kadimah, Istoriko-etnograficheskoe obshchestvo, 1919.
159. The findings of the 1857 commission established by Tsar Alexander II to investigate the blood libel, which included the participation of Daniel Khvolson (a converted Jew on the faculty of the Saint Petersburg Theological Seminary), were not intended for the public. The investigation's results were mixed: although Khvolson refuted the allegation, the Ukrainian historian Nikolai Kostomarov believed in it until the end of his life. On the 1857 commission, see Daniel Chwolson, *O nekotorikh srednevekovikh obvineniakh protiv evreev*, Saint Petersburg: tip. Shtaba otd. korpusa vn. strazhi, 1861.
160. Kelner, "Dubnov, Platonov i drugie," 186–187.
161. Another reason might have been the plan to establish a historical-archival commission, a sort of umbrella Jewish research institution for the study and publication of documents related to the history of Jewish social movements in Russia, the pogroms of the civil war, and ritual murder. See Dubnov, *Kniga zhizni*, 448.
162. Tevye Heilikman, *Geshikhte fun der gezelshaftlekher bavegung fun di yidn in Poyln un Rusland*, Moscow: Tsentraler farlag far di felker fun FSSR, 1926. The book appeared in Russian translation as *Istoriia obshchestvennogo dvizheniia evreev v Polshe i Rossiia*, Moscow: Gos. izd-vo, 1930. Ben Nathans, "On Russian-Jewish Historiography," in *Historiography of Imperial Russia: The Profession and Writing of History in a Multinational State*, ed. Thomas Sanders, New York: Sharpe, 1999, 421. For more information on Heilikman, see Zalmen Rejzen, "Tuvya Heyligman," in *Leksikon fun der yidisher literature, prese un filologye*, vol. 1, Vilna: Kletskin, 1926, 826–827.
163. See Gabriella Safran and Steven J. Zipperstein, eds., *The Worlds of S. An-sky: A Russian Jewish Intellectual at the Turn of the Century*, Stanford, CA: Stanford University Press, 2006; and Eugene M. Avrutin et al., eds., *Photographing the Jewish Nation: Pictures from S. An-sky's Ethnographic Expeditions*, Waltham, MA: Brandeis University Press, 2009.
164. Z.B., "Evreiskaia zhizn v SSSR," *Tribuna*, nos. 4–5, 1927, 40.
165. "Evreiskaia zhizn v SSSR," *Tribuna*, no. 8, 1927, 24.

166. Brian Horowitz, "The Society for the Promotion of Enlightenment among the Jews of Russia, and the Evolution of the St. Petersburg Russian-Jewish Intelligentsia, 1893–1905," in *Jews and the State: Dangerous Alliances and the Perils of Privilege*, ed. Ezra Mendelsohn, Studies in Contemporary Jewry 19, Oxford: Oxford University Press, 2004, 195–213.
167. *Tribuna*, no. 12, 1929, 31–32. Following the liquidation of the remarkable institutions of Russian Jewish culture and scholarship, the last head of the OPE, Saul Ginzburg, fearing arrest, fled for the United States. Beizer, *Evrei Leningrada*, 318–319. The organization published books and brochures in Russian, Yiddish, Ukrainian, and other languages, organized five fund-raising lotteries, and sponsored art exhibitions propagandizing its program. Interestingly, it dropped the word "Jewish" from its title in 1929 and was called simply *Tribuna*.
168. Beizer, *Evrei Leningrada*, 193; Z.B., "Evreiskaia zhizn v SSSR, Gruzinskie evrei," *Tribuna*, nos. 4–5, 1927, 40.
169. Avrutin et al., *Photographing the Jewish Nation*, 192–193.
170. Author of the monumental *Di geshikhte fun der literatur bay yidn* (*A History of Jewish Literature*), from 1919 to 1925, Zinberg taught Jewish literary history and the history ofYiddish at the Jewish People's University in Petrograd. Until 1930, he was among the most prominent leaders of the "bourgeois" Jewish cultural organizations and published articles in Russian-language Jewish periodicals. On his life and work, see Galina Eliasberg, *Odin iz prezhnogo Peterburga: S. L. Tsinberg, istorik evreiskoi literatury, kritik i publitsist*, Moscow: RGGU, 2005.

7. THE FAMILY, THE BODY, AND THE SELF

1. Matveyuk interview.
2. On the ways in which Soviet citizens "lived" the imperative to internalize Soviet ideology, see Christina Kiaer and Eric Naiman, introduction to Kiaer and Naiman, *Everyday Life in Early Soviet Russia*, 10.
3. Ibid., 13.
4. Rachel Polonsky, *Molotov's Magic Lantern: Travels in Russian History*, New York: Farrar, Strauss and Giroux, 2011.
5. Fruma Treivas, "We Were Fighting for an Idea!," in *In the Shadow of Revolution: Life Stories of Russian Women from 1917 to the Second World War*, ed. Sheila Fitzpatrick and Yuri Slezkine, Princeton, NJ: Princeton University Press, 2000, 324, 325.
6. The Rabfak was an educational institution that gave workers preliminary training and prepared them to enter institutions of higher education.
7. Treivas, "We Were Fighting for an Idea!," 325. When they registered, Fruma changed her last name to Treivas-Waltenberg.
8. On Kollontai's progressive and radical Marxist feminism and ideas about women' liberation, see her 1926 *The Autobiography of a Sexually Emancipated Communist Woman*, translated by Salvator Attansio, New York: Herder and Herder, 1971.

9. Harold J. Berman, "Soviet Family Law in the Light of Russian History and Marxist Theory," *Yale Law Journal* 56, no. 26, 1946, 36.
10. This new Soviet life-cycle rite was first launched by Kollontai, who in 1918 married, in a Red Wedding, Pavel Dybenko, people's commissar of naval affairs.
11. Berman, "Soviet Family Law," 27–28.
12. Hoffman, *Red Shtetl*, 70.
13. Matveyuk interview.
14. Anna Shternshis, *When Sonia Met Boris*, New York: Oxford University Press, 2017.
15. Under the Soviets, local klezmer groups, or *kapelyes*, continued to perform at Jewish weddings, whether they were religious or not.
16. "A freylekhe khasene," *Shtern*, April 21, 1927.
17. "Caucasian Official, Charged with Extortion of Jews, Is Acquitted," Jewish Telegraphic Agency, October 12, 1926. Soviet law prohibited girls younger than eighteen to get married, but in the eastern republics, to promote a smoother modernization, it lowered the age to sixteen.
18. Levin, *Collectivization and Social Engineering*, 32–33.
19. Ibid., 33.
20. L. Materson, "Bilder fun der nayer Bukhare," *Di yidishe tsaytung*, October 28, 1924, 5.
21. Liubov Denisova, *Rural Women in the Soviet Union and in Post-Soviet Russia*, London: Routledge, 2010, 71, 84.
22. "Soviet Overrules Rabbi's Decision That Stage Marriage Is Legal," Jewish Telegraphic Agency, June 11, 1924.
23. "A nayer miskher in Rusland," *Dos naye lebn*, April 10, 1922, 4.
24. Z. Vendrof, "Vi azoy es vert gepravet khasene un get in Soviet-Rusland," *Der moment*, January 9, 1925, 7.
25. Rafaeli, *Shirei makhteret*, 23–24.
26. T., "Shteyger, khasene un familye," *Shtern*, March 31, 1926, 4.
27. Denisova, *Rural Women in the Soviet Union*, 71.
28. Anonymous, "What Am I to Do?," in Fitzpatrick and Slezkine, *In the Shadow of Revolution*, 207.
29. Denisova, *Rural Women in the Soviet Union*, 72.
30. Katherine Bliss Eaton, *Daily Life in the Soviet Union*, Westport, CT: Greenwood, 2004, 71.
31. "Der gevezener tenderloin kvartal in Moskve," *Forverts*, September 9, 1920, 4.
32. Z. Vendrof, "Vi azoy es vert gepravet khasene un get in Sovietn Rusland," *Der moment*, January 9, 1925, 7.
33. Richard Stites, "Women and the Revolutionary Process in Russia," in *Becoming Visible: Women in European History*, ed. Renate Bridenthal, Claudia Koonz, and Susan Mosher Stuard, Boston: Houghton Mifflin, 1998, 429.
34. See Wendy Goldman, *Women, the State, and Revolution: Soviet Family Policy and Social Life, 1917–1936*, Cambridge: Cambridge University Press, 1993, in particular chapter 5.

35. On the plight of the *agunot* in other historical contexts, see Haim Sperber, "Agunot 1851–1914: An Introduction," in *Annales de demographie historique* 136, no. 2, 2018, 107–135.
36. Denisova, *Rural Women in the Soviet Union*, 71.
37. Galushteyn, "Dos yunge porfolk," *Shtern*, April 6, 1926, 3.
38. "Kinder-merder," *Der emes*, April 30, 1926, 4.
39. An eygener, "Der katsev mit der katsevte," *Shtern*, April 6, 1926, 3.
40. Ulianova, "A Cross-Examination," in Fitzpatrick and Slezkine, *In the Shadow of Revolution*, 345–346.
41. Bemporad, *Becoming Soviet Jews*, 167; GAMO, f. 162, op. 1, d. 360a, l. 162 ("Autobiography of Communist Party member Rebecca Gimmelshtein, Minsk Province").
42. TsDAGO, f. 1, op. 20, d. 2689, l. 42 ("Doloi antisemitizm, July 14, 1928").
43. See Deborah Yalen, "The Toiling *Froy* and the Speculating *Yidene*: Discourses of Female Productivization in the Soviet Shtetl," in *Jewish History: Jewish Women in Modern Eastern and East Central Europe*, vol. 33, ed. Elissa Bemporad and Glenn Dynner, Cham, Switzerland: Springer, 2022, 187–214.
44. "Intermarriage in Russia Growing, Figures Show," Jewish Telegraphic Agency, September 27, 1926.
45. Yuri Larin, *Evrei i antisemitizm v SSSR*, Moscow-Leningrad: Gosudarstvennoe izd-vo 1929, 1929, 304.
46. In Moscow and Leningrad, in 1939, Jews made up 6 percent of the city population in both cities. See Mordechai Altshuler, *Distribution of the Jewish Population of the USSR 1939*, Jerusalem: Centre for Research and Documentation of East-European Jewry, Hebrew University of Jerusalem, 1993, 28, 30.
47. By 1924, more than 28 percent of German Jews intermarried. The highest intermarriage rate was in Berlin, where in the 1920s one in five Jews intermarried, and less so in rural Germany. See Benjamin Nathans, "Mythologies and Realities of Jewish Life in Prerevolutionary St. Petersburg," in *People of the City: Jews and the Urban Challenge*, ed. Ezra Mendelshon, Studies in Contemporary Jewry 15, New York: Oxford University Press, 2000, 99.
48. "Intermarriage in Russia Growing, Figures Show."
49. On depictions of Jewish women as exotically beautiful in Russian popular songs from the 1920s, see Shternshis, *Soviet and Kosher*, 171.
50. Yiddish poster, printed in the Soviet Union, ca. 1920s, Judah L. Magnes Museum, Berkeley, California.
51. "Only in the Soviet Union Do Jews Have the Right to Work the Land," text by Y. A. Slonim, Society for the Settlement of Jewish Toilers on the Land (OZET), Moscow, 1928, in Yiddish and in Russian, Gift of Mr. and Mrs. Ludwig Jesselson, 1998.617, Collection of Yeshiva University Museum, New York.
52. Shternshis, *Soviet and Kosher*, 172.
53. *Ershte alfarbandishe baratung fun di yidishe sektsyes fun der Al. K. P. B.(b)*, Moscow: Shul un bukh, 1926, 127ff., quoted in Gitelman, *Century of Ambivalence*, 98.

54. A. Lunacharskii, *Ob antisemitizme*, Moscow-Leningrad: Gos. izd-vo, 1929, 46–47, quoted in Slezkine, *Jewish Century*, 180.
55. On the Bolshevik vision of women's liberation, see Goldman, *Women, the State, and Revolution*, 11–13.
56. See Rossiiskii gosudarstvennyi arkhiv literatury i iskusstva (RGALI), f. 2270, op. 1, d. 72. l. 6 (Correspondence between A. Sh. Gurshteyn and N. E. Oyslender, 1926).
57. A Crown Rabbi (*kazennyi ravvin* or *rabiner*) was designated rabbi by the state. His main functions included record keeping, administration, and communal responsibilities, all which outweighed the religious title.
58. In many ways, the Berlin salons that developed over the course of the late eighteenth century owed their existence to the educated Jewish women from well-to-do families searching for a new role in life outside the patriarchal home. See Petra Wilhelmy-Dollinger, "Berlin Salons: Late Eighteenth to Early Twentieth Century," in *The Shalvi/Hyman Encyclopedia of Jewish Women*, December 31, 1999, Jewish Women's Archive, https://jwa.org; and Petra Wilhelmy-Dollinger, "Emanzipation durch Geselligkeit. Die Salons jüdischer Frauen in Berlin zwischen 1780 und 1830," in *Bild und Selbstbild der Juden Berlins zwischen Aufklärung und Romantik*, ed. Marianne Awerbuch and Stefi Jersch-Wenzel, Einzelveröffentlichungen der Historischen Kommission zu Berlin 75, Berlin: Spiess Volker, 1992, 121–138.
59. T., "Shteyger, khasene un familye," *Shtern*, March 31, 1926, 4.
60. D. Volin, "Fraye libe in Sovetn Rusland," *Dos naye lebn*, June 10, 1924, 2–3.
61. Bemporad, *Becoming Soviet Jews*, 163; GAMO, f. 37, op. 1, d. 229, ll. 38–39 ("Construction workers' Party-cell meeting, Minsk, March 1926").
62. Gennady Estraikh, "Khana Levin's Verdict to Free Love," in *Yiddish Poets and the Soviet Union, 1917–1948*, ed. Daniela Mantovan, Heidelberg: Universitatsverlag, 2012, 89; Estraikh, "From 'Green Fields' to 'Red Fields.'"
63. "Der gevezener tenderloin kvartal in Moskve," *Forverts*, November 9, 1920, 4.
64. Dennen, *Where the Ghetto Ends*, 84–85.
65. Yalen, "Toiling *Froy* and the Speculating *Yidene*."
66. On rape during the civil war, see Irina Astashkevich, *Gendered Violence: Jewish Women in the Pogroms of 1917 to 1921*, Boston: Academic Studies Press, 2018.
67. GARF, f. R-1339, op. 1, d. 438, ll. 25–26 ("Doctors' reports from Kyiv province, December 1919"), quoted from Bemporad, "Female Dimension of Violence," 162–163.
68. USHMM, RG 31.058M.0012.00000591 ("Letter from the People's Commissariat of Health to the Department of Healthcare Kyiv province, 1921").
69. Denisova, *Rural Women in the Soviet Union*, 72.
70. "A 'rituele' geshikhte," *Der emes*, April 16, 1926, 4. For more on the ritual murder accusation in Kaniv, see Bemporad, *Legacy of Blood*, 49–54.
71. Estraikh, "Khana Levin's Verdict to Free Love," 90–91.
72. Matveyuk interview.
73. Ibid.

74. See, for example, Anna Sokolova, "Soviet Funeral Services: From Moral Economy to Social Welfare and Back," *Revolutionary Russia* 32, no. 2, 2019, 251–271.
75. Pinkus, *Jews of the Soviet Union*, 105.
76. Elizabeth Wyner Mark, "Crossing the Gender Divide: Public Ceremonies, Private Parts, Mixed Feelings," in *The Covenant of Circumcision: New Perspectives on an Ancient Jewish Rite*, ed. Elizabeth Wyner Mark, Hanover, NH: Brandeis University Press, 2003, xx.
77. On Jewish cemeteries after the war, see Mordechai Altshuler, *Religion and Jewish Identity in the Soviet Union, 1941–1964*, Waltham, MA: Brandeis University Press, 2012, 205–219.
78. Svetlana Malysheva, "Soviet Death and Hybrid Soviet Subjectivity: Urban Cemetery as a Metatext," *Ab Imperio* 3, 2018, 351–385.
79. Nomberg, "Fun mayn rayze in Rusland," 5; "A gelekhter on a zayt," *Oktyabr*, no. 273, December 10, 1936, 6. On Jewish cemeteries in the Soviet Union, see also Gershuni, *Yahadut be-Rusiah ha-Soviyetit*, 93–94; Rothenberg, *Jewish Religion in the Soviet Union*, 195–197; and S. Levin, *Toldot Chabad*, 75, 113, 116.
80. *Di garber un bershter shtime*, no. 1, June 1924, 2.
81. On a clash that erupted between Jewish workers and the Chevrah-Kadisha in 1905, see, for example, Ts. Dolgopolski, "On khevre kadishe," *Oktyabr*, no. 60, March 16, 1936, 3.
82. Nomberg, "Fun mayn rayze in Rusland," 5.
83. "Proposal to Establish Separate Cemeteries for Jewish Communists Discussed," Jewish Telegraphic Agency, March 21, 1926. Tensions around the question of whether uncircumcised children could be buried in Jewish cemeteries predated the establishment of the Soviet Union. See, for example, the 1908 Warsaw scandal discussed by Gershon Bacon in "Religious Compulsion, Freedom of Speech, and Modern Jewish Identity in Poland: Y. L. Peretz, Shalom Asch, and the Circumcision Scandal in Warsaw, 1908," in *Mi-Vilna le-Yerushalayim: Mehkarim be-toledotehem ve-tarbutam shel yehudei mizrah eropa. Mugashim le-profesor Shmuel Werses*, ed. David Assaf, Israel Bartal, Shmuel Feiner, Yehuda Friedlander, Avner Holtzman, and Chava Turniansky, Jerusalem: Magnes, 2002, 167–185.
84. *Der veker*, no. 125, May 31, 1923, 4.
85. "Communist Officials Sentenced to Jail for Terrorizing Jewish Population," Jewish Telegraphic Agency, March 2, 1926.
86. "Soviet Government Allows First Conference of Jewish Religious Communities," Jewish Telegraphic Agency, June 8, 1927. Other questions on the agenda included the establishment of *mikvot* (ritual baths) and yeshivas and the support of rabbis and other synagogue functionaries.
87. "Russian Jews Describe Religious Needs in Memorandum to Government," Jewish Telegraphic Agency, June 26, 1927.
88. "Protest against Building Stables on Cemetery," Jewish Telegraphic Agency, July 21, 1927.

89. "Soviet Official Ousted for Antisemitic Acts," Jewish Telegraphic Agency, January 23, 1928.
90. "Religious Bodies Cannot Control Cemeteries in Russia, New Law Rules," Jewish Telegraphic Agency, June 10, 1929. According to Jewish law, a Jews is to be buried immediately after passing.
91. "Protest against Building Stables on Cemetery."
92. "Vos hert men in der yidisher velt," *Haynt*, July 16, 1929, 4.
93. "Riot in Berditcheff When Ancient Cemetery Transformed into Park," Jewish Telegraphic Agency, July 14, 1929.
94. See Yuliya Len, "Jewish Community of Berdychiv and the Early Soviet Policies," master's thesis, University of Tartu, 2019, 59–60.
95. Richard Stites, "Iconoclastic Currents in the Russian Revolution: Destroying and Preserving the Past," in *Bolshevik Culture: Experiment and Order in the Russian Revolution*, ed. Abbott Gleason, Peter Kenez, and Richard Stites, Bloomington: Indiana University Press, 1981, 2.
96. Ibid., 18.
97. Treivas, "We Were Fighting for an Idea!," 325.
98. Isaac Babel, "Karl-Yankl," in *The Complete Works of Isaac Babel*, New York: Norton, 2002, 619–627.
99. Moshe Kulbak, *Geklibene verk*, New York: CYCO Bikher farlag, 1953, 119–121.
100. Richard Stites, "Bolshevik Ritual Building in the 1920s," in Fitzpatrick, Rabinowitch, and Stites, *Russia in the Era of NEP*, 300.
101. Alexandra Popoff, *Vasily Grossman and the Soviet Century*, New Haven, CT: Yale University Press, 2019, 48–49.
102. On names and Bundist institutions, see Bemporad, *Becoming Soviet Jews*, 58–64. On Hirsh Lekert's role in the Bund and his becoming a legendary hero after death, see J. S. Hertz, *Hirsh Lekert*, New York: Undzer tsayt, 1952; and G. Aronson, S. Dubnov-Erlich, J. S. Hertz, et al., eds., *Di geshikhte fun Bund*, vol. 1, New York: Undzer tsayt, 1960, 231.
103. *Vsia Belarussiia, spravochnaia kniga*, Minsk, n.p., 1924, 51.
104. Alastair Kocho-Williams, *Russian and Soviet Diplomacy, 1900–39*, London: Palgrave Macmillan, 2012, 99–101.
105. Michael Jabara Carley, *Silent Conflict: A Hidden History of Early Soviet Western Relations*, Lanham, MD: Rowman and Littlefield, 2014, 227.
106. Ibid., 227.
107. Ethel Brilliana Tweedie, "Russia as I Saw It. Russia, Siberia, China, 1925–1926," Russia Documents 1924–1930, Trades Union Congress Collection, Warwick Digital Collection.
108. See, for example, G. Sinfield, *The Workers' Sports Movement (Including an Account of the Experiences of the First British Workers' Football Team in Soviet Russia)*, London: G. Sinfield, 1926.
109. Nomberg, "Fun mayn rayze in Rusland," 6.
110. On the specific Jewish house-building and architectural traditions in the shtetl, see Alla Sokolova, "House-Building Tradition of the Shtetl in Memorials and

Memories Based on Materials of Field Studies in Podolia," *East European Jewish Affairs* 41, no. 3, 2011, 111–135; and Alla Sokolova, "The Podolian Shtetl as an Architectural Phenomenon," in *The Shtetl: Image and Reality*, ed. Gennady Estraikh and Mikhail Krutikov, New York: Routledge, 2000, 36–80.

111. Hoffman, *Red Shtetl*, 71.
112. "Fun Bialistok redt men teglekh mit Moskve durkhn telefon," *Haynt*, June 17, 1928, 3.
113. NARB, f. 4, op. 5, d. 409, ll. 45–47 ("Bolshevization and the Bund, Jewish workers' club, February 1926–June 1926").
114. Puah Rakovsky, *My Life as a Radical Jewish Woman: Memoirs of a Zionist Feminist in Poland*, ed. Pula Hyman, Bloomington: Indiana University Press, 2001, 172, 174.
115. Matveyuk interview.
116. Richard Taylor, "The Birth of Soviet Cinema," in Gleason, Kenez, and Stites, *Bolshevik Culture*, 197.
117. Shternshis, *Soviet and Kosher*, 165.
118. For an analysis of *Jewish Luck*, see J. Hoberman, *Bridge of Light: Yiddish Film between Two Worlds*, New York: Museum of Modern Art, 1991. On the construction of a new Soviet Jewish cultural figure through film, see Senderovich, *How the Soviet Jew Was Made*.
119. On the film, cast, and director, see Basin, *Bolshevizm i evrei*, 228, 231. "Beginning on Tuesday, March 20, Belgoskino will feature the great artistic film *Zayn ekselents*. Tickets may be purchased every day from 3 to 11 PM at the movie theater." *Oktyabr*, no. 66, March 18, 1928, 4.
120. "Tsi meg Guzik shpiln in Moskve tsi nisht?," *Grodner moment ekspert*, July 26, 1929.
121. "A gerikht kegn tsvey komiugistn," *Der emes*, March 15, 1928, 4.
122. Shternshis, *Soviet and Kosher*, 69.
123. James von Geldkern and Richard Stites, introduction to von Geldkern and Stites, *Mass Culture in Soviet Russia*, xi; Jeffrey Brooks, "The Breakdown in Production and Distribution of Printed Material, 1917–1927," Gleason, Kenez, and Stites, *Bolshevik Culture*, 153–154, 163.
124. "Moskve leyent," *Khelemer folksblat*, February 8, 1929, 2.
125. Mark Derbaremdiker, interview by Ella Orlikova, Kyiv, 2002, "Mark Derbaremdiker," Centropa (E), Interviews, www.centropa.org.
126. Matveyuk interview.
127. Mikhail Zoshchenko, "The Lady Aristocrat," in von Geldkern and Stites, *Mass Culture in Soviet Russia*, 54–55.
128. M. Sandomirski, "Hoyzarbeterns zaynen nit keyn dinstn!," *Oktyabr*, no. 57, January 7, 1926, 3.
129. Rebecca Spagnolo, "When Private Home Meets Public Workplace: Service, Space, and the Urban Domestic in 1920s Russia," in Naiman and Kiaer, *Everyday Life in Early Soviet Russia*, 241.
130. Faygnberg, "Spektor der privat mentsh," 138.

131. YIVO, H. Leivik Papers, RG 315, file 85 (Letters from H. Leyvik to his wife, 1914–1927).
132. Hoffman, *Red Shtetl*, 71.
133. Ibid., 70–71.
134. On reinventing Jewish dietary laws as a result of the Soviet persecution of religion, see Shternshis, *Soviet and Kosher*, xiii–xiv, 182, 185.
135. "Etlekhe vagonen matses ongekumen in Leningrad un Moskve," *Grodner moment ekspert*, April 11, 1929.
136. See, for example, Elye Kahan, "Tsefaln der matse-podriad," in *Sovetishe Vaysrusland: literarishe zamlung*, ed. Izzy Kharik and Yasha Bronshteyn, Minsk: Melukhe farlag fun Vaysrusland, 1935, 189–191.
137. Derbaremdiker interview.
138. "Vi azoy me makht koshere yidishe maykholim," *Der kustar*, June 15, 1929, 9. On food in the shtetl, see Dobun, *Pravda o evreiakh*, 14, 15.
139. See, for example, Jeffrey Veidlinger, *In the Shadow of the Shtetl: Small-Town Jewish Life in Soviet Ukraine*, Bloomington: Indiana University Press, 2016, 140–143; and Shternshis, "Salo on Challah."
140. Smoliar, *Vu bistu khaver Sidorov?*, 63.
141. On Abram Friman, see Jewish Heroes, "Abram Friman," December 6, 2021, www.jewishheroes.live.
142. Derbaremdiker interview. Of course, the analogy to *marranos* has its limits. Soviet Jews did not face punishment for carrying on Jewish practices to nearly the extent that Judaizers in Spain and Portugal did.

CONCLUSION

1. Sergei Prozorov, "Living Ideas and Dead Bodies: The Biopolitics of Stalin," *Alternatives: Global, Local, Political* 38, no. 3, 2013, 208–227.
2. David Hollinger, "Communalist and Dispersionist Approaches to American Jewish History in an Increasingly Post-Jewish Era," *American Jewish History* 95, no. 1, 2009, 1–32.
3. Quoted in Shlomo Bickel (Shloyme Bikl), "Eliezer Shteynbargs mesholim," in *Rumenye: Geshikhte, literatur-kritik, zikhroynes*, Buenos Aires: Kiyum, 1961, 224.
4. Elye Shekhtman, "Di shtrof fun goylem," *Di goldene keyt*, no. 122, 1987, 20–42.

SELECT BIBLIOGRAPHY

ARCHIVAL COLLECTIONS

Archivio Apostolico Vaticano (CAV), L'archivio di mons. Achille Ratti, visitatore apostolico e nunzio di Varsavia (1918–1921)

Titolo 1, 191, Carteggio di Mon. Ratti Visitatore Apostolico della Polonia, 1918–1919.

Central Archives for the History of the Jewish People (CAHJP), Jerusalem, Israel

MMF, 1058 A/B (Letters of adolescents from the Professional Schools in Odesa, 1924–1925)

Central Zionist Archives (CZA), Jerusalem, Israel

F30 Russia (A. Rafaeli-Zenzipper Collection)

Derzhavnyi arkhyv Kiyvskoi oblasti (DAKO), Kyiv, Ukraine

Fond 3050 Kyiv District Commission of the Jewish Public Committee for Relief for Victims of Pogroms

Gosudarstvennyi arkhiv Minskoi oblasti (GAMO), Minsk

Fond 12 Minsk District Committee of the KP(b)B.

Fond 37 Minsk Municipal District Committee KP(b)B, 1920–1932.

Fond 162 Records of the Local Offices of the Communist Party of Belorussia, Minsk Province, 1921–1930.

Fond 320 Inspector of Public Education of the Minsk District Council, 1923–1930.

Gosudarstvennyi arkhiv Rossiiskoi Federatsii (GARF), Moscow, Russia

Fond 9530, Jewish People's University, 1918–1922

Fond R-1339, All-Russian committee for aid to pogrom victims

Institute for Jewish Research Archives (YIVO), New York

RG 80, Mizrakh Yidisher Historisher Arkhiv (Elias Tcherikower Archive)

RG 89, Gunzburg, Baron Horace de (Naftali Herz)

RG 315, H. Leivik Papers, 1914–1959.

RG 347.7.1, American Jewish Committee, Foreign Affairs Department, Foreign countries
RG 358, Joseph Rosen Papers, 1921–1938
Joint Distribution Committee Archives (JDC), New York
Collection 21/32 Russia
Natsionalnyi arkhiv Respubliki Belarus (NARB), Minsk, Belarus
Fond 4 Central Committee of the Communist Party of Belorussia
Fond 42 Narkompros BSSR
Oral History Division, Hebrew University, Institute for Contemporary Jewry (OHD), Jerusalem, Israel
Interview with Benjamin Gorstein, 1986
Interview with Shterna Ninburg, 12/20/1986
Rossiiskii gosudarstvennyi arkhiv literatury i iskusstva (RGALI), Moscow, Russian Federation
Fond 2270, Gurshteyn, Aron Sheftelevich. Papers, 1900–1957.
Tsentralnyi derzhavniy arkhyv gromadskikh obednan Ukrainy (TsDAGO), Kyiv, Ukraine
Fond 1, Central Committee of the Communist Party of Ukraine
Tsentralnyi derzhavniy arkhyv vishikh organiv vladi ta upravlinnia Ukrainy (TsDAVO), Kyiv, Ukraine
Fond 5, People's Commissariat of Internal Affairs of the Ukrainian SSR, Kyiv
Fond 413, Central Commission of National Minorities, All-Ukrainian Central Executive Committee (VUTsIK)
Fond 2708, Ukrainian Republican Committee of the Trade Union of Art Workers, Kyiv
Fond 2514, Bureau of Newspaper Clippings at the Newspaper Bureau of the Southern Department of Communication, Kharkiv
Tsentralniy nauchnyi arkhiv natsionalnoi akademii nauk Belarusi (TsNANANB), Minsk, Belarus
Fond 72 Institute of National Minorities, Academy of Sciences BSSR
United States Holocaust Memorial Museum Archives (USHMM), Washington, DC
RG 31.057M, Documents of the Kyiv Oblast Commission for Relief to Victims of Pogroms
RG 31.058M, Selected Records Related to the History of Jews and Jewish Communities from the State Archives of Kyiv Region of Ukraine
RG 31.060M, Selected Records Related to the History of the Jews in Zhytomyr Region of Ukraine
RG 31.075M, Selected Records from the State Archives of the Vinnytsia Region Related to the History of the Jewish Communities before WWII

NEWSPAPERS AND PERIODICALS

Af di vegn tsu der nayer shul
Arbeter shtime, Golos pratsi

Bezbozhnik u stanka
Der apikoyres
Der emes
Der moment
Der morgen zhurnal
Der kustar
Der Odeser arbeter
Der veker
Detroit Jewish Chronicle
Di goldene keyt
Di garber un bershter shtime
Di yidishe tsaytung
Dos naye lebn
Evreiskaia starina
Folksshtime
Forverts
Grodner moment ekspert
Haynt
He-avar
Izvestiia
Jewish Telegraphic Agency Daily Bulletin
Khelemer folksblat
Komsomolskaia pravda
Komune
Komunistishe fon
Krigerisher apikoyres
Ogoniok
Oktyabr
Pravda
Proletarii
Proletarskaia pravda
Rabochee ekho
Revoliutsiia i tserkov: Ezhemesiachnyi zhurnal
Robitnik Poltavshchini
Shtern
Sovetish heymland
Sovetskoe iskusstvo
Tribuna evreiskoi sovetskoi obshchestvennosti
Tsaytshrift
Undzer ekspres
Yunge gvardie

INTERVIEWS

Derbaremdiker, Mark. Interview by Ella Orlikova, Kyiv, 2002. "Mark Derbaremdiker," Centropa (E), Interviews. www.centropa.org.

Matveyuk, Asia. Interview by Zhanna Litinskaya, Kherson, 2003. "Asia Matveyuk," Centropa (E), Interviews. www.centropa.org.

PRIMARY SOURCES

APPO Leningradskogo oblastkoma VK(b)B, *Na borbu s antisemitizmom: Materialy dlia agitatorov i besedchikov*. Leningrad: APPO Len. Obk., 1929.

Babel, Isaac. *The Complete Works of Isaac Babel*. New York; London: Norton, 2002.

Ben-Gurion, David. *Igorot David Ben-Gurion*. Edited by Yehuda Erez. Vol. 2. Tel Aviv: Am Oved and Tel Aviv University, 1973.

Berkman, Alexander. *The Bolshevik Myth*. London: Pluto, 1989.

Bezymensky, Aleksander. *Komsomolia: Stranitsy epopei*. Moscow and Leningrad: Gos. Izd-vo, 1927.

Bickel, Shlomo (Shloyme Bikl). "Eliezer Shteynbargs mesholim." In *Rumenye: Geshikhte, literatur-kritik, zikhroynes*, 223–234. Buenos Aires: Kiyum, 1961.

Browder, Robert Paul, and Alexander F. Kerensky. *The Russian Provisional Government 1917: Documents*. Vol. 1. Stanford, CA: Stanford University Press, 1961.

Caro (Krupnik), Baruch. *Yalkut volin, osaf maamarim, reshimot, skirot, teudot vetsilumim*. Tel Aviv, n.p., 1951.

Charny, Danil. *A yortsendlik aza, 1914–1924*. New York: CYCO Bikher Farlag, 1943.

Chwolson, Daniel. *O nekotorikh srednevekovikh obvineniakh protiv evreev*. Saint Petersburg: tip. Shtaba otd. korpusa vn. strazhi, 1861.

Coben, Lawrence. *Anna's Shtetl*. Tuscaloosa: University of Alabama Press, 2007.

Dennen, Leon. *Where the Ghetto Ends: Jews of Soviet Russia*. New York: A. H. King. 1934.

Dobun, Ef. *Pravda o evreiakh*. Leningrad: Krasnaia Gazeta, 1928.

Dubnov, Simon M. *Fun zhargon tsu yidish un andere artiklen: Literarishe zikhroynes*. Vilna: Kletskin, 1929.

———. *Kniga zhizni: Vospominaniya i razmyshleniya: Materialy dlia istorii moego vremeni*. Saint Petersburg: Peterburgskoe vostokovedenie, 1998.

Dubnov, Simon M., and Grigory Ia. Krasnyi-Admony, eds. *Materialy dlia istorii antievreiskikh pogromov v Rossii*. Vol. 1. Petrograd: Kadimah, Istoriko-etnograficheskoe obshchestvo, 1919.

Ehrenburg, Ilia "Burnaia zhizn Lazika Roitshvanetsa." In *Neobychainye pokhozhdenia: Proza*, edited by B. Ia. Frezinskii. Saint Petersburg: Kristall, 2001.

Estraikh, G., and E. I. Melamed. "'O pogrome v Berdicheve' (Novonaidennaia zapiska D. Lipetsa 1919)." In *Arkhiv evreiskoi istorii*, vol. 8, edited by O. V. Budnitskii, Moscow: ROSSPEN, 2016, 157–176.

Even-Shoshan, Sh., ed. *Minsk, ir va-em: Korot, maasim, ishim, havai*. 2 vols. Tel Aviv: Irgun yotse Minsk k u-venotecha be-Yisrael, 1975, 1985.

Faygnberg, Rakhil. *A pinkes fun a toyter shtot (khurbn Dubove)*. Warsaw: Akhisefer, 1926.

———. *Letopis mertvogo goroda*. Leningrad: Priboi, 1928.

———. *Untern hamer*. Tel Aviv: Beiamei zeam, 1942.

Frumkina, M. (Ester). *Doloi ravvinov!* Moscow: Krasnaia nov, 1923.

Ginzburg, Shaul. *Amolike Peterburg: Forshungen un zikhroynes vegn Yidishn lebn in der rezidents-shtot fun tsarishn Rusland*. New York: CYCO Bikher Farlag, 1944.

Glebov, V. *Sovremennyi antisemitizm i borba s nim*. Moscow and Leningrad: Molodaia gvardia, 1927.

Gorev, M. *Protiv antisemitov: Ocherki i zarisovki*. Moscow and Leningrad: Gos. Izd-vo, 1928.

Gusev-Orenburskii, S. I. *Bagrovaia kniga. Pogromy 1919–1920 gg. na Ukraine*. New York: Izd-vo "Ladoga," 1983.

Hadad. *Der tsionizm vi er iz*. Moscow: Farlag shul un bukh, 1925.

Heifetz, Elias. *The Slaughter of the Jews in the Ukraine in 1919*. New York: Thomas Seltzer, 1921.

Heilikman, Tuvia. *Geshikhte fun der gezelshaftlekher bavegung fun di yidn in Poyln un Rusland*. Moscow: Tsentraler farlag far di felker fun FSSR, 1926.

Hodoshevitsh, K., Sh. Yofe, and M. Mogilnitski. *Undzer royte heym: Arbet-bukh af gezelshaftkentenish farn 4tn lernyor*. Moscow, Kharkov, and Minsk: Tsentraler felker farlag fun FSSR, 1931.

Kaminski, Zvi. *Geven a mol a shtot Berdichev*. Paris: Kaminski, 1952.

Kantor, L. M. *Tuzemnye evrei v Uzbekistane*. Samarkand: Uzbekskoe gosudartvennoe izd-vo UzSSR, 1929.

Kaplan, Vera. *K tebe dusha izdaleka: Po vospominaniiam Racheli Blekhman*. Tel Aviv: Piles Studio, 2000.

Kassel, David, ed. *Spektor-bukh*. Warsaw: Akhisefer, 1929.

Khanin, Nokhem. *Soviet Rusland: Vi ikh hob ir gezen*. New York: Farlag Veker, 1929.

Kharik, Izzy, and Yasha Bronshteyn, eds. *Sovetishe Vaysrusland: Literarishe zamlung*. Minsk: Melukhe farlag fun Vaysrusland, 1935.

Khurbn Proskurov: Tsum ondenken fun di heylike neshomes vos zaynen umgekumen in der shreklekher shkhite vos iz ongefirt gevorn fun di Haydamakes. New York: Levant, 1924.

Kollontai, Alexandra. *The Autobiography of a Sexually Emancipated Communist Woman*. Translated by Salvator Attansio. New York: Herder and Herder, 1971.

Kulbak, Moishe. *Geklibene verk*. New York: CYCO Bikher Farlag, 1953.

Kuusinen, Aino. *Gospod nizvergaet svoikh angelov: Vospominaniya, 1919–1965*. Petrozavodsk: Kareliia, 1991.

Lagovier, N. *Antisemitizm i borba s nim*. Moscow: Gosudarstvennoe iuridicheskoe izd-vo, 1930.

Larin, Yurii. *Evrei i antisemitizm v SSSR*. Moscow: Gosudarstvennoe izd-vo, 1929.

Ledat, G. *Antisemitizm i antisemity: Voprosy i otvety*. Leningrad: Priboi, 1929.

Lenin, Vladimir. *Lenin Collected Works*. Vol. 20. Moscow: Progress, 1972.

Leningradskii, S. *Kto i za chto ustraival pogromy nad evreiami.* Moscow: Krasnaia nov, 1924.

Lezman, J. *Fun Seydemenukhe biz Kalinindorf.* Kharkiv and Kyiv: Melukhishe natsmindfarlag bam prezidium fun Vutsik, 1932.

Liadov, L. *O vrazhde k evreiam.* Moscow and Leningrad: Moskovskii rabochii, 1927.

Mariasina, Sara. *Di alte un di naye shul (a bikhl farn masn-leyener).* Minsk: Folkombild fun Vaysrusland tsentral yidish bildung-biuro, 1929.

Materialy i issledovaniia. Vol. 4, *Evrei v SSSR.* Moscow: Emes, 1929.

Miliakova, L. B. *Kniga pogromov: Pogromy na Ukraine, v Belorussii i Evropeiskoi chasti Rossii v period grazhdanskoi voiny: 1918–1922: Sbornik dokumentov.* Moscow: ROSSPEN, 2007.

Mindlin, Z. L. *Evrei v SSSR. Materialy i issledovaniia.* Moscow: Pravlenie vserossiiskogo ORT, 1929.

Narkompros RSFSR. *O borbe s antisemitizmom v shkole.* Moscow: OGIZ, 1929.

Naselenie SSSR. Moscow: Izd-vo politicheskoi literatury, 1983.

Nomberg, H. D. *Mayn rayze iber rusland.* Warsaw: Kultur-lige, 1928.

Obolensky, Dimitry, ed. *The Penguin Book of Russian Verse.* London: Penguin, 1962.

Ostrovskii, Z. S. *Evreiskie pogromy, 1918–1921.* Moscow: Shkola i kniga, 1926.

Petrovsky, D. A. *Voennaia shkola v godi revoliutsii (1917–1924gg).* Moscow: Vissh. voen. red. sovet, 1924.

Prakticheskoe razreshenie natsionalnogo voprosa v Belorusskoi SSR. Minsk: Izdanie tsentralnoi natsionalnoi komissii TsIK BSSR, 1927.

Preigerzon, Zvi. *Memoirs of a Jewish Prisoner of the Gulag.* Boston: Academic Studies Press, 2022.

Program fun yidish un literature far zibnyoriker shul mit metodishe briv tsu der program. Minsk: Folkombild fun Vaysrusland tsentral yidish bildung-biuro, 1927.

Rabinovich, Yitshak. *Me-moskva ad yerushalayim: Ha-maavak ha-yehudi ha-leumi bi-Verit ha-Mo'atsot.* Jerusalem, n.p., 1957.

Rafaeli, Arye (Zenzipper). *Ba-maavak li-geula. Sefer ha-tsiyonut ha-rusit mi-mahapekhat 1917 ad yameinu.* Tel Aviv: Davar ve-ayanot, 1957.

Rafaeli, Leah (Zenzipper). *Shirei makhteret (Umlegale lider): Parodiyot al nasiim me-khaiei ha-makhteret shel ha-noar ha-tsioni be-Rusiah.* Tel Aviv, n.p., 1971.

Rakovsky, Puah. *My Life as a Radical Jewish Woman: Memoirs of a Zionist Feminist in Poland.* Edited by Paula Hyman. Bloomington: Indiana University Press, 2001.

Ravutsky, Abraham. *Wrenching Times in Ukraine: Memoir of a Jewish Minister.* Translated by Sam Revusky and Moshe Kantorowit. St. John's, Newfoundland: Yksuver, 1998.

Rejzen, Zalmen. *Leksikon fun der yidisher literatur, prese un filologye.* Vol. 1. Vilna: Kletskin, 1926.

Rozental-Shnayderman, Ester. *Af vegn un umvegn: Zikhroynes, geshenishn, perzenlekhkaytn.* 3 vols. Tel Aviv: Havatselet, 1972, 1978, 1982.

Rozin, Aharon. *Mayn veg aheym: Memuarn fun an asir-tsiyon in Ratn-Farband.* Jerusalem: Yiddish Culture Association, 1981.

Ryback, Isaakhar. *On the Jewish Field of the Ukraina.* Paris: A. Simon and Cie, 1926.

Sandomirskii, Yurii. *Puti antisemitizma v Rossii*. Moscow and Leningrad: Gosudarstvennoe izd-vo, 1928.

Sheinman, M. M. *O ravvinakh i sinagogakh*. Moscow: Bezbozhnik, 1927.

Shekhtman, Elye. "Di shtrof fun goylem." *Di goldene keyt*, no. 122, 1987, 20–42.

Shif, Betsalel. "Zabveniiu ne podlezhit." *Lechaim*, November (11) 51, 2004. https://lechaim.ru.

Sinfield, G. *The Workers' Sports Movement*. London: G. Sinfield, 1926.

Singer, I. J. *Nay-Rusland: bilder fun a rayze*. Vilna: Kletskin, 1928.

Smoliar, Hersh. *Fun ineveynik: Zikhroynes vegn der "Yevsektsye."* Tel Aviv: Farlag Peretz, 1978.

———. *Vu bistu khaver Sidorov?* Tel Aviv: Farlag Peretz, 1975.

Sosis, Israel. *Di geshikhte fun di yidishe gezelshaftlekhe shtrebungen in Rusland in XIX y.h.* Minsk: Folkombild fun Vaysrusland tsentral yidish bildung-biuro, 1929.

———. *Di sotsial-ekonomishe lage fun di Ruslendishe yidn in der ershter helft fun 19tn yorhundert*. Petrograd: Hevrat mefitse haskalah be-Israel, 1919.

Stalin, Josef. *Marxism and the National and Colonial Question*. New York: International, 1935.

Tcherikower, Elias. *Di ukrainer pogromen in yor 1919*. New York: YIVO, 1965.

———. *In der tkufe fun revolutsye: memuarn, materyaln, dokumentn*. Berlin: Yidisher literarisher farlag, 1924.

———. *Istoriia pogromnogodvizheniia na Ukraine 1917–1921*. Berlin: Ostjudisches Historisches Arkhiv, 1923.

Tsentralnoe statisticheskoe upravlenie. *Vsesoiuznaia perepis naselenia 17 dekabria 1926 g., kratkie svodki*. Vypusk 4. *Narodnost i rodnoy iazyk naselenia SSSR*. Moscow: Izdanie TsSU SSSR, 1928.

Tsvayg, A. R. *Muter shprakh in shul fun der ershter shtufe, metodishe hantbukh*. Moscow: Folkskomissariat far bildung fun RSFSR, tsentrale felker farlag fun FSSR, 1929.

Tweedie, Ethel Brilliana. "Russia as I Saw It. Russia, Siberia, China, 1925–1926." Russia Documents 1924–1930, Trades Union Congress Collection, Warwick Digital Collection.

Vsia Belarussiia, spravochnaia kniga. Minsk, n.p., 1924.

West, Benjamin. *Beyn yoush lo tikvah: Mikhtavim shel asirei-tsiyon be-rusyah ha-sovetit*. Tel Aviv: Arkhion ha-avodah ha-makhlakah le-kheker yahadut Rusiyah, 1973.

———. *He-Halutz be-Rusyah: Le-toldot He-Halutz ha-bilti-legali (Ha-le'umi-amlani)*. Tel Aviv: Mishlahat shel He-Halutz ha-bilti-legali be-Rusyah, 1932.

———. *The Struggle of a Generation: The Jews Under Soviet Rule*. Tel Aviv: Massada pub., 1959.

Yabrov, G. *Di yidishe literatur in frages, ufgabes un temes, a hilfbukh far di eltere grupn fun tsveytn kontsenter, far lerer, studenn fun pedtekhnikum un far shuln fun hekhern tip*. Minsk: Vaysruslendisher melukhe-farlag, 1928.

Yaroslavskii, E. *Razvernutym frontom: O zadachakh i metodakh antireligioznoy propagandy*. Moscow: Bezbozhnik, 1929.

Zhigalin, G. L. *Prokliatoe nasledie (ob antisemitisme)*. Moscow and Leningrad: Molodaia Gvardia, 1927.

Zhitnik, A. I. *Di yidn in Sovetn-Rusland.* Cleveland: Independent, 1925.

SECONDARY SOURCES

Abbott, Gleason, Peter Kenez, and Richard Stites, eds. *Bolshevik Culture: Experiment and Order in the Russian Revolution.* Bloomington: Indiana University Press, 1981.

Abramson, Henry. *A Prayer for the Government: Ukrainians and Jews in Revolutionary Times, 1917–1920.* Cambridge, MA: Harvard University Press, 1999.

Alroey, Gur. *An Unpromising Land: Jewish Migration to Palestine in the Early Twentieth Century.* Stanford, CA: Stanford University Press, 2014.

Altshuler, Mordechai. *Distribution of the Jewish Population of the USSR 1939.* Jerusalem: Centre for Research and Documentation of East European Jewry, Hebrew University of Jerusalem, 1993.

———. "Georgian Jewish Culture Under the Soviet Regime." *East European Jewish Affairs* 5, no. 2 (1975): 21–39.

———, ed. *Ha-Teatron ha-yehudi bi-Verit ha-Moatsot.* Jerusalem: Hebrew University, 1996.

———. *Ha-Yevsektsya bi-Verit ha-Moatsot: Ben leumiut le-komunizm, 1918–1930.* Tel Aviv: Sifriyat poalim, 1981.

———. "The Rabbi of Homel's Trial." *Michael* 6 (1980): 9–61.

———. *Soviet Jewry on the Eve of the Holocaust: A Social and Demographic Profile.* Jerusalem: Center for Research of East European Jewry, the Hebrew University of Jerusalem, 1998.

———. *Soviet Jewry since the Second World War: Population and Social Structure.* Westport, CT: Greenwood, 1987.

———. *Yahadut ba-makhbesh ha-Sovieti: Ben dat le-zehut yehudit bi-Verit ha-Moatsot, 1941–1964.* Jerusalem: Zalman Shazar Center for Jewish History, 2007.

———. *Yehudei Mizrah Kavkaz: Toledot ha-yehudim hahareriim me-reshit ha-meah ha-teshah esreh.* Jerusalem: Mekhon Ben-Tsevi le-heker kehilot Yisrael ba-Mizrah; Makhon le-Yahadut zemanenu, ha-Universitah ha-Ivrit bi-Yerushalayim 1990.

Altshuler, Mordechai, B. Pinkus, and A. Greenbaum, eds. *Pirsumim rusiim al yehudim ve-yahadut bi-vrit ha-moatsot 1917–1967.* Jerusalem: Historical Society of Israel, 1970.

Arad, Yitzhak. *The Holocaust in the Soviet Union.* Translated by Cummings Ora. Lincoln: University of Nebraska Press, 2009.

Armstrong, John Alexander. *The European Administrative Elite.* Princeton, NJ: Princeton University Press, 1973.

Aronson, G., and Ja. G. Frumkin, eds. *Kniga o russkom evreistve, 1917–1967.* Israel: Gesharim, 2002.

Aronson, G., and J. S. Hertz, eds. *Di geshikhte fun Bund.* 4 vols. New York: Undzer tsayt, 1960–1962.

Ashin, Paul. "Wage Policy in the Transition to NEP." *Russian Review* 47, no. 3 (1988): 293–313.

Assaf, David. *Untold Tales of the Hasidim: Crisis and Discontent in the History of Hasidism*. Waltham, MA: Brandeis University Press, 2011.

Assaf, David, Israel Bartal, Shmuel Feiner, Yehuda Friedlander, Avner Holtzman, and Chava Turniansky, eds. *Mi-Vilna le-Yerushalayim: Mehkarim be-toledotehem ve-tarbutam shel yehudei mizrah eropa. Mugashim le-profesor Shmuel Werses*. Jerusalem: Magnes, 2002.

Astashkevich, Irina. *Gendered Violence: Jewish Women in the Pogroms of 1917 to 1921*. Boston: Academic Studies Press, 2018.

Avrutin, Eugene M. "The End of Everything? Pogroms in Wars and Revolution." *Journal of Modern History* 95, no. 3 (September 2023): 669–691.

———. *Jews and the Imperial State: Identification Politics in Tsarist Russia*. Ithaca, NY: Cornell University Press, 2010.

———, ed. *Photographing the Jewish Nation: Pictures from S. An-sky's Ethnographic Expeditions*. Waltham, MA: Brandeis University Press, 2009.

Avrutin, Eugene M., and Elissa Bemporad. *Pogroms: A Documentary History*. New York: Oxford University Press, 2021.

Barber, John. *Soviet Historians in Crisis, 1928–1932*. London: Palgrave Macmillan, 1981.

Baron, Salo. *The Russian Jew under Tsars and Soviets*. New York: Macmillan, 1964.

Basin, Yakov. *Bolshevizm i evrei: Belorussia, 1920-e*. Minsk: Baraskin, 2008.

———. "Delo Girsha Lekerta (1902) i ego interpretatsiia v fil'me Belgoskino *Ego prevoskhoditelstvo*, 1927." *Belarus y XX stagoddzi*, no. 3 (2004): 34–45.

Bauer, Yehuda. *My Brother's Keeper: A History of the American Jewish Joint Distribution Committee, 1929–1939*. Philadelphia: Jewish Publication of America, 1974.

Beizer, Michael. "Antisemitism in Petrograd/Leningrad, 1917–1930." *East European Jewish Affairs* 29, nos. 1–2 (1999): 5–28.

———. "Dubnov's St. Petersburg." In *A Missionary for History: Essays in Honor of Simon Dubnov*, edited by Kristi Groberg and Avraham Greenbaum, 83–87. Minnesota: University of Minnesota, 1998.

———. *Evrei Leningrada, 1917–1939: Natsional'naya zhizn' i sovietizatsia*. Jerusalem and Moscow: Gesharim, 1999.

———. *Relief in Time of Need: Russian Jewry and the Joint, 1914–1924*. Bloomington: Slavica, Indiana University, 2015.

Bemporad, Elissa. *Becoming Soviet Jews: The Bolshevik Experiment in Minsk*. Bloomington: Indiana University Press, 2013.

———. "Da letteratura del popolo a storia del popolo: Simon Dubnov e l'origine della storiografia russo-ebraica." *Annali di storia dell'esegesi* 18, no. 2 (2001): 533–557.

———. "Defying Authority in the Pale: The Making of Soviet Jewish Rituals and the Emergence of Folk Legitimacy." In *Reappraisals and New Studies of the Modern Jewish Experience: Essays in Honor of Robert M. Seltzer*, edited by Brian M. Smollett and Christian Wiese, 62–82. Leiden: Brill, 2015.

Bemporad, Elissa. *Legacy of Blood: Jews, Pogroms, and Ritual Murder in the Lands of the Soviets*. New York: Oxford University Press, 2019.

Bemporad, Elissa and Thomas Chopard, eds. "The Pogroms of the Russian Civil War at 100: New Trends, New Sources." *Quest. Issues in Contemporary Jewish History* 15 (August 2019).

Bemporad, Elissa, and Glenn Dynner, eds. *Jewish Women in Modern Eastern and East Central Europe*. Cham, Switzerland: Springer, 2022.

Bemporad, Elissa, and Joyce Warren, eds. *Women and Genocide: Survivors, Victims, Perpetrators*. Bloomington: Indiana University Press, 2018.

Bergmann, Werner, Christhard Hoffman, and Helmut Walser Smith, eds. *Exclusionary Violence: Antisemitic Riots in Modern German History*. Ann Arbor: University of Michigan Press, 2002.

Berman, Harold J. "Soviet Family Law in the Light of Russian History and Marxist Theory." *Yale Law Journal* 56, no. 26 (1946): 26–57.

Biale, David. *Power and Powerlessness in Jewish History*. New York: Schocken Books, 1986.

Blobaum, Robert. *A Minor Apocalypse During the First World War*. Ithaca, NY: Cornell University Press, 2017.

Borovoi, Saul Ia. *Evreiskaia zemledelcheskaia kolonizatsiia v staroi Rossii: Politika, ideologiia, khoziaistvo, byt*. Moscow: Sabashnikovy, 1928.

Bridenthal, Renate, Susan Stuard, and Merry E. Wiesner-Hanks, *Becoming Visible: Women in European History*. Boston: Houghton Mifflin, 1998.

Bristow, Edward J. *Prostitution and Prejudice: The Jewish Fight against White Slavery 1870–1939*. Oxford, UK: Clarendon, 1982.

Budnitskii, Oleg. "Jews, Pogroms, and the White Movement: A Historiographical Critique." *Kritika: Explorations in Russian and Eurasian History* 2, no. 4 (2001): 1–23.

———. *Russian Jews between the Reds and the Whites, 1917–1920*. Philadelphia: University of Pennsylvania Press, 2012.

Bunyan, James, and H. H. Fisher. *The Bolshevik Revolution, 1917–1918: Documents and Materials*. Stanford, CA: Stanford University Press, 1934.

Byrnes, Robert F. "Creating the Soviet Historical Profession, 1917–1934." *Slavic Review* 50, no. 2 (1991): 297–308.

Carleton, Gregory. *Sexual Revolution in Bolshevik Russia*. Pittsburgh: University of Pittsburgh Press, 2010.

Carley, Michael Jabara. *Silent Conflict: A Hidden History of Early Soviet Western Relations*. Lanham, MD: Rowman and Littlefield, 2014.

Chopard, Thomas. "The First Catastrophe of East European Jewry: Wars, Pogroms, Displacement and Survival, 1914–1924." PhD diss., Ecole des Hautes Etudes en Sciences Sociales (EHESS), 2017.

Cohen, Nathan. *Yiddish Transformed: Reading Habits in the Russian Empire, 1860–1914*. Oxford, UK: Berghahn Books, 2023.

Crews, Robert. "Empire and the Confessional State: Islam and Religious Politics in Nineteenth-Century Russia." *American Historical Review* 108 (2003): 50–83.

Davies, Franziska, Martin Schulze Wessel, and Michael Brenner, eds. *Jews and*

Muslims in the Russian Empire and the Soviet Union. Göttingen: Vandenhoeck and Ruprecht, 2015.

Davies, R. W., ed. *From Tsarism to the New Economic Policy: Continuity and Change in the Economy of the U.S.S.R.* London: Palgrave Macmillan, 1990.

Dean, Martin. *Collaboration in the Holocaust: Crimes of the Local Police in Belorussia and Ukraine, 1941–1944*. London: Palgrave Macmillan/USHMM, 2000.

Dekel-Chen, Jonathan. *Farming the Red Land: Jewish Agricultural Colonization and Local Soviet Power, 1924–1941*. New Haven, CT: Yale University Press, 2005.

Dekel-Chen, Jonathan, David Gaunt, Natan Meir, and Israel Bartal. *Anti-Jewish Violence: Rethinking the Pogrom in East European History*. Bloomington: Indiana University Press, 2010.

Denisova, Liubov. *Rural Women in the Soviet Union and in Post-Soviet Russia*. London: Routledge, 2010.

Dumitru, Diana. *The State, Antisemitism, and Collaboration in the Holocaust: The Borderlands of Romania and the Soviet Union*. New York: Cambridge University Press, 2016.

Dymshits, Valery. *Facing the West: Oriental Jews of Central Asia and the Caucasus*. Amsterdam: Rossisskii etnograficheskii muzei / Joods Historisch Museum, 1998.

Eaton, Katherine Bliss. *Daily Life in the Soviet Union*. Westport, CT: Greenwood, 2004.

———. *Enemies of the People: The Destruction of Soviet Literary, Theater, and Film Arts in the 1930s*. Evanston, IL: Northwestern University Press, 2002.

Eliasberg, Galina. *Odin iz prezhnogo Peterburga: S. L. Tsinberg, istorik evreiskoi literatury, kritik i publitsist*. Moscow: RGGU, 2005.

Engel, Barbara Alpern. *Mothers and Daughters: Women of the Intelligentsia in Nineteenth-Century Russia*. Cambridge: Cambridge University Press, 1985.

Engel, David, ed. *The Assassination of Symon Petliura and the Trial of Sholem Schwarzbard 1926–1927: A Selection of Documents*. Archiv Judischer Geschichte und Kultur / Archive of Jewish History and Culture. Göttingen: V&R Academic, 2016.

Engelstein, Laura. *Russia in Flames: War, Revolution, Civil War, 1914–1921*. New York: Oxford University Press, 2017.

Estraikh, Gennady. "From 'Green Fields' to 'Red Fields': Peretz Hirschbein's Soviet Sojourn, 1928–1929." *Jews in Russia and Eastern Europe* 1 (2006). 60–81.

———. "From Yehupets Jargonists to Kiev Modernists: The Rise of a Yiddish Literary Centre, 1880s–1914." *East European Jewish Affairs* 30, no. 1 (2000): 17–38.

———. *The History of Birobidzhan: Building a Soviet Jewish Homeland in Siberia*. New York: Bloomsbury, 2023.

———. *In Harness: Yiddish Writers' Romance with Communism*. Syracuse, NY: Syracuse University Press, 2005.

———. "Mnogolikii David Lipets: Evrei v russkoi revoliutsii." In *Arkhiv evreiskoi istorii*, vol. 7, edited by Oleg Budnitskii, 225–241. Moscow: ROSSPEN, 2012.

———. *Transatlantic Russian Jewishness: Ideological Voyages of the Yiddish* Daily Forverts *in the First Half of the Twentieth Century*. Boston: Academic Studies Press, 2020.

Estraikh, Gennady, and Mikhail Krutikov, eds. *The Shtetl: Image and Reality*. London: Routledge, 2000.

———, eds. *Yiddish and the Left: Papers of the Third Mendel Friedman International Conference on Yiddish*. Oxford, UK: Legenda, 2001.

Faigan, Susan. "An Annotated Bibliography of Maria Yakovlevna Frumkina (Esther)." PhD diss., Australian National University, 2018.

Feiner, Shmuel. *The Jewish Enlightenment*. Translated by Chaya Naor. Philadelphia: University of Pennsylvania Press, 2002.

Feuer, Lewis S. "American Travelers to the Soviet Union 1917–32: The Formation of a Component of New Deal Ideology." *American Quarterly* 14, no. 2, pt. 1 (Summer 1962): 119–149.

Fishman, David E. "'The Kingdom on Earth Is Like the Kingdom of Heaven': Rabbinic Reactions to Jewish Radicalism in Russia." In *Let the Old Make Way for the New: Studies in the Social and Cultural History of East European Jewry Presented to Immanuel Etkes*, edited by David Assaf and Ada Rapoport-Albert, vol. 2, 227–259. Jerusalem: Shazar Center, 2009.

———. "Preserving Tradition in the Land of Revolution: The Religious Leadership of Soviet Jewry 1917–1930." In *The Uses of Tradition: Jewish Continuity in the Modern Era*, edited by Jack Wertheimer, 85–118. New York: Jewish Theological Seminary of America, 1992.

———. "Rabbi Joseph Isaac Schneersohn: The Making of a Jewish Religious Leader in the USSR." In *Religion and the Russian Revolution of 1917: Conflicts, Encounters, and Transformations*, edited by N. Kizenko. Bloomington: Indiana University Press, forthcoming.

Fitzpatrick, Sheila. "The 'Soft' Line on Culture and Its Enemies: Soviet Cultural Policy, 1922–1927." *Slavic Review* 33, no. 2 (June 1974): 267–287.

Fitzpatrick, Sheila, Alexander Rabinowitch, and Richard Stites, eds. *Russia in the Era of NEP: Explorations in Soviet Society and Culture*. Bloomington: Indiana University Press, 1991.

Fitzpatrick, Sheila, and Yuri Slezkine, eds. *In the Shadow of Revolution: Life Stories of Russian Women from 1917 to the Second World War*. Princeton, NJ: Princeton University Pres, 2000.

Flory, Harriette. "The Arcos Raid and the Rupture of Anglo-Soviet Relations, 1927." *Journal of Contemporary History* 12, no. 4 (1977): 707–723.

Foner, Philip S. *The Bolshevik Revolution: Its Impact on American Radicals, Liberals, and Labour*. New York: International, 1967.

Frankel, Jonathan. *Prophecy and Politics: Socialism, Nationalism and the Russian Jews, 1862–1917*. Cambridge: Cambridge University Press, 1981.

Freeze, ChaeRan Y. *Jewish Marriage and Divorce in Imperial Russia*. Waltham, MA: Brandeis University Press, 2002.

Freeze, ChaeRan Y., and Jay Michael Harris, eds. *Everyday Jewish Life in Imperial Russia: Select Documents, 1772–1914*. Waltham, MA: Brandeis University Press, 2013.

Freeze, Gregory L. "Churching Russian History: Orthodoxy in the Great War and

Revolution." In *Religion and the Russian Revolution of 1917: Conflicts, Encounters, and Transformations*, edited by N. Kizenko. Bloomington: Indiana University Press, forthcoming.

———. *Gubitel'noe blagochestie: Rossiiskaia pravoslavnaia tserkov' i padenie imperii.* Saint Petersburg: Izdatelstvo Evropeiskogo Universiteta, 2019.

Galili, Ziva. "The Soviet Experience of Zionism: Importing Soviet Political Culture to Palestine." *Journal of Israeli History, Politics, Society, Culture* 24, no. 1 (2005): 1–33.

Galili, Ziva, and Boris Morozov. *Exiled to Palestine: The Emigration of Zionist Convicts from the Soviet Union, 1924–1934.* London: Routledge, 2013.

Gershuni, A. A. *Yahadut be-Rusiayh ha-Soviyetit: Le-korot redifot ha-daat.* Jerusalem: Mosad ha-Rav Kuk, 1961.

Gessen, Valerii. *K istorii Sankt-Peterburgskoi evreiskoi religioznoi obshchiny: Ot pervykh evreev do XX veka.* Saint Petersburg: Tema, 2000.

Getzler, Israel. *Kronstadt 1917–1921: The Fate of Soviet Democracy.* Cambridge: Cambridge University Press, 1983.

Gilboa, Yehoshua A. *A Language Silenced: The Suppression of Hebrew Language and Culture in the Soviet Union.* New York: Herzl, 1982.

———. "Tzvi Preigerzon: A Hebrew Writers in the USSR." *Soviet Jewish Affairs* 7, no. 2 (1977): 62–68.

Gilley, Christopher. "Beyond Petliura: The Ukrainian National Movement and the 1919 Pogroms." *East European Jewish Affairs* 47, no. 1 (2017): 45–61.

Gimpelevich, Ziva, and Vital Zajka. "Zmitrok Biadulia: A Belarusian Jewish Writer Who Was Loved by Many." *Tsaytshrift* 8, no. 3 (2013): 131–159.

Gitelman, Zvi. *A Century of Ambivalence: The Jews of Russia and the Soviet Union, 1881 to the Present.* Bloomington: Indiana University Press, 2001.

———, ed. *The Emergence of Modern Jewish Politics: Bundism and Zionism in Eastern Europe.* Pittsburgh: University of Pittsburgh Press, 2003.

———. *Jewish Nationality and Soviet Politics: The Jewish Sections of the CPSU, 1917–1930.* Princeton, NJ: Princeton University Press, 1972.

Gitelman, Zvi, and Yaakov Ro'i, eds. *Revolution, Repression, and Revival: The Soviet Jewish Experience.* Lanham, MD: Rowman and Littlefield, 2007.

Glaser, Amelia. "Maxim Gorky's 'Pogrom': Jewish Victimhood and Russian Revolutionary Thought." *Shofar: An Interdisciplinary Journal of Jewish Studies* 37, no. 2 (2019): 166–190.

Goland, Yurii. "Currency Regulation in the NEP Period." *Europe-Asia Studies* 46, no. 8 (1994): 1251–1296.

Goldin, Semion. *The Russian Army and the Jewish Population, 1914–1917: Libel, Persecution, Reaction.* London: Palgrave Macmillan, 2022.

Goldman, Wendy Z. *Women, the State, and Revolution.* Cambridge: Cambridge University Press, 1993.

Gordienko, Anastasia. *Outlaw Music in Russia: The Rise of an Unlikely Genre.* Madison: University of Wisconsin Press, 2023.

Granick, Jaclyn. *International Jewish Humanitarianism in the Age of the Great War.* Cambridge: Cambridge University Press, 2021.

Greenbaum, A. A. "The Belorussian State Jewish Theater in the Interwar Period." *Jews in Russia and Eastern Europe* 42 (2001): 56–75.

———. *Jewish Scholarship and Scholarly Institutions in Soviet Russia, 1918–1953*. Jerusalem: Hebrew University of Jerusalem, 1978.

Gurevitz, Baruch. "The Liquidation of the Last Independent Party in the Soviet Union." *Canadian Slavonic Papers* 18, no. 2 (1976): 178–186.

Hagen, William. *Anti-Jewish Violence in Poland, 1914–1920*. New York: Cambridge University Press, 2018.

Hanebrink, Paul. *A Specter Haunting Europe: The Myth of Judeo-Bolshevism*. Cambridge, MA: Harvard University Press, 2018.

Herlihy, Patricia. *Odessa Recollected: The Port and the People*. Boston: Academic Studies Press, 2019.

Hertz, Deborah. "Dangerous Politics, Dangerous Liaisons: Love and Terror among Jewish Women Radicals in Czarist Russia." *Histoire, économie & société* 33année(4) (2014): 94–109.

Hertz, J. S., ed. *Doyres Bundistn*. New York: Farlag Undser tsayt, 1956.

———. *Hirsh Lekert*. New York: Undzer tsayt, 1952.

Hirsch, Francine. *Empire of Nations: Ethnographic Knowledge and the Making of the Soviet Union*. Ithaca, NY: Cornell University Press, 2014.

Hoberman, J. *Bridge of Light: Yiddish Film between Two Worlds*. New York: Museum of Modern Art, 1991.

Hoffman, Charles E. *Red Shtetl: The Survival of a Jewish Town under Soviet Communism*. New York: American Jewish Joint Distribution Committee, 2002.

Hoffmann, David L. "Moving to Moscow: Patterns of Peasant In-Migration during the First Five-Year Plan." *Slavic Review* 50, no. 4 (1991): 847–857.

———. *Peasant Metropolis: Social Identities in Moscow, 1929–1941*. Ithaca, NY: Cornell University Press, 1994.

Hollinger, David. "Communalist and Dispersionist Approaches to American Jewish History in an Increasingly Post-Jewish Era." *American Jewish History* 95, no. 1 (2009): 1–32.

Horowitz, Brian. "The Society for the Promotion of Enlightenment among the Jews of Russia, and the Evolution of the St. Petersburg Russian-Jewish Intelligentsia, 1893–1905." In *Jews and the State: Dangerous Alliances and the Perils of Privilege*, edited by Ezra Mendelsohn, 195–213, Studies in Contemporary Jewry 19. Oxford: Oxford University Press, 2004.

Horowitz, Rosemary, ed. *Women Writers of Yiddish Literature: Critical Essays*. Jefferson, NC: McFarland, 2015.

Hosking, Geoffrey A. *The First Socialist Society: A History of the Soviet Union from Within*. Cambridge, MA: Harvard University Press, 1997.

Hundert, Gershon David, ed. *YIVO Encyclopedia of Jews in Eastern Europe*. New Haven, CT: Yale University Press, 2008.

Hutton, Marcelline J. *Russian and West European Women, 1860–1939: Dreams, Struggles, and Nightmares*. Lanham, MD: Rowman and Littlefield, 2001.

Hyman, Paula E. *Gender and Assimilation in Modern Jewish History: The Roles and Representations of Women*. Seattle: University of Washington Press, 1995.

———. "Two Models of Modernization: Jewish Women in the German and the Russian Empires." In *Jews and Gender: The Challenge to Hierarchy*, edited by Jonathan Frankel, 39–54, Studies in Contemporary Jewry 16. New York: Oxford University Press, 2000.

Ivanov, V. V. *Russkie sezony teatra Gabima*. Moscow: Artist-Rezhesser-Teatr, 1999.

Jackson, Brian. *The Black Flag: A Look Back at the Strange Case of Nicola Sacco and Bartolomeo Vanzetti*. London: Routledge, 1981.

Judd, Robin. "The Politics of Beef: Animal Advocacy and the Kosher Butchering Debates in Germany." *Jewish Social Studies* 10, no. 1 (Fall 2003): 117–150.

Kaiser, Robert J. *The Geography of Nationalism in Russia and the USSR*. Princeton, NJ: Princeton University Press, 1994.

Kaplan, Pegelow Thomas. "Reinterpreting Jewish Petitioning Practices during the Shoah: Contestation, Transnational Space, and Survival." *Journal of Holocaust Research* 35, no. 4 (2021): 306–325.

Kelner, V. E. *Ocherki po istorii russko-evreiskogo knizhnogo dela vo vtoroi polovine XIX-nachale XX v*. Saint Petersburg: Rossiiskaia natsionalnaia biblioteka, 2003.

Kenez, Peter. "Lenin's Concept of Culture." *History of European Ideas* 11, nos. 1–6 (1989): 359–363.

Kerler, Dov-Ber, ed. *Politics of Yiddish: Studies in Language, Literature and Society*. Lanham, MD: AltaMira, 1998.

Kiaer, Christina, and Eric Naiman, eds. *Everyday Life in Early Soviet Russia: Taking the Revolution Inside*. Bloomington: Indiana University Press, 2006.

Klier, John Doyle. *Imperial Russia's Jewish Question, 1855–1881*. Cambridge: Cambridge University Press, 2005.

Kochan, Lionel, ed. *The Jews in Soviet Russia Since 1917*. London: Oxford University Press, 1970.

Kocho-Williams, Alastair. *Russian and Soviet Diplomacy, 1900–39*. London: Palgrave Macmillan, 2012.

Koenker, Diane. "Urbanization and Deurbanization in the Russian Revolution and Civil War." *Journal of Modern History* 57, no. 3 (September 1985): 424–450.

Koller, Sabine, Gennady Estraikh, and Mikhail Krutikov, eds. *Joseph Opatoshu: A Yiddish Writer between Europe and America*. Oxford, UK: Legenda, 2017.

Kolonitsky, Boris. "Antibourgeois Propaganda and Anti-'Burzhui' Consciousness in 1917." *Russian Review* 53 (1994): 183–196.

Kostyrchenko, G. V. *Tainaia politika Stalina: Vlast' i antisemitizm*. Moscow: Mezhdunarodnye otnosheniia, 2001.

Kotkin, Stephen. *Magnetic Mountain: Stalinism as a Civilization*. Berkeley: University of California Press, 1995.

Kozerod, Oleg. *Jewish Women in Ukraine: Writers, Zionists, Leaders in the 1920s*. Warsaw: European World, 2019.

Krichevsky, Lev "Evrei v apparate VChK-OGPU v 20-e gody." *Vestnik evreiskogo universiteta*, 1 (8) (1995): 104–140.

Kupfer, Matthew. "Zvi Preigerzon: The Soviet Union's Secret Hebrew Writer." *Odessa Review*, November 17, 2017.

Lederhendler, Eli. *Road to Modern Jewish Politics: Political Tradition and Political Reconstruction in the Jewish Community of Tsarist Russia*. New York: Oxford University Press, 1989.

Len, Yuliya. "Jewish Community of Berdychiv and the Early Soviet Policies." Master's thesis, University of Tartu, 2019.

Leshchinsky, Yaakov. *Ha-Yehudim be-Rusyah ha-Sovyetit: Mi-mahpekhet Oktober ad milhemet-ha-olam ha-sheniyah*. Tel Aviv: Am oved, 1942.

Levin, Mordechai. *Erchei hevrah ve-kalkalah be-ideologiah shel tkufat ha-haskalah*. Jerusalem: Bialik Institute, 1975.

Levin, Nora. *The Jews of the Soviet Union: A Paradox of Survival*. Vol. 1. New York: New York University Press, 1990.

Levin, Sholem Dovber. *Toldot Chabad be-Rusiah ha-Soviyetit*. Brooklyn, NY: Kehot Publication Society, 1989.

Levin, Vladimir. *Mi-mahpekhah le-milhamah: Ha-politikah ha-Yehudit be-Rusyah, 1907–1914*. Jerusalem: Merkaz Zalman Shazar, 2016.

Levin, Zeev. *Collectivization and Social Engineering: Soviet Administration and the Jews of Uzbekistan, 1917–1939*. Leiden: Brill, 2015.

———. "The Khujum Campaign in Uzbekistan and the Bukharan Jewish Women." In *Gender Politics in Central Asia: Historical Perspectives and Current Living Conditions of Women*, edited by Christa Ehrmann-Hammerle, 95–113. Köln: Böhlau-Verlag, 2008.

Levine, Hillel. *Economic Origins of Anti-Semitism: Poland and Its Jews in the Early Modern Period*. New Haven, CT: Yale University Press, 1991.

Levitin, Anatoli, and Vadim Shavrov. *Ocherki po istorii Russkoi tserkvnoy smuty*. 3 vols. Kusnacht: Institut Glaube in der 2 Welt, 1978.

Lipsky, Seth. *The Rise of Abraham Cahan*. New York: Schocken, 2013.

Litvak, Olga. *Conscription and the Search for Modern Russian Jewry*. Bloomington: Indiana University Press, 2006.

Livne-Liberman, Zvi. *Ikarim yehudim be-Rusyah*. Tel Aviv: Aleph, 1967.

Lohr, Eric. "The Russian Army and the Jews: Mass Deportation, Hostages, and Violence during World War I." *Russian Review* 60, no. 3 (2001): 404–419.

Lumer, Hyman. *Lenin on the Jewish Question*. New York: International, 1974.

Mahler, Raphael. *Hasidism and the Jewish Enlightenment: Their Confrontation in Galicia and Poland in the First Half of the Nineteenth Century*. Philadelphia: Jewish Publication Society, 1985.

Makaryk, Irena, and Virlana Tkacz. *Modernism in Kyiv: Jubilant Experimentation*. Toronto: University of Toronto Press, 2010.

Malysheva, Svetlana. "Soviet Death and Hybrid Soviet Subjectivity: Urban Cemetery as a Metatext." *Ab Imperio* 3 (2018): 351–385.

Mantovan, Daniela. *Yiddish Poets in the Soviet Union, 1917–1948*. Heidelberg: Heidelberg Universitatsverlag, 2012.

Maor, Yitzchak. *Ha-tnua ha-tziyonit be-rusya me-reshita ve-ad yameinu*. Jerusalem: Ha-sifriya ha-tziyonit and Magnes 1973.

Margolis, R. E. "A Tempest in Three Teapots: Yom Kippur Balls in London, New York and Montreal." *Canadian Jewish Studies / Études Juives Canadiennes* 9 (2001): 38–84.

Marshall, Alex. *The Caucasus under Soviet Rule*. London: Routledge, 2010.

Martin, Terry. *The Affirmative Action Empire: Nations and Nationalism in the Soviet Union, 1923–1939*. Ithaca, NY: Cornell University Press, 2001.

Mawdsley, Evan. *Thunder in the East: The Nazi-Soviet War 1941–1945*. New York: Bloomsbury, 2005.

Mazower, Mark. *What You Did Not Tell: A Russian Past and the Journey Home*. New York: Penguin Books, 2018.

McGeever, Brendan. *Antisemitism and the Russian Revolution*. Cambridge: Cambridge University Press, 2019.

McMeekin, Sean. *History's Greatest Heist: The Looting of Russia by the Bolsheviks*. New Haven, CT: Yale University Press, 2009.

———. *The Russian Revolution: A New History*. London: Profile Books, 2017.

Medding, Peter Y., ed. *Jews and Violence: Images, Ideologies, Realities*. Studies in Contemporary Jewry 18, New York: Oxford University Press, 2003.

Meir, Natan. *Kiev, Jewish Metropolis: A History, 1859–1914*. Bloomington: Indiana University Press, 2010.

Melamed, Efim. "The Fate of the Archives of the Kiev Institute of Jewish Proletarian Culture: Puzzles and Discoveries." *East European Jewish Affairs* 42, no. 2 (August 2012): 99–110.

Meleshkina, Irina. *Mandrivni zori v Ukraini: Storinki istorii evreiskogo teatru*. Kyiv: Dukh i litera, 2019.

Mendelsohn, Ezra, ed. *Essential Papers on Jews and the Left*. New York: New York University Press, 1997.

———, ed. *Jews and Other Ethnic Groups in a Multi-ethnic World*. Studies in Contemporary Jewry 3. Jerusalem: Hebrew University of Jerusalem, 1987.

———, ed. *People of the City: Jews and the Urban Challenge*. Studies in Contemporary Jewry 15. New York: Oxford University Press, 2000.

Meyers, Joshua. "A Portrait of Transition: From the Bund to Bolshevism in the Russian Revolution." *Jewish Social Studies* 24, no. 2 (Winter 2019): 107–134.

Miccoli, Giovanni. "Santa Sede, questione ebraica e antisemitismo tra Otto e Novecento." In *Storia d'Italia. Annali 11/2. Gli ebrei in Italia*, edited by Corrado Vivanti, 1371–1574. Turin: Einaudi, 1997.

Mintz, Mattityahu. "Illegal Zionist Organizations in Ukraine, 1924–1925." *Jews in Eastern Europe* 31, no. 3 (Winter 1996): 46–66.

Mitsel, Mikhail. *Poslednaiaia glava: Agro-Joint v gody bolshogo terrora*. Kyiv: Dukh i litera, 2012.

Moss, Kenneth B. *Jewish Renaissance in the Russian Revolution*. Cambridge, MA: Harvard University Press, 2009.

Moss, Kenneth B., Benjamin Nathans, and Taro Tsurumi, eds. *From Europe's East to the Middle East: Israel's Russian and Polish Lineages*. Philadelphia: University of Pennsylvania Press, 2021.

Murav, Harriet L. *A Dust of the Earth: The Literature of Abandonment in Revolutionary Russia and Ukraine*. Bloomington: Indiana University Press, 2024.

Murav, Harriet L., Gennady Estraikh, and Myroslav Shkandrij, eds. *Building Modern Jewish Culture: The Yiddish Kultur-Lige*. Oxford, UK: Legenda, 2023.

Nadell, Pamela Susan, and Kate Haulman. *Making Women's Histories: Beyond National Perspectives*. New York: New York University Press, 2013.

Naiman, Oleksander Iakovich. *Evreiski partiy ta obednannia Ukrainy, 1917–1925*. Kyiv: Natsionalna akademia nauk Ukrainy, Institut politichnikh i etnonatsionalnikh doslidzhen, 1998.

Nathans, Benjamin. *Beyond the Pale: The Jewish Encounter with Late Imperial Russia*. Berkeley: University of California Press, 2002.

Novershtern, Avraham. "Hundert yor Dovid Bergelson: Materialn tsu zayn lebn un shafn." *Di goldene keyt* 115 (1985): 44–58.

Novikova, Liudmila. *An Anti-Bolshevik Alternative: The White Movement and the Civil War in the Russian North*. Translated by Seth Bernstein. Madison: University of Wisconsin Press, 2018.

O'Keeffe, Brigid. *The Multiethnic Soviet Union and Its Demise*. New York: Bloomsbury Academic, 2022.

———. "The People's Ambassadress: The Forgotten Diplomacy of Ivy Litvinov." *Aeon*, March 29, 2021. https://aeon.co.

———. "The Woman Always Pays: The Lives of Ivy Litvinov." *Slavonic and East European Review* 97, no. 3 (July 2019): 501–528.

Patt, Avinoam, Atina Grossman, Linda G. Levin, and Maud S. Mandel, eds. *JDC at 100: A Century of Humanitarianism*. Detroit: Wayne State University Press, 2019.

Penslar, Derek J. *Zionism: An Emotional State*. New Brunswick, NJ: Rutgers University Press, 2023.

Peris, Daniel. *Storming the Heavens: The Soviet League of the Militant Godless*. Ithaca, NY: Cornell University Press, 1998.

Petrovsky-Shtern, Yohanan. *The Anti-Imperial Choice: The Making of the Ukrainian Jew*. New Haven, CT: Yale University Press, 2009.

Phillips, Hugh. "From a Bolshevik to a British Subject: The Early Years of Maxim Litvinov." *Slavic Review* 48, no. 3 (Autumn 1989): 388–398.

Pines, D. *Hehalutz be-kur ha-mahapekha: Korot ha-histadrut he-haluts be-Rusiya*. Tel Aviv: Davar, 1938.

Pinkus, Benjamin. *The Jews of the Soviet Union: The History of a National Minority*. Cambridge: Cambridge University Press, 1988.

Polonsky, Antony. *Jews in Poland and Russia: A Short History*. Liverpool: Liverpool University Press, 2020.

Polonsky, Rachel. *Molotov's Magic Lantern: Travels in Russian History*. New York: Farrar, Strauss and Giroux, 2011.

Popoff, Alexandra. *Vasily Grossman and the Soviet Century*. New Haven, CT: Yale University Press, 2019.

Pospielovsky, Dimitry. *A History of Soviet Atheism in Theory, and Practice, and the Believer*. Vol. 1, *A History of Marxist-Leninist Atheism and Soviet Anti-Religious Policies*. New York: St. Martin's, 1987.

Prozorov, Sergei. "Living Ideas and Dead Bodies: The Biopolitics of Stalin." *Alternatives: Global, Local, Political* 38, no. 3 (2013): 208–227.

Quigley, John. "The 1926 Soviet Family Code: Retreat from Free Love." *Soviet and Post-Soviet Review* 6, no. 1 (1979): 166–174.

Rabinovitch, Simon. "Russian Jewry Goes to the Polls: An Analysis of Jewish Voting in the All-Russian Constituent Assembly Elections of 1917." *East European Jewish Affairs* 39, no. 2 (2009): 205–225.

Radkey, Oliver H. *Russia Goes to the Polls: The Election to the All-Russian Constituent Assembly, 1917*. Ithaca, NY: Cornell University Press, 1990.

Regelson, Lev. *Tragediia Russkoi tservki, 1917–1945*. Paris: YMCA Press, 1977.

Rein, Leonid. *The Kings and the Pawns: Collaboration in Byelorussia during World War II*. New York: Berghahn Books, 2011.

Rogger, Hans. *Jewish Policies and Right-Wing Politics in Imperial Russia*. Berkeley: University of California Press, 1986.

Ro'i, Yaakov, ed. *Jews and Jewish Life in Russia and the Soviet Union*. New York: Routledge, 1995; 2nd ed., 2016.

Roslof, Edward E. *Red Priests: Renovationism, Russian Orthodoxy and Revolution, 1905–1946*. Indianapolis: Indiana University Press, 2002.

Rothenberg, Joshua. *The Jewish Religion in the Soviet Union*, New York: Ktav, 1971.

Rubenstein, Joshua. *Leon Trotsky: A Revolutionary Life*. New Haven, CT: Yale University Press, 2011.

Rubenstein, Joshua, and Vladimir Pavlovich Naumov, eds. *Stalin's Secret Pogrom: The Postwar Inquisition of the Jewish Anti-Fascist Committee*. New Haven, CT: Yale University Press, 2001.

Rudling, Per Anders. *The Rise and Fall of Belarusian Nationalism, 1906–1931*. Pittsburgh: University of Pittsburgh Press, 2014.

Rürup, Reinhard. "A Success Story and Its Limits: European Jewish Social History in the Nineteenth and Early Twentieth Centuries." *Jewish Social Studies* 11, no. 1 (2004): 3–15.

Russkaia literatura XX veka. Prozaiki, poety, dramaturgi. Vol. 1. Moscow: Olma Press Invest, 2005.

Safran, Gabriella, and Steven J. Zipperstein, eds. *The Worlds of S. An-Sky: A Russian Jewish Intellectual at the Turn of the Century*. Stanford, CA: Stanford University Press, 2006.

Sanders, Thomas, ed. *Historiography of Imperial Russia: The Profession and Writing of History in a Multinational State*. New York: Sharpe, 1999.

Schwarz, Solomon. *The Jews in the Soviet Union*. Syracuse, NY: Syracuse University Press, 1951.

Senderovich, Sasha. *How the Soviet Jew Was Made*. Cambridge, MA: Harvard University Press, 2022.

Shapira, Anita. "Labor Zionism and the October Revolution." *Journal of Contemporary History* 24, no. 4 (October 1989): 623–656.

Shcherbakova, Marina. "K voprosu o kontseptualnom razvitii evreiskogo muzeia i etnografii evreev na territorii Ukrainy v 1917–1941gg." *Judaic-Slavic Journal*, no. 1 (2) (2019).

Shechtman, J. B. "Sovetskaia Rossia, sionizm i Izrail." In *Kniga o russkom evreistve, 1917–1967*, edited by J. G. Frumkin, G. J. Aronson, and A. A. Goldenveizer, 315–344. New York: Soiuz russkikh evreev, 1968.

Shepherd, Naomi. *A Price below Rubies: Jewish Women as Rebels and Radicals*. Cambridge, MA: Harvard University Press, 1998.

Sherman, Joseph, Gennady Estraikh, David Shneer, and Jordan Finkin, eds. *A Captive of the Dawn: The Life and Work of Peretz Markish*. London: Routledge, 2020.

Shmeruk, Khone. "Ha-kibbuts ha-yehudi veha-hityashvut ha-haklait ha-yehudit be-Bielorusiah ha-sovetit, 1918–1932." PhD diss., Hebrew University, 1961.

Shneer, David. "Who Owns the Means of Cultural Production? The Soviet Yiddish Publishing Industry of the 1920s." *Book History* 6 (2003): 197–226.

———. *Yiddish and the Creation of Soviet Yiddish Culture*. Cambridge: Cambridge University Press, 2004.

Shrayer, Maxim, ed., *An Anthology of Jewish-Russian Literature, 1801–1953: Two Centuries of Dual Identity in Prose and Poetry*. Vol. 1. New York: M. E. Sharpe, 2007.

Shternshis, Anna. "Salo on Challah: Soviet Jews' Experience of Food in the 1920s–1950s." In *Jews and Their Foodways*, edited by Anat Helman, 10–27, Studies in Contemporary Jewry 28. New York: Oxford University Press, 2016.

———. *Soviet and Kosher: Jewish Popular Culture in the Soviet Union, 1923–1939*. Bloomington: Indiana University Press, 2006.

———. *When Sonia Met Boris*. New York: Oxford University Press, 2017.

Silver, Matthew. *Louis Marshall and the Rise of Jewish Ethnicity in America: A Biography*. Syracuse, NY: Syracuse University Press, 2013.

Skubii, Iryna. "Wealth in Soviet Times: The Material World of the Ukrainian Economic Elite, 1920s–1930s." *Res Historica* 48 (2019): 193–213.

Slezkine, Yuri. *The House of Government: A Saga of the Russian Revolution*. Princeton, NJ: Princeton University Press, 2017.

———. *The Jewish Century*. Princeton, NJ: Princeton University Press, 2004.

Sloin, Andrew. *The Jewish Revolution in Belorussia: Economy, Race, and Bolshevik Power*. Bloomington: Indiana University Press, 2017.

———. "Speculators, Swindlers, and Other Jews: Regulating Trade in Revolutionary White Russia." *East European Jewish Affairs* 40, no. 2 (2010): 103–125.

Smele, Jonathan D. *Civil War in Siberia: The Anti-Bolshevik Government of Admiral Kolchak, 1918–1920*. Cambridge: Cambridge University Press, 1996.

Smilovitsky, Leonid. *Jewish Life in Belarus under Stalin: The Final Decade of the Stalin Regime (1944–1953)*. Budapest: Central European University Press, 2014.

Smith, Helmut Walser. *The Continuities of German History: Nation, Religion, and Race across the Long Nineteenth Century*. Cambridge: Cambridge University Press, 2008.

Smolkin, Victoria. *A Sacred Space Is Never Empty: A History of Soviet Atheism*. Princeton, NJ: Princeton University Press, 2018.

Sobolevskaia, Olga, and Vladimir Gancharov. *Evrei Grodnenshchiny: Zhizn do katastrofy*. Donetsk: Nordpress, 2005.

Sokolova, Alla. "House-Building Tradition of the Shtetl in Memorials and Memories Based on Materials of Field Studies in Podolia." *East European Jewish Affairs* 41, no. 3 (2011): 111–135.

Sokolova, Anna. "Soviet Funeral Services: From Moral Economy to Social Welfare and Back." *Revolutionary Russia* 32, no. 2 (2019): 251–271.

Sover, Arie, ed. *The Languages of Humor: Verbal, Visual, and Physical Humor*. New York: Bloomsbury, 2018.

Soyer, Daniel. "Back to the Future: American Jews Visit the Soviet Union in the 1920s and 1930s." *Jewish Social Studies* 6, no. 3 (2000): 124–159.

Spektor, Shmuel, ed. *The Encyclopedia of Jewish Life before and during the Holocaust*. Vol. 1, New York: New York University Press, 2002.

Sperber, Haim. "Agunot 1851–1914: An Introduction." *Annales de demographie historique*, 136, no. 2 (2018): 107–135.

Stanislawsky, Michael. *For Whom Do I Toil? Judah Leib Gordon and the Crisis of Russian Jewry*. New York: Oxford University Press, 1988.

———. *Tsar Nicholas I and the Jews: The Transformation of Jewish Society in Russia, 1825–1855*. Philadelphia: Jewish Publication Society, 1983.

Stites, Richard. *The Women's Liberation Movement in Russia: Feminism, Nihilism, and Bolshevism, 1860–1930*. Princeton, NJ: Princeton University Press, 1978.

Suny, Ronald Grigor, and Terry Martin, eds. *A State of Nations: Empire and Nation-Making in the Age of Lenin and Stalin*. New York: Oxford University Press, 2001.

Szajkowski, Zosa. *Jews, Wars and Communism*. Vol. 1, *The Attitude of American Jews to World War I, the Russian Revolutions of 1917, and Communism (1914–1945)*. New York: Ktav, 1971.

Tanny, Jarrod. *City of Rogues and Schnorrers: Russia's Jews and the Myth of Old Odessa*. Bloomington: Indiana University Press, 2011.

Teller, Adam. *Money, Power, and Influence in Eighteenth-Century Lithuania: The Jews on the Radziwill Estates*. Stanford, CA: Stanford University Press, 2016.

Ury, Scott. *Barricades and Banners: The Revolution of 1905 and the Transformation of Warsaw Jewry*. Stanford, CA: Stanford University Press, 2012.

Van den Bercken, William. *Ideology and Atheism in the Soviet Union*. New York: Mouton de Gruyter, 1989.

Veidlinger, Jeffrey. *In the Midst of Civilized Europe: The Pogroms of 1918–1921 and the Onset of the Holocaust*. New York: Metropolitan Books, 2021.

———. *Jewish Public Culture in the Late Russian Empire*. Bloomington: Indiana University Press, 2009.

Veidlinger, Jeffrey. *The Moscow Yiddish State Theater: Jewish Culture on the Soviet Stage*. Bloomington: Indiana University Press, 2000.

Von Geldkern, James, and Richard Stites, eds. *Mass Culture in Soviet Russia: Tales, Poems, Songs, Movies, Plays and Folklore, 1917–1953*. Bloomington: Indiana University Press, 1995.

Von Hagen, Mark. *Soldiers in the Proletarian Dictatorship: The Red Army and the Soviet Socialist State, 1917–1930*. Ithaca, NY: Cornell University Press, 1990.

Weinberg, Robert. "Demonizing Judaism in the Soviet Union during the 1920s." *Slavic Review* 67, no. 1 (Spring 2008): 120–153.

———. *Stalin's Forgotten Zion: Birobidzhan and the Making of a Soviet Jewish Homeland, an Illustrated History, 1928–1996*. Berkeley: University of California Press, 1998.

Wilhelmy-Dollinger, Petra. "Emanzipation durch Geselligkeit. Die Salons jüdischer Frauen in Berlin zwischen 1780 und 1830." In *Bild und Selbstbild der Juden Berlins zwischen Aufklärung und Romantik*, edited by Marianne Awerbuch and Stefi Jersch-Wenzel, 121–138, Einzelveröffentlichungen der Historischen Kommission zu Berlin 75. Berlin: Spiess Volker, 1992.

Wixman, Ronald. *Peoples of the USSR: An Ethnographic Handbook*. New York: Routledge, 1984.

Wyner Mark, Elizabeth, ed. *The Covenant of Circumcision: New Perspectives on an Ancient Jewish Rite*. Waltham, MA: Brandeis University Press, 2003.

Yona, Rona. "From Russia to Palestine via Poland: The Shifting Centre of Interwar Labour Zionism." *Contemporary European History* 30, no. 4 (2021): 513–527.

Young, Glennys. *Power and the Sacred in Revolutionary Russia: Religious Activists in the Village*. University Park: Penn State University Press, 2008.

Zand, Michael. "Notes on the Culture of the Non-Ashkenazi Jewish Communities under Soviet Rule." In *Jewish Culture and Identity in the Soviet Union*, edited by Yaakov Ro'i and Avi Beker, 378–445. New York: New York University Press, 1991.

Zeltser, Arkadi. "Belorusizatsiia 1920-x gg.: Dostizheniia i neudachi." In *Evrei Belarusi: Istoriia i kultura*, vols. 3–4, 60–93. Minsk: Otkrityi universitet Izrailia v Belarusi, 1998.

———. *Evrei sovetskoi provintsii: Vitebsk i mestechki, 1917–1941*. Moscow: ROSSPEN, 2006.

Zeltser, Arkadi, and V. Selimenev. "The Jewish Intelligentsia and the Liquidation of Yiddish Schools in Belorussia, 1938." *Jews in Russia and Eastern Europe* 43 (2001): 78–97.

———. "The Liquidation of Yiddish Schools in Belorussia and Jewish Reaction." *Jews in Russia and Eastern Europe* 41 (2001): 74–111.

Zierler, Wendy. "Chariot(ess) of Fire: Yokheved Bat-Miriam's Female Personifications of Erets Israel." *Prooftexts* 20, nos. 1–2 (Winter–Spring 2000): 111–138.

Zinger, V. *Di yidishe bafelkerung in SSSR*. Moscow: Emes, 1930.

Zipperstein, Steven J. *The Jews of Odessa: A Cultural History, 1794–1881*. Stanford: Stanford University Press, 1986.

INDEX

Photo insert images are indicated by *p1*, *p2*, *p3*, etc.

ABOUT THE AUTHOR

ELISSA BEMPORAD is Jerry and William Ungar Chair in Eastern European Jewish History and the Holocaust and Professor of History in the Department of History at Queens College and The Graduate Center–CUNY. She is a two-time winner of the National Jewish Book Award. She is the author of *Becoming Soviet Jews: The Bolshevik Experiment in Minsk* (2013), and *Legacy of Blood: Jews, Pogroms, and Ritual Murder in the Lands of the Soviets* (2019). She is the coeditor of four volumes, including *Pogroms: A Documentary History* (2021).